BUSINESS NETWORKS IN EAST ASIAN CAPITALISMS

Elsevier

Asian Studies Series

Series Editor: Professor Chris Rowley,
Cass Business School, City University, London, UK;
Institute of Hallyu Convergence Research, Korea University, Korea
Griffith Business School, Griffith University, Australia
(email: c.rowley@city.ac.uk)

Elsevier is pleased to publish this major Series of books entitled Asian Studies: Contemporary Issues and Trends. The Series Editor is Professor Chris Rowley of Cass Business School, City University, London, UK and Department of International Business and Asian Studies, Griffith University, Australia.

Asia has clearly undergone some major transformations in recent years and books in the Series examine this transformation from a number of perspectives: economic, management, social, political and cultural. We seek authors from a broad range of areas and disciplinary interests covering, for example, business/management, political science, social science, history, sociology, gender studies, ethnography, economics and international relations, etc.

Importantly, the Series examines both current developments and possible future trends. The Series is aimed at an international market of academics and professionals working in the area. The books have been specially commissioned from leading authors. The objective is to provide the reader with an authoritative view of current thinking.

New authors: we would be delighted to hear from you if you have an idea for a book. We are interested in both shorter, practically orientated publications (45,000+words) and longer, theoretical monographs (75,000–100,000 words). Our books can be single, joint or multi-author volumes. If you have an idea for a book, please contact the publishers or Professor Chris Rowley, the Series Editor.

Dr Glyn Jones
Email: g.jones.2@elsevier.com

Professor Chris Rowley
Email: c.rowley@city.ac.uk

BUSINESS NETWORKS IN EAST ASIAN CAPITALISMS

Enduring Trends, Emerging Patterns

Edited by

JANE NOLAN

CHRIS ROWLEY

MALCOLM WARNER

ELSEVIER

AMSTERDAM • BOSTON • CAMBRIDGE • HEIDELBERG
LONDON • NEW YORK • OXFORD • PARIS • SAN DIEGO
SAN FRANCISCO • SINGAPORE • SYDNEY • TOKYO
Chandos Publishing is an imprint of Elsevier

CP
CHANDOS PUBLISHING

Chandos Publishing is an imprint of Elsevier
50 Hampshire Street, 5th Floor, Cambridge, MA 02139, United States
The Boulevard, Langford Lane, Kidlington, OX5 1GB, United Kingdom

Library of Congress Cataloging-in-Publication Data
A catalog record for this book is available from the Library of Congress

British Library Cataloguing-in-Publication Data
A catalogue record for this book is available from the British Library

ISBN: 978-0-08-100639-9 (print)

For information on all Chandos publications
visit our website at https://www.elsevier.com/

Publisher: Glyn Jones
Acquisition Editor: Glyn Jones
Editorial Project Manager: Tessa De Roo
Production Project Manager: Omer Mukthar Moosa
Cover Designer: Maria Inês Cruz

CONTENTS

CONTRIBUTOR BIOGRAPHIES

Tim G. Andrews, PhD, is an associate professor based at Thammsat Business School, Thammasat University in Bangkok, Thailand. His current scholarly interests include international brand management, indigenous culture constructs, and economic inequality for organizations doing business in Southeast Asia (particularly Thailand and Myanmar). He has authored numerous international journal articles and books, including *Building Brands in Asia: From the Inside-out* to be published by Routledge (forthcoming). He is co-editor of the *Working in Asia* book series (also with Routledge).

Heidi Dahles (PhD in social sciences in 1990, Radboud University Nijmegen, Netherlands) is Professor and Head of the Department of International Business and Asian Studies at Griffith Business School, Griffith University, Australia. Prior to moving to Australia, she was a professor in organizational anthropology at *Vrije Universiteit* Amsterdam, Netherlands. Her research interest is in Chinese business networks, small-scale and micro business, business resilience, and the informal economies of Southeast Asia. Heidi has published in peer-reviewed journals, such as *Asia-Pacific Business Review, Culture & Organization, East Asia – An International Quarterly, Asian Ethnicity, Journal of Entrepreneurial Communities, the Journal of Small Business & Entrepreneurship, Journal of Social Entrepreneurship,* and *Journal of Contemporary Asia.* Among her co-edited volumes are *Capital and Knowledge, Changing Power Relations in Asia* (2003), and *Multicultural Organizations in Asia* (2006).

Robert Fitzgerald, PhD, is located at Royal Holloway, University of London, United Kingdom. His research interests include business history, economic development, comparative management, Asia Pacific and Japanese business, employment relations and labour history, corporate governance, business-state relationships, marketing, and multinational enterprise. Recent publications, among others, are articles in leading academic journals on a comparison of Japanese and Chinese multinationals and the global strategies of Japanese multinationals, *Operating in Emerging Markets: a Guide to Management and Strategy in the New International Economy* (Financial Times Press, 2013), and *The Rise of the Global Company: Multinational Enterprise and the Making of the Modern World* (Cambridge University Press, 2015). He is currently working on the historical early globalization of the electrical industry and its implications, the historical and comparative development of Chinese banking, and flexible specialization among Japanese SMEs.

Sven Horak, PhD, teaches and researches in the field of international business and management at The Peter J. Tobin College of Business at St. John's University in New York City, New York, United States. His research interests include the analysis of informal social network structures, interpersonal relationships and social ties, managerial behaviour, informal management, and distinctive socio-cultural aspects of management in an international context. His recent studies have addressed, among other things, the impact of variables related to cultural context on managerial decision-making behaviour, analysed through a cross-cultural experimental research design, the dynamics of formal-informal institutional interactions and their co-evolution in transitional, as well as advanced economies, challenges to social responsibility and sustainability, and questions concerning ethical behaviour within informal social network structures in an international business context.

Khin Thi Htun, PhD, is currently Director of Builder's International Trading Ltd based in Bangkok, Thailand. A Burmese national with a background in medicine, she is also a member of the Myanmar Women Entrepreneurs Association (MWEA) in Yangon. Her research interests focus on the role of women in a changing Burma, as well as the experiences of base-of-the-pyramid employees in Burmese organizations working abroad.

Keith Jackson, PhD, MBA, MA, holds a PhD in International Human Resource Management from the School of Oriental and African Studies (SOAS), University of London, United Kingdom. He has worked at SOAS since 1993, most recently as a tutor on MSc (distance learning) programmes in public sector management, and international management (China, Japan, Middle East, and North Africa). He is currently working as a Professor of Sustainable Human Resource Management at Doshisha University in Japan. Keith is founding co-editor and author of the Routledge 'Working in Asia' series. He works as a reviews editor for the journals *Asia Pacific Business Review* and *China in Comparative Perspectives Network (CCPN) Global* and is an editor on the *South Asian Journal of Global Business Research* and *Journal of Management Sciences.* Keith has worked as a consultant in cross-cultural communication and leadership development in China, Japan, Singapore, Switzerland, Turkey, and the United Kingdom.

Shigeru Matsumoto, PhD, is a professor at Doshisha graduate school of business in Japan. He obtained his PhD degree from Kobe University by conducting an in-depth study of Japanese cross-border Mergers and Acquisitions (M&As). With the award of a Fulbright Scholarship, he gained an MBA degree from Thunderbird School of Global Management (United States). Matsumoto has more than 15 years of experience in investment banking and in advisory roles at global institutions, including HSBC, Macquarie Capital, and PwC. During his career, he has advised on more than 50 Japan-related cross border M&A transactions in twenty countries, including the United States, the United Kingdom, France, China, and Vietnam. In 2015, he won the 9th M&A Forum Grand Prize with his recent publication about Japanese cross border acquisition: Matsumoto, S. (2014) *海外企業買収　失敗の本質　戦略的アプローチ* [Japanese foreign acquisitions: why do they fail?] Tokyo: Toyo Keizai.

David R. Meyer, PhD, is Senior Lecturer in Management at Olin Business School, Washington University in St. Louis, Missouri, United States, teaching international business with a focus on Asia. Prior to this, he was Professor of Sociology & Urban Studies at Brown University. He received his PhD from the University of Chicago. His publications include five books and monographs and over sixty articles and book chapters. His book, *Hong Kong as a Global Metropolis* (Cambridge University Press, 2000), interpreted that city as the pivot of Asian business networks. Recent publications deal with the transformation of Hong Kong as a financial centre, China's financial centre networks, job mobility of financiers coming to Hong Kong, network governance at the State Banks of China, the banking networks of Asian financial centres, private wealth management in Asia, and high-frequency trading on exchanges, including on Hong Kong's and Singapore's.

Stephen L. Morgan is Dean of Social Science at the University of Nottingham Ningbo China (UNNC) and Professor of Chinese Economic History at the University of Nottingham, United Kingdom. His research is mostly focused on Chinese economic and business history, along with an interest in contemporary economic development, international business, and strategic management. He was formerly the editor-in-chief of the *Australian Economic History Review*, a journal of economic, business, and social history of the Asia-Pacific region. He is the co-author of *Business strategy and corporate governance in the Chinese consumer electronics sector* (2011) and his articles have appeared in *Business History*, *China Quarterly*, *Economics* *and Human Biology*, *Explorations in Economic History*, and the *World Economy*, among others.

Jane Nolan, PhD, is a Senior Member of Newnham College, Cambridge, United Kingdom and was also a Senior Research Fellow at Magdalene College, Cambridge, and a Nuffield Foundation New Career Fellow at the Department of Sociology, University of Cambridge. She has also lectured at Aberystwyth University and the University of Leicester, United Kingdom. Her research interests include: globalisation and institutional change; organisational justice; transnational and national business networks; corporate governance and corporate social responsibility; and gender and employment studies. Her work has appeared in numerous internationally respected journals, including *The International Journal of Human Resource Management*, *Gender Work and Organisation*, *Asia Pacific Business Review*, and the *International Journal of Aging and Human Development*.

Katja Restel is currently pursuing her PhD at the Marcator School of Management at the University of Duisburg-Essen, Germany, and her research so far is concerned with the characteristics and theoretical embedment of Asian informal networks and their influence on Human Resource Management. She is also interested in the issues of Asian Diversity Management, as well as Organizational Attractiveness.

Chris Rowley, PhD, has affiliations at IHCR, Korea University, Korea and IBAS, Griffith University, Australia as well as IAPS, Nottingham University, United Kindgom and Cass Business School, City University, London, United Kingdom, and has been a Korea Foundation Research Fellow. He is editor of the journals *Asia Pacific Business Review* and *Journal of Chinese Human Resource Management* and also series editor of the *Working in Asia and Asian Studies* book series. He has given a range of talks and lectures to universities and companies internationally, with research and consultancy experience with unions, business, and government. He has been published widely in the area of Human Resource Management and Asian business, with over 500 articles, books, chapters, and practitioner pieces, as well as being interviewed and quoted in a range of practitioner reports and magazines, radio, and newspapers globally.

Sununta Siengthai, PhD, is a full Professor of the School of Management, Asian Institute of Technology, Thailand. She obtained her PhD in 1984 from the I.L.I.R, University of Illinois at Urbana-Champaign, United States. She was a JSPS research fellow at the Kyoto Institute of Economic Research in 1986, a Citibank Research Fellow at the Kenan Institute of Private Enterprise, University of North Carolina at Chapel Hill in 1992 and a senior Fulbright research fellow at the Center of Southeast Asian Studies, University of Michigan at Ann Arbor, United States in 1998. She teaches and researches in Organizational Behaviour and HRM, Performance Management, and Industrial Relations in the New Economy. Some of her publications include *Changing Face of Management in Thailand*, *Multi-dimensions of Industrial Relations in the Asian Knowledge-Based Economies*, and articles in *Administrative Science Quarterly*, *International Business Review*, *Journal of Intellectual Capital*, *International Journal of Productivity and Performance Management*, *International Journal of Project Management*.

Wai Ling So, PhD, obtained her PhD in History from the School of Oriental and African Studies (London, United Kingdom) in 2014. Prior to her PhD, she worked as a researcher in the Jebsen History Project, as well as the head of the Jebsen History Project Library. Both positions inspired her to further her studies in business and economic history. Her doctoral research cites the case study of a medium-sized German company called Diederichsen and Jebsen, and discusses colonialism, protection, and economic development in the German colony of Qingdao (China) from 1898 to 1908. Her doctoral dissertation has been revised and will be published in the form of a monograph. Her other research interests include: Sino-German relations and international relations, political economy, network studies and institutional economics. Currently, she acts as a co-investigator for a research project that maps governance as a multi-partite network in the welfare sector of Hong Kong, an initiative of the ExCEL3 of HKU, and continues to actively develop new research projects.

Yuliani Suseno, PhD, is the Course Coordinator and a Senior Lecturer in the School of Business and Law at Edith Cowan University, Australia. She is on the Editorial Board of the *Asia Pacific Business Review*. Her research interests are in the areas of social capital and social networks, professional service firms, knowledge management, and international HRM. Dr Suseno has published in the areas of innovation, social capital, HRM and strategic management of professional-service firms in journals including the *International Journal of Human Resource Management*, *Journal of Organisational Change Management*, and *Employee Relations*. Dr Suseno is a member of the

Centre for Innovative Practice at Edith Cowan University, Australia, and the Australian Human Resources Institute (AHRI).

Pattanee Susomrith, BBus, MBA, PhD, is currently a lecturer at Edith Cowan University (ECU), Western Australia. She lectures on HRM units, including Organisational Behaviour. Pattanee's research interests include HR outsourcing, employee turnover, training and development, and innovation. Pattanee is a member of the School's Centre of Innovative Practice (CIP, ECU) and Australian Human Resources Institute (AHRI).

Quang Truong, PhD (Emeritus Professor), obtained his MPAs from the National Institute of Administration, Saigon, Vietnam and Institute of Social Studies, the Hague; his *doctorandus* in Political Science and PhD in Social Sciences (1987) from the Free University, Amsterdam, the Netherlands. Prior to his academic career, Quang worked for IBM-Netherlands and Europe for 15 years (1978-1993) in several managerial positions. Between 1995 and 2006, he was Associate Professor at the School of Management, Asian Institute of Technology in Bangkok, Thailand. He taught at several postgraduate programs in Thailand, Germany, China, and lately in Africa, the Middle East, and Central America. He joined Maastricht School of Management (MSM), the Netherlands in 2006 as Professor of Organizational Behaviour and Human Resource Management, and retained his position as Emeritus Professor at MSM after retirement in 2011. Quang Truong has authored and co-authored more than 60 articles in internationally refereed journals, book chapters, and edited three books.

Natenapha Wailerdsak, PhD, is Assistant Professor in Management at Thammasat Business School, Bangkok, Thailand and the Chair of the Japanese Studies Center, Institute of East Asian Studies, Thammasat University. She holds a PhD in economics from the University of Tokyo, Japan. Before joining the Thammasat University in 2011, she worked for three years as a Research Associate for the Institute of Oriental Culture, the University of Tokyo. Her publications include *Managerial Careers in Thailand and Japan* (Silkworm Books, 2005), *Business Groups and Family Businesses in Thailand: Before and After Asian Financial Crisis 1997* (BrandAgebooks, 2006, in Thai) and *Japanese Employment Practices and Human Resource Management in an Ultra-Aging Society: Lesson for the Future Thailand* (Japanese Studies Center and Japan Foundation, 2016, in Thai). Her latest articles have appeared in *Asian Pacific Journal of Management*, *Oxford Handbook of Asian Business Systems*, and *Oxford Handbook of Business Groups*. She is editor of *Japanese Studies Journal*, Thammasat University.

Barbara X. Wang, BA MBA, is a Professor of Practice in Leadership and Client & Programme Director at Ashridge Executive Education, at Hult International Business School, United Kingdom. Barbara's interests are in cross-cultural leadership/management, Chinese leadership & executive coaching. She has extensive experience in management training and consulting, and has developed and conducted customised programmes for companies across industries, as well as teaching in MBA/EMBA programmes at Ashridge and Chinese universities. Before she joined Ashridge in 2011, Barbara's commercial experience extended to working for multinational companies in China where she was in a senior managerial position for several companies, such as Western Management Institute of Beijing, Louis Vuitton group, and DHL. Barbara graduated with a BA and MBA, and her recent PhD research is situated in cross-cultural leadership/management. She has qualified in many leadership psychometric tools. Her book 'Chinese Leadership' was published by Palgrave Macmillan in September 2011.

Malcolm Warner, PhD, is currently an Emeritus Professor and Fellow of Wolfson College, Cambridge and Cambridge Judge Business School, University of Cambridge. Prior to joining Cambridge Judge Business School, Professor Warner was a Research Fellow at a number of US universities, including Stanford and Columbia. He has also held appointments at the London Business School and the Brunel University-Henley Management College Joint Graduate Programme. He has also held the Halevy Visiting Professorship at Sciences Po' in Paris. He now holds a Visiting Professorial appointment at Cass Business School. He is Joint Editor of *Asia Pacific Business Review*, and was previously Editor-in-Chief of the *International Encyclopedia of Business and Management*. His most recent publication is *Understanding Management in China: Past, Present and Future*, Routledge, 2014.

Vimolwan Yukongdi, BBA, MBA, PhD, is Assistant Professor of HRM & Organisational Behaviour in the School of Management at Asian Institute of Technology (AIT) in Thailand. Dr Yukongdi has spent the bulk of her career teaching at universities in Australia for many years and has also held academic appointments in New Zealand and Thailand. Her research interests are in leadership, participative decision-making, teams, cross-cultural differences, and diversity management. Her research work has appeared in books, journals, and conference proceedings. She is the joint editor of research-based books, *The Changing Face of Women Managers in Asia* and *Women in Asian Management.* Dr. Yukongdi holds a PhD degree in Organisational Behaviour from the University of Melbourne, Australia and an MBA from the University of Pittsburgh, United States. She has lived in nine countries, including Australia, Denmark, Japan, Kenya, Malaysia, New Zealand, Pakistan, Thailand, and the United States. She has worked at Esso (ExxonMobil) and as a consulting manager in the consulting industry.

Shaoyu Zhao is a current PhD candidate in Contemporary Chinese Studies within the School of Contemporary Chinese Studies at University of Nottingham, United Kingdom. She received her master in Management in Contemporary China also from the School of Contemporary Chinese Studies. She completed a bachelor degree of Business Administration with a major in Management and a minor in Finance within the Business Faculty at Hong Kong Polytechnic University. Her PhD research project is about the role of social networks in helping Chinese private firms to establish and maintain competitive advantages. She is interested in Chinese business and management, the private sector, and social network analysis.

FOREWORD

The study of management in recent decades has matured substantially as the complexities of globalization have brought new conceptual challenges, and the growing need for explanation is felt by managers. One of the newly emerged fields has been the study of different systems of capitalism. In this new field, a number of studies have become classics and they have set the frameworks for the detailed enquiries that have since flourished. One of these classics has been Richard Whitley's 1992 study, 'Business Systems in East Asia' and, along with other authoritative models, it is referenced extensively in this volume.

In that approach, Whitley started from the standpoint he once explained to me in a seminar in 1971, when I asked him to define what management theory was all about. He said, 'it is the study and improvement of forms of cooperation in changing socioeconomic structures'. I had just spent ten years in British industry and could sense immediately what he meant. Since then, that guiding definition has grown into a theory that explains how forms of cooperation evolve differently society by society, not just in firms, but in larger systems containing firms. And these larger 'complex adaptive systems' themselves change through time. In later Asian fieldwork for his 1992 book, the question was settled as to how such 'business systems' could be most straightforwardly described. The answer was to consider the organizational response that came to typify a society (such a type being a simplification and there might be more than one) by seeing it as a fusion of three elements. First is the form of ownership that pulls together the components into a manageable unit such as a firm, or a conglomerate, or a joint venture. Second is the way in which such units relate to others in the society, and whether there are bonds of cooperation that might disturb the basic economic assumption of perfect competition. In other words, what kinds of networks (either intercorporate, interpersonal, and/or political) might influence organizational forms and behaviour? Third is the way in which management typically (within the overall type) arranges cooperation within the firm.

This set of components remains at the core of subsequent theorizing by a large number of scholars. The book you are now reading takes the second of these components – cooperation across the system, or business networks – and subjects it to an extensive review and updating. The book is about the modes of cooperation, or otherwise, that one finds in the various business systems of Asia. Because the larger societal systems are dynamic, it is always necessary to keep such theories adjusted and fine-tuned. It is also necessary to test the logic and if need be, replace it.

Behind the facts in these accounts lies a matter of wider interest. It is that as societies develop, they do not follow a single path. What works to hold together an economic system in advanced cases such as the United States or Germany, is essentially a set of institutions, such as the rule of law, regulation, professions, accountability, and the managing of a high state of competition. These are not universals. Other societies do not have such influences, nor have them to the same degree, nor have them in forms of an indigenous kind. So a high state of cooperativeness across an economy in the West may rest on what Weber called a distinct and peculiar rationality infusing the system. In Asia, it may rest on an entirely different structure: that of networked relationships. Of course, there are always degrees of both. But it is crucial to understand the variations in the degrees of both, especially if you are setting out to do business, or to explain to people setting out to the region, what they might expect to find.

The editors and writers of this book have addressed these issues with new studies, across a wide set of societies, and industries. The understanding of this core issue within Asian business is moved forward substantially with this work.

Gordon Redding
Professor Emeritus, University of Hong Kong
Adjunct Professor of Asian Business, INSEAD
Visiting Professorial Fellow, UCL

ACKNOWLEDGEMENTS

We have long been interested in how business networks operate in *East Asia*, and for a number of years now, we have investigated the intertwining of cultural and institutional factors in network formations and their subsequent influence on management practice in our respective research endeavours.

In this edited volume, we aim both to revitalise the empirical evidence used in the study of business networks and to push forward theoretical frameworks. Specifically, we seek to extend the geographical scope of the study of *East Asian* business networks by presenting contemporary research, not just on China, Japan, and South Korea, but also on some of the key emerging economies of South East Asia, including Myanmar, Thailand, and Vietnam.

We also aim to establish an *interdisciplinary* theoretical perspective which draws on analytical tools developed in the fields of political economy, history, social psychology, sociology, and law, as well as on the conventional approaches found in management and business studies. This, of course, means accepting insights from studies based on a range of methodologies and not being restricted by dogmatic convictions to one particular epistemological or ontological standpoint.

We believe that such *a pluralistic, pragmatic approach* can only deepen and enrich our understanding of this crucial topic. The book may be used by both undergraduate and postgraduate students in international management and business, as well as by those engaged in the study of the social sciences more generally. It will also be of interest, we hope, to academics and practitioners concerned with understanding the latest developments in business networks in the region.

We would like to offer our deepest thanks to all of the contributors to this volume. They are all experts in their fields and have worked on the project with tireless commitment and enthusiasm. They come from a variety of backgrounds; some hail originally from the region, others are Western-born and raised. Professionally, they are now located in universities and professional associations across the globe, including Australia, Germany, Japan, Myanmar, the Netherlands, PRC, Singapore, South Korea, Thailand, the United Kingdom, and the United States, among others.

Finally, we would like to acknowledge the support given to us by a number of institutions and individuals. Dr Jane Nolan would like to acknowledge the Universities of Cambridge and Leicester for their support, and to thank the Nuffield Foundation for the award of a fellowship to support her fieldwork. Professor Chris Rowley would like to acknowledge the Korea Foundation for its support and to thank it for the award of a fellowship for field research. Professor Malcolm Warner would like to acknowledge the Cambridge Judge Business School and Wolfson College for their support.

We also wish to thank the editorial and production teams at Elsevier for their professionalism and patience.

ENDORSEMENTS

If we want to understand any social phenomena, particularly ones that are less familiar, we need multidisciplinary experts to summarise what we know and to guide us through the complexity. In this book, three experts have drawn together an excellent team to do exactly that in relation to East Asia. Using both cultural and institutional analyses the text offers clear outlines of the issues and provides new evidence and insights. This book will become a touchstone for researchers on East Asia.

Chris Brewster, Professor of International HRM, University of Reading, United Kingdom

This book provides a typology of the variety of networks across East and Southeast Asia. Most intriguingly it shows how patterns of interrelationships have evolved within the indigenous, predominantly Confucian, ASEAN Chinese communities as well as in Japan and Korea, and among the Buddhist cultures of Southeast Asia. This is a remarkable effort to weave together research by scholars on a significant theme, a most timely resource to enhance your networking skills.

Check Teck Foo, Professor at Sun Tzu Institute, Singapore

Business Networks in East Asian Capitalism is a must read book for everyone interested in learning more, much more, about the major countries in the East Asia region of the world. It is expertly written by three of most outstanding and respected scholars of the region. With years of experience and a deep academic understanding of the region, the authors provide insights and comparisons into the social and business networks used within and across countries in East Asia, as well as with those in Europe and the Americas.

Randall S. Schuler, Distinguished Professor of Strategic International Human Resource Management, Rutgers University, United States

This edited book of readings presents a comprehensive survey of traditional as well as emerging trends in business networks in the East Asian context. A must read for all who seek to understand and benefit from greater understanding of these unique business relationships in the Asia Pacific region.

Rosalie L. Tung, Professor of International Business, Simon Fraser University, Canada

CHAPTER 1

Key Debates in Business Networks in East Asian Capitalisms: An Introduction

J. Nolan*, C. Rowley[†,‡,§,¶,a], M. Warner[//]
[*]Newnham College, Cambridge, United Kingdom
[†]Korea University, Seoul, Korea
[‡]Griffith University, Nathan, QLD, Australia
[§]Nottingham University, Nottingham, United Kingdom
[¶]City University, London, United Kingdom
[//]University of Cambridge, Cambridge, United Kingdom

1.1 INTRODUCTION

Many scholars have argued that understanding capitalism in East Asia requires a close examination of the dynamics of business networks (see Boisot & Child, 1996; Hamilton, 1996; Hamilton & Shin, 2015; Rowley & Warner, 2006; Tung & Worm, 2001; Warner, 2013). A common view is that if Western capitalist economies are "firm-based," East Asian capitalist economies are "network-based" and thus, networks should be recognized as the *institutional* foundation of economic organization in the region. However, throughout the region, different networks and organizational strategies are used in different contexts, which draw our attention to the way in which "efficiency" in management practices and the various "rationales" underpinning organizational forms may be socially constructed. While some forms of East Asian networks share a common grounding in cultural values which emphasize harmony and hierarchy in relationships, they do, nevertheless, vary in systematic ways based on historical, institutional, and political differences (Redding, 1990; Rowley & Warner, 2006; Warner, 2014; Walter & Zhang, 2012; Whitley, 1992; Witt & Redding, 2013a, 2013b).

The aim of this edited book is to build on the foundational studies of East Asian business networks conducted in the 1990s and 2000s (Boisot & Child, 1996; Hamilton, 1996; Redding, 1990; Tung & Worm, 2001; Whitley, 1992) by gathering together empirical and theoretical work which explores these themes in a contemporary comparative perspective. We have adopted an interdisciplinary

[a]The support of the Korea Foundation is acknowledged.

http://dx.doi.org/10.1016/B978-0-08-100639-9.00001-3

approach to this task and our international authors draw on a variety of historical, economic, political, sociological, and psychological frameworks.

In terms of country focus, contributions to the volume concentrate on business network activity in China, Japan, and South Korea (hereafter Korea), as well as developments in South East Asia, including the Straits region (comprising Singapore and parts of Malaysia and Indonesia), Thailand, Myanmar, and Vietnam. While necessarily selective, the range of countries examined certainly provides us with sufficient scope to investigate the nature of change and continuity in business networks in East Asia. Furthermore, this allows us to also contribute to the wider and more macro-convergence and globalization debates.

The following sections of this chapter will introduce readers to the variety of definitions of "business networks" used by contributors to the volume, including interpersonal networking, intercorporate networking, and political and elite networks. We will also outline the different theoretical frameworks used to examine the organization and development of capitalist societies, including the "varieties of capitalism" (VOC) and "comparative businesses systems" approaches, with a particular focus on how they might apply to developing an understanding of East Asian capitalisms. This will be followed by on overview of the structure of the book and summaries of each chapter.

1.2 DEFINING BUSINESS NETWORKS

It is important to appreciate that there are different kinds of business networks, each of which may require investigation at a different level of analysis. In this book we consider the influence and intersection of the following kinds of networks: (i) interpersonal, reciprocity-based networks which may be based on cultural preferences, as well as historical and institutional conditions; (ii) intercorporate networking and various forms of horizontal firm coordination; and (iii) political networks which may permeate and influence both interpersonal and intercorporate networks and may be identified with rent-seeking, particularly when formal institutions are not well established. These forms of networking are, of course, mutually influential, but they are worth distinguishing here as our authors place differing emphases on the explanatory power of each kind of network.

1.2.1 Interpersonal Networking

Much research on East Asian business networks makes a foundational assumption that countries in the region have particularistic, collectivistic societies—where social norms towards paternalism, authority, and individualism may vary from those generally found in the West (Hofstede, 1984; House, Hanges, Javidan, Dorfman, & Gupta, 2004; Trompenaars, 1993). Some of the consequences of these norms for business networking behavior are that people may be closely bound to particular in-groups across their life course, they may demonstrate respect for age seniority and hierarchical position regardless of individual merit, and they may demonstrate a preference for group cooperation and harmony over the pursuit of individual achievement. That said, there are distinctive differences within the region in terms of how these norms may influence networks. For example, in China the emphasis is on dyadic connections with kin and close friends; in Japan, connections may focus on longstanding relationships established in the workplace; in Korea, kin-based, especially "blood" relationships, may dominate (Rowley, 2013; Rowley & Paik, 2009); and in the Theravada Buddhist-influenced countries of Southeast Asia an acceptance of situations, such as inequalities in power and deference to authority figures may mean less social activism and the development of networks which are resistant to change and outside influences (Alston, 1989; Nolan, 2013; Yukongdi, 2008).

1.2.2 Intercorporate Networking and Firm Coordination

Horizontal firm-to-firm networking may be defined as groups of firms which are coordinated by multiple ties to achieve mutually beneficial objectives. These ties may be based on ownership structure, state economic policy, and/or social networks, such as family, kinship, and friendship ties (Rowley, 2013; Warner, 2014; Zhang & Whitley, 2013). In most Western economies horizontal firm networking is considered important for the acquisition of knowledge, capital, product, and talent (Witt & Redding, 2013b). Certainly, in Japan and Korea, much has been made of the role of horizontal networking and conglomerates in establishing business success (Rowley, Bae, & Sohn, 2002; Rowley & Bae, 2004). Horizontal firm-to-firm networking in China is less common however, especially in the sensitive sectors of the economy, such as energy, communications, and finance, where the state remains heavily involved. This pattern has its roots in the industrial organization of the past and the political structure of the present. Thus, there is a tendency towards vertical networking which is partly a remnant of the planned economy. Similar patterns may be found in some of the emerging economies of South East Asia, such as Myanmar and Vietnam (Giroud, 2007; Lim, 1996; Rowley & Truong, 2009; Truong & Rowley, 2014).

1.2.3 Political and Elite Networks

Reciprocity-based interpersonal networking may lead to favoritism in a range of business outcomes, including recruitment and promotion within an organization through to supply chain development and licensing agreements (Gu & Nolan, 2015; Perkins, 2000; Zhang, 2016). While nepotism and favoritism are key elements of cronyism, these behaviors are not confined to East Asia and also feature in many forms of informal networking in the West (eg, the politically and economically influential "old boy" networks commonly associated with the British public school system) (Khatri, 2006; Watters, 2016). However, wherever they are studied, the relationship between reciprocity-based personal networks and political processes takes us beyond the micro-level social psychological study of networks into an examination of the institutional processes of elite power. The term "crony capitalism" was widely used in the financial press during the Asian Financial Crisis in 1997 to describe the ties which had developed between elite business families and government officials who had jointly extracted wealth from public goods for personal material advancement, a conventional definition of corruption. Marketization, in and of itself, does not eliminate clientelism and may actually reinforce the mutual dependency of officials and entrepreneurs connected through interpersonal networks (Wank, 2001; Weatherbee, 2014). Moreover, it requires explanation through an examination of global power relations in an historical and political framework.

1.3 DEFINING EAST ASIAN CAPITALISMS

East Asian capitalisms can be seen within the historical and broader macro perspectives and debates on convergence (Rowley, 1998; Rowley & Benson, 2004) and within that the streams on globalization from a range of disciplines (Rowley & Oh, 2016), as well as types of capitalism. The study of variation in economic and societal organization has been examined through a number of different models, including the VOC approach, largely the focus of political economists (see for example, Hall & Soskice, 2003; Hall & Thelen, 2009; Walter & Zhang, 2012) and "comparative business systems" frameworks, usually favored by sociologists and management scholars (Whitley, 1999; Witt & Redding, 2013a). In the VOC literature the emphasis has been on identifying dimensions of difference in the institutions of advanced capitalist economies, such as company attitudes towards industrial relations, vocational training, corporate governance, and interfirm relations. While there is no absolute consensus (Allen, 2004; Deeg & Jackson, 2007), most accept the distinctions made between the activities of coordinated market economies (Germany, Continental Northern Europe, and Japan), liberal market economies (Anglo-Saxon economies such as the United States and the United Kingdom) and mixed or state-led market economies (France and Latin European countries). However, much of this work has focused on industrialized nations in the West, with the notable exception of the inclusion and analysis of Japan (Hall & Soskice, 2003; Hall & Thelen, 2009).

Walter and Zhang (2012) consider that the VOC model is relevant to the study of East Asia and they identify four particular VOCs in East Asia: co-governed, state-led, networked, and personalized, which vary along the dimensions of business systems, financial architectures, and labor market regimes. On the other hand, Witt and Redding (2013a) are less convinced of the utility of the VOC model when studying East Asia. They focus particularly on Asian business systems, identifying five particular forms of capitalism: (post-) socialist, advanced city, emerging South East Asian, advanced North East Asian, and Japanese. Their study is based on 13 countries, including India, which is beyond the scope of this book. Nevertheless, their model is a useful interpretive framework for the material presented here. They argue for the fundamental importance of studying social capital, culture, informal relationships, and "multiplexity," defined as the presence of multiple business systems within one country (eg, the co-existence of the state-owned and the private sector in China, each of which follows different "rules of the game"). For Witt and Redding (2013a), each feature ensures that Asian capitalisms are fundamentally distinct from Western varieties and, consequently, the VOC framework is of little relevance when studying Asian economies (apart from Japan). Not all our contributors agree with this assertion and some defend the contribution which could be made by using VOC models when studying East Asian Business networks (see for example Yukongdi's and Rowley's chapter on business networks in Thailand). That said, the dimensions identified by Witt and Redding (2013a) make for a useful guiding framework for analyzing the contributions in this volume and we will return to examine these dimensions in more detail in our conclusion.

1.4 STRUCTURE OF THE BOOK AND CONTRIBUTIONS TO THE VOLUME

The book begins with an overview of the historical development of East Asian business networks. We then have three separate sections focusing on business networks in (i) China, (ii) Japan and Korea, and (iii) South East

Asia (including a discussion of Chinese migration in the Straits region, and in-depth coverage of network development in Thailand, Myanmar, and Vietnam). An overview of each chapter is provided below and interlinkages between chapters are discussed in Chapter 15, "Making Sense of Enduring Trends and Emerging Patterns in Business Networks in East Asian Capitalisms: A Conclusion."

In Chapter 2, "The Historical Development of East Asian Business Networks: Trade, Colonialism, and the State," Robert Fitzgerald surveys the region as a whole, demonstrating how adopting a historical perspective offers valuable insights into the origins and purposes of interfirm networks and business groups, questioning simple distinctions between "marketized" Western and "networked" East Asian systems. The 19th century witnessed a rapidly expanding global economy and the spread of colonialism, and Western multinational companies (MNCs) and indigenous enterprises significantly influenced each other's development. Both relied on networks of trust relationships, shared investments, and entrepreneurial deal-making suited to Asia's developing trade-orientated economies. After the Second World War, decolonization forced Western MNCs to withdraw and reformed and newly established nation states encouraged the growth of local business groups. Analysis demonstrates the importance of international and market factors in shaping business systems and subsequently, the relevance of both government policy and external influences. Therefore, the reliance of MNCs on global networks since the 1990s has historical antecedents, and re-emphasizes the impact of international trends on national business systems. Following Fitzgerald's insightful overview, which draws our attention to the importance of international or cross-border factors in shaping business systems and to the difficulties of considering national or cultural issues in isolation, we turn to our first section on the role of business networks in China.

1.4.1 Section 1: Business Networks in China

In Chapter 3, "Business to Government Networks in Resource Acquisition: The Case of Chinese Private Enterprises," Shaoyu Zhao and Stephen Morgan demonstrate that business to government (B2G) networks in transition countries are an important channel for firms to access strategic government-controlled resources. They explore how Chinese private entrepreneurs perceive the role of B2G networks in their business strategies, with a focus on acquiring financial resources and new technology. They distinguish the quite different roles of local government connections and distant government connections. Drawing on a sample of Chinese private entrepreneurs in Guangdong, they show the continuing importance of B2G networks for the acquisition of financial resources and new technology, despite the progress of market reforms. Local government ties enable private entrepreneurs to connect with state-owned banks, which reduce the cost of information processing, and results in higher loans concluded in a shorter time. Local government connections also help private firms obtain subsidies to support research and development (R&D). Distant government ties facilitate approval of the use of new technology developed by private firms and help them to tap information about new technologies in state-owned enterprises (SOEs). The findings demonstrate the role of different types of B2G networks in the business strategies of private firms in China.

In Chapter 4, "Bank of China International in Hong Kong: Social Status and Network Access," David Meyer demonstrates that the Bank of China International (BOCI), a subsidiary of the prestigious Bank of China (Beijing), has difficulties integrating with the networks of global elite investment banks because government ownership transmits that BOCI is subject to political influence. The chief executive officers (CEOs) of BOCI exemplify why the bank struggles to enter the ranks of top investment banks in Hong Kong. They possess high social status as an educated elite, but this does not transfer to BOCI. Prior to becoming CEO, few bankers had experience in engaging with major global bankers. CEOs who had careers after completing their service are important financiers, but that does not retroactively benefit BOCI's social status among Hong Kong's investment banks. Most CEOs possessed ties to powerful Chinese Communist Party (CCP) cadres prior to taking their posts, while they were CEOs and/or subsequently in their careers. This raises the social status of the bank in the CCP. Nevertheless, these CCP network ties do not enhance the social status of BOCI among Hong Kong's banks. Instead, CCP ties confirm the low social status of the bank because they signify that government and CCP leaders may directly influence it.

In Chapter 5, "Business Networks and the Emergence of *Guanxi* Capitalism in China: The Role of the 'Invisible Hand'" (*kan bujian de shou*) Barbara Wang and Chris Rowley review elements of Chinese business history, attitudes towards business and the "Five Classified Relationships" (*Wulun*) of Confucian ethics to explore how *guanxi* capitalism emerged, evolved, and dominated the economic system. They note that it is widely recognized that *guanxi* plays an important role in the Chinese social-economic system. Nevertheless, they argue that how and why "*Guanxi* Capitalism" emerged in China is still somewhat underplayed in the literature. Their chapter examines *guanxi* capitalism in detail in order to reveal the features of China's economic system which is embedded deeply in its cultural-social-political environment. They aim to develop a conceptual framework of the "*Guanxi* Capitalism Structure" building on the "Differential Mode of Association" (*Chaxugeju*) theory and using the concept of "Central Managed Capitalism," as well as the "Network of *Guanxi* Circles" framework, illustrating the fundamental role of *guanxi* as the "invisible hand" in China.

In Chapter 6, "Networking Strategies of the Jebsens and Chinese Merchants in the Late 19th and early 20th Centuries," Wai Ling So demonstrates that it is possible to discern different models of cooperation between German and Chinese merchants in late Qing China. The chapter identifies a diversity of networking modes in the business communities in Qing China and shows how local norms and practices varied from one community to another. In the case of the Jebsens (a German import/export company) and their business community, trust within the network ruled the quality of personal and business unions, influencing their business endeavors in East Asia. At the same time, informal ties established between families through marriage and shared culture enabled more extensive delegation. This, in turn, increased the possibility of joint venture success, with the likelihood of building a common pool of resources, information, and capital at a low risk. On the other hand, Chinese merchants developed formal networks over time to regulate mercantile activities. Wai Ling So argues that this process of formalizing networks justifies some of the assumptions of Social Exchange Theory, specifically the assertion that the collective actions of people can alter social structures and institutions. In this case, direct government intervention in the economy, as well as political competition in the government, acted as the force of changing social norms and behaviors of Chinese merchants. As Chinese informal networks became institutionalized according to their respective bases of clan and birthplace, it enhanced administrative efficiency, while conforming to the rules and governance of the Chinese government. With written rules specifying treatment for undesirable behavior, these organizations ensured compliance among members who otherwise lacked personal trust in conducting business.

1.4.2 Section 2: Business Networks in Japan and Korea

In Chapter 7, "Business Networks in Japan: The Impact of Exposure to Overseas Markets," Keith Jackson and Shigeru Matsumoto discuss the distinctive features of the development of business networks in Japan. They focus particularly on the type of *keiretsu* networks that continue to shape and influence strategic thinking and decision-making in Japanese business. Presenting case study examples contextualized by data describing current responses of Japanese business networks to exposure in overseas markets, they identify enduring trends and emerging patterns in how these networks operate. One enduring trend appears to be the drawing of performance strength from socially and institutionally embedded network relationships, while an emerging pattern appears to be towards more horizontal forms of organization, as Japanese business networks stretch and develop competitive positions in global markets.

In Chapter 8, "Can Informal Networks Positively Influence Economic Growth and Development?," Katja Restel and Sven Horak investigate the use of *yongo* networks in South Korea. They note that, conventionally, the influence of informal networks is considered a factor dampening, or even preventing, the effectiveness of formal institutions. By drawing on Informal Social Network Theory, they introduce and outline the characteristics and antecedents of Korean *yongo* networks that are assumed to have exerted a positive influence on Korea's economic rise. They argue that, while informal networks may enable corruption (depending on the quality of formal institutions), they can also reduce transaction costs and enable efficient economic coordination. The chapter draws attention to the fact that *yongo* networks have so far been a largely overlooked dimension in analyzing Korea's fast economic development and they argue that informal networks need greater attention in order to explain Korea's success.

1.4.3 Section 3: Business Networks in Southeast Asia

In Chapter 9, "Chinese Capitalisms in Southeast Asia: Diverging Institutional Legacies of Southeast Asian Chinese Business Communities," Heidi Dahles notes that on China's reentry into the world economy, investments in countries with a substantial ethnic Chinese population, such as in South East Asia, were among the first steps taken outwards into an international business environment. Conversely, ethnic Chinese business people from South East Asia were among the first who took their business to China in the 1990s. The ethnic Chinese in South East Asia soon realized their potential to act as a bridge between China and their respective countries of residence. Dahles argues that a key question in this area of research is how ethnic Chinese networks reflect economic integration into the Chinese-dominated regional market and shape the particular variety of Chinese capitalism across Southeast Asia. To answer this question, her chapter draws on literature on ethnic Chinese business communities in the Straits region comprized of

Singapore and parts of Malaysia and Indonesia. These three ethnic Chinese communities can be identified in terms of a common origin, a shared but diverse migration history, colonial legacy, and "diasporic" condition. Based on a comparative literature review, the chapter argues that a comparative analysis of the historical dimensions of ethnic Chinese capitalism in South East Asian countries is vital to understand diverging perceptions and relations that ethnic Chinese businesses in the Straits maintain with China.

In Chapter 10, "Business Networks in Thailand: Import Substitution, Export Orientation, and Expansion in ASEAN Economic Community (AEC)," Natenapha Wailerdsak and Sununta Siengthai discuss the way in which socioeconomic development in Thailand is characterized by a post-developmental capitalism which is private sector led. They describe the characteristics of Thai business networks and the relationships between the government, business, and other organizations that have played a significant role in the economy. The first section of their chapter describes the development of Thai business networks from the beginning of the industrialization process in Thailand during the 1960s through to the current expansion of business into ASEAN in the 2010s. The second section explains the development and building up of business networks into the AEC. The third section reviews government investment policy (ie, Board of Investment Regulations) and other relevant business laws. In the fourth section, they briefly discuss the current anticorruption movement of the private business sector and business ethics issues. Finally, they examine how Thai business networks can be further developed within the AEC.

In Chapter 11, "Business Networks and VOC in Thailand: Adding the Context of History, Political Structures and Social and Cultural Values," Vimolwan Yukongdi and Chris Rowley consider how the VOC framework can be further developed. They note that interest, debate, and criticism across the social sciences of theories and models that seek to describe and analyse the development and types of capitalism has a long history. They also note that, despite critiques of the VOC approach, an examination of an often ignored and under researched example, Thailand, shows VOC remains a useful analytical framework. This is especially so when VOC is grounded in its history and researchers seek to push the theory forward. In this chapter, they seek to do this by adding a new sphere of "Context," defined as historical and political background, as well as social and cultural values and beliefs.

In Chapter 12, "Social capital and the Social Context of Business Networks: The Case of Thailand," Pattanee Susomrith and Yuliani Suseno focus on the importance of exploring the nature of social context when examining Thai business networks and, in particular, how this enables social capital to be developed, utilized, and maintained. Like many of its neighboring countries, Thailand's businesses function in an environment dominated by complex networks encompassing social and business interactions. They argue that the extent of this interweaving of social and business networks is far beyond that which is experienced in Western cultures and has only recently attracted the attention of researchers. Thailand's business networks are shaped as a result of the nation's cultural characteristics, such as collectivism, Buddhist philosophy, particularism, reluctance to change, relationship orientation, and hierarchical structure. These characteristics enable the creation, utilization and maintenance of structural, relational, and cognitive social capital.

In Chapter 13, "Business Networks in Myanmar: *kjei zu*, Corrosion and Reform," Tim Andrews and Khin Thi Htun explore the foundations, characteristics, evolution, and implications of business networks (*a hse a thwe*) in Myanmar. Their central proposition is that, although deeply grounded in national cultural and Buddhist principles, the common workings of *a hse a thwe* have become corrupted under military control—indirectly serving to shape the particular variety of economic capitalism that has emerged over the past three decades. They examine how these networks operate within the sphere of organizational processes and practices and how, in turn, they have grown to shape and delimit what constitutes "normal" business activity at both intra and interorganizational levels (particularly government). Drawing on rich, detailed qualitative research with participants from the realms of private business, the civil service, and academia, they explore how *a hse a thwe* influences organizational processes, practices, and (ultimately) performance. They focus in particular on the role of networks on recruitment, appraisal, dismissal, and governmental relations.

In Chapter 14, "The Network-based Economy in Vietnam: Business Networks in Context and Over Time," Quang Truong and Chris Rowley demonstrate that after two decades of comparably high growth post-1990, Vietnam has entered a declining phase. This decline is so significant that it could virtually nullify all the previous achievements and end the promise to transform Vietnam into an industrialized country by 2020. They argue that the "ideology vs. reality" dilemma is the main obstacle to moving toward a more qualitative and sustainable development phase. This is because the government continues to insist on building "a market economy with socialist orientation." In fact, the "socialist" model of development, typical of a state capitalist or network-based economy, still favors SOEs as the "pillars" of the economy, which drains resources and limits the private sector. They argue that the state has created and nurtured a breeding ground for corruption, cronyism, favoritism, and nepotism that leaves little room for private innovation, efficient production, and effective management so that products can compete and grow sustainably in international markets. They suggest that, in the final analysis, what Vietnam really needs to become more sustainable, is a development-oriented market economy and a public administration for development. Furthermore, they call for a check-and-balance mechanism to allow the participation of a more active civil society which may counter the excessive abuse of power brought about by a corrupted network that caused severe threats to the economic sustainability of the country.

1.5 CONCLUSIONS

In this volume, we have adopted in interdisciplinary approach to investigate the variety of business networks which are used in East Asian capitalisms. Contributors have discussed the specific characteristics of business networks in the country, or countries, under investigation, drawing on a range of different academic disciplines, including social psychology, economics, history, and law as well as politics, management, and sociology.

They agree that "culture matters," but each chapter is sensitive to the specificities of institutional heritage and historical and political process. Moreover, a number of chapters have discussed in detail how business networks reflect integration into regional and global markets and need explanations which extend beyond conventional definitions of nation state boundaries.

In sum, the collection draws our attention, not just to the usual explanatory factors such as cultural norms in influencing interpersonal networking, but it also emphasizes the importance of understanding networks through the historical processes of colonialism and postcolonialism, the development of business to government networking, and the emergence of formal institutions in specific historical, political, and economic contexts.

REFERENCES

Allen, M. (2004). The varieties of capitalism paradigm: Not enough variety? *Socio-Economic Review*, *2*(1), 87–108.

Alston, J. P. (1989). Wa, guanxi, and inhwa: Managerial principles in Japan, China, and Korea. *Business Horizons*, *32*(2), 26–31.

Boisot, M., & Child, J. (1996). From fiefs to clans and network capitalism: Explaining China's emerging economic order. *Administrative Science Quarterly*, *41*(4), 600–628.

Deeg, R., & Jackson, G. (2007). Towards a more dynamic theory of capitalist variety. *Socio-Economic Review, 5*(1), 149–179.
Giroud, A. (2007). MNEs vertical linkages: The experience of Vietnam after Malaysia. *International Business Review, 16*(2), 159–176.
Gu, F., & Nolan, J. (2015). Performance appraisal in Western and local banks in China: The influence of firm ownership on the perceived importance of guanxi. *International Journal of Human Resource Management*, http://dx.doi.org/10.1080/09585192.2015.1089063.
Hall, P. A., & Soskice, D. (2003). *Varieties of capitalism and institutional complementarities*. New York: Springer (pp. 43–76).
Hall, P. A., & Thelen, K. (2009). Institutional change in varieties of capitalism. *Socio-Economic Review*, 7(1), 7–34.
Hamilton, G. G. (Ed.), (1996). *Asian business networks*. Berlin and New York: Walter de Gruyter.
Hamilton, G. G., & Shin, S. I. (2015). Demand-responsive industrialization in East Asia: A new critique of political economy. *European Journal of Social Theory*, http://dx.doi.org/10.1177/1368431014568425.
Hofstede, G. (1984). *Culture's consequences: International differences in work-related values* (Abridged ed.). Thousand Oaks, CA: Sage.
House, R. J., Hanges, P. J., Javidan, M., Dorfman, P. W., & Gupta, V. (2004). *Culture, leadership, and organizations: The GLOBE study of 62 societies*. Thousand Oaks, CA: Sage.
Khatri, N. (2006). Cronyism: A cross-cultural analysis. *Journal of International Business Studies, 37*(1), 61–75.
Lim, L. (1996). Southeast Asian business systems: The dynamics of diversity. In A. E. Safarian & W. Dobson (Eds.), *East Asian capitalism: Diversity and dynamism* (pp. 91–110). Toronto, ON: University of Toronto Press.
Nolan, J. (2013). Continuity and change in guanxi networks in East Asia. In M. Warner (Ed.), *Managing across diverse cultures in East Asia: Issues and challenges in a changing globalized world* (pp. 168–182). London: Routledge.
Perkins, D. H. (2000). Law, family ties, and the East Asian way of business. In L. Harrison & S. Huntington (Eds.), *Culture matters: How values shape human progress* (pp. 232–243). New York: Basic Books.
Redding, S. G. (1990). *The spirit of Chinese capitalism*. Berlin and New York: Walter de Gruyter.
Rowley, C. (1998). *HRM in the Asia pacific region: Convergence questioned*. London: Frank Cass.
Rowley, C. (2013). The changing nature of management and culture in South Korea. In M. Warner (Ed.), *Managing across diverse cultures in East Asia: Issues and challenges in a changing globalized world* (pp. 122–150). London and New York, NY: Routledge.
Rowley, C., & Bae, J. (2004). Big business in South Korea: The reconfiguration process. *Asia Pacific Business Review, 10*(3–4), 302–323.
Rowley, C., Bae, J., & Sohn, T. W. (Eds.), (2002). *Managing Korean businesses: Organization, culture, human resources and change*. London: Frank Cass.
Rowley, C., & Benson, J. (2004). *The management of HR in the Asia pacific region: Convergence reconsidered*. London: Frank Cass.
Rowley, C., & Oh, I. (2016). Business ethics and the role of context: Institutionalism, history and comparisons in the Asia pacific region. *Asia Pacific Business Review, 22*, 1–13.
Rowley, C., & Paik, Y. (2009). *The changing face of Korean management*. London and New York, NY: Routledge.
Rowley, C., & Truong, Q. (2009). *The changing face of Vietnamese management*. London and New York, NY: Routledge.
Rowley, C., & Warner, M. (2006). Business and management in South East Asia: Studies in diversity and dynamism: Introduction: Setting the scene. *Asia Pacific Business Review, 12*(4), 389–401.
Trompenaars, F. (1993). *Riding the waves of culture*. London: Nicholas Brealey.

Truong, Q., & Rowley, C. (2014). Post-state capitalism. In M. Witt & G. Redding (Eds.), *The Oxford handbook of Asian business systems* (pp. 283–309). Oxford: Oxford University Press.

Tung, R. L., & Worm, V. (2001). Network capitalism: The role of human resources in penetrating the China market. *International Journal of Human Resource Management, 12*(4), 517–534.

Walter, A., & Zhang, X. (2012). *East Asian capitalism: Diversity, continuity, and change*. Oxford: Oxford University Press.

Wank, D. L. (2001). *Commodifying communism: Business, trust, and politics in a Chinese city. Vol. 14*. Cambridge: Cambridge University Press.

Warner, M. (2013). *Managing across diverse cultures in East Asia: Issues and challenges in a changing globalized world*. London and New York, NY: Routledge.

Warner, M. (2014). *Understanding Chinese management: Past, present and future*. London and New York, NY: Routledge.

Watters, S. (2016). Old boy networks. In A. Koh & J. Kenway (Eds.), *Elite schools: Multiple geographies of privilege* (pp. 101–121). London and New York, NY: Routledge.

Weatherbee, D. E. (2014). *International relations in Southeast Asia: The struggle for autonomy*. London: Rowman & Littlefield.

Whitley, R. (1992). *Business systems in East Asia: Firms, markets and societies*. Thousand Oaks, CA: Sage.

Whitley, R. (1999). *Divergent capitalisms: The social structuring and change of business systems*. Oxford: Oxford University Press.

Witt, M. A., & Redding, G. (2013a). Asian business systems: Institutional comparison, clusters and implications for varieties of capitalism and business systems theory. *Socio-Economic Review, 11*(2), 265–300.

Witt, M. A., & Redding, G. (2013b). *The Oxford handbook of Asian business systems*. Oxford: Oxford University Press.

Yukongdi, V. (2008). Trade unions in Thailand. In J. Benson & Y. Zhu (Eds.), *Trade unions in Asia: An economic and sociological analysis* (pp. 216–235). London and New York, NY: Routledge.

Zhang, X. (Ed.), (2016). *Changing Asian business systems: Globalization, socio-political change, and economic organization*. Oxford: Oxford University Press.

Zhang, X., & Whitley, R. (2013). Changing macro-structural varieties of East Asian capitalism. *Socio-Economic Review, 11*(2), 301–336.

CHAPTER 2

The Historical Development of East Asian Business Networks: Trade, Colonialism, and the State

R. Fitzgerald
Royal Holloway University of London, Egham, Surrey, United Kingdom

2.1 HISTORY, NATION STATES, AND THE INTERNATIONAL ECONOMY

Emphasis on the 'networked' characteristics of East Asian business has been contrasted with the 'firm-based' priorities of Western economies and the Anglo-American model in particular (Boisot & Child, 1996; Gerlach, 1992; Hamilton, 1996; Shiba & Shimotani, 1997; Tung & Worm, 2001). The distinction highlights a fundamental difference in the strategies, organization, and objectives of business and in the nature of commercial and social transactions. We should ask, nonetheless, to what extent this broad East-West difference is a valid one, and, in addition, whether variations in business structures and practice across East Asia are bigger than the similarities. Scholars have identified regionally-shared Confucian values founded on family, hierarchies and harmony as influencing firms and the relations between firms, but acknowledge that they must be operationalized in the specific national-level historical, political, institutional, and economic contexts that significantly shape business systems (Redding, 1990; Whitley, 1992). Networks have been portrayed as inter-personal relationships that substitute or supplement the market-based dealings and competitive strategies associated with Western-style capitalism. But they have evolved in different ways within national environments, and, in turn, must be understood through their interaction with multiple political, institutional, economic, and cultural factors (Hamilton, 1996).

Although the long-term circumstances that shape economic systems and business networks are frequently noted, detailed historical explanation and analysis are normally absent. Yet they are needed if we are to understand the emergence of national systems, and they can illuminate the origins and purposes of business networks. This will broaden our understanding of the chapters

Business Networks in East Asian Capitalisms
http://dx.doi.org/10.1016/B978-0-08-100639-9.00002-5

which follow, many of which take a country-specific approach to the analysis of business networks. In this short survey, the aim will be to highlight the most significant historical changes in the nature of business networks, especially in East Asia, and trends and changes of direction over time. Expanding global trade and colonialism were intimately and increasingly linked, from the 19th century onwards. Large-scale European multinationals transformed established trade routes in Asia, and had an impact on the operations and organization of businesses from India to Japan. It is revealing that the European firms that traded in the undeveloped or developing economies of Asia and Latin America, and then subsequently Africa, operated in substantially different ways to European firms that remained in their home markets. They relied overseas on networks of firms that facilitated diversification and entrepreneurial opportunism, and, while they often had the singular advantage of imperial favouritism, they relied within Asia on links with indigenous local and regional business networks. The marked expansion of international trade in the 19th century was connected closely to industrialization and colonialism, and cross-border networks affected directly the development of national economies. Despite, between 1914 and 1945, two worldwide conflicts and the consequences of the Great Depression, an international political economy based on imperialism, trade, and foreign direct investment (FDI) in natural resources and within developing territories continued into the post-war decades. Decolonization thereafter established nation states which associated their newly-won sovereignty with regaining control of their economies, and transformed polities, such as Japan and South Korea, acknowledged that their long-term viability as nation states required programmes of industrialization. There were, during the post-war decades, critical shifts in the geographical location and sectoral composition of global FDI. Across Asia, the developmental state model curtailed market mechanisms and encouraged business networks, but, although often ignored or denied, there were historical precedents and external influences. Governments supported and favoured business groups that led economic development, but international networks and alliances continued to be integral to their strategies, organization, and success. Perceptions of trends since the 1990s have largely determined contemporary discussion of 'globalization' or 'emerging economies', but tend to overlook an extensive history of international trade and FDI. Multinational enterprises have progressively abandoned directly-managed subsidiaries and vertical cross-border organization for a complex horizontal network of owned businesses, contracted operations and off-shoring. A long-term perspective questions if these trends are new or innovative, and re-emphasizes the task of assessing national business systems in their international contexts.

World or international history is not simply a compilation of national histories, but an exploration of common themes and the means by which cross-border factors have determined human development. Its aim is to challenge deeply-embedded or popular assumptions about discrete national histories, or, more worryingly, politically-biased national missions or 'special' national characteristics (Evans, 2005; Saunier, 2013). The quickening pace of the international economy and the rise of the global company since the mid-19th century remind us that cross-border interaction and the transfer of capital, technology, and business practices have determined the fortunes of countries and their industries. The process has been neither even nor smooth over time, and, while fostering or imposing interdependence, it has caused or heightened divisions and inequalities between and within polities. Nations modernize by emulation of global best practice, but, through adaptations and learning, and because their contexts differ and circumstances change, they can never modernize in exactly the same way.

2.2 BUSINESS NETWORKS AND THE INTERNATIONAL ECONOMY: 1820–1950

The growth in trade during the 19th century was associated with the first industrial revolution and to the related rising demand of advanced economies for raw materials and consumer goods not available at home. Differences in wealth and power established an international division of labour between manufacturing nations and commodity producers, and brought colonization to large parts of Asia and Africa. Multinational trading companies, largely from Europe, organized the bulk of this burgeoning global commerce, and played a central role in imperialist ventures. Trade explains the investments made by multinationals from industrialized nations in mines, plantations, and transport infrastructure in emerging territories. Economically underdeveloped and militarily-weaker regions, as a result, were turned into colonies or zones of influence. The European powers abandoned the international commercial system of mercantilism, based upon protectionism, government-sponsored monopolies and slavery, and advocated instead the principles of markets, competition, and free labour, although practice did not always match principles. Industrial companies, in this period, were inclined overall to rely on exports rather than FDI to meet overseas demand from nations with comparatively high living standards, but firms operating in economically undeveloped territories normally required a different strategic response. The transfer of European capital and technology and the establishment of trade routes and facilities required FDI, and, furthermore, the creation of cross-border and local business networks. With overseas investment orientated towards natural resources and trade-related infrastructure, the regions of Asia, Africa, or Latin America became hosts to some 60% of FDI assets from the end of the 19th century until the 1930s. Asia held 20.9% of inward FDI by 1914, with most flowing to China (accounting for 7.8% of the global total) and to India and Ceylon (about 3.2%) (Fitzgerald, 2015). In Asia, and subsequently in Africa, commercial interests, treaties with local rulers, and disputed jurisdictions could create unstable borders and international disputes, persuading European states to intervene and colonize. The securing of raw materials overseas, as industrial competition intensified, provided an important additional reason (Fieldhouse, 1965). Colonial regimes could install governance rules and business systems with which European multinationals were familiar, and the legal and military protection of property rights lowered the risks for international investors. Institutional bias, personal networks, and tariffs could and did unfairly favour enterprises from the imperial country, but, despite handicaps, non-European traders and investors continued to play a vital role in Asia's colonial economies. International trade and European FDI formed in the 19th century the most important trend and influence on business organization and networks in the region. They affected merchant and financial networks in individual territories and across regional diaspora networks. In China, they transformed banking and comprador systems; in Japan, they extensively determined the evolution of Japanese trading firms (*sogososha*) and business groups (*zaibatsu*). Overall, economic development in Asia was closely linked to the evolution of trading and merchant enterprises, European and indigenous, and to the expansion of a merchant class (Latham & Kawakatsu, 1994; McVey, 1992).

What is striking about multinational enterprise in the 19th century is the free-standing company (FSC), whose home nation 'base' was limited to being a source of capital investment and the formal place of registration. From the outset, operations were conducted only in an overseas market, and the formal headquarters in the country of origin had no management function. FSCs were investment vehicles designed to exploit the opportunities of a booming world economy and imperial expansion. Some grew into multi-activity businesses. Most tended to focus on a single core activity, commodity, or service, but they could overcome any lack of scope or size through strategic alliances, cross-directorships, and business groups joined by equity (Wilkins & Schroter, 1998). Trading, banking, and financing in distant locations suited the FSC form, allowing for on-the-spot entrepreneurship and flexible deal-making. To succeed, traders relied on business networks, and built trust relationships with clients. Individual entrepreneurship, reputation, contacts, and market knowledge fostered and secured deals. Personal connections, private partnerships and flexible methods of working amounted to necessary competitive strengths. FSCs, as they grew in operational size and geographical scope, were capable of evolving international management structures and headquarters functions, many doing so by the end of the 19th century, and experienced administrative teams oversaw transcontinental commercial interests. As a result of industry-specific factors, British shipping lines did not develop into hierarchical, integrated enterprises, and many were closely linked to trading firms (Boyce, 1995).

The accelerating Indian economy in the 1860s was a natural lure for British merchants, most of whom settled in the commercial hub of Calcutta (Fieldhouse, 1965). Prominent British examples were Andrew Yule & Co., Bird & Co., and Shaw Wallace, and Volkart Brothers Winterthur, originally from Switzerland, was another prominent case (Guex, 1998; Jones, 1998).[1] Expatriate businessmen imitated or participated in networks founded by local Indian entrepreneurs and financiers, and quickly evolved beyond simple trading. They acquired plantations in jute, tea, coffee, and sugar, as well as cotton; they dug and extended coal, copper, and tin mines; and amongst much else, they held assets in flour-milling, oil, trams, light railways, and coastal shipping. British trading firms preferred to found multiple and legally separate mining, plantation, or industrial enterprises, usually registered locally, and they then frequently provided highly profitable management agency services to partner enterprises. Informal Indian capital markets and business networks supplied much of the investment, but the City of London was a vital source, too. By 1911, seven 'agency houses' controlled nearly a half to two-thirds of India's jute, tea, and coal companies. Bird & Co. and Andrew Yule expanded into the largest business groups in India (Bagchi, 1972; Ray, 1979). Outside the textile sector, expatriate finance in India proved significantly greater in size and impact than indigenous capital (Tomlinson, 1993). Leading trading companies evolved into diversified international business groups; in order to raise capital for their expanding operations, several founded a headquarters in London, such as

[1]Volkart Brothers Winterthur, E.D. & F. Man, Aug. 2009, 'A History of Volcafe'; Ralli Brothers, London Metropolitan Archives, Business Papers, 1822–1914, and 'Historical notes, 1899–52'.

David Sasoon (in 1872), Dalgety (1884) and Dodwell, Carlill (1891) (Allen & Donnithorne, 1957; Fitzgerald, 2015).[2] Harrisons and Crosfield had enterprises from India to China, Australia, and North America, coordinated through its London headquarters. It was involved in commodity trading, insurance and finance, and shipping services. The firm placed each plantation and timber venture into a separate firm, appointing board members with personal connections to each concern, and it floated some 40 rubber plantation businesses on the London market between 1903 and 1914. The largest firm of them all, Mackinnon Mackenzie, was a myriad of associated trading agencies, shipping lines, and commodity processors, operating locally in and internationally across Arabia, India, Australasia, and South East and East Asia. In 1914, its chairman, Lord Inchcape, arranged the merger with P&O that created the world's largest shipping group (Allen & Donnithorne, 1957; Jones, 1998, 2000). Internal strife left China vulnerable to the incursions of Western powers and their business interests, notably around the Yangste delta. The US commission agent and shipper, Russell & Co., was founded in Shanghai as early as 1824, and it created the Shanghai Steam Navigation Company in partnership with Chinese financiers and merchants.[3] Jardine Matheson and then Butterfield & Swire, associated with John Swire & Sons, emerged as the most important international trading firms in China, and their commercial activities depended on the networks they cultivated with local merchants (Liu, 1962). Jardine Matheson invested, furthermore, in railways, silk, sugar, harbours, shipping, insurance, and banking, and in China's first cotton mill. It fulfilled its global ambitions by working with agencies in which it had partial ownership or shared partners. In London, it was represented by Matheson & Company, with which it merged and incorporated in 1906, founding a multinational headquarters (Allen & Donnithorne, 1954; Chapman, 1992; Jones, 2000).[4]

Organization and strategies adopted in India and China were replicated in South East Asia, where Indian and particularly Chinese diaspora were well entrenched. Wallace Brothers, in 1865, created the Bombay Burmah Trading Corporation with a group of Indian merchants, and the business was concerned with felling and dealing in teak. When it challenged Bombay Burmah's illegal logging activities, the remnant kingdom of Burma

[2]Dodwell, Carlill, London Metropolitan Archives, Dodwell & Company, Private Notebooks of G.B. Dodwell, 1891–1914.

[3]Dent & Co., HSBC Archives, Branch Correspondence, 1867.

[4]Jardine Matheson, University Library, Cambridge University, Correspondence, 1820–1914, and Miscellaneous Papers; Jardine Skinner, Calcutta Office, 1843–73, and Correspondence.

gave Britain a pretext to begin, in 1885, a third war between the two countries. British commercial interests had long eyed the natural resources of the Upper Irrawaddy Valley and a possible new trade route to China. At Rangoon, T.D. Findlay & Son built and worked through a complex of local shipping lines, for which it provided a global trading and sales network (Fitzgerald, 2015; Myint-U, 2001). The Federated Malay States were formed, in 1886, as a means of installing British control of the peninsula. The trading firm of Guthrie arrived in the same year, opting to invest in coffee, and, in partnership with a local Chinese businessman, rubber. Dealings between British firms and Chinese entrepreneurs and financiers were common. The sizeable Chinese community, moreover, supplied the labour which worked in Malaya's mines, mills, and docks (Fitzgerald, 2015). Yap Ah Loy, called the Kapitan China of Kuala Lumpur, was by the 1890s the peninsula's richest individual through his ownership of mines, plantations, and shops (Andaya & Andaya, 1982; Chew & Lee, 1991). Malaya would be transformed, from the 1890s, first by rubber plantations, and soon thereafter by the cultivation of palm oil. In 1902, Sime Darby was founded as a trading firm in Malacca, with the active participation of local Chinese entrepreneurs. It initiated palm oil cultivation, in 1910, and Sime Darby would have a major and long-term impact on Malaya's landscape and economy.[5] The Danish-owned Andersen & Co., from 1886 onwards, built strong commercial interests in Siam, one of the few Asian nations to remain formally independent, and it operated through Chinese officials and merchants appointed by the Siamese king. Anderson & Co. was a forerunner to the East Asiatic Company, registered in 1897, which expanded globally and notably in China, Singapore, and Malaya (Guex, 1998).[6]

Borneo offers the most explicit cases of business imperialism. The former East India Company officer, James Brook, made himself Rajah of Sarawak, and granted special privileges to Borneo Company Ltd., founded during 1856 in Singapore by a group of Glasgow merchants. Yet its success depended on a network of Chinese investors and merchants. From 1879, it was allowed to buy out the Burmese gold mines owned by Chinese businessmen, and, from 1884, it became Thailand's largest teak company after the Bombay Burmah Trading Company. In Sabah, in northeast Borneo, several powers contended for the right to rule. The lease on the territory changed hands several times, after 1865, until the British government in 1882

[5] Sime Darby, Jul. 2009, 'A short history of Sime Darby'.

[6] East Asiatic Company, Odense University, Vol. 164, 'The life and memoirs of Hon State Councillor A.N. Andersen', 1993.

forestalled the risk of German intervention by granting a royal charter and commercial guarantees to the British North Borneo Company (BNBC). As was frequently the case, BNBC worked locally through established Chinese merchants (Allen & Donnithorne, 1957; Fitzgerald, 2015; Jones, 1998, 2000).[7] In the Dutch East Indies, during 1824, the Nederlandsche Handel-Maastschappij (NHM) was founded in Batavia, and its operations extended as The Netherlands conquered the rest of the archipelago. At first, it utilized trading outposts and agreements with local rulers, but ultimately Netherlands multinationals, working with indigenous and Chinese business interests and agents, took control of the territory's economy. After 1870, Deli-Maatschappij and Tabaksmaatschappij 'Arendsberg' developed interests in tobacco, cinchona, copra, rubber, tin, coal, and light railways, and they worked with financial concerns such as the Nederlandsche-Indische Handelsbank and the Rotterdamsche Bank. Internationale Crediet- en Handelsvereeniging (Internatio), Borneo-Sumatra Handelsmaatschappij (Borsumij), George Wehry, Lindeteves, and Jacobson & Van Den Bergh were the Big Five colonial houses doing business in the Dutch East Indies before 1914 (Jonker & Sluyterman, 2005).

Trading firms were closely associated with the most important overseas bank in Asia during this period, the Hongkong Bank, which was established in 1865 (and it was the predecessor to HSBC, or the Hong Kong and Shanghai Bank).[8] The Banque d'Indochine, founded in 1875, helped the French government manage colonial assets in South East Asia, where it dominated commerce and investment. From 1900, it was transacting trade between France and China, and it could be found in Shanghai, financing projects such as the Shangahi Power Company and Shanghai Tramways. Deutsche Bank formed branches in Shanghai and Yokohama, as early as 1872. In partnership with Disconto-Gesellschaft and Bleichroder, in 1889, Deutsche Bank created the Deutsch-Asiatische Bank. Their new subsidiary fruitfully cooperated with the Hongkong Bank in financing Chinese government loans and railway building within China. The business of international finance dissolved national identities and loyalties. Both local and expatriate businessmen founded the National Bank of India, and, while the officers of the Hongkong Bank were predominantly British, its founders included German, US, and Indian firms (Fitzgerald, 2015). In the 1920s, economic conditions posed severe challenges to trading firms that relied on

[7]British North Borneo Company, School of Oriental and African Studies, Reports, and Press Cuttings, 1880–1914.

[8]HSBC Archives, Sep. 2009, 'HSBC's history'.

the financing, production, and shipping of commodities. In India, British trading companies lost market share to new competitors from Japan, and Ralli Brothers decided to form a Japanese majority-owned firm, Showa Menka, to sell Indian cotton in Japan. From Switzerland, Diethelm-Keller acquired interests in machinery, chemicals, pharmaceuticals, and automobiles, and extended its operations to Malaysia and Hong Kong (Jones, 1998). In 1919, a French textile group established Optorg to increase its sales in Russia and Asia, and, by the end of the 1930s, it had evolved into one of the five largest businesses in Indo-China.[9] Paribas, Banque de l'Indochine, Banque Lazard, and the Chinese government established, in 1925, the Banque Franco-Chinoise pour le Commerce et l'Industrie (BFCCI) to take over the assets of the Banque Industrielle de Chine: it founded offices in Beijing, Shanghai, and Tientsin, plus eight in Indo-China, including Saigon, Hanoi, and Phnom Penh, and three in France.[10]

2.3 ASIAN BUSINESS NETWORKS: 1820–1950

Western firms in Asia had numerous financial, technological, managerial, and colonially-based advantages. They transformed transcontinental and intra-regional commerce, but additionally bolstered or established networks with the Indian, Chinese, and Arab merchants who had historically pioneered the region's trade routes. Indian growers and shippers had been deeply involved in the opium trade, and, for a period, the Cowasjee family had connections and resources that rivalled those of Jardine Matheson, Dent, or Russell. They had access, moreover, to trading and finance agencies located around the Indian Ocean (Lombard & Austin, 2000). The economy of the Raj depended on the raising of local as well as international capital to fund the development of mining, plantations and trade (Bagchi, 1972). As we have seen, Western companies such as Birds and Yule both imitated and transformed established business networks. Repeated deal-making and shared personnel connected operatively-flexible and formally-independent enterprises, facilitated the spread of commercial information, and dispersed commercial risks. Indian merchants were major participants in the Bombay Burmah Trading Corporation and the Indo-Burma Petroleum Company, as well as the National Bank of India, or the Hongkong Bank. In Malaya, dealings between British partners and the Chinese business diaspora were the starting point for Sime Darby, and Chinese and British businesses jointly

[9]Optorg, 'A long history of distribution in Africa', Sep. 2010.
[10]BNP Paribas, 'History of the group', May 2010.

dominated several industrial sectors, and particularly tin-mining. The Straits Steamship Company had its origins, during 1890, in an agreement between Mansfield & Co. and wealthy Singaporean tycoons Tan Jiak Kim, Tan Keong Saik, and Lee Cheng Yan. It took cargoes in tin ore, coffee, pepper, rice, rubber, and tobacco, and brought Chinese labourers to work in the tin mines and rubber estates stretched along the Malayan peninsular. We know that ownership of the Shanghai Navigation Company was divided equally between a US shipping line, British financiers, and Chinese bankers and merchants. Within China, but especially outside the treaty ports, Western traders relied on local partners, investors, buyers, sales agents, and managers. Jardine Matheson and Butterfield and Swire's success importing to and exporting from mainland China rested on indigenous agents. To trade deep in China, multinationals evolved a network of 'compradors' to supply finance and make deals. In time, many compradors gained enough experience and resources to establish themselves as independent commission agents. As the control of Chinese agents over business transactions increased, profits for Western businesses declined. Jardine Matheson eventually withdrew from trading inside China, turning instead to international financial and shipping services, Butterfield and Swire also relocated its commercial interests, from 1902 onwards.[11] Although their approach was not typical, a few multinational importers responded with directly-owned distribution networks, storage facilities, and transport, in their attempt to reach some 400 m Chinese customers: notable were Britain's ICI (Imperial Chemical Industries); Standard Oil's highly-promoted kerosene for use as lamp-oil; and British American Tobacco (BAT), which formed the Union Trading Company with a Chinese partner, in 1911, and created an impressive marketing organization to sell its brands of rolled cigarettes. Japanese trading firms, too, gradually replaced compradors with directly-employed Mandarin-speaking Japanese managers (Chan, 1982; Cox, 2000; Fitzgerald, 2015; Yonekawa, 1990; Yonekawa & Yoshihara, 1987). Foreign banks such Deutsch Asiastische and the Hongkong Bank used traditional national *qianzhuang* financial networks to do business across China, and these multinationals became the model for banking reform, following defeat in the Sino-Japanese War during 1895. The Qing government employed Western

[11]Jardine Matheson, University Library, Cambridge University, Correspondence, 1820–1914, and Miscellaneous Papers; Jardine Skinner, Calcutta Office, 1843–73; Swire Group, School of Oriental and African Studies, London Office Correspondence, and Organization Papers, 1867–1914; Butterfield and Swire, School of Oriental and African Studies, 'Swire: our story'.

examples of 'best practice', based on joint-stock enterprise and limited liability, to restructure China's banking system, as would the Republican and Nationalist regimes that replaced the monarchy after 1911.

As part of the Self-Strengthening Movement against Western aggression, China's government had founded the China Merchants' Steam Navigation Company (CMSNC) in 1872. It wanted to halt foreign penetration of its coastal trade, and the CMSNC, as China's first joint-stock enterprise, was a watershed in national business practice (Lai, 1994). The Ministry of Agriculture, Industry and Commerce—to finance China's modernization—sought to raise international capital through the regional Chinese diaspora. The tin magnate, Foo Chee Chun, supported projects in Kwangtung and Fujian, and an overseas Chinese consortium funded the Teochew-Swatow Railway. However notable they were, such cases were rare. Chang Pi-Sheh, who emigrated to the Dutch East Indies in 1856, founded a steamship line between Penang and North Sumatra, and later gained fame as one of the world's richest Chinese. He had a contract from the Dutch navy, flew the Dutch flag, and competed effectively against Western shipping lines. Fujian was a rich source of emigrant merchant enterprises, and its entrepreneurs built Chinese trading networks throughout East Asia. Zhang Baojing, for example, left Xiamen to trade in the Dutch East Indies, and he founded the Yiho tea firm. Guo Chunyang would build trading enterprises in Taiwan, Hong Kong, Xiamen, Zhangzhou, Shanghai, and Tianjin. He owned sugar plantations in China, and refined the commodity in Hong Kong. Politically pragmatic, Guo had good relations with both the imperial Qing government and its Republican successor. He was involved with the Taiwan Oolong tea trade, from 1888, exporting the Baozhong scented variety to the Chinese populations located throughout the Dutch East Indies and Thailand. When Japanese forces occupied Taiwan, in 1895, Guo took Japanese nationality, and his Taiwanese enterprises received greater legal protection and reduced taxation; anti-Chinese sentiment in the Dutch East Indies was another motive. Guo's younger brother first encountered Mitsui as a comprador for Jardine Matheson, and this major Japanese trading company began selling Guo's Oolong tea in the United States from 1898 (Fitzgerald, 2015; Lin, 2001).

Because British companies had been slow to invest in tin-mining in Malaya, they had left the initiative to others. It is estimated that, before 1912, some 80% of the capital employed in the industry in Malaya were Chinese, although there were no Chinese-owned tin mines in the Dutch East Indies. The fact that Malayan tin was near the surface and easy to mine reduced the capital costs involved. As it contained few impurities, it could be used by most smelters, which had small incentive to integrate backwards and buy up Malayan mines. During the 1920s, international investment achieved economies of scale in the dredging of tin held in Malaya's alluvia deposits, and British-owned tin production finally overtook that of the Chinese operators. Tin companies, like their rubber counterparts, used the FSC form to raise capital in London and to operate overseas. Many of the medium to small rubber estates in Malaya, the Dutch East Indies, and Siam were Chinese-owned. Leading Chinese groups operated between Malaya, Siam, and the Dutch East Indies, involved in shipping, docks, insurance, and banking, as well as commodity trading. Khaw Soo Cheang and his family became major figures in the mining, smelting, and exporting of Siamese tin. For this, they established close relations with the government: they collected taxes, took up appointments as regional governors, imported Chinese labour, and harshly re-established royal authority in Ranong province when workers revolted against the conditions in which they laboured. In Siam, leading Chinese business groups dominated the export of rice and teak, much of it going to Singapore and Hong Kong. Thio Thiau Siat, in Sumatra, received contracts from the Netherlands colonial authorities, developed shipping enterprises, and participated in the founding of the Deli Bank of Medan and the Batavian Bank (Fitzgerald, 2015). Throughout South East Asia, Chinese merchants were pivotal in financing, procuring, processing, and distributing rice and fish, and they remained influential in shipping, insurance, fruit, vegetables, poultry, pigs, tea, hemp, and timber throughout the inter-war years. In Singapore, the regional centre for processing and trading, small Chinese factories produced beer, aerated waters, ice, food, furniture, and building materials (Barnett, 1943). On the other hand, as The Netherlands increased its political and economic grip on the East Indies, investments in plantations and steamship lines created a scale of operations that disadvantaged Chinese merchants and producers. Military and political events had their impact elsewhere, too. Japanese gunboat diplomacy in Korea (copying Western empires) had led to the Treaty of Ganghwa, in 1876, and opened up the peninsula to more trade. Despite growing Japanese influence, trading skills maintained the large presence of Chinese merchants, active in the exporting of goods such as ginseng and specie, and in importing Chinese silks and medicines as well as Western matches, kerosene, soap, and cotton textiles. Only Japan's full occupation of Korea in 1905 and its later annexation in 1910 dislodged the position of Chinese enterprises (Fitzgerald, 2015; Larsen, 2000).

The Western powers forced Japan to trade and to follow China in signing during 1858 the 'unequal' Ansei treaties and opening treaty ports. As a result, from that year, multinational traders and banks began to establish themselves in Japan. A Jardine Matheson representative, Thomas Blake Glover, founded his own firm of Glover & Co., in 1861, in Nagasaki. He was instrumental in smuggling administrators from the domain of the Choshu *daimyo* out of Japan, and many of them used the knowledge they gained of the West when they later became some of Japan's most important ministers. Glover also supplied the armaments that the forces of the Choshu and Satsuma *daimyo* needed to modernize, securing the victory that brought about the Meiji Restoration of 1868. Glover & Co. was the model for Mitsubishi Shoji (now called Mitsubishi Corporation), and Glover himself stayed in Japan to be an adviser to the Mitsubishi *zaibatsu*.[12] In reforming its economy and staving off colonization, the first aim of the Japanese government was not industrialization, but taking control of its trade. Japan had lost the right to set its own tariffs, and, by the 1880s, foreign trading firms and shipping lines oversaw some nine-tenths of its external trade. At the treaty ports, Japanese merchants had to deal with foreign traders who controlled international shipping routes, insurance facilities, and access to finance. The first firm to export Japanese rice was the US's Walsh, Hall & Co., in 1872, and E. Fischer & Co. organized much of the coal trade out of Yokohama. The British-based Marcus Samuel & Co. targeted specialist trading lines and luxury goods. From 1875, the government sought to establish competitive Japanese trading firms, assisted by the Tokyo Marine Insurance Company (founded in 1879) and the exchange and credit facilities from the Yokohama Specie Bank (established 1880). Following the Sino-Japanese War of 1894–95, an empowered Japan was able to fix its own tariffs, and, in 1899, it abolished the port settlements. By 1911, the country directly controlled 51% of its exports and 64% of its imports. Significant trading companies (*sogoshosha*) were often arms of business conglomerates (*zaibatsu*), whose emergence required government sponsorship and contacts. They provided the overseas expertise and knowledge much of Japanese business lacked, and by dealing in many products, and acting for many clients, their scale became one source of advantage against international competitors that remained at this point more experienced and better connected (Fitzgerald, 2015; Fruin, 1994; Yonekawa, 1990; Yoshihara, 1988).

[12]Mitsubishi Corporation, 'Mitsubishi Corporation: a history', and 'Mitsubishi Corporation and the Japanese Economy'.

The size and diversity of the *sogoshosha* have been viewed as unique, but (as we have seen) many British and European traders evolved into multi-product global enterprises by 1914. While European trading firms mostly operated outside their 'home' economy, the *sogoshosha* were central to the Japanese economy. Moreover, while the *sogososha* built management hierarchies, European traders retained their network of agency houses, partnerships, and cross-shareholdings, even when they founded headquarters operations (Fitzgerald, 2015; Yamazaki, 1987; Yonekawa, 1990; Yoshihara, 1988). Mitsui Bussan, established in 1876, was linked through shared political and personal connections to Okada & Company, a cotton producer and Japan's largest manufacturer. In overseas markets, it relied on cooperation with foreign enterprises, including E.B. Watson, originally from the United States, and it created offices in London and New York by 1896 in partnership with R.W. Irwin. In Bombay, it worked with Ralli Brothers in the export of raw cotton. In Japan, it acted as representatives for Carnegie Steel, the American Locomotive Company, and the world leader in cotton textile machinery, Britain's Platt Brothers. Mitsui Bussan accounted, by 1912, for 80% of the nation's machinery imports. Between 1893 and 1908, Mitsui Bussan established offices throughout Asia (especially China), Siberia, the United States, Australia, and Germany. Close relations with Mitsui Bank, another part of its parent conglomerate, and Yokohama Specie Bank, assisted its growth. Like other Japanese traders, and in a parallel pattern to their European counterparts, Mitsui Bussan played a central part in the economic development and integration of Japan's colonies, through its investments in manufacturing and natural resources. It became a major investor in Taiwanese sugar plantations and in the island's sugar exports, and it owned cotton and flour mills in Shanghai. During years in which British and European traders were losing control over their trade in inland China, Mitsui Bussan was among the *sogoshosha* that replaced its network of independent agents with a directly-owned distribution organization (Fitzgerald, 2015; Yonekawa, 1990).

While European traders in the inter-war period retracted, the presence of the *sogoshosha* in world markets increased, and notably so in Latin America, the Middle East, and the Soviet Union. Japan, before the First World War, looked to Germany for lessons in rapid industrialization, and admired German technology. Companies such as Siemens & Halske and Deutsche Bank lost extensive FDI assets as a result of the conflict. Short of capital in the inter-war decades, they sought to re-establish export markets, often using traders, or they attempted to exploit their product and technological advantages through licensing. C. Illies & Co. rebuilt its network of representative offices throughout Asia, and, in Japan, met the huge demand for construction materials following the Great Kanto earthquake of 1923. German exports equipped Japan's rapidly-expanding heavy industry and chemicals sector, and armed its growing army and navy.[13] During the 1920s, Japan reaffirmed its openness to inward FDI, but, as an industrializing country, its government used import licensing, tariffs, and quotas to foster domestic manufacturing. It especially encouraged joint ventures with foreign investors in the expectation that they would promote the transfer of technology and management. Siemens and Halske, in 1923, founded a subsidiary called Fuji Denki Seizo, or, in later years, simply Fuji Electric, in partnership with Furukawa Electric, itself part of a large zaibatsu (Fitzgerald, 2015; Kudo, 1994).[14] During the First World War, the Japanese government had sequestrated the Haber-Bosch process for producing artificial fertilizer and explosives from German firms, and leading *zaibatsu* had formed the Toyo Chisso Kumiai, or the Oriental Nitrogen Association, to exploit the technology. In the inter-war period, however, the firm had to commission technical assistance from Interessengemeinschaft or IG Farben, the successor conglomerate to the companies that had 'lost' their patent rights in Japan (Kudo, 1994). For their significant impact on Japanese industrialization, German companies began to share the credit with US multinationals. General Electric kept its stake in the Shibaura Engineering Works, which was linked to the Mitsui Bank, and, therefore, to the Mitsui *zaibatsu*, and it had shares in the Tokyo Electric Company (the subsidiaries would be merged, in 1939, into the Tokyo Shibaura Electric Company or Toshiba). The Mitsubishi *zaibatsu* incorporated Mitsubishi Electric, during 1921, with Westinghouse as a shareholder. Western Electric further expanded its subsidiary, Nippon Electric Company (NEC), with which it formed a business alliance with the Sumitomo *zaibatsu*. Western Electric sold its interest in NEC, during 1925, to International Telephone & Telegraph (ITT). When pro-military groups took control of the Japanese Diet, in 1930, they initiated a change in both domestic politics and foreign policy that led, in the following year, to the invasion of Manchuria. A nationalist-militarist government instinctively sought to reduce the influence of overseas capital. Disinvestment accelerated after the invasion of China in 1937. General

[13]C. Illies, 'History: 1859–2010', Aug. 2010.

[14]Siemens, 'Siemens history', 'Our history in 51 countries'.

Motors, Ford, Chrysler, General Electric, and ITT were amongst the multinationals undertaking total or partial withdrawal. All enemy assets were sequestrated following the attack on Pearl Harbor in 1941 (Fitzgerald, 2015).[15]

2.4 THE NEW INTERNATIONAL ECONOMIC ORDER: 1950–80

The post-war acceleration in trade was especially pronounced between developed economies, and offered fewer opportunities for European trading firms operating in colonial or post-colonial markets. The ending of empires in Asia and Africa undermined the foundations on which many of them had constructed their businesses. The governments of developing countries—frequently former colonies—wanted to control the production and sale of local commodities, the very mainstay of their economies. They had a panoply of options—the promotion of local businesses, state marketing and export companies, nationalization, import substitution policies, exchange controls, taxation, and the revision of natural resource concessions—with which to curtail the influence of foreign traders. Newly-established nation states sought to promote indigenous enterprises and business groups. Every case of decolonization had its own particularities, but the overall international pattern was evident.

Multinationals increasingly turned away from India, in the post-war period. The heavier taxation imposed on private firms, from 1949, was highly inimical to British traders. Jawaharlal Nehru, India's first Prime Minister, pursued state controlled heavy industry, electrification, and infrastructure in a series of 5-year plans, beginning in 1951, and was instinctively suspicious of inward investment. In that year, having been forced to divest, American & Foreign Power exited. A 1956 law limited the operations of managing agencies, most foreign owned, and further legislation in 1967 abolished the system. The coal industry, organized through investment networks and agency houses, was nationalized in 1970. The Foreign Exchange Regulation Act, passed in 1973, placed restrictions on all firms that were 40% or more foreign-controlled (Roy, 2006). Traders James Finlay completed, in 1976, the sale of one of the world's largest tea businesses to Tata, amongst India's biggest business groups (Jones, 2000; Tomlinson, 1993).[16] The Borneo Company declared, in 1953, its intention to shift from Asia to

[15] ITT, 'History of ITT', May 2010, and Annual Reports 1933–40, 1945, 1948; NEC, 'NEC Corporation: the first 80 years'.

[16] James Finlay, Glasgow University, Managers' Letters, Administrative Records 1948–64, and 'History and company overview'.

commercially safer territories. Guthries and Harrisons & Crosfield at first retained their place in Malaysia's rubber business, due to their control over R&D and the large costs associated with the process of replanting. Sime Darby, Boustead, the Unilever subsidiary United Africa Company (UAC), Harrisons and Crosfield, and Guthries held extensive palm oil interests in a sovereign Malaya, from 1957, and then Malaysia, after 1965.[17] In 1971, the government introduced its New Economic Policy, in favour of transferring wealth and business ownership to native Malays, and discriminating against the local Chinese and Indian populations. It wanted, furthermore, to reduce overseas influence: in 1976, the government bought a 10 per cent stake in Sime Darby, an enterprise in the engine-room of the Malaysian economy, and forced out all its British directors.[18] It likewise terminated British control over Guthries, in 1981.[19] The Japanese attack on China and, subsequently, South East Asia had inevitably damaged international trading and investment firms. Butterfield and Swire and Jardine Matheson recovered successfully from the Pacific War, but sought to be less reliant on the politically precarious and strategically vulnerable colony of Hong Kong, and on a China in which the Communists had seized power in 1949. Butterfield & Swire developed numerous businesses, including airlines, soft drinks, tea, sugar, shipping, distribution, and retailing, and it reincorporated as John Swire & Sons in 1972.[20] Jardine Matheson tried to work with the Communists, in Shanghai, in 1950, but eventually wrote off the considerable assets that were nationalized.[21] In Hong Kong, the Chinese hongs used comparable organizational forms and operational methods, and developed into serious competitors of the commercial establishment. Yue-Kong Pao's World Wide Shipping Group grew by diversification, as did Li Ka Shing's Cheung Kong, the first Chinese enterprise to buy, in 1979, a British hong, Hutchinson Whampoa (Fitzgerald, 2015). Netherlands trading firms returned to Indonesia, which achieved independence in 1949, hoping the new government would value their capabilities and know-how. Indonesia restricted imports and profit transfers, and gave preference to indigenous merchants. Internatio, Borsumij and Hagemeyer, as a result, concentrated

[17]Harrisons and Crosfield, London Metropolitan Archives, 'Administrative/biographical history'; United Africa Company of Nigeria, http://www.uacnplc.com/company/history.htm.

[18]Sime Darby, 'A short history of Sime Darby', Jun. 2010.

[19]Guthries, SOAS Archives, 'Corporate history'.

[20]Swire Group, SOAS, London Office Correspondence, Organization Papers, and 'Swire: our story'.

[21]Jardine Matheson, 'Jardines—175 years of looking to the future', 2007.

on expanding elsewhere in Asia, and, in 1957, Indonesia nationalized all Netherlands capital (Jonker & Sluyterman, 2005). Optorg, from 1963, pulled out of South East Asia, the centre of geopolitical turmoil, in favour of Africa (Fitzgerald, 2015).

Developing countries, through the United Nations Conference on Trade and Development (UNCTAD), fashioned a set of proposals to replace the Bretton Woods system, and the General Assembly adopted the Declaration for the Establishment of a New International Economic Order (NEIO), in 1974. The declaration stated the right of sovereign nations to regulate and control multinationals, and to nationalize or expropriate foreign property on favourable terms. With the sanction of UN resolutions, national sovereignty and government policy were given precedence over international property rights. With some justification, supporters of the NEIO perceived international trade and investment as mostly benefiting the North, and, to redress the balance, they associated progress and national sovereignty with central planning and import controls. Liberated nations wanted to tackle the historical wrongs of colonialism, and to overcome slow progress in economic and social development (Fitzgerald, 2015). In practice, most developing economies continued to depend on the technological, financial, managerial, and marketing capabilities of foreign multinationals. Small states were especially vulnerable, and a high export dependency on a single or small range of commodities similarly undermined autonomy (Stopford & Strange, 1991). Third World countries showed a preference for socialist planning in conjunction with a wariness of foreign-owned companies. Clashes between a multinational and the host nation were, therefore, capable of acquiring an ideological edge. Multinationals posed questions about the benefits of open trade and investment, and, in the era of the Cold War, about the advantages of very different economic systems. Nor was the Communist or socialist model the only challenger to Western or US-led political economy. Japan illustrated a mix of state activism and markets—based on the notion that only government could initiate the process of industrialization, and protect industries during their growth stage—and it fashioned a distinct Asian or developmental state model. The approach placed more emphasis on networks and business groups than in the case of the developed and more market-based economies of North America and Western Europe. In this respect, the re-establishment or founding of nation states represented historical continuity rather than a break with the past (Fitzgerald, 2015).

From the late 19th century onwards, breakthroughs in the nature of manufacturing required mass production and large-scale organization, and firms gained a competitive advantage over rivals through their ownership of scientific, financial, organizational and human resources and through the integration and systemization of processes and decision-making within the firm. These manufacturers might have proprietary rights over technology or brands, and they developed the capacity to exploit returns to scale or synergies from multiproduct operations. Deals with other firms risked loss of technological leadership, product quality, or brand reputation. In transferring their core capabilities to foreign subsidiaries, large-scale manufacturing multinationals showed a preference for creating mini-versions of the parent business in foreign markets, as evidenced by important examples in the inter-war period, and more significantly by overall trends in post-war global FDI. Investments by US manufacturers in the 1950s and 1960s altered the global flow of FDI and the structure of the international economy. In 1978, FDI asset totals were distributed as manufacturing at 52%, services at 26%, and natural resources as 22%; by 1980, in contrast to the world economy before the Second World War, developed economies were host to 61% of FDI assets compared to the remaining 39% in developing economies. The giant, integrated, and managerial US manufacturing multinational greatly influenced the emergence of FDI theory in this period, and became a model for all multinationals (Fitzgerald, 2015). Just as the diverse and geographically differentiated experience of multinational enterprise in the 19th and early 20th century was overlooked, the practice of multinational enterprise outside manufacturing and in developing regions such as East Asia became downplayed. In Japan before 1971, inward FDI was prohibited, and remained in practice difficult after that date. But cross-border alliances continued to be pivotal. Fujitsu required technological cooperation with IBM from 1961 in order to develop its computing business.[22] Isuzu, allied in turn to Subaru, Mitsubishi Motors and Nissan, exchanged equity and signed a model and technology sharing agreement with General Motors.[23] From 1954, long-established family-owned business groups (*zaibatsu*) that had been dissolved by the United States after the war began to reconstitute themselves, this time as looser groupings of independent businesses run by professional managers (*kigyo shudan*). Newly-formed *kigyo shudan*

[22]Fujitsu, 'History of Fujitsu', Mar. 2010, and 'Company history', 1989.
[23]General Motors, 'History and Heritage'; GM Holden, 'Holden History', Jun. 2013.

coalesced around major banks. By pooling capital and managerial resources, and spreading commercial risks, they could assist bold plans in investment, manpower and output, as made at the Ministry of International Trade and Industry, to bring about Japan's rapid industrialization. The United States had similarly broken up the *sogososha*. To re-establish their role as efficient multinationals, and to obtain the flow of materials needed for economic recovery, Japanese trading companies had to re-acquire scale, and recreate their overseas offices and commercial networks. Mitsui Bussan was in effect revived as Mitsui & Co. by 1958, and, overseas, it cooperated with foreign and Japanese mining, oil and chemical firms.[24] Mitsubishi Shoji was reunited in a series of mergers, by 1954, and worked with foreign and Japanese businesses in oil, chemicals, tourism, mining, and automobiles. It anglicized its name into Mitsubishi Corporation in 1971. Japanese FDI was markedly concentrated in the post-war period in East Asia, led by the *sogososha* acquiring the natural resources, components and machinery sought by Japan's consumers and manufacturing businesses (Fitzgerald, 2005).[25]

2.5 GLOBALIZATION, THE STATE, AND BUSINESS NETWORKS

We can draw out a number of conclusions from an historical survey of the international economy, multinationals, governments, and business networks. There are, firstly, questions about the origin and nature of business networks, and the extent to which they are rooted in specific national, cultural, and institutional characteristics. For East Asia, Confucian values and prevalent institutional structures are seen as producing business systems that are more 'networked' and less 'marketized' than those in the West (Hamilton, 1996; Redding, 1990). Whitley has argued that key social institutions, such as the state, the financial system, or educational provision during the processes of industrialization critically determined national business systems. He does add that kinship groups, trust networks, and authority structures constitute secondary determinants. On the other hand, capital intensity levels, markets, transaction costs, or 'general processes of economic development' have been minor in their influence (Whitley, 1992, see also Maurice, Sellier, & Silvestre, 1986; Orru, Biggart, & Hamilton, 1997; Sorge & Warner, 1986). Economic and business historians, by contrast, give due weight to

[24]Mitsui & Co., 'History of Mitsui & Company Ltd', Jun. 2009.

[25]Mitsubishi Corporation, Jun. 2009, 'Mitsubishi Corporation: a history', and 'Mitsubishi Corporation and the Japanese economy'.

shifts in resources, technology, and markets as well as institutional factors. In some cases, they have looked at the relationship between the macroeconomic and political background and business organization, management and networks (Fruin, 1994; Meier, 1989). As we have seen, globalization and colonization constituted a major influence on Asian economic development from the 19th century onwards. Multinational trading companies operated through complex networks of international and local alliances, repeat contracting, trust relationships, kinship ties, and shared partners and personnel, in which personal contacts, market intelligence and deal-making were critical competitive tools. They enabled the global transfer of capital, effected transcontinental trade and marketing, and invested in mines, plantations, transport, infrastructure, and industry (Chapman, 1992; Jones, 1998, 2000). The characteristics of trading and finance businesses before the Second World War—and notably in Asia—underlines the relevance of multinationals that did not depend on a large parent firm and subsidiaries overseen by a management hierarchy (Fitzgerald, 2015). Multinational trading companies extended business, network, and partnership opportunities for indigenous Asian entrepreneurs, and had an impact on the strategies and organization of local and native business networks and the Japanese *sogososha*. In turn, Asian business networks had an impact on the strategies and organization of European multinationals. Historical analysis places an emphasis on studying business networks in East Asia and Asia generally and not, as such, Asian business networks: it points to the importance of international or cross-border factors in shaping business systems, and to the impossibility of considering national or cultural issues in isolation; it suggests, too, that European multinationals and local enterprises adopted similar forms of organization and operation, and that the market and policy circumstances of developing and commodity-exporting economies were more determinant than the cultural or the institutional.

There is no doubt that the economic leadership achieved by the West, in combination with colonialism, enabled multinational traders and investors to achieve their commercial dominance across Asia. Research indicates that links with colonial administrations were as important to the rise of significant Chinese businesses in South East Asia as the later contacts they forged with independent governments after the era of imperialism (MacIntyre, 1990; McVey, 1992; Robison, 1986; Yoshihara, 1988). We can argue, secondly, that government policy has in developing and commodity-exporting economies encouraged international and local business networks, and it follows that the end of colonialism and the founding of new nation states marked an important trend in which indigenous trading or business groups were favoured. From the inter-war period, but particularly in the post-war period, there was a shift in global FDI patterns, and investment from manufacturing and US multinationals accelerated. Large industrial companies had to maintain, utilize and monitor the loyalty and expertise of managers through administrative structures, since they were employed for their specialized knowledge of tangible products and process technologies. They demonstrated a growing inclination towards the internalization of process stages, multiproduct production, and integrated managerial hierarchies. Certain types of manufacturers and service firms in general showed a greater inclination towards business groups and networks, but post-war Western business and multinationals revealed an overall trend towards internalization and management integration and away from networks (Fitzgerald, 2000, 2003, 2015). On the other hand, state-directed industrial policy, regulated or government-owned financial systems, international technology transfer, and import and exchange controls underpinned rapid or 'late' industrialization in developing economies and, most prominently, in East Asia. State-business networks and cooperation were integral to the policy, and governments promoted particular business groups. Vertical and horizontal links between firms and within business groups, moreover, facilitated economic development and diversification. The absorption of new technologies required factories with minimal process stages, and networks offered compensating economies of scale and negotiating power. Business groups and networks were alternatives to inchoate markets, and they served as effective means of transferring capital, technology, and management. They provided a means of spreading the risks inherent in rapid growth through shared ownership and secure supply and distribution chains (Amsden, 1989, 1994; Cho, 1995; Fruin, 1994; Fukusaku, 1992; Gerlach, 1992; Suehiro, 1993). Nation states in East Asia had a detectable impact on the development of business systems in the post-war period, yet international factors such as strategic alliances, transfers of technology and managerial know-how, joint ventures and shared equity remained influential, too.

Historical insights into the international economy and business networks, thirdly, pose doubts about much of the commentary on the 'new' era of 21st century globalization. It is a period in which, with obvious exaggeration, the disappearance of the nation state has been predicted. Trends in multinational business organization demonstrate trends away from the integrated and hierarchical parent-subsidiary model, in which large-scale manufacturing enterprises had overall once shown a strategic preference for equity ownership and direct control of overseas subsidiaries, thereby facilitating the transfer and safeguarding of technology and managerial know-how. From the 1980s, and more notably from the 1990s, manufacturing multinationals found that they could utilize the production resources of locations all over the world, as well as compete for every major market. FDI and the relocation of production serviced greater returns to scale and efficiencies for each production stage, and created complex cross-border value chains. Multinationals showed greater inclination to adopt licensing, franchising, subcontracting, or strategic alliances, and other collaborative arrangements that supported outsourcing and off-shoring in competitive locations (Fitzgerald, 2015). Cross-border production networks used a mix of inter-firm and intra-firm transactions; those in automobiles, aircraft, electrical machinery, and computers were producer-driven chains; those in clothing and shoes were buyer-driven by large retailers and brand-name merchandisers (Gereffi, 1994). There was, by the 1980s, acknowledgement of the impact of Japanese manufacturing multinationals on the global economy and the emergence of their 'regional' and 'global production networks'. The Japanese *sogososha*, well placed to take advantage of Asian growth and develop new types of business, continued to utilize networks of alliances, joint ventures, suppliers, and buyers. To secure the resources needed for industrialization, the Korean government followed the Japanese example of appointing and assisting official trading enterprises, such as Hyundai Corporation or Samsung Corporation, which were, in addition, members of family-owned business groups or *chaebol*. The growing scale and incidence of cross-border production chains and outsourcing strategies meant that contract manufacturers grew in size and underpinned the workings of the global economy. Li and Fung emerged as a well-known example in fashion and textiles, as were the cases of Foxconn and Flextronics in electronics and Denso in auto-parts (Fitzgerald, 2015). As we have seen, cross-border networks have long antecedents, and historical perspective indicates that there has been a return to greater reliance on international networks. It suggests a need to analyse the relationship between trends in the international economy and multinational business organization, on the one hand, and national business networks and business groups on the other.

REFERENCES

Allen, G. C., & Donnithorne, A. G. (1954). *Western enterprise in far eastern economic development: China and Japan*. London: Allen & Unwin.

Allen, G. C., & Donnithorne, A. G. (1957). *Western enterprise in far eastern economic development: Indonesia and Malaysia*. London: Routledge.

Amsden, A. H. (1989). *Asia's next giant: South Korea and late industrialization*. Oxford: Oxford University Press.

Amsden, A. H. (1994). Staying behind, stumbling back, sneaking up, and soaring ahead: Late industrialization in historical perspective. In W. J. Baumol, R. R. Nelson, & E. N. Wolff (Eds.), *Convergence of productivity: Cross national studies and historical evidence*. Oxford: Oxford University Press.

Andaya, B. W., & Andaya, L. Y. (1982). *A history of Malaysia*. Basingstoke: Palgrave.

Bagchi, A. K. (1972). *Private investment in India, 1900–39*. Cambridge: Cambridge University Press.

Barnett, P. G. (1943). The Chinese in Southeastern Asia and the Philippines. *Annals of the American Academy of Political and Social Science*, *226*, 32–49.

Boisot, M., & Child, J. (1996). From fiefs to clans and network capitalism: Explaining China's emerging economic order. *Administrative Science Quarterly*, *41*, 600–628.

Boyce, G. (1995). *Information, mediation and institutional development: The rise of large-scale enterprise in British shipping, 1870–1914*. Manchester: Manchester University Press.

Chan, W. K. K. (1982). The organizational structure of the traditional Chinese firm and its modern reform. *Business History Review*, *56*, 218–235.

Chapman, S. D. (1992). *Merchant enterprise in Britain from the industrial revolution to the World War I*. Cambridge: Cambridge University Press.

Cheng, L. (2003). *Banking in modern China: Entrepreneurs, professional managers, and the development of Chinese banks, 1897–1937*. Cambridge: Cambridge University Press.

Chew, E. C. T. & Lee, E. (Eds.), (1991). *A history of Singapore*. Oxford: Oxford University Press.

Cho, D. S. (1995). A dynamic approach to international competitiveness: The case of Korea. In R. Fitzgerald (Ed.), *The competitive advantages of far eastern businesses*. London: Frank Cass.

Cox, H. (2000). *The global cigarette: Origins and evolution of British American tobacco, 1880–1945*. Oxford: Oxford University Press.

Evans, R. J. (2005). *In defence of history*. London: Granta Books.

Fieldhouse, D. K. (1965). *Colonial empires: A comparative survey from the 18th century*. New York: Delacorte Press.

Fitzgerald, R. (2000). The competitive and institutional advantages of holding companies: British business in the inter-war period. *Journal of Industrial History*, 1–30.

Fitzgerald, R. (2003). Corporate governance, business organization and competitiveness: British and Japanese business in the inter-war period. In E. Abe & R. Fitzgerald (Eds.), *The development of corporate governance in Japan and Britain*. London: Ashgate/Gower Press.

Fitzgerald, R. (2015). *The rise of the global company: Multinationals and the making of the modern world*. Cambridge: Cambridge University Press.

Fruin, W. M. (1994). *The Japanese enterprise system: Competitive strategies and cooperative structures*. Oxford: Clarendon Press.

Fukusaku, Y. (1992). *Technology and industrial development in pre-war Japan: Mitsubishi Nagasaki Shipyard, 1884–1934*. London: Routledge.

Gereffi, G. (1994). *Commodity chains and global capitalism*. Westport: Praeger.

Gerlach, M. (1992). *Alliance capitalism: The strategic organization of Japanese business*. Berkeley, CA: University of California Press.

Guex, S. (1998). *Switzerland and the great powers, 1914–1945*. Geneva: University of Geneva.

Hamilton, G. G. (Ed.), (1996). *Asian business networks*. Berlin: De Gruyter.

Jones, G. (1998). *The multinational traders*. London: Routledge.

Jones, G. (2000). *Merchants to multinationals*. Oxford: Oxford University Press.

Jonker, J., & Sluyterman, K. (2005). *At home on the world markets: Dutch trading international trading companies from the 16th century to the present*. Montreal: McGill Queen's University Press.

Kudo, A. (1994). IG Farben in Japan: The transfer of technology and managerial skills. *Business History*, *36*, 159–183.

Lai, C. K. (1994). China Merchants' Steam Navigation Company, 1872–1902. *Journal of Economic History, 54*, 432–434.

Larsen, L. (2000). Seizing the opportunities: Chinese merchants in Korea, 1876–1910. *Chinese Business History*, 7, 142–167.

Latham, A. J. & Kawakatsu, H. (Eds.), (1994). *The evolving structure of the East Asian economic system since 1700: A comparative analysis*. London: Routledge.

Lin, M. H. (2001). Overseas Chinese merchants and multiple nationality: A means of reducing commercial risk, 1895–1935. *Modern Asian Studies, 35*, 985–1009.

Liu, K. C. (1962). *Anglo-American rivalry in China, 1862–74*. Cambridge, MA: Harvard University Press.

Lombard, D., & Austin, J. (2000). *Asian merchants and businessmen in the Indian Ocean and the China Sea*. Oxford: Oxford University Press.

MacIntyre, A. (1990). *Business and politics in Indonesia*. St Leonards: Allen & Unwin.

Maurice, M., Sellier, F., & Silvestre, J. J. (1986). *The social bases of industrial power*. Cambridge, MA: MIT Press.

McVey, R. (Ed.), (1992). *South East Asian capitalists*. Ithaca, NY: Cornell South East Asian Studies Program.

Meier, G. M. (1989). *Leading issues in economic development*. New York: Oxford University Press.

Myint-U, T. (2001). *The making of modern Burma*. Cambridge: Cambridge University Press.

Orru, M., Biggart, N. W., & Hamilton, G. G. (1997). *The new institutionalism in organizational analysis*. London: Sage.

Ray, R. K. (1979). *Industrialization in India*. Oxford: Oxford University Press.

Redding, S. G. (1990). *The spirit of Chinese capitalism*. New York: Walter De Gruyter.

Robison, R. (1986). *Indonesia: The rise of capital*. Sydney: Allen & Unwin.

Roy, T. (2006). *The economic history of India, 1857–1947*. Oxford: Oxford University Press.

Saunier, P.-Y. (2013). *Transnational history*. London: Palgrave Macmillan.

Shiba, T., & Shimotani, M. (Eds.), (1997). *Beyond the firm: Business groups in international and comparative perspective*. Oxford: Oxford University Press.

Sorge, A., & Warner, M. (1986). *Comparative factory organization*. Aldershot: Gower.

Stopford, J. M., & Strange, S. (1991). *Rival states, rival firms*. Cambridge: Cambridge University Press.

Suehiro, A. (1993). Family business reassessed: Competition, structure and late-starting industrialization in Thailand. *The Developing Economies, 31*, 378–407.

Tomlinson, B. R. (1993). *The new Cambridge history of India: The economy of modern India, 1860–1970*. Cambridge: Cambridge University Press.

Tung, R., & Worm, V. (2001). Network capitalism: The role of human resources in penetrating the China market. *International Journal of Human Resource Management, 12*, 517–534.

Whitley, R. (1992). *Business systems in East Asia*. London: Sage.

Wilkins, M., & Schroter, H. (1998). *The free-standing company in the world economy, 1830–1914*. Oxford: Oxford University Press.

Yamazaki, H. (1987). The logic of general trading companies in Japan. In S. Yonekawa & H. Yosihara (Eds.), *Business history of trading companies*. Tokyo: Tokyo University Press.

Yonekawa, S., & Yoshihara, H. (1987). *Business history of general trading companies*. Tokyo: University of Tokyo Press.

Yonekawa, S. (Ed.), (1990). *General trading companies: A comparative and historical study*. Tokyo: Tokyo University Press.

Yoshihara, K. (1988). *Sogo Sosha: The vanguard of the Japanese economy*. Oxford: Oxford University Press.

PART 1

Business Networks in China and Hong Kong

CHAPTER 3

Bank of China International in Hong Kong: Social Status and Network Access

D.R. Meyer
Washington University in St. Louis, St. Louis, MO, United States

During the decade following economic reforms of the 1980s, China's government turned its attention to reforming financial markets. This effort was essential to maintain the pace of economic growth because financial reform would improve the allocation of capital to economic decision makers. Nonperforming loans (NPLs), especially from state-owned enterprises (SOEs), had become a drain on the banking system; therefore, banks were given authority to write off loans. In 1994, the government established policy banks which released the state banks of China (SBOCs) from direct policy lending. The SBOCs were recapitalized in the late 1990s, and substantial amounts of NPLs were shifted to asset management companies, one for each of the four largest SBOCs: Agricultural Bank of China, Bank of China, China Construction Bank, and Industrial and Commercial Bank of China. These reforms paved the way for initial public offerings (IPOs) of stock on the Hong Kong and Shanghai exchanges between 2002 and 2010 (Brean, 2007; Chiu & Lewis, 2006, pp. 186–224; Wines, 2010).

Financial reforms provided the basis for incorporation of Bank of China International (BOCI) to operate as an investment bank in Hong Kong in 1998 as a wholly owned subsidiary of Bank of China (Beijing) (Bank of China International, 2012; Loong, 2000). This inserted a unit of a mainland China SBOC into the intensely competitive environment of Hong Kong, dominated by investment banking units of leading global banks headquartered in London, New York, Zurich, Frankfurt, and Paris. BOCI offers a full range of investment banking services to institutional clients, including stock and bond issuance, mergers and acquisitions, private equity, syndicated lending, derivatives, commodity trading, and asset management. For private clients, the bank offers services such as stock and bond trading, private wealth

Business Networks in East Asian Capitalisms
http://dx.doi.org/10.1016/B978-0-08-100639-9.00003-7

management, and fund investments. Other international units of BOCI are in London, New York, and Singapore (Bank of China International, 2015).

The parent company, Bank of China (Beijing), is a prestigious SBOC in mainland China, but this does not translate into a source of strength in the Hong Kong environment dominated by elite global investment banks. As noted in Chapter 4, the development of government relationships is a priority for Chinese business networks, with relatively less effort given to the cultivation of international connections. The thesis proposed here is that BOCI's tie to its parent company, rather than being a benefit, confers lower status among investment banks. This undermines the bank's capacity to participate in elite investment banking networks.

3.1 IMPACT OF FINANCIAL REFORM ON THE SOCIAL STATUS OF BANKS

China's reforms included policies to allow limited access of foreign financial institutions to the country's markets as a mechanism to introduce international standards of governance, technology, and management to Chinese financial institutions. The transfer mechanism operated through the introduction of competition and through small ownership stakes that foreign institutions took in the large state banks (Brean, 2007; Chiu & Lewis, 2006; Levy & Meyer, 2012; Nolan, 2011). By improving the professional operations of Chinese banks, the goal was to make them more sophisticated collaborators with foreign institutions on transactions, such as issuing stocks and bonds, IPOs, mergers and acquisitions, and syndicated loans, thus enhancing the expertise of China's banks.

Foreign experts assisted Chinese regulators at the China Banking Regulatory Commission (CBRC) to develop laws that would improve the governance of Chinese banks. Nevertheless, banks have few external incentives to improve their governance practices. The political-economy of China discourages banks from pushing for bankruptcy of nonfinancial firms, and bank bankruptcy will not be allowed by the government. From the perspective of foreign bankers, the regulatory system is opaque, and *guanxi* networks are viewed as more important for understanding the regulatory system than formal rules and institutions. Few foreign nonexecutive directors are on bank boards of directors, and those on the board possess little or no power to influence the banks because government-appointed directors from state agencies dominate the boards. Ownership stakes of foreign banks do not generate much influence on banks (Levy & Meyer, 2012; Nolan, 2010). While technical knowledge was transferred through ownership stakes of foreign banks, limited improvements were made in the more strategic areas of credit ratings and risk management. In any case, foreign banks reduced their ownership stakes to insignificant levels. Chinese banks appear more concerned with gaining legitimacy than with fundamental management reform (Nolan, 2010).

The Chinese Communist Party (CCP) commands the levers of state power in China; therefore, the Party controls the SBOCs. Borrowing Heilmann's (2005b, p. 1) framing, the CCP employs Leninist institutions that "include the pervasive presence and elaborate hierarchy of Party organs in administrative bodies and state-controlled firms, rigid rules of cadre surveillance and recruitment as well as methods of extra-judicial disciplinary supervision." This institutional approach as applied to the financial system, however, does not mean the Party exerts tight control over the administration of financial institutions. Instead, the CCP focuses on cadre recruitment, appointment, and supervision (Heilmann, 2005a, 2005b).

Political patronage within the Party impacts appointments of financial executives and boards of directors. When top Party cadres obtain leadership positions in financial institutions, their political power within the Party insulates them, to a degree, from the discipline inspection committees. This allows them to pursue profit-making opportunities as would be followed in the "western" financial institutions, even as their power might also allow opportunities for corruption (Shevchenko, 2004). The increasing number of financial institutions (banks, fund management companies, private equity) that are led by family members of leading CCP cadres introduces highly networked financial leaders who can exert political influence that exceeds their cadre status (Andreosso-O'Callaghan & Gottwald, 2013).

The CCP exerts pervasive control over appointments of all top executives of financial institutions and of their regulatory bodies—People's Bank of China (PBOC), China Securities Regulatory Commission (CSRC), CBRC, and China Insurance Regulatory Commission (CIRC). Consequently, this reinforces the view of "foreign" financiers and their firms that whenever they deal with top financiers in China's institutions and regulatory agencies, they are dealing with individuals who are beholden to the Party. While these Chinese financiers and their regulators do not comprise a monolithic entity—many competing entrenched interests exist, final resolution of major financial issues will be resolved within the CCP, and, if necessary, at the level of the State Council and the Politburo Standing Committee (Andreosso-O'Callaghan & Gottwald, 2013). Network ties of foreign financiers with their peers in Chinese financial institutions, therefore, ultimately are impacted by this web of ties within the CCP and its members in senior positions in finance.

The government's control of the large SBOCs through the mechanism of the CCP's recruitment, appointment, and supervision of cadres, combined with the intertwined Party control of financial regulators, all under the oversight of the State Council, contributes to the belief that the government will not let any banks fail. This belief may explain why the SBOCs—that is, those directly controlled by the government—take more risks than banks in which the majority ownership is held by SOEs or by private-sector investors. The SBOCs are subject to direct intervention by the government, and the bankers are not incentivized to engage in prudent management (Dong, Meng, Firth, & Hou, 2014). From the perspective of foreign financiers, this structural condition of the SBOCs undermines their status and that of their financiers.

Foreign bankers who operate in China utilize *guanxi* networks to access information and expertise from public and private sector actors. One mechanism bankers use for gaining this access is to hire Chinese who have prior relationships that they can leverage for their bank. This type of *guanxi* has similarities to conditions in most, if not all, countries whenever relationships are required for successful operation of a business. On the other hand, some bankers have experience with the bad form of *guanxi* in which favors are exchanged, such as hiring bankers recommended by government officials with the expectation that the officials would reciprocate in the future (Nolan, 2011). When foreign bankers engage in this type of *guanxi*, which involves a large state bank, the likelihood is that the foreign bankers rate the Chinese bankers as possessing lower status. Regardless of whether or not *guanxi* networks are used by foreign bankers, some of their experiences working with Chinese bankers in SBOCs leads them to rank these banks less desirable in which to work and they lag international standards (Levy & Meyer, 2012).

China's reforms have strengthened the financial system, and substantial improvements have been implemented to make banking adhere more to international standards of governance, market-orientation, and management. Nonetheless, the government exerts continued direct control over the largest state banks (SBOCs). This telegraphs that these banks must respond to policy initiatives when ordered to do so by the government. Furthermore, leadership of these banks comes from the ranks of Communist Party cadres, which signifies that they must negotiate within the political realm of the Party. Foreign bankers must use networks that employ *guanxi* to engage with Chinese banks, as well as with government officials. The consensus is that foreign bankers have had minimal influence on the practices of Chinese banks, except in the realm of technology. China's SBOCs have a reputation for taking more risks, probably because they know the government will not let them fail.

In sum, foreign bankers view China's banks as possessing lower status in international banking. This leads to the hypothesis that BOCI in Hong Kong, a subsidiary of Bank of China (Beijing), possesses a lower status in investment banking circles. Lower status contributes to BOCI's weak integration with elite investment banking networks. The theoretical literature on social status of firms and the impact of status on their network ties provides a basis for analyzing BOCIs' position in investment banking networks.

3.2 THEORETICAL LENS ON SOCIAL STATUS AND NETWORKS

3.2.1 Social Bases of Status

The status of a firm is a subjective assessment of its social rank which members of a group draw from their hierarchy of values. The group's status judgment is based on perceptions and is ascribed to the firm; it does not earn the status. This evaluation is socially shared and represents a consensus of the group. The firm's status always is with reference to its rank in the group. Status ranking of members offers them possibilities to gain opportunities and to exert constraint on other members (Pearce, 2011; Piazza & Castellucci, 2014).

The quality of a firm's performance, its expertise, and its power may influence the ascription of status that group members assign to it, but these are imprecise indicators of the firm's status (Pearce, 2011). Quality, expertise, and power are not always directly observable, and the correlation of them with status may be weak. Social processes and relations mediate the link between status and these measures (Podolny, 1993).

Status, which is based on a social ranking of firms and creates unearned privileges and social esteem, is distinguished from reputation, which is based on differences in actual or perceived quality or merit that generate rewards for the firm (Washington & Zajac, 2005). Status identifies a firm's relative position within an industry, whereas reputation relates to its attributes (Jensen & Roy, 2008). When choosing a partner for exchange, status operates as a mechanism for screening potential partners by their market identity within a social group, while reputation may be used for final selection (Jensen, Kim, & Kim, 2011).

3.2.1.1 *Social Status as a Relational Asset*

The degree of social prestige and deference conferred on a firm impacts the level of status it holds within a group. Status is an asset that indicates the expectations about the firm's attributes, such as quality and its capacity to perform. Past recognition given to the firm will be an asset that encourages others to recognize it in the future (Granados & Knoke, 2013). Affiliations of a firm indicate its degree of attractiveness to others. A firm's status is enhanced to the degree that it affiliates with higher-status firms; conversely, linkages with lower-status firms reduce one's status (Podolny, 1993).

Instances of lower-status firms affiliating with higher-status firms occur (Piazza & Castellucci, 2014; Tortoriello, Perrone, & McEvily, 2011). Nevertheless, the principle of status homophily—firms affiliate with others that have similar status—is more prevalent (Chung, Singh, & Lee, 2000; Jensen et al., 2011). Similar status firms have congruent ways of behaving and comparable capabilities, and, if uncertainty about results of interfirm transactions is high, collaborating with firms of similar status helps mitigate uncertainty. Higher-status firms prefer to avoid affiliating with lower-status firms to minimize threats to their status (Benjamin & Podolny, 1999; Piazza & Castellucci, 2014).

The relative stability of status undergirds it as a relational asset. The tendency of group members to develop a consensus about their assessments of the relative status of members contributes to reproducing the status hierarchy (Gould, 2002). Nevertheless, this hierarchy is not rigid; upper levels do not gain all of the benefits. Lower-status members keep their deference within limits to minimize unreciprocated gestures of approval from higher-status members. Still, cumulative advantages accrue to higher-status firms because other firms commit resources to the former, allowing it to improve performance and enhance status (Podolny & Phillips, 1996). The higher-status firm gains benefits, such as raising its capacity to produce better quality outputs for a given cost.

3.2.2 Network Status

The relative social rank or prominence of the positions that firms occupy in networks of firms who are directly or indirectly linked and compete in a market is termed network status (Jensen, 2003; Podolny, 1993). These linkages are the "pipes" through which status flows. Firms employ linkages to identify others' status as well as to communicate their own status. Likewise, pipes are conduits for firms in the network to access resources (advice, cooperative agreements, business knowledge), and these network resources are unique to a given network (Owen-Smith, Cotton-Nessler, & Buhr, 2015; Podolny, 2001). The firm's network status in a given market may be only partially transferrable to another market because firms in that market have limited knowledge about the status of the firm that joins the network.

The structure of networks impacts flows of status and resources through the networks. From an individual firm's perspective, its "reach" is the degree to which the firm can access potential partners. This reach is impacted by the position of the firm in the network (Gulati, Lavie, & Madhavan, 2011). A firm that is a network hub has connections to other firms in the network, and these connections may be mechanisms for exerting influence or power over other firms and accessing valuable resources. This may occur when the firm bridges to two other firms that have no links to each other; thus, a structural hole exists between them. The firm building the bridge, not only gains access to nonredundant information, but it can also exploit control over information and resources and exert structural constraint on them. Similarly, a firm may build bridges to two or more clusters of firms, each of which has links among firms in the cluster. When these clusters are not connected, that is, structural holes exist among them, the firm gains the benefits of control. In both cases, the firm building the bridge becomes the *tertius gaudens*, the controller of information and resource flows (Burt, 1992, 2004, 2010).

A firm aims to exploit its brokerage position in networks to accumulate status and enhance its market performance (Kogut, 2000; Shipilov & Li, 2008). It acquires information about new business opportunities and potential partners with whom to cooperate and collaborate on deals. High-status firms view this firm as an attractive partner, thus allowing the firm to boost its status because it associates with high-status firms. Nevertheless, in an open network with structural holes, firms cannot fully assess the cooperativeness and quality of the firm. This leads to doubts about the trustworthiness of the firm and/or its capacity to perform in a manner which generates revenues/profits. Knowledge about cooperativeness and quality is chiefly available in cohesive networks where numerous links among members permit extensive sharing of deep insight about each other.

High-status firms are perceived to have more valuable resources and access to business opportunities. This gives the high-status firm more power in exchange relations with low-status firms (Thye, 2000). These unequal relations are enhanced when the high-status firm possesses brokerage advantages in networks and bridges structural holes, as well as when the firm has substantial internal capabilities—high quality resources for executing strategies (Zaheer & Bell, 2005). A high-status firm in a strong brokering position, therefore, will initiate ties to low-status firms—build heterophilous ties—so long as it gains access to resources and business opportunities, yet does not diminish its status.

These theoretical concepts are employed to interpret the integration of BOCI into the elite networks of global investment banking. The collective performance of leading financiers in the firm contributes to the social status of the bank and its integration into premier networks. Nevertheless, the chief executive officers (CEOs) of BOCI are the external "face" of the bank. Thus, their social status and integration into elite investment banking networks offer an important window into the network position of BOCI as an organization.

3.3 CHIEF EXECUTIVE OFFICERS OF BOCI

3.3.1 An Educated Elite

The upper levels of the CCP have been transformed into an educated elite (Bian, Shu, & Logan, 2001; Walder, 2004; Zhang, 1998), and the CEOs of BOCI exemplify this change (Table 3.1). Following degrees at a major Chinese university in Beijing, the first CEO, Gao Xiqing (1998–1999), earned a J.D. degree from Duke University's elite law school. Both Li Shan (2001–2005) and Wang Yan (2005–2011) hold undergraduate degrees from prestigious Chinese universities and doctorates from the world's top universities—Li Shan from Massachusetts Institute of Technology and Wang Yan from Peking University. Fang Fenglei (2000–2001), arguably the most famous financier to hold the position of CEO, earned his undergraduate degree from Sun Yat-sen, a top university in Guangzhou, China. The current CEO, Li Tong (2012–2015), holds an EMBA degree from a major global business school, Australian Graduate School of Management.

While the high social status of the CEOs based on their academic pedigrees benefits them personally in interactions with other financiers and with clients, it is doubtful that this transfers much to the social status of BOCI itself. Academic degrees are not indicative of the quality of the financier's investment banking prowess, nor of the financier's positioning in investment banking networks. Consequently, they could not transfer high social status to BOCI. Furthermore, their limited strong linkages (or "pipes") provided weak access for BOCI to network resources (expertise, knowledge, opportunities to execute deals).

Table 3.1 Chief Executive Officers (CEOs) of Bank of China International (BOCI) until 2015

Date	Name	Education
1998–1999	Gao Xiqing	B.A., M.S., University of International Business and Economics, Beijing; J.D., Duke University
1999–2000	Liang Xiaoting	Unknown
2000–2001	Fang Fenglei	B.A., Sun Yat-sen University
2001–2005	Li Shan	B.A., Tsinghua; M.A., University of California, Davis; Ph.D., Massachusetts Institute of Technology
2005–2011	Wang Yan	B.A., M.S., Beijing University; Ph.D., Peking University
2012–2015	Li Tong	B.A., Dongbei University of Finance and Economics; EMBA, Australian Graduate School of Management

Based on various newspapers and websites.

3.3.1.1 Careers Prior to Becoming CEO

Few CEOs of BOCI brought significant networks from elite global financial firms when they took over the top position (Table 3.2). Gao Xiqing, the first CEO, had no direct experience in investment banking. After a brief stint as a lawyer in New York, his early career consisted of legal positions in government regulatory agencies in China. Arguably, Fang Fenglei (2000–2001) possessed the best networks to top global firms prior to becoming CEO. During the 1980s and early 1990s, Fang worked as a provincial-government trade official and in several Chinese financial institutions. In the early 1990s, Fang convinced his boss and mentor, Wang Qishan, that China should establish an investment bank modeled after United States' banks (Anderlini & Tucker, 2009; Stein & Areddy, 2007). Wang already was a senior Party official, including positions in China Construction Bank and the PBOC (Wang, 2015). In 1995, China International Capital Corporation (CICC) started as a joint-venture between Morgan Stanley and China Construction Bank (Barboza, 2014).

Fang brought to CICC his extensive network ties to senior government officials, including those in the SOEs (nonfinancial) and the SBOCs. These firms were candidates for IPOs, such as China Telecom (now called China Mobile), mergers and acquisitions, and stock and bond underwriting (CICC, 2015). With Morgan Stanley, a top United States investment bank, as a partner, Fang had access to the global network of elite investment

Table 3.2 Careers of CEOs of Bank of China International (BOCI) until 2015

Name	Date	Career
Gao Xiqing	1987	Associate, Mudge, Rose, Guthrie, Alexander & Ferdon, New York
	1990	General counsel, Securities Exchange Executive Council, Beijing
	1993–1995	General counsel, China Securities Regulatory Commission
	1998–1999	CEO, Bank of China International
	1999–2003	Vice-chairman, China Securities Regulatory Commission
	2003–2007	Vice-chairman, National Council for Social Security Fund
	2006–2007	Vice-chairman, China Securities Regulatory Commission
	2007–2014	Vice-chairman, China Investment Corporation
Liang Xiaoting	1993–1994	General manager, China Development Finance, Hong Kong
	1995–1999	General manager, Bank of China, Hong Kong
	1999–2000	CEO, Bank of China International
	2002	Arrested on corruption and embezzlement charges
	2004–2008	Sentenced to prison
	2010	Employed by property developer, Beijing
Fang Fenglei	1995–2000	China International Capital Corporation, founder and Deputy chief executive
	2000–2001	CEO, Bank of China International
	2002–2003	CEO, ICEA Finance Holdings, Hong Kong
	2004–2008	Partner, Goldman Sachs, owner and Chairman, Gao Hua Securities, Beijing (joint venture with Goldman Sachs)
	2007–2015	Owner, Hopu Investment Management, private equity firm
Li Shan	1993	Trader, Credit Suisse, New York
	1994–1998	Investment banker, Goldman Sachs, New York, Hong Kong, London
	1999–2001	Investment banker, Lehman Brothers, Hong Kong
	1998–2001	Owner, Soufun Holdings, online real estate information
	2001–2005	CEO, Bank of China International
	2005–2015	Owner, San Shan Capital Partners, private equity firm

Table 3.2 Careers of CEOs of Bank of China International (BOCI) until 2015—Cont'd

Name	Date	Career
Wang Yan	2000–2005	Deputy General Manager, Industrial and Commercial Bank of China (Hong Kong)
	2005–2011	CEO, Bank of China International
	2011–2015	CEO, China Merchants Securities
Li Tong	1993–2004	Various positions, Bank of China International
	2005–2008	Managing director, Bank of China International
	2009–2010	Deputy chief executive, Bank of China International
	2010	Manager, private equity fund, Bank of China International
	2010–2011	Executive president, Bank of China International
	2012–2015	CEO, Bank of China International

Note: Dates and titles are approximations based on sources.
Based on various newspapers and websites.

bankers who were active in Asia. Fang was a highly sought-after financier because he bridged the structural hole separating the Chinese and foreign financial networks; that is, he was a *tertius gaudens* financier. Consequently, after 5 years of participating in major financial transactions, he was a hub of financial networks in Asia that included China, and this was transmitted to CICC. It acquired hub status, bridging the Chinese and foreign networks. Fang brought these network ties to BOCI when he became CEO in 2000. Alas, his tenure was short, and within a year or so, he had resigned. Fang, therefore, had little time to enhance the social status of BOCI in investment banking networks of firms in Hong Kong and in Asia and to elevate it to hub status as the bridge between the Chinese and foreign firm networks.

Li Shan (2001–2005) was the only banker who worked at a major global investment bank prior to becoming CEO, and his experience covered 8 years; nonetheless, this experience was limited. He had a 6-month stint as a trader for Credit Suisse in New York in 1993, and then he joined Goldman Sachs as an international economist in early 1995. While this position involved some aspects of investment banking, direct work on advising and on deals, the more prestigious activities, did not commence for 18 months. That included brief work in Hong Kong and then in London, but Li soon moved to Beijing in 1998 to work on plans for a Chinese investment bank that would become BOCI. The bureaucratic wrangling on the committee finally led Li to resign; he then worked for Lehman Brothers in Hong Kong as an investment banker for just under 2 years. In 2001, he was hired as CEO of BOCI (Li Shan's mission impossible, 2003).

Li had built network ties with investment bankers at three global banks—Credit Suisse, Goldman Sachs, and Lehman Brothers, and he spent time in each of the leading global financial centers—London, New York, and Hong Kong (Meyer, 2014). Because he spent limited time in each center, he could not build deep network ties to investment bankers, both within the firms in which he worked and in other firms he collaborated with on deals. His modest experience generated few opportunities to build strong network relations with the most senior investment bankers. Li, therefore, was not a hub of investment banking networks. Consequently, when he became the CEO of BOCI in 2001, he brought neither high status nor network brokerage power to the bank which would have been recognized by other elite investment banks in Hong Kong.

BOCI, therefore, could not exploit high status to access network resources, such as hiring elite bankers and accessing the most lucrative business opportunities through cooperative and collaborative relations. Top investment banking firms in Hong Kong ascribed low status to BOCI because it was an affiliate of BOC (Beijing), a state bank of China. They would view BOCI as susceptible to influence from the parent bank and from the Chinese regulatory authorities, such as CBRC, CSRC, and PBOC. These organizations report to the State Council and the Politburo Standing Committee, whose members are the most powerful in the CCP. Consequently, investment banks in Hong Kong know that BOCI must adhere to policies of the Party regarding banking activities and must support efforts such as funding government programs. While global investment banks recognize the power and high status of these government and Party organizations within China, that high status does not transfer to BOCI's relative status position in Hong Kong's cluster of elite investment banks (Li Shan's mission impossible, 2003).

Half of the CEOs of BOCI—Liang Xiaoting, Wang Yan, and Li Tong, whose tenure accounts for 70% of the time since its founding, built most of their banking careers in a state bank of China prior to becoming CEO (Table 3.2). The current CEO, Li Tong, advanced in the ranks of BOCI over a period of about 18 years. While these executives, especially Wang Yan and Li Tong, developed skills as administrators and investment bankers, their financial networks were constrained by their positions within BOCI. These executives, therefore, had limited "reach" to sophisticated global investment bankers. Likewise, most of their peers did not have significant network ties (or reach) to top bankers because they did not work in those firms. These CEOs, therefore, did not raise BOCI's social status among global investment banks.

BOCI's membership in a cohesive group of SBOCs, whose social status has an extraordinary degree of stability, would continue to influence its status. They possess high-status homophily within China as the country's leading banks; however, that status is not transferable to Hong Kong. Instead, the SBOCs retain low-status homophily as perceived by global investment banks in Hong Kong. The SBOCs' frequent affiliations with each other in funding SOEs reinforce their standing as low-status banks. Consequently, high-status banks only will affiliate with BOCI, as a subsidiary of Bank of China (Beijing), if they need to involve it on deals as required by China's financial rules, or if it brings special access to an investment deal with a Chinese firm.

The low status of BOCI among investment banks in Hong Kong undermines its capacity to hire and retain bankers who have experience in elite firms (Wilson, 2013). BOCI's own bankers, and, collectively, the bank, therefore, cannot effectively access resources of knowledge, expertise, and deal opportunities which are nested within high-status banks. The absence of these ties of BOCI's bankers with elite global bankers also means that the latter cannot adequately assess the quality of most of the investment bankers in BOCI, with the exception of those they occasionally collaborate with on deals. Thus, BOCI's reputation, at least based on the internal capabilities of its bankers, is obscure, even though objectively, its bankers may be quite talented in executing deals. This low status of BOCI is an ascribed characteristic; a low correlation may exist between that status and the internal quality of its bankers.

Liang Xiaoting resigned from being CEO in 2000 (Wang, 2001). Ultimately, he was charged with corruption, sentenced, and served a prison term from 2004 to 2008 (Rosenthal, 2002; Yam, 2010). Certainly, his downfall contributed to the view among global investment bankers, especially in Hong Kong, that BOCI possessed low status. While the full charges against Liang did not surface officially for more than another year after his resignation, rumors surely were rampant among investment bankers in Hong Kong. This would reinforce the low social status of BOCI. Nevertheless, the appointment of Fang Fenglei as Liang's successor brought in one of the top deal makers in Asia, especially involving Chinese firms. This quickly changed the focus from a corrupt CEO to an elite investment banker (Wang, 2000). Yet, Fang's short tenure could not raise BOCI's social status among Hong Kong investment banks.

3.3.1.2 Careers After Resigning as CEO

The CEOs—Gao Xiqing, Fang Fenglei, Li Shan, and Wang Yan—who had careers after completing their term at the head of BOCI, took divergent paths. Gao Xiqing moved on to a distinguished public career that included service as Vice-chairman of CSRC for two terms covering about 7 years in total (Table 3.2). Prior to becoming CEO, he had served as General Counsel of CSRC for about 3 years and must have impressed senior Party leaders that he would serve well in a top leadership position in the CSRC. It has been a critical agency for the opening of China's equity markets to global investors, as well as encouraging domestic investors to participate. In between the two terms, he served as Vice-chairman of the National Council for Social Security Fund (2015) for about 5 years. The fund serves as support for various social security and pension programs of the central government and provinces. Gao's CSRC position provided high visibility in global investment banking networks. He met with many of the senior executives of global investment banks, both in China on their visits and in conferences and forums outside China.

Nonetheless, Gao Xiqing's service as Vice-chairman of China Investment Corporation (CIC) from 2007 to 2014 thrust him even more directly into global investment banking networks. He was one of the first set of Vice-chairs for CIC in its inauguration in September 2007. The corporation invests the foreign exchange reserves of China, acting as a sovereign wealth fund, and commenced operations with an initial capital of US$200 billion. At that time, Central Huijin Investment Corporation, which had been the vehicle of China's government to inject capital into domestic financial institutions, was merged into CIC (China's state forex investment company debuts, 2007).

Gao became the president and chief investment officer of CIC, which made him the target of global investment bankers, among other financiers, who sought capital from CIC, because it allocated substantial sums to investments outside of China. He was a bridge between foreign firms and CIC. One of its investments was in Blackstone, the large New York-headquartered private equity and real estate firm. The senior hires of CIC also included top financiers such as Collin Lau, a Starr International executive, and Zhou Yuan, who had been the China head of UBS (CIC reportedly hires, 2008). Consequently, Gao cemented network ties to global financial firms through CIC's investments, as well as through the access he obtained from the global network ties of financiers he hired.

The prominence of CIC as a major sovereign wealth fund also created opportunities for Gao to be a leading spokesperson in global meetings regarding finance in China. In 2011, he was at the World Economic Forum in Davos, Switzerland (CIC defends its investments, 2011). A year later he chaired a major investment conference that CIC sponsored in Hong Kong (Sender, 2012). By the time Gao stepped down from CIC in 2014 the fund had grown to almost US$600 billion, indicative of the deep global financial network ties that he accumulated during his 8-year tenure and which CIC possessed as his employer (Sender, 2014). Nevertheless, Gao's high status as a pivotal actor in global financial networks and the high status of CIC could not retroactively be transferred back to BOCI after his resignation as CEO.

Fang Fenglei's recognition in global investment banking networks advanced significantly when he became a partner in Goldman Sachs (Table 3.2). He joined with the bank to found Gao Hua Securities (Beijing), an investment bank licensed to operate in China (Goldman Sachs wins approval for its China venture, 2004). Fang's deep ties to leaders in the Chinese government and in the CCP provided the network bridge which Gao Hua Securities leveraged to participate in some of the largest deals involving Chinese firms, such as purchases by China National Offshore Oil Company (CNOOC) of oil assets or China Construction Bank's IPO in Hong Kong in 2005 (Wright & Wilson, 2007). Gao Hua Securities, for which Fang was a leading dealmaker, provided the organizational network bridge to Goldman Sachs' Asia-Pacific headquarters in Hong Kong, as well as to its Singapore Southeast Asia headquarters, London—the international banking headquarters, and New York—the global headquarters (Goldman Sachs, 2015). As opportunities arose, Fang could access Goldman Sachs' elite global bankers.

Even as Fang Fenglei continued in the role of nonexecutive chairman in Gao Hua Securities to the present (2015), he departed in 2007 from active business and founded a private equity firm, Hopu Investment Management. This was a partnership with Temasek, the Singapore sovereign wealth fund (Fang, 2015; Fang to set up $2bn fund with Temasek, 2007). Headquartered in Beijing, Hopu's investments range widely across businesses in Africa, China, Indonesia, and Mongolia, to name a few (Chen, 2013; China Goldman spinout makes first investment in Mongolia, 2008; Steger & McMahon, 2013; TPG, GIC dig deep, 2010). In many of these investments, Fang leveraged his deep ties to China's political leadership, its state-owned banks, and other SOEs. Still, Fang's investments also place him into network relations with many top global financiers. His continued involvement in global finance, however, has no impact on the social status of BOCI because he has few, if any, ties to it.

Similar to Fang Fenglei, Li Shan entered the private sector following his 5-year term as CEO of BOCI (Table 3.2). In 2005, he founded

San Shan Capital Partners, a firm that he runs at the present time (2015) from Hong Kong (San Shan Capital Partners, 2015). His team of professionals has included several Goldman Sachs bankers, reflecting his access to Hong Kong's elite investment bankers while he was CEO of BOCI (Lee, 2010). Nonetheless, his personal networks probably did little to raise the social status of BOCI as an organization. Its membership in the cohesive group of SBOCs meant that global investment banks ascribed low status to it. Li's firm primarily invests in China. As with Fang, Li's current banking business does not contribute to raising BOCI's social status.

In 2011, when Wang Yan resigned as CEO from BOCI, his approximately 7-year tenure made him the longest-serving CEO in the firm's short history (Table 3.2). Almost immediately, he took over the position of CEO of China Merchants Securities, which is headquartered in Shenzhen, just north of the Hong Kong border. It is a subsidiary of China Merchants Group, the venerable SOE which dates back to the 19th century (Chen, 2012). China Merchants Securities has a Hong Kong unit, thus inserting itself directly into the local investment banking networks. The firm has a strategic alliance with the Hong Kong Exchanges and its unit, London Metals Exchange, dealing with commodities. This comports with the expertise of the parent company, China Merchants Group, in logistics and warehousing (HKEx Group & China Merchants Group sign MOU, 2014; Sanglap, 2015).

While CEO of BOCI, Wang had a reputation as a dealmaker; nonetheless, when he departed for China Merchants Securities, he took one of his investment banking teams (Wilson, 2013). The shift of a specialized team from one bank to another is not unusual, but when the CEO takes a team, that signals a major transfer of talent. That move undermines the social status of BOCI because it indicates a loss of financial networks of the CEO and his team.

BOCI has had important CEOs, and its current one, Li Tong, provides strong leadership for the bank. Nonetheless, its social status as measured by rankings in key areas of high-profile investment banking—equity capital markets and mergers and acquisitions—remains low. From 2006 to 2014, BOCI rarely ranked among the top-ten investment banks in Asia-Pacific (Dealogic, 2015). Some of the bank's CEOs, however, possess high social status within networks of the CCP, and, conceivably, some of this higher status was transferred to the bank's social status within the Party hierarchy.

3.4 CEOS' SOCIAL STATUS IN THE CCP

All CEOs of government-controlled banks in China must be members of the CCP, and BOCI is no exception. The Party ties of the CEOs, therefore, reinforce the view that the bank is controlled by the government and subject to its policy decisions. That government control would contribute to the low status of BOCI as perceived by top global investment bankers and their firms. BOCI cannot operate as freely as private-sector firms and allow its bankers to pursue market opportunities with little restraint.

While BOCI may be perceived as low status by global bankers and their firms, networks of the CEOs in the Party contribute to the high status of the bank within the Party and among major government organizations, the leaders of which also are important Party cadres. Most of the CEOs of BOCI possessed powerful Party ties prior to taking over as head of investment banking, during their tenure as CEO, and/or subsequently. Gao Xiqing's Party ties, especially, derived from his senior positions at the CSRC and CIC (Table 3.2). Both positions placed him into relationships with the chairs of these organizations, as well as ongoing ties to the heads of major financial ministries. These leaders are among the most important Party members because of the significance of the organizations. While at CIC, Gao worked under Lou Jiwei, who had been allied with former premier Zhu Rongji, and then Lou resigned to become the Minister of Finance (Ren, 2013). Most of Gao's high-status Party ties came after he was CEO of BOCI; consequently, Gao's career could not confer high status on the bank within the CCP.

Fang Fenglei's career prior to becoming CEO of BOCI consisted of movement up the bureaucratic ladder in provincial-government trade organizations and in some Chinese financial institutions during the 1980s and early 1990s. One of his most important Party network ties derived from his work with Wang Qishan who was his boss, mentor, and personal friend (Anderlini & Tucker, 2009; Leahy, 2006; Stein & Areddy, 2007). Arguably, Wang is among the most influential members of the CCP with leadership positions in finance (China Construction Bank, PBOC), political office (Mayor of Beijing), and most recently, a member of the Politburo Standing Committee, which includes the bosses of the CCP and the government. Wang also chairs the Central Committee for Discipline Inspection, which is the most powerful watchdog of Party members (Wang, 2015; Wang Qishan highlights Party discipline in anti-corruption effort, 2015).

Thus, Fang currently possesses extraordinary networks to the top leadership of the CCP. Although BOCI benefited somewhat in terms of high status within the CCP based on Fang's ties to Wang prior to becoming CEO, Fang was only in that position for about a year. Most of Fang's benefits in terms of high status within the CCP derive from his ties to Wang after Fang resigned from BOCI. These were personal benefits, as well as gains that accrued to Gao Hua Securities (Goldman Sachs joint venture) and to Fang's own firm, Hopu Investments, to the present. These firms acquired high status from their affiliation with Fang.

Zhu Rongji, arguably one of the most prominent members of the CCP, provided some heft to Li Shan's network ties to the Party. While Li was a student at Tsinghua University, he appears to have had contact with Zhu who served as an honorary dean. In any case, Li knew Zhu well enough such that he lobbied Zhu to set up an investment bank under the control of Bank of China (Hong Kong). In 1998, Zhu invited Li to Beijing to work on the idea with a special committee (Li Shan's mission impossible, 2003). At that time, Zhu was on the verge of beginning his approximately 6-year term as premier of China. Prior to that, he had served as mayor of Shanghai and in numerous powerful positions during the 1990s which were involved with the economic reforms of China, especially during his service as Vice-premier of China from 1991 to 1996. Zhu had numerous protégés who went on to major positions in China's government (China leaders consult old master Zhu Rongji over reform, 2015; Zhu, 2015).

Although it is unclear how much direct contact Li Shan had with Zhu Rongji subsequently, Li's ties with such a prominent member of the Party and one who continues to be highly respected for his leadership in the economic reforms of China, certainly must have benefited Li. Zhu would have been a source of referrals, both while Li was CEO of BOCI, which overlapped Zhu's position as premier of China, and as a member of the Politburo Standing Committee, and, later, when Li formed San Shan Capital Partners (Table 3.2). Zhu's networks extend to the top of the government's financial organizations, including the Ministry of Finance and the PBOC (China leaders consult old master Zhu Rongji over reform, 2015). Thus Li's CCP network ties during his tenure as CEO of BOCI would position the bank as high social status in the eyes of the CCP. Nevertheless, this would not accrue as high social status among global investment bankers.

The ties of Wang Yan to elite CCP members must be inferred from his education and positions. With a doctorate from Peking University, he would have been networked with some of the leading students who are Party members and would go on to major positions in the government and the Party (Table 3.1). His banking positions with Industrial and Commercial Bank of China, and as CEO of BOCI, likewise would bring him into contact with top Party people. Most likely, however, his current position as CEO of China Merchants Securities positions him in important CCP networks because the firm is a unit of China Merchants Group, one of the most powerful SOEs. Its leaders typically have high Party rank, although the current Chairman, Li (2015b), has spent much of his career as an executive of logistics and shipping companies—a key part of China Merchants Group. Nonetheless, Wang's CCP networks would not have distinguished him much from other major financiers while he was CEO of BOCI. Consequently, Wang did not contribute much to raising the position of BOCI to high status in Party networks.

Li Tong, the current CEO of BOCI, spent most of her career in the bank and rose up through the ranks to her present position. Certainly, her networks in the Party have rested, in part, on her father, Li (2015a). He had a long, distinguished career in Party posts at the provincial level, and, by the late 1990s, he was on the Central Committee of the Party, including service on the Politburo Standing Committee from 2007 to 2012. Li Tong's close ties to the upper ranks of the Party confer high status on BOCI in CCP networks. As CEO, she takes a leading role in promoting Chinese investments in Asia, exemplified when she was the head of the Chinese delegation to Pakistan in 2014, which included Chinese firms. Illustrating her high status as a financial executive, which is transferred to BOCI, she also met with the state bank of Pakistan to discuss improving financial ties between that country and China (China likes to strengthen banking ties, 2014).

Li Tong used her stature as head of BOCI, as well as close ties to the CCP leadership, to strengthen collaborative ties between her bank and the Singapore Stock Exchange (SGX) in areas of Renminbi programs—which comports with the Chinese government's goal of internationalizing the Renminbi (Bank of China, 2015). She also raises the stature of BOCI in the CCP and the government through supporting the country's "One Belt, One Road" initiative. BOCI led a large Silk Road bond issuance in multiple currencies. While known as staying out of the media spotlight, her personal stature is growing such that she was identified as among the top-25 women in Asia-Pacific (Top 25 women in Asia Pacific, 2015). The extent that her activities are raising the social status of BOCI among global investment bankers is less certain. Most likely, however, her social status within the

CCP and the top levels of China's government, as well as the social status of BOCI within the views of the Party leadership, is rising.

3.5 CONCLUSIONS

BOCI is a subsidiary of the prestigious Bank of China (Beijing) on the Mainland. The goal was to create an investment bank that would join the ranks of elite global firms. Its incorporation in Hong Kong inserted it into the third most significant agglomeration of top investment banks, after London and New York. China's bank reforms had the admirable goal of transforming them into globally competitive institutions through raising their standards of corporate governance, enhancing risk management, improving operations, and modernizing technology systems. Mechanisms for this transformation included the sale of small ownership stakes to foreign banks and bringing outside directors to the boards of the banks as means to raise them to global standards.

Nevertheless, the government's continued ownership through various entities of virtually all of the stock of the four major SBOCs—Agricultural Bank of China, Bank of China, China Construction Bank, and Industrial and Commercial Bank of China—transmits the fact that these banks are directly subject to central government policy. Furthermore, the continued control of the banks at the top levels by senior CCP cadres reinforces the view that political decisions, ultimately, will govern bank strategy.

Consequently, this raised a conundrum for BOCI. On the one hand, it has high social status within China as a subsidiary of Bank of China (Beijing) and concurrently its top executives, including the CEO, possess high social status within the CCP. On the other hand, these same conditions mean that BOCI has low social status within the global investment banking hub of Hong Kong. The ties to the parent and to the CCP are reminders that the bank reports to the upper levels of China's government, including its ministries and regulatory agencies, and to the heads of the Party—the State Council and the Politburo Standing Committee. These conditions, therefore, hinder the transformation of BOCI into a globally competitive investment bank.

The CEOs of BOCI provide a window to explain why the bank continues to struggle to enter the ranks of elite global investment banks in Hong Kong. They possess high social status as an educated elite, consistent with the transformation of the upper ranks of the CCP. While that social status confers prestige value in interpersonal relations with clients and among financiers, it does not transfer to BOCI because that background has little, if any, impact on success as an investment banker.

Prior to becoming CEO of BOCI, few of them possessed much experience operating with global investment bankers. Fang Fenglei brought the most experience from his leadership in CICC, but this firm could not freely function as an elite investment bank because it was a joint venture between Chinese institutions and Morgan Stanley. In any case, Fang's tenure as CEO was too short to influence the social status of BOCI. Li Shan worked in major investment banks; nevertheless, his career was brief, and he spent only a few years directly gaining expertise as a banker at the top level. Half of the CEOs acquired experience was in SBOCs prior to becoming head of investment banking at BOCI. Overall, therefore, the CEOs of BOCI brought limited network ties to elite global investment bankers; arguably, Fang Fenglei was the only one with such ties, albeit as a bridge across networks—a *tertius gaudens* financier. Consequently, the CEOs could not raise the social status of BOCI among global investment banks in Hong Kong. The bank remained affiliated with the cohesive SBOCs which have high social status in China, yet low social status in Hong Kong.

The four CEOs who had careers after completing their service with BOCI worked as major financiers; unfortunately, that was too late to benefit BOCI's social status in investment banking circles in Hong Kong. Gao Xiqing's long-running tenure as Vice-chairman of CIC inserted him directly into global investment banking networks. Fang Fenglei became more tightly integrated into elite networks through his ties to Gao Hua Securities, aligned with Goldman Sachs, and his own Hopu Investment Fund. Li Shan formed his own private equity fund and operates in the Hong Kong financial networks. Wang Yan shifted to heading China Merchants Securities, a unit of China Merchants Group, where he has more freedom to operate as an investment banker. Thus, a stark contrast exists between the careers of these bankers prior to becoming CEO, when they possessed minor network ties to elite investment bankers, and their careers afterward, when they became more tightly integrated into global investment banking networks. Arguably, Gao and Fang, as well as their organizations, moved into hub status and acted as bridges across the structural holes separating the Chinese and foreign financial networks of firms.

Membership of the CEOs in the CCP is a requirement for holding the leadership position. Most of the CEOs possessed Party ties to powerful cadres prior to taking the post, while they were CEO, and/or subsequently in their career. Li Tong, the current CEO, continues in that pattern. Definitely, these CCP ties raise the social status of BOCI within the government and among Party leaders. Li Tong's current efforts in support of China's "One Belt, One Road" initiative, including the affiliated Asian Infrastructure Investment Bank, surely must strengthen the high social status of the bank in the eyes of the government and top Party leaders.

Nevertheless, these CCP network ties do not contribute to raising the social status of BOCI among global investment banks in Hong Kong. Instead, the CCP ties reinforce the low social status of the bank because they serve as a reminder that it is subject to direct influence from the government and the Party leadership. Consequently, these conditions do not make the bank attractive to elite bankers as an employer because they anticipate that they will not have the same freedom to operate as they do in top-tier investment banks.

The social status and network position of BOCI among global investment banks demonstrates that the context in which a bank operates impacts its position. Within China, BOCI retains high social status and is extensively networked among the banks. Its leaders consistently possess superb networks to the highest levels of the government and the Party. While these characteristics are attractive to Chinese financiers, they are unattractive to global investment bankers. BOCI, therefore, is not well integrated into the networks of elite banks and their financiers. To be integrated that way, the bank has to hire and retain these bankers because they bring their networks from their previous employers. This lack of integration hinders the access of BOCI to resources of expertise, knowledge, and deal opportunities.

The low social status of BOCI as a global investment bank in Hong Kong is an ascribed characteristic; this is unrelated to the quality of its bankers. Certainly, Chinese financiers in the bank possess superb credentials in the techniques of banking, in building critical relationships, and in designing and implementing deals. They execute their investment banking efforts with many Chinese firms. Nonetheless, that does not mean the bank can readily rise to high social status among the elite global investment banks. Arguably, the only way that transformation could occur would be if BOCI no longer was owned by the government and headed by top Party cadres.

REFERENCES

Anderlini, J., & Tucker, S. (2009). The rise of China's ultimate dealmaker. Financial Times, May 14.

Andreosso-O'Callaghan, B., & Gottwald, J.-C. (2013). How red is China's red capitalism? Continuity and change in China's financial services sector during the global crisis. *Asia Pacific Business Review*, *19*, 444–460.

Bank of China. (2015). BOC International Holdings and SGX expand collaboration on Renminbi and market developments. ACN Newswire, April 17.
Bank of China International. (2012). http://www.bocigroup.com/pub/en/. Accessed 19.01.12.
Bank of China International. (2015). http://www.bocigroup.com/pub/en/. Accessed 23.10.15.
Barboza, D. (2014). Longtime chief leaves C.I.C.C., a major Chinese investment bank. New York Times, October 14.
Benjamin, B. A., & Podolny, J. M. (1999). Status, quality, and social order in the California wine industry. *Administrative Science Quarterly, 44*, 563–589.
Bian, Y., Shu, X., & Logan, J. R. (2001). Communist Party membership and regime dynamics in China. *Social Forces, 79*, 805–841.
Brean, D. J. S. (2007). *Bank reform in China*. Toronto: Asia Pacific Foundation of Canada.
Burt, R. S. (1992). *Structural holes: The social structure of competition*. Cambridge: Harvard University Press.
Burt, R. S. (2004). Structural holes and good ideas. *American Journal of Sociology, 110*, 349–399.
Burt, R. S. (2010). *Neighbor networks: Competitive advantage local and personal*. Oxford: Oxford University Press.
Chen, G. (2012). CMS considering Hong Kong offering. South China Morning Post, July 18.
Chen, G. (2013). CDB backs Congo potash project. South China Morning Post, June 22.
China Goldman spinout makes first investment in Mongolia. (2008). PrivateEquityOnline.com, April 30.
China leaders consult old master Zhu Rongji over reform. (2015). Bloomberg News, September 15.
China likes to strengthen banking ties. (2014). Plus News Pakistan, October 21.
China's state forex investment company debuts. (2007). Xinhua General News Service, September 29.
Chiu, B., & Lewis, M. K. (2006). *Reforming China's state-owned enterprises and banks*. Cheltenham: Edward Elgar.
Chung, S., Singh, H., & Lee, K. (2000). Complementarity, status similarity and social capital as drivers of alliance formation. *Strategic Management Journal, 21*, 1–22.
CIC defends its investments. (2011). China Economic Review, January 28.
CIC reportedly hires former Starr International exec to lead RE funds. (2008). Private Equity Asia, December 4.
CICC. (2015). http://www.cicc.com. Accessed 30.10.15.
Dealogic. (2015). ap.dealogic.com. Accessed 27.10.15.
Dong, Y., Meng, C., Firth, M., & Hou, W. (2014). Ownership structure and risk-taking: Comparative evidence from private and state-controlled banks in China. *International Review of Financial Analysis, 36*, 120–130.
Fang, F. (2015). http://www.bloomberg.com/research/stocks/private/person.asp?personld=41080670&privcapld=50251078. Accessed 27.10.15.
Fang to set up $2bn fund with Temasek. (2007). PrivateEquityOnline.com, December 5.
Goldman Sachs. (2015). http://www.goldmansachs.com. Accessed 31.10.15.
Goldman Sachs wins approval for its China venture. (2004). SinoCast China Financial Watch, December 7.
Gould, R. V. (2002). The origins of status hierarchies: A formal theory and empirical test. *American Journal of Sociology, 107*, 1143–1178.
Granados, F. J., & Knoke, D. (2013). Firm status growth and structure: An alliance network analysis. *Social Networks, 35*, 62–74.
Gulati, R., Lavie, D., & Madhavan, R. (2011). How do networks matter? The performance effects of interorganizational networks. *Research in Organizational Behavior, 31*, 207–224.
Heilmann, S. (2005a). Policy-making and political supervision in Shanghai's financial industry. *Journal of Contemporary China, 14*, 643–668.

Heilmann, S. (2005b). Regulatory innovation by Leninist means: Communist Party supervision in China's financial industry. *China Quarterly*, *181*, 1–21.
HKEx Group and China Merchants Group sign MOU. (2014). Exchange News Direct, October 23.
Jensen, M. (2003). The role of network resources in market entry: Commercial banks' entry into investment banking, 1991–1997. *Administrative Science Quarterly*, *48*, 466–497.
Jensen, M., Kim, B. K., & Kim, H. (2011). The importance of status in markets: A market identity perspective. In J. L. Pearce (Ed.), *Status in management and firms* (pp. 87–117). Cambridge: Cambridge University Press.
Jensen, M., & Roy, A. (2008). Staging exchange partner choices: When do status and reputation matter? *Academy of Management Journal*, *51*, 495–516.
Kogut, B. (2000). The network as knowledge: Generative rules and the emergence of structure. *Strategic Management Journal*, *21*, 405–425.
Leahy, C. (2006). Two sneak through. Euromoney, September.
Lee, M. (2010). San Shan Capital, Ping an to launch RMB fund. Greater China Private Equity Review Daily, November 8.
Levy, T., & Meyer, D. R. (2012). Challenges of network governance at the state banks of China. *Journal of Contemporary China*, *21*, 481–498.
Li, C. (2015a). http://www.chinavitae.com/biography/Li_Changchun/career. Accessed 03.11.15.
Li, J. (2015b). http://wwwen.cmhk.com/n124/n136/n137/c12381/content.html. Accessed 03.11.15.
Li Shan's mission impossible. (2003). Institutional Investor, September 1.
Loong, P. (2000). The newest jewel in China's crown. *Asiamoney*, *11*(9), 34–41.
Meyer, D. R. (2014). The banking networks of Asian financial centers. In D. L. Kuo Chuen & G. N. Gregoriou (Eds.), *Handbook of Asian finance: Financial markets and sovereign wealth funds: Vol. 1.* (pp. 37–52). Oxford, England: Academic Press.
National Council for Social Security Fund. (2015). http://www.ssf.gov.cn/Eng. Accessed 31.10.15.
Nolan, J. (2010). The influence of western banks on corporate governance in China. *Asia Pacific Business Review*, *16*, 417–436.
Nolan, J. (2011). Good *guanxi* and bad *guanxi*: Western bankers and the role of network practices in institutional change in China. *The International Journal of Human Resource Management*, *22*, 3357–3372.
Owen-Smith, J., Cotton-Nessler, N. C., & Buhr, H. (2015). Network effects on organizational decision-making: Blended social mechanisms and IPO withdrawal. *Social Networks*, *41*, 1–17.
Pearce, J. L. (2011). Introduction: The power of status. In J. L. Pearce (Ed.), *Status in management and firms* (pp. 1–22). Cambridge: Cambridge University Press.
Piazza, A., & Castellucci, F. (2014). Status in firm and management theory. *Journal of Management*, *40*, 287–315.
Podolny, J. M. (1993). A status-based model of market competition. *American Journal of Sociology*, *98*, 829–872.
Podolny, J. M. (2001). Networks as the pipes and prisms of the market. *American Journal of Sociology*, *107*, 33–60.
Podolny, J. M., & Phillips, D. J. (1996). The dynamics of firm status. *Industrial and Corporate Change*, *5*, 453–471.
Ren, D. (2013). Ex-wealth fund guru's career turns full circle. South China Morning Post, March 17.
Rosenthal, E. (2002). Bank of China's mounting problems. New York Times, February 1, Section W, p. 1.
Sanglap, R. (2015). LME Clear ink MOU to ease China's access to commodities market. European Financials Daily, October 26.

Sender, H. (2012). China's state fund faces new challenges. Financial Times, March 29.
Sender, H. (2014). Gao to pass on the reins at CIC. Financial Times, January 23.
San Shan Capital Partners. (2015). http://www.bloomberg.com/research/stocks/private/snapshot.asp?privcapId=36593986. Accessed 31.10.15.
Shevchenko, A. (2004). Bringing the party back in: The CCP and the trajectory of market transition in China. *Communist and Post-Communist Studies*, *37*, 161–185.
Shipilov, A. V., & Li, S. X. (2008). Can you have your cake and eat it too? Structural holes' influence on status accumulation and market performance in collaborative networks. *Administrative Science Quarterly*, *53*, 73–108.
Steger, I., & McMahon, D. (2013). Hopu Investment is back in the private equity game with $1.1bn fund. Private Equity News, November 11.
Stein, P., & Areddy, J.T. (2007). Goldman, China partner are in talks about a split. Wall Street Journal Europe, September 18.
Thye, S. R. (2000). A status value theory of power in exchange relations. *American Sociological Review*, *65*, 407–432.
Top 25 women in Asia Pacific. (2015). Finance Asia, July 20.
Tortoriello, M., Perrone, V., & McEvily, B. (2011). Cooperation among competitors as status-seeking behavior: Network ties and status differentiation. *European Management Journal*, *29*, 335–346.
TPG, GIC, dig deep into Indonesian coal miner (2010). Private Equity International, December 20.
Walder, A. G. (2004). The party elite and China's trajectory of change. *China: An International Journal*, *2*, 189–209.
Wang, X. (2000). Bank of China snares top listing deal-maker. South China Morning Post, January 10, Business Post, p. 2.
Wang, X. (2001). Top executives quit BOC. South China Morning Post, January 17, Business Post, p. 1.
Wang, Q. (2015). Wang Qishan. China Vitae, http://www.chinavitae.com/biography/Wang_Qishan/. Accessed 30.10.15.
Wang Qishan highlights Party discipline in anti-corruption effort. (2015). China Daily, May 10.
Washington, M., & Zajac, E. J. (2005). Status evolution and competition: Theory and evidence. *Academy of Management Journal*, *48*, 282–296.
Wilson, E. (2013). China: "I" has trouble with teams in HK. Euromoney, May 1.
Wines, M. (2010). China bank I.P.O. raises $19 billion. New York Times, July 6.
Wright, C., & Wilson, E. (2007). Fang Fenglei and Fred Hu: One bank, two rainmakers. Euromoney, April.
Yam, S. 2010. Jail not the end for disgraced high-flyers. South China Morning Post, May 22, Business, p. 8.
Zaheer, A., & Bell, G. G. (2005). Benefiting from network position: Firm capabilities, structural holes, and performance. *Strategic Management Journal*, *26*, 809–825.
Zhang, X. (1998). Elite transformation and recruitment in post-Mao-China. *Journal of Political and Military Sociology*, *26*, 39–57.
Zhu, R. (2015). China Vitae, http://www.chinavitae.com/biography/Zhu_Rongji/career. Accessed 03.11.15.

CHAPTER 4

Business to Government Networks in Resource Acquisition: The Case of Chinese Private Enterprises

S. Zhao*, S.L. Morgan†
*University of Nottingham, Nottingham, United Kingdom
†University of Nottingham, Ningbo, China

4.1 INTRODUCTION

Social networks play a pivotal role in the strategic management of firms in emerging economies. Business-to-business (B2B) and business-to-government (B2G) networks serve distinctly different roles in the strategies of firms. B2B ties with suppliers, buyers, and competitors are market oriented, facilitating contracting and sales. B2G ties, by way of contrast, serve to overcome constraints that arise from the underdeveloped market mechanisms and institutional environment that allow the government to greatly influence market activities. In China, the allocation of many strategic resources, such as land, finance, utility services, and so on, are controlled or influenced by the government, which affects the competitiveness of firms (Chow & Fung, 2012; Hsueh, Lin, & Li, 2010; Wei, Hou, Wang, & Wang, 2011; Zhu, Wittmann, & Peng, 2012). Chinese private firms are therefore disadvantaged when competing with state-owned enterprises (SOEs) and foreign-invested firms, which are more favoured by the Chinese government (Haggard & Huang, 2008). In the face of these particular difficulties private firms spend heavily on cultivating informal networks with government officials in order to access resources (ACFIC, 2007). Understanding how private entrepreneurs perceive the role of B2G networks in their strategic decisions of resource acquisition is an important topic for understanding the contemporary Chinese style of management.

This study will explore the role of B2G networks in helping private firms to access financial resources and new technology. Drawing on data from 418 private firms in Guangdong in 2013, our results firstly distinguish between local government connections and distant government connections.

http://dx.doi.org/10.1016/B978-0-08-100639-9.00005-0

Local government connections measure the personal ties with officials in local government departments and SOEs, which typically have more influence on the daily operations of the focal firms. Distant government connections measure personal ties with officials in provincial or central government, or in the state-affiliated departments that less affect the day-to-day operations. Using these two types of government connections in our logistic regression models, the results show that local government ties, compared to distant government ties, play a more significant and important role in helping private firms to acquire financial resources and new technology. Although the Chinese state-owned banks are supposed to operate on an independent commercial basis, their lending decisions are still influenced by personal networks and the rule of reciprocating favours common to *guanxi* relationships, the Chinese term for social connections. The enduring influence of informal networks for accessing key resources is a common theme in the analysis of East Asian business networks and is discussed in detail in Chapters 5, 7, 8, 11 and 14. For access to new technology, both local government connections and distant government connections help private firms obtain subsidies and approval for the application of new technology. Access to financial resources and new technology enhances the performance of the private firms through improved internal capabilities and competitive advantage in the market.

The remainder of this chapter is divided into four sections. Section 4.2 will review the existing literature that examines social networks and resource acquisition. Section 4.2 will also discuss the role of government in transition countries that control the resource allocation, which motivates private firms to rely on informal networks to acquire resources. Section 4.3 will discuss the research method and data. It will also present the descriptive statistics of the sample. Section 4.4 will discuss the regression results, combined with the interview data. Section 4.5 will summarize our conclusion.

4.2 LITERATURE REVIEW

A resource can take many forms and contribute in various ways to the profit of a firm. The resource-based view (RBV) argues that a firm's sustained competitive advantage is based on its valuable, rare, inimitable, and nonsubstitutable resources (Barney, 1991). The capability of firms to create or acquire these resources affects their performance and competitiveness over their competitors. In a transition country like China, where the government controls many important strategic resources, state-affiliated firms are granted preference to access these resources. For example, existing researches show that less than 10% of bank loans were extended to the private sector (Firth, Lin, Liu, & Wong, 2009); Kwong (2009). Zhu et al. (2012) indicated that the lack of government support and protection for innovations is an institutional barrier to research and development (R&D) in small and medium-sized enterprises, the majority of which are private firms. Private enterprises are discriminated by the government and state-affiliated firms in resource allocation.

Social networks, which mean *guanxi* in the Chinese context, connect private entrepreneurs with other stakeholders in society. The personal networks of an entrepreneur affect how the firm acquires resources and generates value during this process. B2G networks, which refer to connections between private entrepreneurs and government officials (Park & Luo, 2001), are important as they allow private firms to access resources easier. From the RBV perspective, the government connections of the private entrepreneurs are a form of internal capability for their firms. Close ties with government officials enable the private firms to better communicate with the regulatory agencies, which increase the trust between the firms and the government departments that influence the allocation of resources.

Institutional theory also suggests that social networks supplement formal institutional mechanisms (Potter, 2002). Informal organizations and rules help to deal with issues that are ambiguous in the laws and regulations. The implementations of policies in China are subject to the interpretation of government officials. This motivates private entrepreneurs to use personal connections to evade regulations and access resources and preferential treatments (Guthrie, 1999). The improvement of the institutional environment and market mechanism may gradually reduce the importance of government connections in business transactions (Peng & Zhou, 2005).

Other literature, however, suggest the use of social networks is deeply embedded in the Chinese business culture (Chung & Hamilton, 2001; Luo, 2007). Chung and Hamilton (2001) highlight three dimensions of *guanxi* relationships in business: normative, affective, and instrumental. The normative dimension describes the expected obligation that arises from relationships such as those of kin. The affective dimension broadly covers the bonds of friendship that establish and maintain a relationship. The instrumental dimension emphasizes a quid pro quo consideration of cost and benefit of a relationship. When a social network is established, the people who are involved in that network become familiar with one another, which sets up expected obligations among connected members (Chung & Hamilton, 2001).

A person who has received a favour is expected to return it in some form at some time in the future (Lovett, Simmons, & Kali, 1999). This rule of reciprocity requires connected members to give and return favours to others in order to maintain their own face and to avoid making others lose face. The logic of reciprocal favours motivates people to invest in a relationship first and to acquire a favour that will be returned by others in the future. This unique cultural trait has significant influence on how Chinese connect to others. The rule of reciprocity means that B2G networks in China are not narrowly transaction-based in general. Both entrepreneurs and government officials weigh the costs and benefits of relationships as well as their obligations toward the relationships, balancing the normative, affective, and the instrumental dimension of *guanxi*. From the perspective of government officials and regulatory departments, B2G networks enable them to find support from private firms in terms of economic development or personal benefits, which increases their willingness to invest in B2G networks to support private firms (Ma, Lin, & Liang, 2012).

This study focuses on the perception of private entrepreneurs of the role of B2G networks in helping them to access financial resources and new technology. Existing literature show that connections with government officials and managers in state-owned banks help firms to acquire financial capital (Gu, Hung, & Tse, 2008). Relationships with government officials help private firms to forecast policy changes, and therefore, they can invest in new technology in advance to gain a first-mover advantage (Li, Zhou, & Shao, 2009). Government connections also helps private firms to access government assistance, such as subsidies and support for R&D (Wei et al., 2011). However, existing research views government connections as homogeneous. It does not distinguish connections with officials in different regulatory departments and state-affiliated organizations, or between officials in local government and those in higher-level government. However, these different state-related identities may differently influence how private firms are treated. Since the private sector is an important contributor to local economic development and employment, local government officials have a stronger incentive to maintain a good relationship with private entrepreneurs and seek their supports for policy implementation (Ma et al., 2012). Haggard and Huang (2008) suggested that officials in higher-level government favour private firms less compared with state or foreign firms. We further investigate whether private entrepreneurs' ties with officials in regulatory departments differ in how they help private firms to access resources.

4.3 METHOD AND DATA

4.3.1 Sample

Our primary data comes from a survey involving 418 private firms in Guangdong and 53 interviews with entrepreneurs who had also completed the survey. The data was collected between March and August 2013. The survey instrument was first developed in English, translated into Chinese, and back-translated to ensure validity. Before we distributed the questionnaires, we conducted a pilot study with five Guangdong entrepreneurs. They were asked to provide suggestions on the structure and content of the questionnaires. We then made minor corrections to the survey instrument and prepared the core questions for the interviews. The interviews used a semi-structured approach to ensure commonality of questions across interviews.

Three channels were used to distribute the survey: an online survey using the Survey Monkey; physical questionnaires distributed to respondents, and questionnaires completed during the interviews. The online survey and the physical questionnaires were distributed with the assistance of seven cooperative business chambers and four trade fairs focused on manufacturing industries held in Guangzhou. Five of the seven cooperative business chambers are provincial-level chambers located in Guangzhou. Three chambers have multi-industry membership and two are for manufacturing industries. We also used two local area business chambers in Shenzhen and Jiangmen, respectively. On our behalf, the business chambers selected sample companies for distribution of the surveys according to our definition of private enterprises.[1] The initial respondents who participated in the interviews were either contacted through these business chambers, or introduced through personal connections of the authors. Other interviewees were obtained based on snowball sampling from recommendations of previous interviewees.

Among the 418 collected questionnaires, 188 were from the online survey; 177 were hardcopy questionnaires collected through the business

[1]We adopted a narrow definition of private enterprises, which includes the forms: the private-funded enterprise (*siying duzi qiye* 私营独资企业), private partnership enterprise (*siying hehuo qiye* 私营合伙企业), private limited liability corporation (*siying youxian zeren gongsi* 私营有限责任公司), and private share-holding corporate limited (*siying gufen youxian gongsi* 私营股份有限公司). The Company Law in China states that companies registered using the above four forms should have at least 51% of shares in the hands of private entrepreneurs. This definition ensures the private owners exercise control over the firms.

Table 4.1 Summary statistics of respondents' attributes

Variables	Percentage	Observations
Gender		
Male	68.00	418
Female	32.00	418
Age		
Under 30	6.00	417
30–39	40.00	417
40–49	39.00	417
50–59	12.00	417
Above 60	3.00	417
Highest qualification		
Primary school	1.00	416
Middle school	5.00	416
High school	14.00	416
College or Bachelor degree	74.00	416
Postgraduate degree	6.00	416
Experience in current job (years)	7.17	418
Former cadre	5.00	409
Former state-owned firm manager	22.00	409
CCP membership	23.00	416

Based on survey data.

chambers, or completed at the trade fairs; and the remaining 53 were completed during the interviews. Some of surveys were incomplete, which left us with a sample size of 405 for the regression analysis below. Table 4.1 shows the summary statistics of respondent's attributes. Our sample entrepreneurs were young and well-educated. More than two-thirds of our sample entrepreneurs were male. Nearly 80% of them were younger than 49 years, and 75% held college or higher degrees. On average, they had been in their current jobs for 7 years, 23% of them were CCP members, 22% were former mangers in SOEs, and 5% were former cadres in government agencies.

Table 4.2 summarizes the characteristics of the sample companies. Our sample firms ranged in size from very small enterprises to large-scale firms that employed more than 5000 people. The sample includes firms established in the 2013 survey year, as well as firms that have operated for more than

Table 4.2 Summary statistics of firms' attributes

Variables	Mean	SD	Min	Max	Observations
Firm age (years)	11.93	6.54	0	35	418
Annual sales (million yuan)	146.96	408.31	0.02	6200	413
Employment (persons)	278.24	534.95	2	5400	417
Net profit (million yuan)	14.57	70.93	−225	1300	410
Total assets (million yuan)	203.09	1438.90	0.05	27,594	406
Total debts (million yuan)	58.14	248.51	0	3000	405
Percentage of bank loans to total debts	42.50	40.31	0	100	405
Industry					
Primary industry (%)	7.00				418
Manufacturing industry (%)	60.00				418
Construction (%)	1.00				418
Service industry (%)	31.00				418

Based on survey data.

30 years. The average firm age of our sample is 11.93 years, which is relatively old compared to the average of 7 years for private firms reported in a 2004 national survey (ACFIC, 2007). The older average age of our sample firms suggests that they are survivors in the Chinese market and probably more successful on average than many private firms. Manufacturing firms account for 60% of the sampled firms. This bias partly arises because respondents were accessed at trade fairs for manufacturing industries, and two of the seven cooperative business chambers drew their membership exclusively from manufacturing industries.

Our sample firms were located in the two deputy-provincial level cities of Guangzhou and Shenzhen and 10 prefecture-level cities.[2] Table 4.3 shows the distribution of sample companies by their locations and the level of economic development of these cities. The two subprovincial cities are the most developed cities in the province. Both had a gross regional product (GRP) higher than one trillion yuan and per capita GRP higher than 100,000 yuan in 2013. The remaining cities are classified into two groups, the Pearl River

Table 4.3 Distribution of sample firms by locations and the GRP of each location

	City	GRP in 2013 (million yuan)	Per capita GRP in 2013 (yuan)	Percentage of sample firms
Two deputy-provincial level cities	Guangzhou	1,542,014	119,695	12.9
	Shenzhen	1,450,023	136,948	8.9
Pearl River Delta prefecture-level cities	Foshan	701,017	96,310	7.2
	Dongguan	549,002	66,109	6.0
	Huizhou	267,835	57,144	3.1
	Zhongshan	263,893	83,393	12.7
	Jiangmen	200,018	44,546	30.4
	Zhuhai	166,238	104,798	7.9
Peripheral prefecture-level cities	Maoming	216,017	36,063	2.4
	Zhanjiang	206,001	28,859	1.7
	Shantou	156,590	28,661	1.7
	Qingyuan	109,304	28,928	5.3

The GRP and per capita GRP data from Guangdong Statistical yearbook 2014.

[2]Deputy-provincial level cities are half a rank higher than prefecture-level cities. They have independent authority to plan social and economic development. Their governments have province-style power related to local production, distribution of energy and materials, development of local transportation and postal services, import and export, investment in fixed assets, local wages, and other policy aspects.

Delta prefecture-level cities, which are relatively well-developed, and the peripheral cities, which are less developed and distant from the provincial economic centre. In our sample, 22% of respondent firms are located in the two subprovincial cities, 67% are in the Pearl River Delta cities, and 11% are in the peripheral cities. Our sample is biased to the Pearl River Delta. The over representation of firms in Jiangmen arises from the help of the local business chambers in distributing survey questionnaires.

4.3.2 Measurement Variables

This study explores how Chinese private entrepreneurs perceive the role of B2G networks in helping their firms to acquire financial resources and new technology. In the survey questionnaires, we used two statements to examine the perceptions of entrepreneurs regarding the use of B2G networks to acquire financial resources and new technology. Table 4.4 shows these two statements and a descriptive summary of the responses. Both statements received slightly positive view from private entrepreneurs (financial resources: mean = 3.26, new technology: mean = 3.16 on a five-point scale). This result is consistent with existing literatures indicating that B2G networks help private firms to access strategic resources (Sheng, Zhou, & Li, 2011; Wei et al., 2011; Wu, Wu, Zhou, & Wu, 2012). In this study, we further explore

Table 4.4 Descriptive statistics of the perceptions of private entrepreneurs about B2G networks in acquiring resources

	Mean	SD	No.	Positive responses[a] (%)	Negative responses[a] (%)
1. Good connections with government officials enable my company to acquire financial resources easier (1–5)[b]	3.26	1.02	405	38.00	20.20
2. Good connections with government officials enable my company to acquire new technology easier (1–5)[b]	3.16	1.04	405	33.80	24.70

[a]The percentage of positive responses is the combination of the percentages of those who 'agree' and 'strongly agree' with the questionnaire statement. The percentage of negative responses is the combination of the percentages of those who 'disagree' and 'strongly disagree' with the questionnaire statements.
[b]Respondents were asked to access each of these four statements on a five-point scale, from 1 (strongly disagree) to 5 (strongly agree).
Based on survey data.

how embeddedness in different types of B2G networks affects entrepreneurs' perception of using B2G networks to acquire resources. The agreement of entrepreneurs with the two statements showed in Table 4.4 are recoded into dummy variables with scores higher than 3 recoded as 1 for positive responses, and scores equal to or lower than 3 as 0 for nonpositive responses. These two dummy variables are used in the regression models as dependent variables.

The independent variables try to measure how private entrepreneurs connect to officials in different levels of the government. In our survey questionnaire, we have 10 items that examine the intensity of connections between respondents and officials in different government departments or managers in state-affiliated firms. These 10 items and their correlation are all shown in Table 4.5. Each item uses a five-point scale from 1 for 'no relation' to 5 for 'very intensive' use of that kind of personal connection. Since all of the correlations are higher than 0.3 and none are higher than 0.9, the sample and all of the 10 variables are suitable for factor analysis (Field, 2013). We thus conducted a principal component analysis of the 10 variables to examine the underlying pattern of using different types of B2G networks.

Table 4.6 shows the results of the factor analysis after rotation. Two factors were extracted from the data. They explain 62.04% of the variance in combination. The first factor includes personal connections with government officials in regulatory and supporting organizations, local government leaders, and managers in state-owned banks and state-owned utility companies. This factor is named 'local government connections': it measures the relationships with local authorities, or managers in state-affiliated firms that affect the day-to-day operation of the focal firms. The second factor includes personal connections with leaders in central and provincial governments, staffs in public-sector organizations, managers in SOEs in the same sector, and members in business chambers. These organizations are less likely to affect the daily operation of private firms. Thus we have classified them as 'distant government connections'.

The results of the factor analysis distinguish the intensity of connections between private entrepreneurs and officials in different hierarchies of government departments. The two new factors allow us to examine whether the embeddedness of private entrepreneurs in distant or local government connections affect their perceptions of the role of B2G networks in accessing resources. We thus used the Anderson-Rubin method to calculate the composite score for all cases on these two factors to avoid collinearity in regression analysis (Field, 2013). The two new variables measure the

Table 4.5 Descriptive statistics and pearson correlation coefficients of different personal ties utilized by private entrepreneurs

Types of personal ties	Mean	SD	1	2	3	4	5	6	7	8	9
1. With SOEs Managers in the Same Sector	0.28	1.10									
2. With State-Owned Banks Managers	2.70	1.11	0.42***								
3. With State-Owned Utility Companies Managers	2.45	1.10	0.53***	0.56***							
4. With Business Chambers Members	2.55	1.15	0.36***	0.33***	0.47***						
5. With Central Government Leaders	1.68	0.96	0.46***	0.39**	0.40***	0.40***					
6. With Provincial Government Leaders	1.82	1.03	0.44***	0.35***	0.38***	0.43***	0.82***				

Continued

Table 4.5 Descriptive statistics and pearson correlation coefficients of different personal ties utilized by private entrepreneurs—cont'd

Types of personal ties	Mean	SD	1	2	3	4	5	6	7	8	9
7. With Local Government Leaders	2.74	1.24	0.29***	0.39***	0.40***	0.42***	0.42***	0.56***			
8. With Regulatory Organizations Officials	2.80	1.18	0.32***	0.55***	0.49***	0.37***	0.30***	0.39***	0.63***		
9. With Supporting Organizations Officials	2.73	1.13	0.39***	0.54***	0.51***	0.42***	0.32***	0.39***	0.59***	0.75***	
10. With Public-Sector Organizations Staffs	2.15	1.04	0.48***	0.38***	0.49***	0.39***	0.46***	0.46***	0.28***	0.31***	0.41***

$n = 412$.
*$p < 0.10$; **$p < 0.05$; ***$p < 0.01$.
Based on survey data.

Table 4.6 Summary of exploratory factor analysis results for the frequency of using personal B2G ties for business purpose

	Rotated factor loadings	
Types of personal B2G connections	**Local government connections**	**Distant government connections**
With Regulatory Organizations Officials	**0.88**	
With Supporting Organizations Officials	**0.86**	
With State-Owned Banks Managers	**0.69**	
With Local Government Leaders	**0.68**	
With State-Owned Utility Companies Managers	**0.56**	0.50
With Central Government Leaders		**0.88**
With Provincial Government Leaders		**0.82**
With SOEs Managers in the Same Sector		**0.65**
With Public-Sector Organizations Staffs		**0.66**
With Business Chambers Members	0.42	**0.48**
Eigenvalues	4.965	1.239
% of variance	49.652	12.388
a	0.854	0.807

Note: Highest factor loading for each variable appears in bold.
$n = 412$.
Based on survey data.

frequency of utilization of local government connections and distant government connections. They are the main predictors in the regression models.

In addition to the two main predictors that measure the intensity of different types of B2G networks, we use two control variables in the regression models. The first control variable is the location of the firm. Existing literature show that people in more developed and marketized regions rely less on informal networks to acquire resources and protect their own interests (Gu et al., 2008; Park & Luo, 2001). Firms located in cities which are far away from the administrative centre of the province may also have less opportunity to establish connections with officials in provincial and central governments. Thus, they are forced to rely more on local government connections to access resources. It is meaningful to explore the regional difference of the perception of different B2G networks by private entrepreneurs.

The second control variable is firm size. Larger firms have more formal ties with different stakeholders in the market, which enable them to tap market resources and establish legitimacy with government agencies easier (Freeman, Carroll, & Hannan, 1983; Park & Luo, 2001; Peng & Luo, 2000). Compared to large firms, smaller firms lack bargaining power and are weaker. They are more likely to rely on informal networks with officials to win government acceptance in order to increase their capability in resource acquisition. We thus control for firms size to explore how that affects the perception of entrepreneurs about using B2G networks. Firm size in the regression model is the natural log of annual sales.

4.3.3 Estimation Strategy

Since both dependent variables are dummy variables that measure the intensity of the distant and local government connections of entrepreneurs, we use a binary logistic regression model. The general logistic regression equation is shown below:

$$P(Y) = \frac{1}{1 + e^{-Z_n}} \tag{4.1}$$

Where

$$Z_n = b_0 + b_1 X_1 + b_2 X_2 + \cdots + b_n X_n \tag{4.2}$$

We rewrite the above equations into Eq. (4.3). It takes the natural log of the odds ratio, the probability of Y, $P(Y)$, divided by the probability of not-Y, $(1 - P(Y))$, which is known as the logit and which has a linear relationship with the right-hand dependent variables (Field, 2013; Gujarati, 1995, pp. 554–563).

$$\ln\left[P(Y)/\left(1 - P(Y)\right)\right] = b_0 + b_1 X_1 + b_2 X_2 + \cdots + b_n X_n \tag{4.3}$$

The logistic regression predicts the probability of Y occurring for predictors of Xs, where b_0 is the constant, X_1, X_2 ... X_n are predictor variables and b_1, b_2 ... b_n are their coefficients. In this study, Y is the probability that the private entrepreneurs give a positive response to the two statements used as the dependent variables to examine whether entrepreneurs agree B2G networks help their firms to access financial resources and new technology. The two main predictors are LGC, which is the frequency of local government connections, and DGC, which is the frequency of distant government connections. Model 1 uses the two main predictors. Model 2 adds the control variables LO for firm location and SI for firm size. For firm locations, the reference group is the two main cities (Guangzhou and Shenzhen).

$$\ln\left[P(Y)/\left(1 - P(Y)\right)\right] = b_0 + b_1 \text{LGC} + b_2 \text{DGC} \tag{model 1}$$

$$\ln\left[P(Y)/\left(1 - P(Y)\right)\right] = b_0 + b_1 \text{LGC} + b_2 \text{DGC} + b_3 \text{LO}_1 + b_4 \text{LO}_2 + b_5 \text{SI} \tag{model 2}$$

4.4 RESULTS AND DISCUSSION

Table 4.7 shows the logistic regression results. Model 1a and 2a examine the determinants of the view of entrepreneurs about B2G networks in helping private firms to access financial resources. Model 1b and 2b focus on access to new technology. The model χ^2 shows that all models are significant ($p<0.01$).

For access to financial resources, only local government connection is significant in model 1a ($p<0.01$). In a logistic regression, the odds ratio is the change in odds of the dependent variable resulting from a unit change of the independent variables (Field, 2013). The odds ratio of local government connections is 1.74 in model 1a and decreases slightly to 1.72 in model 2a after controls for firm locations and sizes. The odds

Table 4.7 Logistic regression examining the determinants of private entrepreneurs' perception of B2G networks to acquire resources

	B2G networks to access financial resources		B2G networks to access new technology	
	Model 1a	Model 2a	Model 1b	Model 2b
	b (odds ratio[a])	b (odds ratio[a])	b (odds ratio[a])	b (odds ratio[a])
Local Government Connections	0.55 (1.74)***	0.54 (1.72)***	0.39 (1.47)***	0.41 (1.50)***
Distant Government Connections	0.17 (1.19)	0.17 (1.18)	0.24 (1.27)**	0.24 (1.29)**
Location[b]				
Pearl River Delta Cities		−0.64 (0.53)**		−0.07 (0.93)
Peripheral Cities		0.25 (1.29)		0.18 (1.19)
Firm characteristics				
Size		−0.07 (0.93)		−0.01 (0.91)*
Constant	−0.52 (0.59)***	0.12 (1.13)	−0.71 (0.49)***	−0.33 (0.72)
Model χ^2	28.06***	41.23***	17.15***	20.69***
Cox & Snell R^2	0.07	0.1	0.04	0.05

[a]The odds ratio is calculated based on 95% confidence interval.
[b]Reference category for location is Guangzhou and Shenzhen.
$n=405$.
*$p<0.10$; **$p<0.05$; ***$p<0.01$.
Based on survey data.

ratio indicates that entrepreneurs who connect to local government officials frequently are 1.74 times more likely to agree that B2G networks help their firms to access financial resources. This result demonstrates the significant role of local government in helping private firms to access financial resources.

In interviews, most entrepreneurs affirmed that the state-owned banks in China operate commercially and independently. Their lending decisions are influenced less by government officials since the reform of the state-owned banks in the early 2000s (Jiang, Yao, & Feng, 2013). Banks managers are under more strict supervision and are less likely to approve loans based purely on personal connections. However, the close relationship between bank managers and local government officials enables government leaders to retain considerable influence over financial resource allocation. One entrepreneur who from one of the two deputy-provincial level cities mentioned:

> *The managers in local bank branches work and live in local cities. They have to give face to local government officials. Even if the local government does not appoint them, the job arrangement of their family members or the education of their children might be related to local authorities. (Interview 40)*

From the viewpoint of this entrepreneur, the influence of government leaders over lending decisions is not through direct requirement of loan approvals, but instead works through the rule of reciprocity, which is deeply embedded in Chinese culture (Chung & Hamilton, 2001). Bank managers who give favours to local leaders are entitled to ask for something in return in the future, such as access to better jobs for their family members, or a better school for their children as mentioned in the above quotation. The rule of reciprocity motivates people to invest in relationships first in order to stockpile favours that should be returned. The exchange of favours between different connected people helps private firms to expand their networks and access resources through indirect connections, in which government officials act as the middle agent connecting the private firms with banks. Another entrepreneur also highlighted the role of government officials in conveying positive information about the private firms to the banks, such that these ties can be seen as a kind of intangible asset that support the private firm's application for loans (Interview 9). Both private firms and banks can thus reduce the cost of processing information in loan approvals.

In addition to support for loan approval, B2G networks also help private firms to acquire larger loans than they otherwise would through the influence over the asset evaluation process. One entrepreneur who owns a manufacturing firm said:

> *When the companies face different problems, they can use guanxi with asset evaluation companies to influence the estimation of their asset value in different ways. For example, the evaluated value of a piece of land owned by a factory can be quite different in different cases. When the firm needs to report the value of the land to the tax bureau, the value can be estimated as lower. But when the firm needs to use the land as the collateral for bank loans, the value can be much higher. However, besides the guanxi with the asset evaluation company, firms also need to maintain good guanxi with the tax bureau and the banks. Otherwise, they can reject the asset evaluation report and refuse to grant the loan. (Interview 39)*

The above example reveals that although B2G networks are no longer able to influence the lending decisions directly, good connections with local government are an advantage for private firms that fulfil the basic requirements of loan applications. Connections with local government officials who are knowledgeable about the operations of the focal firms and are well known in the local city are helpful to reduce the time taken to approve loans or to obtain higher loans. For these reasons, entrepreneurs who use local government connections frequently are more likely to agree that B2G networks help private firms to access financial resources.

For the control variables, only location had a partially significant effect on the perception of entrepreneurs. The odds ratio of Pearl River Delta cities is 0.53. This indicates that entrepreneurs whose firms are located in the Pearl River Delta cities are less likely to agree that B2G networks are useful in acquiring financial resources, compared with their counterparts in Guangzhou and Shenzhen. This contradicts our initial expectations and existing literature, which suggest ties will be more frequent in less developed areas (Lu, 2012; Park & Luo, 2001).

We suspect one reasonable explanation for this finding is the composition of external financing. Bank loans are the most important channel of external financing for Chinese private firms (Allen, Qian, Zhang, & Zhao, 2012). However, existing literature has reported that firms in developed regions access bank loans easier and rely less on informal financing, compared to their counterparts in smaller cities (Ayyagari, Demirgüç-Kunt, & Maksimovic, 2010). Firms in less developed regions rely more on informal financial institutions and their business partners to solve financial problems. The reliance on informal financing might imply that entrepreneurs in smaller cities feel less confidence to acquire loans from state-owned banks. Thus, they are less motivated to use other methods, including B2G networks, to access financial resources in the banks.

Access to new technology is a challenge for private firms. Models 1b and 2b in Table 4.7 examine the determinants that affect the perceptions of private entrepreneurs' use of B2G networks to acquire new technology. Both local government connections and distant government connections are significant factors at $p < 0.01$ and $p < 0.05$, respectively. The odds ratio of local government connections is 1.47 in model 1b, and for distant government connections, slightly lower at 1.27. Entrepreneurs who have frequent connections with local government officials are 1.47 times more likely to agree that B2G networks help their firms to acquire new technology, compared to entrepreneurs who use local government connections less frequently. In model 2b, which controls for firm location and sizes, the odds ratios of both local and distant government connections increase slightly, but otherwise similar to model 1b. The control variables are discussed below.

The regression results show local government connections and distant government connections greatly assisted private firms to acquire new technology. Acquisition of new technology can be interpreted either as support for R&D, or as a means to acquire an existing new technology developed by other firms.

For R&D, interviewees mentioned that insufficient capital was an important reason why many private firms did not invest in new technology (Interviews 30, 39, 51), which is consistent with the existing literature on the institutional barriers to the innovation capability of small and medium-sized enterprises (Zhu et al., 2012). As highlighted above, B2G networks help private firms to access financial resources in general. In addition, local government connections provide private firms with information about subsidies and loans to support the development of new technology (Interviews 29, 32). This information allows the private firms to better prepare the application for subsidies and loans, which increases the probability they will obtain financial support for R&D.

Besides using B2G networks to finance technology, interviewees also emphasized the role of government in approving the use of new technology. One entrepreneur who invested in the wholesale and retail industry said:

> *In China, government connections not only affect whether the firm can receive funding for R&D. It also affects whether the new technology developed by the firm can be applied in production. For many industries, firms need to seek approval or pass certain tests before they can use the new technology in daily production. And obviously, the power of examination and approval is in the hands of the government. (Interview 51)*

Several interviewees mentioned the uncertainty surrounding the application of a new technology in production (Interviews 39, 45, 51). B2G networks help firms to reduce the time needed for administrative approval, and overcome unclear and confusing regulations in the application of new technology. Distant government connections may be more helpful in this respect. The departments that have the power to approve the application of a new technology may not have local sub-branches. Entrepreneurs who have distant government connections have the advantage here in cultivating relationships with officials in higher-level government agencies. This explains why entrepreneurs who use distant government connections frequently are more likely to agree that B2G networks help private firms to acquire new technology.

In addition to helping with R&D, government connections also help private firms to acquire new technology developed by other firms. Interviewees reported that B2G networks provided information especially about new technologies developed by SOEs (Interviews 41, 49). Compared to private firms, one interviewee said that SOEs have looser control over their new technologies (Interview 41). Information about new technologies acquired through the private firm's connections with managers in the SOEs increased the competitiveness of the focal firms in the market.

For the control variables, firm size is significant at $p<0.1$, and it is negatively correlated to the perception of private entrepreneurs about the role of B2G networks in acquiring new technology. The larger the firm, the less likely their owners perceive that B2G networks are significant to help their firms to access new technology. Larger firms usually have deeper pockets and are able to access financial resources, which lessen the burden of investment in R&D. They therefore rely less on B2G networks to develop and acquire new technology. Large firms also usually receive more support from local government because they contribute more than small firms to local employment and economic development (Park & Luo, 2001). There is, thus, less incentive for large firms to cultivate connections with government officials.

Overall, these results illustrate the importance of B2G networks in helping private firms to access both financial and technological resources. Local government connections and distant government connections assist private firms to access resources in different respects. Both connections constitute an important channel for private firms to increase their capabilities to acquire resources and to compete in the market.

4.5 CONCLUSION

This research explores the role of B2G networks in helping Chinese private firm to access financial resources and new technology. We have examined the intensity of government connections between private entrepreneurs and officials in different regulatory agencies or state-affiliated organizations. Using factor analysis, we have distinguished between local government connections and distant government connections. The logistic regression results showed that connections with local government officials help private firms to acquire higher loans in a shorter time. The rule of reciprocity embedded in Chinese culture motivates both entrepreneurs and local government officials to invest in and maintain a stable relationship that might benefit them in the future. People take a future orientation towards personal relationship. Thus, local government officials retain influential power over lending decisions through their influence on the career development or other aspects of the life of bank managers. In addition, local government connections transmit information between firms and state-owned banks, which reduce the cost of information asymmetry in making lending decisions. In general, B2G networks favour connected private firms in terms of access to financial resources.

While private entrepreneurs emphasized the importance of local government connections in accessing financial resources, both local and distant government connections help private firms to acquire new technology. Connections with local government officials assist private firms to obtain subsidies and government supports in R&D. Distant government connections enable private firms to ensure the application of new technology through speeding up the approval process, and provide information about technologies developed by other companies.

Our findings reaffirm the important role the government plays in resource allocation in China. Although new policies in recent decades have improved the market and institutional environment and circumscribed the conduct of government officials, officials still influenced the allocation of resources, especially those officials in local government. In addition to the institutional environment, the rule of reciprocity in Chinese culture also motivates people to cultivate personal relationships and hold a future-orientation towards potential benefits that might accrue from the maintenance of personal connections.

APPENDIX: LIST OF INTERVIEWEES CITED IN TEXT

Number	Gender	Position of interviewee	Years with the position	Age of the company (years)	Industry	Location of headquarter
9	M	Owner	17	17	Real Estate	Guangzhou and Shenzhen
29	M	Owner	9	9	Wholesale and Retail Trade	Pearl River Delta Cities
30	M	Owner	16	16	Manufacturing	Pearl River Delta Cities
32	M	Owner	7	7	Manufacturing	Pearl River Delta Cities
39	M	Vice Manager	4	8	Manufacturing	Pearl River Delta Cities
40	M	Owner	10	10	Manufacturing	Guangzhou and Shenzhen
41	M	Owner	12	12	Manufacturing	Peripheral Cities
45	F	Owner	19	19	Agriculture, Forestry, Animal Husbandry, and Fishery	Peripheral Cities
49	M	Owner	12	12	Manufacturing	Guangzhou and Shenzhen
51	M	Owner	21	21	Wholesale and Retail Trade	Guangzhou and Shenzhen

REFERENCES

ACFIC (All China Federation of Industry and Commerce 中华全国工商业联合会). (2007). 1993–2006 the large-scale survey on private enterprises in China (1993–2006 中国私营企业大型调查). Beijing: China Industry & Commerce Associated Press (中华工商联合出版社).

Allen, F., Qian, J., Zhang, C., & Zhao, M. (2012). China's financial system: Opportunities and challenges, National Bureau of Economic Research Working Paper No. 17828. Cambridge, MA: National Bureau of Economic Research.

Ayyagari, M., Demirgüç-Kunt, A., & Maksimovic, V. (2010). Formal versus informal finance: Evidence from China. *Review of Financial Studies, 23*(8), 3048–3097.

Barney, J. B. (1991). Firm resources and sustained competitive advantage. *Journal of Management, 17*(1), 99.

Chow, C. K. W., & Fung, M. K. Y. (2012). Investment opportunity set, political connection and business policies of private enterprises in China. *Review of Quantitative Finance and Accounting, 38*(3), 367–389.

Chung, W.-K., & Hamilton, G. G. (2001). Social logic as business logic: Guanxi, trustworthiness, and the embeddedness of Chinese business practices. In R. P. Appelbaum, W. L. F. Felstiner, & V. Gessner (Eds.), *Rules and networks: The legal culture of global business transactions* (pp. 325–346). Oxford: Hart Publishing.

Field, A. (2013). *Discovering statistics using IBM SPSS statistics* (4th ed.). London: SAGE Publication.

Firth, M., Lin, C., Liu, P., & Wong, S. M. L. (2009). Inside the black box: Bank credit allocation in China's private sector. *Journal of Banking & Finance, 33*(6), 1144–1155.

Freeman, J., Carroll, G. R., & Hannan, M. T. (1983). The liability of newness: Age dependence in organizational death rates. *American Sociological Review, 48*(5), 692–710.

Gu, F. F., Hung, K., & Tse, D. K. (2008). When does Guanxi matter? Issues of capitalization and its dark sides. *Journal of Marketing, 72*(4), 12–28.

Gujarati, D. N. (1995). *Basic econometrics* (3rd ed.). USA: McGraw Hill. International Edition.

Guthrie, D. (1999). *Dragon in a three-piece suit: The emergence of capitalism in China*. Princeton, NJ: Princeton University Press.

Haggard, S., & Huang, Y. (2008). The political economy of private sector development in China. In L. Brandt & T. G. Rawski (Eds.), *China's great economic transformation* (pp. 337–374). Cambridge: Cambridge University Press.

Hsueh, J.-T., Lin, N.-P., & Li, H.-C. (2010). The effects of network embeddedness on service innovation performance. *Service Industries Journal, 30*(10), 1723–1736.

Jiang, C., Yao, S., & Feng, G. (2013). Bank ownership, privatization, and performance: Evidence from a transition country. *Journal of Banking & Finance, 37*(9), 3364–3372.

Kwong, C. C. L. (2009). From commercialization to WTO accession. *Chinese Economy, 42*(5), 8–20.

Li, J. J., Zhou, K. Z., & Shao, A. T. (2009). Competitive position, managerial ties, and profitability of foreign firms in China: An interactive perspective. *Journal of International Business Studies, 40*(2), 339–352.

Lovett, S., Simmons, L. C., & Kali, R. (1999). Guanxi versus the market: Ethics and efficiency. *Journal of International Business Studies, 30*(2), 231–247.

Lu, L.-T. (2012). Guanxi and renqing: The roles of two cultural norms in Chinese business. *International Journal of Management, 29*(2), 466–475.

Luo, Y. D. (2007). *Guanxi and business*. Singapore: World Scientific Publishing Co. Pte. Ltd.

Ma, H., Lin, S., & Liang, N. (2012). *Corporate political strategies of private Chinese firms*. London: Routledge.

Park, S. H., & Luo, Y. D. (2001). Guanxi and organizational dynamics: Organizational networking in Chinese firms. *Strategic Management Journal, 22*(5), 455–477.

Peng, M.W., & Luo, Y. (2000). Managerial ties and firm performance in a transition economy: The nature of a micro-macro link. *Academy of Management Journal, 43*(3), 486–501.
Peng, M. W., & Zhou, J. Q. (2005). How network strategies and institutional transitions evolve in Asia. *Asia Pacific Journal of Management, 22*(4), 321–336.
Potter, P. B. (2002). Guanxi and the PRC legal system: From contradiction to complementarity. In T. B. Gold, D. Guthrie, & D. L. Wank (Eds.), *Social connections in China: Institutions, culture, and the changing nature of Guanxi* (pp. 179–196). New York: Cambridge University Press.
Sheng, S., Zhou, K. Z., & Li, J. J. (2011). The effects of business and political ties on firm performance: Evidence from China. *Journal of Marketing, 75*(1), 1–15.
Wei, Z., Hou, J., Wang, D., & Wang, L. (2011). How can SMEs leverage political ties and technological innovation capability to acquire government assistance in a transition economy? *Journal of General Management, 36*(4), 3–22.
Wu, W., Wu, C., Zhou, C., & Wu, J. (2012). Political connections, tax benefits and firm performance: Evidence from China. *Journal of Accounting and Public Policy, 31*(3), 277–300.
Zhu, Y., Wittmann, X., & Peng, M. W. (2012). Institution-based barriers to innovation in SMEs in China. *Asia Pacific Journal of Management, 29*(4), 1131–1142.

CHAPTER 5

Business Networks and the Emergence of *Guanxi* Capitalism in China: The Role of the 'Invisible Hand'

B.X. Wang[*], C. Rowley[†,‡,§,¶]
[*]Ashridge-Hult International Business School, Ashridge, United Kingdom
[†]Korea University, Seoul, Korea
[‡]Griffith University, Nathan, QLD, Australia
[§]Nottingham University, Nottingham, United Kingdom
[¶]City University, London, United Kingdom

5.1 INTRODUCTION

The continuously growing importance of China's economy can be seen in its rapid growth and recent establishment of Asian Infrastructure Investment Bank (AIIB) in 2015 to support the building of infrastructure in the Asia Pacific region, as well as the Renminbi's joining the elite basket of currencies (United Nations, 2015). This has partly driven concern about global economic governance (United Nations Financing for Development Office, 2015). Given these circumstances, there is an urgent need to better understand China's political and economic system. We undertake this task by grounding developments historically and developing the idea of *guanxi* capitalism.

As an indigenous Chinese social-cultural phenomena *guanxi*—although the notion is similar to Western-termed interpersonal relationships or social networks—possesses much broader implications—the concept per se has been widely accepted in academia (Ambler, Styles, & Xiucun, 1999; Barnes, Yen, & Zhou, 2011; Chen & Chen, 2004; Chen, Chen, & Huang, 2013; Chua & Wellman, 2015; Fan, 2002; Fan, Woodbine, & Scully, 2012; Farh, Tsui, Xin, & Cheng, 1998). Despite its traditions, whether the *guanxi* phenomenon would continue to prevail alongside globalisation and modernisation of Chinese companies and society has provoked a wide-ranging debate (Hsu & Saxenian, 2000; Kwock, James, & Tsui, 2013; Lu & Reve, 2011; Luo & Chen, 1997; Michailova & Worm, 2003; Zhang & Zhang, 2006). In this collection, Chapters 10, 12 and 13 are also concerned with understanding whether or not culturally rooted, informal networks are sustainable over the long term in capitalist societies.

Business Networks in East Asian Capitalisms
http://dx.doi.org/10.1016/B978-0-08-100639-9.00006-2

Our chapter examines *guanxi* capitalism in order to reveal the features of China's economic system embedded deeply in its cultural-social-political environment. We will explore how *guanxi* capitalism emerged, evolved, and dominated the economic system by reviewing Chinese business history, understanding attitudes toward business, and elaborating the 'Five Classified Relationships' (FRC) (*Wulun*) of Confucian ethics. The aim, therefore, is to develop a conceptual framework of the '*Guanxi* Capitalism Structure' building on the theory of 'Differential Mode of Association' (DMA) (*Chaxugeju*) developed by Chinese sociologist Fei (1992), and using the concept of 'Central Managed Capitalism' (CMC) (Lin, 2010) as well as the framework of 'Network of *Guanxi* Circles' (Wong & Huang, 2015). This framework illustrates the fundamental role of *guanxi* as the 'invisible hand' in China.

Guanxi capitalism has been fiercely debated since Hamilton (1989) first deployed this term in his study of political economies in Taiwan. Mcnally (2011, p. 1) further defined *guanxi* capitalism as 'a unique conceptual blend infused with seemingly incongruous cultural and historical meanings drawn from both Chinese and Western roots, which encompasses both contradictory and complementary institutional logics'.

Other scholars (Borja, 2014; Liu, Noel, Rollins, & Gao, 2014; Peck & Zhang, 2013) addressed the important role that *guanxi* plays in the Chinese social-economic system. Nevertheless, how and why *guanxi* capitalism emerged in China is somewhat underplayed in the literature. This chapter develops a conceptual framework of the *guanxi* capitalism structure based on the analysis of Confucian ethics in FCR (*Wulun*), DMA (*Chaxugeju*) and using the concept of CMC the framework of 'Network of *Guanxi* Circles'. Among debates in relations to the origin of *guanxi*, some scholars contended that FCR (*Wulun*) is the basic norms of *guanxi* (Fei, 1992; Hwang, 1987; Nuang, 1992; Wong & Huang, 2015), Fei (1992) conceptualised DMA to illustrate that *guanxi* extended from the kinship system. Thus, Wong and Huang (2015) developed the framework of 'Network of Gunaxi Circles'. Therefore, we further develop the notion of '*guanxi* knot' and '*guanxi* web', which we believe provides the foundation of CMC.

Weber (1920, p. xxi) claimed that 'greed for gain' is 'as old as the history of man', which includes the '*greed* of mandarins in China'. He further emphasised the crucial role of cultural values, in particular, the significant impact of protestant ethics as the 'spirit of capitalism' and organisational life in the West, where capitalism is carried by powerful social networks consisting of both commercial elites and self-made parvenus (Weber, 1920). In China, *guanxi* was derived from Confucian ethics on human relationships which underpin the Chinese social-political structure (Chen et al., 2013; Dunning

& Kim, 2007) and carries capitalism. The spirit of capitalism is formulated and cultivated by *guanxi* holders who are composed of influential people at all levels of the social and political hierarchies.

Since Kanter (1995) identified the three assets (concept, competition, and connection) of the global economy, developing networks came to be seen as one of the competitive advantages for Western multinational companies (MNCs). This is of particular importance for their endeavours in China where *guanxi* capitalism has become the root of business. Business networks in China are underpinned by a variety of weak to strong links that range from the formal to the informal kind, such as *guanxi*. Studies (Ambler et al., 1999; Chua & Wellman, 2015; Fan et al., 2012) have validated the importance of *guanxi* as a systemic modus operandi in understanding the role and functions of networks in Chinese business culture.

Guanxi, a network featuring 'face-to-face' and 'face-for-face' interpersonal relationships, has been one of the most crucial elements of Chinese culture and remains relevant, although the 'dark side' (corruption-related) of *guanxi* has been acknowledged. Despite the fact that capitalism has been embraced since China reopened to the world in the 1980s and that the economy is termed 'state capitalism', the ideology of the Chinese Communist Party toward business is derived from Marxism as well as an historically biased view. Nevertheless, as a result of pragmatism being a key component of Chinese culture and the psychological justification initiated by Mao Zedong: 'apply ancient knowledge into current practice, apply Western knowledge into Chinese practice', *guanxi* capitalism has emerged as one of the 'Chinese characteristics' of the economic development.

Mcnally (2011) argued that *guanxi* capitalism realigns the interests of the state and capital in China, and bridges the divide between freewheeling capitalist accumulation and authoritarian control prevalent in a state-dominated economy. Mcnally (2011) was able to evaluate China's economic transition and avoid the more common and narrower understanding of capitalism. For this reason, he proposed that as far as his primary observations are concerned, China was generating a 'new' form of capitalism.

Despite Confucianism having been marginalised since the New Cultural Movement in the 1920s and vilified during the Cultural Revolution of the 1960s (Zhang & Schwartz, 1997), in 2005 a campaign of Confucian 'Harmonious Society' (Zheng & Tok, 2007) was launched by the Chinese government to establish social order by emphasising cultural values and social responsibility, since increasing economic disparity in the country was endangering the stability of the state and social morality. In particular, Chinese president Xi Jinping has so elevated Confucianism that he convened a 'collective study' session of the ruling Politburo at which he said that traditional culture should act as a 'wellspring' nourishing the Party's values. In 2013, Mr. Xi paid homage at the Confucius temple in Qufu (Confucius' birthplace), and he is the first Party chief to attend a birthday celebration for Confucius, born 2565 years ago (The Economist, July 2015).

5.2 CHINESE BUSINESS HISTORY

One of the challenges in understanding Chinese businesses is that some neglect the importance of history, making it impossible to fully understand. Tong (2014, p. 5) quoted Berger and Luckmann: 'Institutions always have a history of which they are products. It is impossible to understand an institution adequately without an understanding of the historical process in which it is produced'. In terms of history, we can place analysis within the older and wider theories and debates around convergence-divergence, models of capitalism, varieties of capitalism, business systems, and globalisation, etc. For example, universalism's convergence versus contingency's divergence concerns the central proposition of a possible global tendency for political, social, and economic forces to push toward uniformity of systems and practices. Such views have a long antecedence (eg, Kerr, Dunlop, Harbison, & Myers, 1962) and regularly re-emerge. Earlier ideas of the 'best way' include, *inter alia*, scientific management, and Fordism in the United States, indicative planning in France (1960s), corporatism in Scandinavia (1980s), lean production, Toyotism, and Japanisation (1990s) and the post-cold war prescriptions, as well as in the Excellence and Flexible Specialisation literatures (Rowley, 1994).

Such universalistic ideas are seen in the globalisation debate with its singular world view of market unification and institutional convergence leading to the 'one best way' in a range of areas. Theories from different subjects seek to explain globalisation: Global Capitalism, Network Society, Space and Place, Transnationality and Transnationalism, Modernity and Postmodernity to Global Culture and World-Systems (Robinson, 2007). For example, the multidisciplinary World-Systems Theory (Wallerstein 1974, 2004) does not emphasise nation-states, but rather historical processes, as they unfold over time, key moments, and that the world-system is a social reality comprised of interconnected firms, households, classes, and identity groups. However, world-systems simplistically collapse cultural forces into political systems, although the independent influence of cultural forces cannot be reduced to different characteristics of political systems (Robinson, 2007).

Universalism has many sceptics, producing a literature with a similarly long lineage (Hofstede, 1980, 1984; Lawrence & Lorsh, 1967; Woodward, 1965).

For example, comparisons of the United Kingdom with other economies often found national differences in areas such as business organisation and structure, management, technology utilisation, etc., including not only with Japan (Dore, 1974), but also Germany and France. Similarly, System, Society and Dominance Theory (Smith & Meiksins, 1995) organised influences on work organisation as: production modes; institutional patterns; best practice or universal modernisation strategies. This argued convergence was unlikely as structural pressures were conveyed through national histories and cultural contingencies. Indeed, mediation of local actions through traditions at a national level meant rounds of institutional change were built on, resulting in place-specific recombinant formations, each with their own distinctive properties (Sorge, 2005).

Other historically grounded contingency type views can be seen in Modes of Exchange (Lie, 1992) with its 'Manorial', 'Market', 'Entrepreneurial' and 'Mercantile' exchanges. Then there is the capitalist variety (Hall & Soskice, 2001; Hancke, Rhodes, & Thatcher, 2007) and comparative capitalism (Berger & Dore, 1996; Boyer, 2005; Coates, 2000; Crouch, 2005; Hollingsworth & Boyer, 1997; Kitschelt, Lange, Marks, & Stephens, 1998) literature distinguishing various different 'types' of capitalisms. These include: 'Stock Market' and 'Welfare' (Dore, 2000); 'Competitive Managerial', 'Personal', and 'Cooperative Managerial' (Chandler, 1990); 'Liberal' and 'Alliance' (Gerlach, 1992); 'Neo-American' and 'Rhinish' (Albert, 1993); 'Managerial', 'Propriety', and 'Collective' (Lazonick, 1990, 1991, 1998); 'Market-based', 'Social-democratic', 'Continental European', 'South European', and 'Asian' (Amable, 2003). A fivefold typology of Asian capitalism diversity (Harada & Tohyama, 2012) was: 'City' (Singapore, Hong Kong), 'Insular Semi-Agrarian' (Indonesia, Philippines), 'Innovation-Led' (Japan, Korea, Taiwan), 'Trade-Led Industrializing' (Malaysia, Thailand), and 'Continental Mixed' (China) and three types of North East Asian capitalism were: 'Fragmented', 'State-Organised', and 'Collaborative' (Whitley, 1999). Indeed, 'Variegated Capitalism' was concerned with the combined and uneven development of capitalism '...and the polymorphic interdependence of its constituent regimes' (Peck & Theodore, 2007, p. 733).

Other related models of relevance include business systems (Redding, 2005; Whitley, 1999, 2007, 2014). Whitley (1992) used a threefold framework of variation of impacts from: 'Firms' (management styles and structures, decision-making processes, owner-employee relations, patterns of growth and development); 'Markets' (customer, supplier and inter-firm relations, financial sector and market and industry development); 'Societies' (social influences on business evolution such as education, systems of power and status and family structures) to examine Asia (Japan, Korea, Taiwan, Hong Kong). Witt and Redding (2014, p. 686) argued theories needed to incorporate social capital, culture, informality, and 'multiplexity' and '... variations in the extent of informality in a business system and its interplay with formal institutions'. By social capital they meant 'trust', interpersonal or relational; as well as institutionalised or system (with triple components: control; trust; morality) trust. Their framework included the role of the state, financial system, ownership and corporate governance, internal structure of the firm, employment relations, education and skills formation, interfirm relations, and social capital. This framework has been used to analyse countries, including Vietnam (Truong & Rowley, 2014).

The current principles guiding business and daily life in the West have evolved from ancient Greek philosophies, which originate from a different ideological root from the Chinese. Indeed, 'The ancient Chinese and Greek philosophers not only lived under different geographic conditions, but different economic ones as well' (Fung, 1948, p.17). As a continental country, agriculture was the dominant economy for thousands of years in China, and so from a social and economic perspective, agriculture was the 'root' and commerce or business the 'branch'. Therefore, throughout millennia of Chinese civilisation, social-cultural norms and economic systems have all tended to emphasise the root and slight the branch (Graham & Lam, 2003), a doctrine of 'pro-agriculture and anti-commerce', which originated in the Qin Dynasty some 2200 years ago. Consequently, business people dealing with the 'branch' were at the bottom of the social class after scholars, farmers and artisans.

The first commercial activities emerged in China around BC475 and the privatisation of land was first institutionalised in BC216. The beginnings of industrialisation were developed around BC221 during the Qin Dynasty when China was unified by Emperor Qin Shihuang. The new empire with a unified written language, currency, a measuring system, and a bureaucracy facilitated business activities across all regions in China (Qian, 2013). Beginning in the Han dynasty (BC206–AD220) until the 1450s, the Silk Road was established to facilitate business from China to the West, largely through the missions and explorations of Chinese imperial envoys. Trade on the Silk Road was a significant factor in the development of the civilizations of China, the Indian subcontinent, Persia, Europe, the Horn of Africa, and Arabia, opening long-distance political and economic relations between them. In addition to economic trade, the Silk Road served as a means of carrying out cultural exchange among the civilizations along its network (Bentley, 1993). The Tang Dynasty (618–907) was the most open era (until three decades ago) in Chinese history, welcoming merchants and entrepreneurs from Persia, Rome, Arabia, and India.

When the British broke down the door to China in 1840 by winning the Opium War, a group of Chinese intellectuals appealed for changing the 'anti-commerce' mindset, and for strengthening and saving China by boosting commercialization. They proposed the adoption of the practices of Western capitalism and industrialisation. In 1903, the Commerce Ministry was established and Commercial Law was enacted. The first generation of national capitalists was created and was expected to save China from poverty and the oppression of foreign countries. Most of them were from landlord families and were well-educated: the merchant had ascended to second place, next to the scholar. However, this did not last (in mainland China, anyway): in 1949 Mao Zedong came to power, and implemented Marxist socialism and rooted the business community out of China.

When Deng Xiaoping took control in 1978, he implemented a 'Social market economy with Chinese characteristics'. He encouraged common people to pursue individual wealth through a pragmatic approach: (No matter if it is a white cat or a black cat, it is a good cat if it catches mice.) Another phrase of his was 'Cross the river by touching the stones', which implied there was no common business practice or culture to follow at that point.

As illustrated in Table 5.1, given the mind-set of anticommerce embedded in Chinese society for more than 2000 years, the concept of Western-termed business is still relatively new to the Chinese. In spite of the economic growth in China over the past three decades, positions in the leading class are still not open to members of the business community.

5.3 ATTITUDES TOWARD BUSINESS

Notwithstanding the history of business in China, there were complex attitudes toward business, derived from Chinese traditional schools of philosophy. Daoism was against materialism, and one faction of Legalism strongly opposed commercial pursuit. A Confucian planned economy dominated in Imperial China, despite the concerns of Sima Qian (135–86 BC), the Chinese historian of the Han dynasty who advocated a free and individualised economy (Qian, 2013). Confucianism highly praised agricultural activities, but mentioned no business life as 'Confucius seldom spoke of profit, destiny, and benevolence' (Analects C9). He further spoke of associating 'profit' (the purpose of business) with 'the small man' (vulgar man):

Table 5.1 Evolution of business concepts in China

Stage	Anti-commerce	Infancy of capitalism	Anti-capitalism	State capitalism with Chinese characteristics
Time	BC500–1903 (2403 years) Imperial China	1903–1948 (45 years) Semi-feudal and semi-colonial	1949–1977 (28 years) Cultural revolution	1978–present (36 years) Reform and opening up
Main ideology	Confucianism	Confucianism Capitalism	Socialism	Socialism Capitalism Confucianism
Leading class	Aristocrat Scholar-officials	Anarchy	Military/ worker-official	Scholar-officials
Social status	Business people ranked at the bottom of social stratum	– Established Ministry of Commerce – First generation of national capitalists emerged from landlord background – Business class ascended to second place next to the scholar	– Business and business class were ruined completely – Planned economy	– Business and economic development is the top priority – From planned economy to market economy – Government plays the key role – State-owned enterprise is most privileged among all business organisations

Derived from Fung, Y.-L. (1948). A short history of Chinese philosophy: A systematic account of Chinese thoughts from its origins to the present day. New York: The Free Press, A Division of Simon & Schuster Inc. and Qian, M. (2013). History of Chinese economy (in Chinese). Beijing United Publishing Co. Ltd., Beijing.

While the gentleman cherishes virtue, the small man cherishes the property. While the gentleman cherishes the legality, the small man cherishes the profit. (Analects C4)

If one acts with one's own profit, there will be much resentment. (Analects C4)

The gentleman knows what is right, the small man knows what is profitable. (Analects C4)

In Confucian society, the conviction of 'scholarly/official superiority' steers people to pursue higher education in order to get a position in the government. Even though the legendary Tao Zhugong (517–? BC) is considered the first business person in China and prototyped the 'Money God' (*Cai Shen*), his leaving a high-ranking position for business was to avoid a dispute at court and potential murder by the king. Even now the ultimate promotions and rewards for the Chinese are the top positions and ranks in the party and the state in Beijing (Lin, 2010). The loyalty of corporate executives is ultimately to the party and the state, not the board of directors, shareholders, or stakeholders. For example, 'Of course, one significant criterion for being promoted is performance in the marketplace. In this manner capitalism is linked to rewards in the political realm as well' (Lin, 2010, p. 76).

Thanks to the economic growth over the past three decades, the business community has grown rapidly and some successful business leaders are admired enormously by some.[1] Business Studies is the first choice by many college students, and the MBA/EMBA market has been overheating for a decade. However, many entrepreneurs still want their children to become scholars first and then inherit their business as a second choice. 'No businessman trades without fraud' is still somehow deeply rooted in the Chinese subconscious. As a result, business organisations classify themselves into four hierarchies, which are, in order of status (Wang & Chee, 2011):

- State-Owned Enterprise (SOE): led by government, the Chairman or CEO is also an official who should be an expert in some academic field or at least have a higher education degree.
- Western MNE and JVs: possess advanced technology from the West and are superior in business savvy and management practices.
- Chinese Private Company and SMEs: established by former officials or scholars, who have achieved in the political or academic field and then manage their private business, strongly connected with government.
- Chinese Family Business: established by non-intellectuals, the undereducated entrepreneurs from the grassroots.

[1]Based on participants and entrepreneurs coached by the authors.

The current social society is implicitly structured as scholar, business person, worker, and farmer. The demographic of government officials is dominated by scholars or intellectuals.[2]

5.4 CONFUCIAN ETHICS

Due to the holistic feature from the Chinese Yin-Yang culture, there are no clear boundaries among the political, economic, and social apparatus in human life—as a whole, it is guided by a general principle which is Confucian ethics (Fung, 1948). Confucius created a rational and humane ethical system, as opposed to a legal institution, to govern and stabilise the country by mobilising, rather than repressing people's emotions. Accordingly, he established a comprehensive ritual procedure (礼) for people to follow the *formal* rules, and instituted human ethical relations (人伦) as a basis for *informal* personal interactions. Therefore, the Western-termed rational and logical economic system does not apply to China. Rather, *guanxi* capitalism is the indigenous and highly dynamic system integrated and intertwined with both rational and emotional variables, which is the most effective, if not the best way to operate in China.[3]

As Russell (1961, p. 41) stated: 'To understand an age or a nation, we must understand its philosophy'. In addition, the Chinese philosopher Fung (1948, p. 7) stated: 'The Chinese philosophy, regardless of its different schools of thought, is directly or indirectly concerned with government and ethics about daily functions of human relations, not hell and heaven; with man's present life, but not his life in a world to come'. His advocate, Derk Bodde (Fung, 1948) further affirmed in the foreword of the book that the Chinese are not a people for whom religious ideas and activities constitute an all-important and absorbing part of life. It is ethics (especially Confucian ethics), and not religion that provided the spiritual basis in Chinese civilization and nurtured Chinese institution and culture.

The Confucian system of ethics is the fundamental motivation of all pursuits in life in society and has been embedded in civilisation for two millennia. This is the philosophical root of doing business: following the ethics of the 'rule of man' rather than the 'rule of law' is common business practice for firms. In other words, decision-making through complex social processes engenders an institutional environment constructed by *guanxi*. In general, ethics driven by *guanxi* rather than law determines the way of doing business.

[2]Based on the author's personal views as well as conversation with scholar in China.
[3]Based on the author's own opinions.

The Chinese philosopher of neo-Confucianism, Liang Shuming (1893–1988) encapsulated two main differences between Chinese and Western national characteristics. Chinese society is driven by 'individual interacts with individual' (Liang, 2010, p. 171) based on 'personal ethical emotions and lofty ideals' (p. 172); Western society is driven by 'people interact with things' (p. 172) based on 'scientific technology and social organisation' (p. 173). Wang (2008) noted that there exists a union of emotions and reason in Confucian ethics. According to Confucians, the ethical significance of emotions lies in the point that an ethical life is also emotional and virtues are inclinational, which constitutes a challenge to Western ethical theories engaged in seeking justifications for abstract moral rules.

Warner (2004) noted that China's national identity is thus deep-rooted in its history and culture. Every day the Chinese media feature a reference to historical analogies or precedents, whether in business, economics, or management. Viewed from another perspective, the miracle of China has been its astonishing unity. The key reason is due to the coherent Confucian culture. Many scholars, such as *inter alia* Styles and Ambler (2003), Lin (2011), Warner (2004), noted that Confucianism has actually developed from the interactions of a single ethnic group, the Han people, which has largely distanced itself from other ethnic groups for many centuries. According to the census in 2011, 91.51% of the population in China is Han ethnic. Han culture has been dominant in China for many thousands of years, which can be regarded as synonymous with Chinese culture. Despite two dynasties (Yuan and Qing) being ruled by minorities (Mongolian and Manchu), the ruling class embraced Han culture completely and governed the country following mainly Confucian ethics.

Two prominent Chinese philosophers, Fung (1948) and Wei (2009), emphasised the important social and political role that family plays in China, given the agricultural nature of the country and Confucian culture. In Imperial China, as an agriculture-oriented country, scholars, who are landlords and farmers, were the driving force for social and economic development and both of them must live on their land, which is immovable. Also, the whole family of several generations needed to live together for economic reasons, from which the Chinese family system has developed. Confucius made tremendous efforts to rationalise and theorise this social system, which is 'one of the most complex and well-organised in the world' (Fung, 1948, p. 21). The family apparatus has been adopted naturally in both social-cultural and political-economic systems and facilitated the synchronising of these two systems. Hence, Confucianism became the orthodox philosophy in imperial China and has remained as such into the present time.

Both Confucius and Aristotle shared the same theory of the family as a model for the organisation of the state. It either explains the structure of certain kinds of state in terms of the structure of the family (as a model or as a claim about the historical growth of the state), or it attempts to justify certain types of state by appealing to the structure of the family. In contrast, Aristotle drew a sharp distinction between the *economic* relationships of the family and the *political* relationships of the state (Schochet, 1975), while Confucius integrated the relationship of family and state. The Chinese word for state is composed of two characters (国家), which are literally 'state' and 'family', because only the notion of family can evoke the sense of belonging in Chinese people.

5.5 FIVE CLASSIFIED RELATIONSHIPS (*WULUN*)

The Confucian ideal is to harmonise the world by passing through each stage of cultivating self, regulating family, and governing the state. A stable state and harmonious society is based on regulated families, where each member self-cultivates obedience to the rule of the FCR ('*Wulun*', 五伦), which are those between: (1) ruler and subject, (2) father and son, (3) elder and younger brother, (4) husband and wife, (5) friend and friend. Three of these are direct family relationships—however, the relationship between ruler and subject can be conceived as that between father and son, and that between friend and friend can be conceived as that between brothers (Fung, 1948). The rules are: 'Between father and son, there should be affection, between ruler and subject, there should be righteousness, between husband and wife, attention to their separate functions; between old and young, a proper order; and between friends, good faith' (Mencius, 2004, p. 60).

Different rules are applied in accordance with the classification of relationships and so we use the term FCR. Confucian ethics is embedded in social life as well as institutionalised for governing the country. FCR is the essence of Confucian ethics, which determines that the Chinese have a strong sense of self-needs and dyadic personal relationship within the family as an in-group, but not with an out-group, such as state, society, or organisations. There is no relationship between an individual and an out-group. Barkema, Chen, George, Luo, and Tsui (2011) indicated that collectivists also tend to make sharp distinctions between in-group and out-group members among the Chinese, which reflects particularism rather than universalism (Schwartz, 1992), but as do Koreans (Rowley, 2013; Rowley, Bae, & Sohn, 2002). Thus, Chinese people typically believe that it is acceptable

to treat people differently depending on their *guanxi* with themselves. The psychological contract of the Chinese is to be treated as 'reasonable' rather than 'fair'. Chinese is neither a Western-termed collective nor individual culture, rather it is particularistic and pluralistic.

5.6 CONCEPTUALISATION OF *GUANXI*

The *guanxi* construct, therefore, originated from FCR (Wong & Huang, 2015), which is the underpinning of not only the social-cultural, but also the political-economic system in China. It would be challenging to build loyalty and trust in Chinese for any relationship outside of FCR, given that the 'rule of law' has not prevailed in China. Hence, to establish business and raise capital it is necessary to go through *guanxi*.

Summarising previous studies (Chen & Chen, 2004; Chen et al., 2013; Chua & Wellman, 2015; Dunning & Kim, 2007; Fan, 2002; Fan et al., 2012; Hsu & Saxenian, 2000; Kwock et al., 2013; Lu & Reve, 2011; Luo & Chen, 1997; Michailova & Worm, 2003), the difference between Western-termed interpersonal relationships and *guanxi* is illustrated in Table 5.2.

Table 5.2 *Guanxi* and Western interpersonal relationships

	Interpersonal relationships/ social network	*Guanxi* (differential interpersonal relationships)
Context	West	China
Social order	Equality, universal love	Particularity, differentiated love according to classification of personal relationships based on FCR
Social structure	Organisational mode of association	Differential mode of association
Social pursuit	Society benefit, teamwork	Family benefit, self-achievement
Social hub	Society/organisation	Individual/family
Interaction	Dyadic or multiple group	Dyadic, personal
Purpose	Reciprocate, neutral feelings, short-time, occasional meeting	Reciprocate, strong affections, long-term, periodical or frequent meeting

5.7 DIFFERENTIAL MODE OF ASSOCIATION (*CHAXUGEJU*)

Fei (1992) developed the concept of DMA (*Chaxugeju*) to distinguish Chinese social structure from Western 'organisational mode of association' (*Tuantigeju*), and also noted that families in the West are organisations with distinct boundaries. However, the Chinese pattern: '…is like the circles that appear on the surface of a lake when a rock is thrown into it. Everyone stands at the centre of the circles produced by his or her own social influence. Everyone's circles are interrelated. One touches different circles at different times and places' (Fei, 1992).

In Chinese society the most important relationship is kinship, which is a social relationship formed through marriage and reproduction. The networks woven by marriage and reproduction can be extended to embrace countless numbers of people—in the past, present, and future. Each network is like a spider's web in the sense that it centres on oneself. Everyone has this kind of a kinship network, but the people covered by one network are not the same as those covered by any other. The web of social relationships linked with kinship is specific to each person. 'Each web has a self as its centre, and every web has a different centre. This pattern of organisation in Chinese traditional society has the special quality of elasticity' (Fei, 1992, p. 62).

This describes how *guanxi* is developed from one individual as a centre to expand in a circular form to facilitate the social process. Therefore, this social structure created the 'egocentrism but not individualism' in Chinese culture. Confucian ethics reinforces the central person of *guanxi* in the social order, which both public officials and private persons use to define the context of their actions (Fei, 1992). Therefore, in Confucian culture, the boundary between public and private is blurred. The concept of public is ambiguous: the state is seen as the Emperor's family. Thus: 'The state and the public are but additional circles that spread out like the waves from the splash of each person's social influence' (Fei, 1992, p. 63). Therefore, the whole society is connected by *guanxi* circles. *Guanxi* is fundamentally self-centred and personal, which determines the social-cultural and political-economic dynamics in China.

Consequently, in order to balance self-interest and social responsibility, the starting point of Confucian ethics is the self-cultivation of 'Subdue the self and follow the rites. From the Son of Heaven (the ruler) down to ordinary people, all must consider the cultivation of the person as the root of everything' (Confucius (Chinese), 2014, p. 836) in order to inculcate the individual's value and conduct one's behaviours. Therefore, as Confucian ethics are all about

human relationships, *guanxi* is embedded with ethical principles of filial piety, fraternal duty, loyalty, and sincerity according to its classification. Thus: 'The degree to which Chinese ethics and laws expand and contract depend on a particular context and how one fits into that context' (Fei, 1992, p. 65).

From 1949 to 1978, China implemented socialism which tried to move people's interests from individual and family to the Communist party and build collective culture in Communist party-centred society. In doing so, the government conceptualised 'Parent-like officials', 'Big family of Socialism', and 'Brotherly and sisterly colleagues' to project 'family roles' onto organisations and society, and, therefore, to stretch *guanxi* out of family boundaries and lay the psychological foundation to gain trust and loyalty. Up to the present, in many Chinese companies, a well-respected CEO would be considered a 'father', colleagues with good *guanxi* call each other 'brother' and 'sister' and a successful organisation in China is the one which makes its employees feel they work if not for themselves at least for their families.[4]

5.8 THE FUTURE ROLE OF *GUANXI* IN BUSINESS

Leung (2008) noted that to understand the behaviour of Chinese people, it is important to examine the interplay between contemporary social forces and traditional values and beliefs. Materialistic achievement may be more relevant for *economic* behaviour, whereas the *social* behaviour of the Chinese is still guided by traditional values and beliefs. *Guanxi*, one of the key cultural and managerial values exercised by Chinese managers is, to some extent, the 'best practice' of Chinese business and management, which has been studied extensively over the past two decades.

Guanxi is historically contingent and context-dependent (Tong, 2014). According to his 25-year (1987–2012) research study on family business in China, Tong (2014) concluded that together with the economic rise of China, *guanxi* continues to play an important, if not greater, role in doing business there. Trust was the fundamental element of doing business between parties: in the West, the system of 'the rule of law' would provide trust to both parties, however, in China, the protocol of 'the rule of man' provides trust through *guanxi*. Consequently, it is much easier in the West to establish

[4]Based on participants and entrepreneurs trained and coached by the authors.

business first without personal connection, but it is much safer in China to have *guanxi* first before doing any business.

Fligstein and Zhang (2011) analysed the different viewpoints among scholars toward the role of *guanxi* in Chinese development. One group (Nee, 1989; Nee, Opper, & Wong, 2007) are sceptical about *guanxi* and believe that the Chinese government should try its best to remove it from the economy to enhance 'the rule of law'; while another group provide reasons for *guanxi* to continue to play important roles in China's economic development. The advantages and disadvantages of *guanxi* are listed in Table 5.3.

Table 5.3 Pros and cons of *Guanxi* practice

Pros	Cons
• Pivotal to the success of local economies and, particularly, to newly emerged private sector where there is relative lack of legal infrastructure and insufficient capital market structures and high institutional uncertainty during transition (Peng & Heath, 1996; Peng & Luo, 2000; Wank, 1999; Xin & Pearce, 1996)	• As part of a process of profit-seeking whereby firms with the right connections can produce abnormal gains for themselves (Zhang & Keh, 2010)
• Ties between firms and between entrepreneurs and government officials allow firms to successfully overcome barriers of old command system, gain access to critical resources and find and exploit market opportunities (Krug & Hendrischke, 2008; Wank, 1999; Zhou, 1996)	• Is about paying bribes in order to obtain good deals from transaction partners or to persuade government to help control competitors (Fligstein & Zhang, 2011)
• Offers greater capacities for generating and transmitting new information (Boisot & Child, 1999). These scholars believe that social networks will accomplish this	• Often seen as an impediment to economic growth because it stifles competition, does not allow for efficient allocation of capital, prevents right kinds of investments from being made, and leads to transaction breakdown due to opportunism (Luo, 2006)
• To establish a happy life, harmonious organisation, stable society, and a peaceful world (Zhang, 2014)	• May disappear or decline as no longer need ties to the state to attain their objectives (Guthrie, 1998)

The vigorous anticorruption movement launched by the central government since 2013 has tried to enforce 'the rule of law' approach in all aspects of Chinese life, including the legal, political, and business systems. Undoubtedly, the 'dark side' of *guanxi* will be reduced to some degree—it might be the tipping point for a shift of business behaviour from following 'the one you know' to 'the *good* one you know'. Nevertheless, the 'human touch' at a personal level will continue to endure in business to underpin *guanxi* capitalism, given the 'official' reinforcement of Confucian values from the government.

For Confucius, filial piety was the first virtue a person must have, but in recent times this has begun to decline. In 2012, the local government in Zhejiang province made 'filial piety to parents' as one of the promotion criteria for officials, and the national government legislated that parents have the right to sue their children for visiting them too infrequently. No matter whether it aims to restore family relationships or project affection and obligation onto the 'parent' of government, it is believed such actions would improve the social order.

Yik (2010) argued that people from the Aristotelian cultural tradition (the West) tend to endorse an *independent* self-construal, consisting of inner attributes that make an individual distinct from others—the mission is to become independent from others and to pursue personal goals. People from the Confucian cultural tradition (the East) tend to endorse *interdependent* self-construal, which is characterised by the belief that the self cannot be separated from the social context—*guanxi*. The self is embedded in circles of *guanxi* and people regulate their emotions and thoughts to fit the agendas of others. The ideal is to maintain harmony with others. Lee, Aaker, and Gardner (2000) suggested that people with interdependent self-construals are prevention-focused, that is they focus on information that prevents them from disturbing harmony.

5.9 CENTRAL MANAGED CAPITALISM

Mcnally (2013) argued that China's remodelled state capitalism represents a complex fusion of Western, Asian, socialist and Chinese historical and modern elements, because China's historical background as both imperial and socialist frames its state-centric approach to economic management. Most fundamentally, China's emergent capitalism encompasses a unique duality of state-led capitalism juxtaposed with entrepreneurial *guanxi* capitalism. Top-down, state-guided development dominates, but bottom-up, a myriad of medium- and small-sized private firms have used entrepreneurial strategies to create highly flexible production and knowledge networks with global reach (Mcnally, 2013).

Lin (2010) noted that China exhibited two unique features which are not usually identified with capitalism. First, the state itself acts as a capitalist, and second, economic activities are heavily embedded in *guanxi*. He then coined the term CMC for the continuously emerging economy in which China continues to develop capitalistic capacities, and the party-state increasingly tightens control of the economy and synchronised political and economic stratification. The combination of state guidance with informal *guanxi* enables Chinese businesses to connect with each other and with officialdom at various levels and build trust and harmony for long-term mutual benefit and stability in both business and social aspects.

5.10 NETWORK OF *GUANXI* CIRCLES

Wong and Huang (2015) applied Fei's 'ripple effect' of Chinese *guanxi* circles to explore the underlying mechanism of *guanxi*. Their ISOLINK network of *guanxi* circles illustrated that *guanxi* circles link up and this process continues until all the related similarities are utilised and all possible circles are connected. For example, as the circles of individuals Z3 and Z5 (Appendix) are linked up, they become a bigger circle.

5.11 CONCEPTUAL FRAMEWORK: *GUANXI* CAPITALISM STRUCTURE

Referring to the previous analysis of rationale underpinning *guanxi* capitalism in this chapter and building on Lin's (2010) theory of CMC, in which political and economic stratification are synchronised and Wong and Huang's (2015) network of *guanxi* circles, we develop the following framework of *Guanxi* Capitalism Structure (see Fig. 5.1) to explore the force of *guanxi* dynamic on social-economic system:

***Guanxi* holder**: the person who stands at the centre of circles produced by their own social influence (Fei, 1992).

***Guanxi* circle**: the group of people who are led by one *guanxi* holder, the people in the inner circle have closer relationships with the *guanxi* holder (Fig. 5.1).

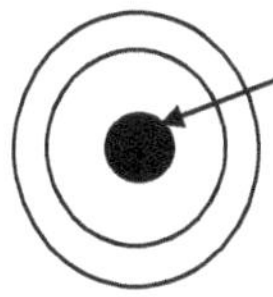

Fig. 5.1 *Guanxi* circle.

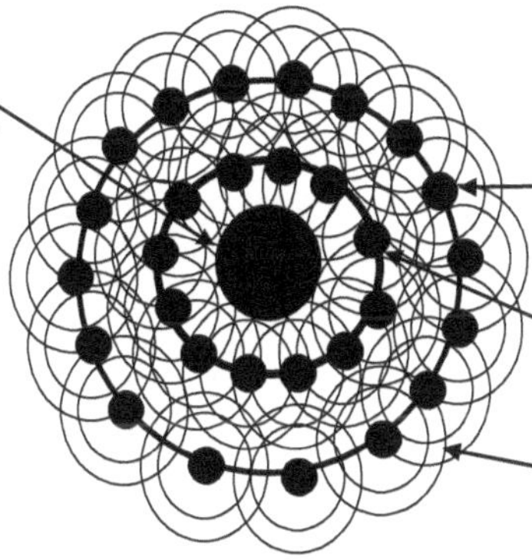

Fig. 5.2 *Guanxi* knot.

***Guanxi* knot**: interlinked *guanxi* circles influenced by Tier 1 *guanxi* holder (Fig. 5.2).
***Guanxi* web**: a dynamic system composed of numerous *guanxi* knots in which all *guanxi* holders constantly interact and change their tiers depending on circumstances.

Fig. 5.3 illustrates that under the central state system, the political system and economic system are synchronised through key players provided by the *guanxi* web rotating between two systems. The structure of the system is formal, but the key players are *guanxi* holders operating the systems to get things done through informal *guanxi* at a personal level. To achieve results, they need to go through both a *formal* process and hierarchy (Confucian rite) and an *informal* communication and interaction with *guanxi* (Confucian human ethical relations). Both political and economic systems in terms of structure and policy are slow to take effect, yet the *guanxi* web is highly dynamic with constant changes of personnel flow and *guanxi* holders. This results in a flexible and rapid response to external circumstances: however, it can give rise to unpredictable problems and inconsistencies in ethical standards.

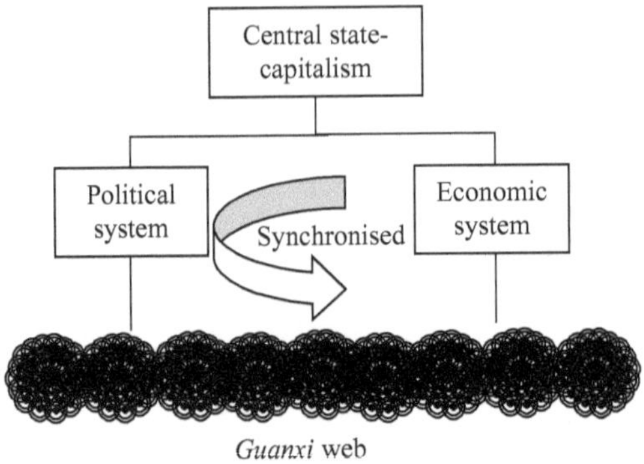

Fig. 5.3 *Guanxi* capitalism structure.

The *guanxi* web is composed of numerous *guanxi* knots, which illustrates the 'ripple effect' extending *guanxi* from the 'Tier 1 holder' to 'Tier *n* holder', and each holder can be Tier 1 or Tier *n* depending on who 'creates the ripple' at a time. *Guanxi* is a dyadic personal interaction and each single *guanxi* movement involves two holders at a time. The influencing or power of the Tier 1 holder will be reduced by passing through each circle, which requires constant maintenance of *guanxi* between adjacent holders.

Furthermore, as *guanxi* is conducted in the DMA according to the classification of relationships, the way to maintain *guanxi* is to treat each holder differently in terms of layer of circles, which means the Tier 1 holder should keep the closest relationship and strongest intimacy with the Tier 2 holder. This might not be 'equal or fair' to holders of other layer of circles, but it would be 'reasonable' and keep the entire *guanxi* web in equilibrium. However, if the Tier 1 holder has a closer relationship with the Tier 3/Tier *n* holder than the Tier 2 holder, it might upset the Tier 2 holder and endanger *guanxi*. The equilibrium of the *guanxi* web is critical to stabilise the entire capitalism system that requires each holder to follow the social order carefully to create harmony. *Guanxi* is the 'invisible hand' in China.

5.12 CONCLUSION

We have looked at the development and conceptualisation of *guanxi* capitalism in China. To help in this, we have used the concepts and ideas of: (1) FCR, (2) DMA, (3) CMC, (4) Network of *guanxi* circles in order to further construct the term of *guanxi* knot and *guanxi* web to develop a *guanxi* capitalism structure concept.

Although it appears that China is highly centralised, in fact China is extremely diverse and very pluralistic, and in many ways very decentralised (Jacques, 2012). It is almost impossible for central government to control everything, given its 1.4 billon people spread over 30 provinces. In particular, on the surface it appears that formality governs all aspects of business due to Confucian principles, whereas in reality communications and activities are conducted through the informal *guanxi* web. Here, each holder has their own power under different circumstances and the central government or the headquarters of a business organisation acts as the Tier 1 holder, and drives things through different tiers of holders inside *guanxi* circles.

Despite the awareness of the disadvantageous and dysfunctional elements of *guanxi*, the commitment to a more personal mode of management is still quite strong among Chinese business people (Tong, 2014). Even though many Chinese firms have adopted Western management techniques by recruiting professional executives, nevertheless, the fundamental rules of ownership, control and decision-making, and the continued reliance on *guanxi* remain central in Chinese business practice.[5]

Over the past 150 years, China has imported and implemented the Western ideologies of Marxism, socialism, and capitalism, which function in the economic and political domain to some degree, but can disrupt social norms because of their aspects of counter-Confucianism. In order to catch up with the West, China grows like an adolescent with a Western appearance and an ancient, yet troubled soul. The rehabilitation of Confucian values would help a great deal for those unsettled by China's rapid pace of change.

The Chinese government has embarked on the strategy and framework of 'One Belt, One Road' since 2013, focusing on connectivity and cooperation among countries primarily in Eurasia, which is to rehabilitate the historical and long-term relationship and regain the affections with those countries benefited trading with China through 'Silk Road' from 114 BC to 1450. This strategy underlines China's push to take a bigger role in global affairs through *guanxi* capital. Thus, *guanxi* will continue to play a key role in the Chinese social-political-economic system, probably in a different way, and *guanxi* capitalism might prove to be the most effective, if not the best, system in China.

[5]Based on the author's own experience of working with those companies.

APPENDIX

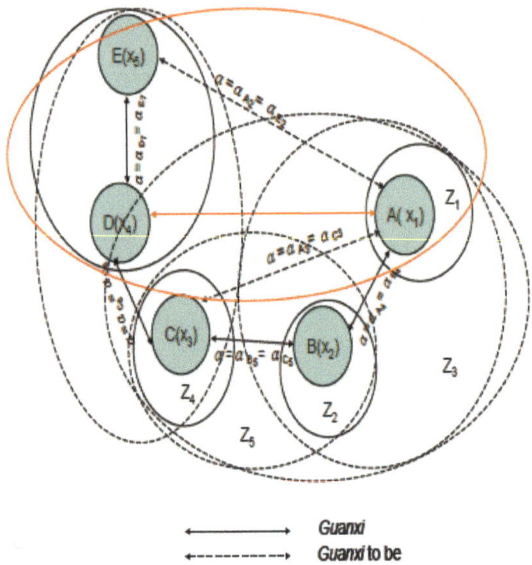

The ISOLINK network development of *Guanxi Chuens* (Circles). From Wong, M., & Huang, P. (2015). Culturally embedded mechanism, *Guanxi* in marketing. *Open Journal of Social Sciences, 3*, 154–158.

REFERENCES

Albert, M. (1993). *Capitalism against capitalism*. London: Whurr.

Amable, B. (2003). *The diversity of modern capitalism*. Oxford: Oxford University Press.

Ambler, T., Styles, C., & Xiucun, W. (1999). The effect of channel relationships and guanxi on the performance of inter-province export ventures in the People's Republic of China. *International Journal of Research in Marketing, 16*, 75–87.

Barkema, H., Chen, X.-P., George, G., Luo, Y., & Tsui, A. (2011). West meets East: New concepts and theories. *Academy of Management Journal, 54*(3), 642–644.

Barnes, B. R., Yen, D., & Zhou, L. (2011). Investigating guanxi dimensions and relationship outcomes: Insights from Sino-Anglo business relationships. *Industrial Marketing Management, 40*(4), 510–521.

Bentley, J. (1993). *Old world encounters: Cross-cultural contacts and exchanges in pre-modern times*. New York: Oxford University Press.

Berger, S. & Dore, R. (Eds.), (1996). *National diversity and global capitalism*. Ithaca, NY: Cornell University Press.

Boisot, M., & Child, J. (1999). Organizations as adaptive systems in complex environments: The case of China. *Organization Science, 10*(3), 237–252.

Borja, A. L. A. (2014). China's emergent political economy: Capitalism in the dragon's lair. *Philippine Political Science Journal, 35*, 37–41.

Boyer, R. (2005). How and why capitalisms differ. *Economy and Society, 34*, 509–557.

Chen, X. P., & Chen, C. C. (2004). On the intricacies of the Chinese guanxi: A process model of guanxi development. *Asia Pacific Journal of Management, 21*(3), 305–324.

Chandler, A. (1990). *The invisible hand: The managerial revolution in American business.* Cambridge: Belknap Press.

Chen, C. C., Chen, X.-P., & Huang, S. (2013). Chinese guanxi: An integrative review and new directions for future research. 中国人的关系：综合文献回顾及未来研究方向, *Management and Organization Review, 9*(1), 167–207.

Chua, V. & Wellman (2015). Social network in in East and Southeast Asia I: National Characteristics, Institutions, Network Capital, and Guanxi, American Behavioral Scientist 2015, *59*(8), 903–913.

Coates, D. (2000). *Models of capitalism: Growth and stagnation in the modern era.* Cambridge: Cambridge University Press.

Confucius. (Chinese), (2014). *The four books and five classics.* Beijing: Xian zhuang Publishing. The Book of Rite, 836.

Crouch, C. (2005). *Capitalist diversity and change: Recombinant governance and institutional entrepreneurs.* Oxford: Oxford University Press.

Dore, R. (1974). *British factory-Japanese factory: The origins of national diversity in industrial relations.* London: Allen and Unwin.

Dore, R. (2000). *Stock market capitalism: Welfare capitalism: Japan and Germany versus the Anglo-Saxons.* Oxford: OUP.

Dunning, J. H., & Kim, C. (2007). The cultural roots of Guanxi: An exploratory study. *World Economy, 30*, 329–341.

Fan, Y. (2002). Questioning guanxi: Definition, classification and implications. *International Business Review, 11*, 543–561.

Fan, Y. H., Woodbine, G., & Scully, G. (2012). Guanxi and its influence on the judgments of Chinese auditors. *Asia Pacific Business Review, 18*(1), 83–97.

Farh, J. L., Tsui, A. S., Xin, K., & Cheng, B. S. (1998). The influence of relational demography and guanxi: The Chinese case. *Organization Science, 9*(4), 471–488.

Fei, X. (1992). *From the soil: The foundations of Chinese society.* Translated by Hamilton, G.G. and Wang, Z. Berkeley: University of California Press.

Fligstein, N., & Zhang, J. (2011). A new agenda for research on the trajectory of Chinese capitalism. *Management and Organization Review*, 7(1), 39–62.

Fung, Y.-L. (1948). *A short history of Chinese philosophy: A systematic account of Chinese thoughts from its origins to the present day.* New York: The Free Press, A Division of Simon & Schuster Inc.

Gerlach, M. (1992). *Alliance capitalism: The social organization of Japanese business.* London: University of California Press.

Graham, J. L., & Lam, M. N. (2003). The Chinese negotiation. *Harvard Business Review, 81*, 1–869.

Guthrie, D. (1998). The declining significance of guanxi in China's economic transition. *The China Quarterly, 154*, 254–282.

Hall, P. A., & Soskice, D. (2001). An introduction to varieties of capitalism. In P. A. Hall & D. Soskice (Eds.), *Varieties of capitalism: The institutional foundations of comparative advantage* (pp. 1–68). Oxford: Oxford University of Press.

Hamilton, G.G. (1989). Patterns of Asian capitalism: The cases of Taiwan and South Korea. Program in East Asian Culture and Development Research Working Paper Series, No. 28, Institute of Government Affairs, University of California.

Hancke, B., Rhodes, M., & Thatcher, M. (Eds.), (2007). Introduction. *Beyond varieties of capitalism: Conflict, contradictions, and complementarities in the European economy.* Oxford: Oxford University Press.

Harada, Y., & Tohyama, H. (2012). Asian capitalisms: Institutional configuration and firm heterogeneity. In R. Boyer, H. Uemura, & A. Isogai (Eds.), *Directions and transformations in Asian capitalisms* (pp. 243–263). Abingdon: Routledge.

Hofstede, G. H. (1980). *Culture's consequences: International differences in work-related values.* Newbury Park, CA: Sage.
Hofstede, G. (1984). *Culture's consequences: International differences in work-related values* (abridged ed.). Beverly Hills: Sage.
Hollingsworth, J. P. & Boyer, R. (Eds.), (1997). *Contemporary capitalism: The embeddedness of institutions.* Cambridge: Cambridge University Press.
Hsu, J.Y., & Saxenian, A. (2000). The limits of guanxi capitalism: Transnational collaboration between Taiwan and the USA. *Environment and Planning A, 32*(11), 1991–2005.
Hwang, K.-K. (1987). Face and favor: Then Chinese power game. *American Journal of Sociology, 92*, 944–974.
Jacques, M. (2012). *When China rules the World.* London: Penguin Books.
Kanter, R. M. (1995). *World class: Thriving locally in the global economy.* New York: Simon & Schuster.
Kerr, C., Dunlop, J., Harbison, F., & Myers, C. (1962). *Industrialism and industrial man.* London: Heinemann.
Kitschelt, S., Lange, P., Marks, G., & Stephens, J. (Eds.), (1998). *Continuity and change in contemporary capitalism.* Cambridge: Cambridge University Press.
Krug, B., & Hendrischke, H. (2008). Framing China: Transformation and institutional change through co-evolution. *Management and Organization Review, 4*(1), 81–108.
Kwock, B., James, M., & Tsui, A. (2013). Doing business in China: What is the use of having a contract? The rule of law and guanxi when doing business in China. *Journals of Business Studies Quarterly, 4*(4), 56–68.
Lawrence, P., & Lorsch, J. (1967). *Organisation and environment.* Cambridge, MA: Harvard University Press.
Lazonick, W. (1990). *Competitive advantage on the shopfloor.* Cambridge: Harvard University Press.
Lazonick, W. (1991). *Business organization and the myth of the market economy.* New York: Cambridge University Press.
Lazonick, W. (1998). Organisational learning and international competition. In J. Michie & J. Grieve Smith (Eds.), *Globalization, growth, and governance* (pp. 204–238). Oxford: OUP.
Lee, A. Y., Aaker, J. L., & Gardner, W. L. (2000). The pleasures and pains of distinct self-construals: The role of interdependence in regulatory focus. *Journal of Personality and Social Psychology, 78*, 1122–1134.
Leung, K. (2008). Chinese culture, modernization, and international business. *International Business Review, 17*, 184–187.
Liang, S. (2010). *The fate of Chinese culture.* Beijing: China CITIC Press (in Chinese).
Lie, J. (1992). The concept of mode of exchange. *American Sociological Review, 57*(4), 508–523.
Lin, N. (2010). Capitalism in China: A centrally managed capitalism (CMC) and its future. *Management and Organization Review,* 7(1), 63–96.
Lin, L. (2011). Cultural and organizational antecedents of *Guanxi*: The Chinese cases. *Journal of Business Ethics, 99*(3), 441–451.
Liu, A. H., Noel, A., Rollins, M., & Gao, H. (2014). Industrial marketing management role conflict and ambiguity confronting transnational business networkers: Contrasting social stigma and relational risks for Chinese and Western boundary spanners. *Industrial Marketing Management, 43*(6), 911–919.
Lu, R., & Reve, T. (2011). Guanxi, structural hole and closure. *Journal of Strategy and Management,* 4(3), 275–288.
Luo, Y. (2006). Opportunism in inter-firm exchanges in emerging markets. *Management and Organization Review, 2*(1), 121–147.
Luo, Y., & Chen, M. (1997). Does guanxi influence firm performance? *Asia Pacific Journal of Management, 14*, 1–16.

Mcnally, C. A. (2011). China's changing guanxi capitalism: Private entrepreneurs between Leninist control and relentless accumulation. *Business and Politics*, *13*, 1–31. Berkeley Electronic Press.

Mcnally, C. A. (2013). How emerging forms of capitalism are changing the global economic order. *AsiaPacific Issues*, *107*, 1–8. Analysis from the East-West Center USA.

Mencius. (2004). *Mencius (Penguin Classics)*. London: Penguin Books.

Michailova, S., & Worm, V. (2003). Personal networking in Russia and China: Blat and guanxi. *European Management Journal*, *21*(4), 509–519.

Nee, V. (1989). A theory of market transition: From redistribution to markets in state socialism. *American Sociological Review*, *54*(5), 663–681.

Nee, V., Opper, S., & Wong, S. (2007). Developmental state and corporate governance in China. *Management and Organization Review*, *3*(1), 19–53.

Nuang, D. T. (1992). Contemporary human relationship and interaction. *LongJian Social Science*, *6*, 64–67.

Peck, J., & Theodore, N. (2007). Variegated capitalism. *Progress in Human Geography*, *31*, 371–372.

Peck, J., & Zhang, J. (2013). A variety of capitalism with Chinese characteristics? *Journal of Economic Geography*, *13*, 357–397.

Peng, M. W., & Heath, P. S. (1996). The growth of the firm in planned economies in transition: Institutions, organizations, and strategic choice. *Academy of Management Review*, *21*(2), 492–528.

Peng, M. W., & Luo, Y. D. (2000). Managerial ties and firm performance in a transition economy: The nature of a micro–macro link. *Academy of Management Journal*, *43*(3), 486–501.

Qian, M. (2013). *History of Chinese economy*. Beijing: Beijing United Publishing (in Chinese).

Redding, G. (2005). The thick description and comparison of societal systems of capitalism. *Journal of International Business*, *36*, 123–155.

Robinson, W. (2007). Theories of globalization. In G. Ritzer (Ed.), *The blackwell companion to globalization*. Oxford: Blackwell.

Rowley, C. (1994). The illusion of flexible specialisation: The domesticware sector of the ceramics industry. *New Technology Work & Employment*, *9*(2), 127–139.

Rowley, C. (2013). The changing nature of management and culture in South Korea. In M. Warner (Ed.), *Managing across diverse cultures in East Asia: Issues & challenges in a changing globalized world* (pp. 122–150). London: Routledge.

Rowley, C., Bae, J., & Sohn, T. (2002). *Managing Korean businesses: Organization, culture, human resources and change*. London: Frank Cass.

Russell, B. (1961). *History of Western philosophy*. New York: George Allen & Unwin Ltd.

Schochet, G. J. (1975). *Patriarchalism in political thought: The authoritarian family and political speculation and attitudes, especially in seventeenth-century England*. New York: Basic Books.

Schwartz, S. H. (1992). Universals in the content and structure of values: Theory and empirical tests in 20 countries. In M. Zanna (Ed.), *Advances in experimental social psychology. Vol. 25* (pp. 1–65). New York: Academic Press.

Smith, C., & Meiksins, P. (1995). System, society and dominance effects in cross-national organisational analysis. *Work, Employment & Society*, *9*, 241–267.

Sorge, A. (2005). *The global and the local: Understanding the dialectics of business systems*. Oxford: Oxford University Press.

Styles, C., & Ambler, T. (2003). The coexistence of transaction and relational marketing: Insights from the Chinese business context. *Industrial Marketing Management*, *32*, 633–642.

The Economist. (2015), Confucius says, Xi does, 25th July.

Tong, C. K. (2014). *Rethinking guanxi and trust in Chinese business networks, Chinese business*. New York: Springer.

Truong, Q., & Rowley, C. (2014). Vietnam: Post-state capitalism. In M. Witt & G. Redding (Eds.), *The Oxford handbook Asian business systems*. Oxford: Oxford University Press.

United Nations. (2015). World economic situation and prospects 2015.

United Nations Financing for Development Office. (2015). Global economic governance.

Wallerstein, I. (1974). *The modern world-system: Capitalist agriculture and the origins of the European world-economy in the sixteenth century*. New York: Academic Press.

Wallerstein, I. (2004). *World-systems analysis*. Durham: Duke University Press.

Wang, Y. (2008). Confucian ethics and emotions. *Frontiers of Philosophy in China, 3*(3), 352–365. Higher Education Press and Springer-Verlag.

Wang, B., & Chee, H. (2011). *Chinese leadership*. London: Palgrave Macmillan.

Wank, D. L. (1999). *Commodifying communism: Business, trust, and politics in a Chinese city*. New York: Cambridge University Press.

Warner, M. (2004). *Management in China: Past, present and future*. London: Routledge. p. 41.

Weber, M. (1920). The protestant ethic and the spirit of capitalism the expanded 1920 version authorized by Max Weber. Roxbury Publishing Company, Los Angeles, California, 2002.

Wei, Z. (2009). *The Chinese wisdom*. Changchun: Jilin Publishing Corp (in Chinese).

Whitley, R. (1992). *Business systems in East Asia: Firms, markets and societies*. London: Sage.

Whitley, R. (1999). *Divergent capitalisms: The social structuring and change of business systems*. Oxford: OUP.

Whitley, R. (2007). *Business systems and organizational capabilities*. Oxford: OUP.

Whitley, R. (2014). Change and continuity in East Asian business systems. In M. Witt & G. Redding (Eds.), *The Oxford handbook Asian business systems* (pp. 626–657). Oxford: Oxford University Press.

Witt, M. & Redding, G. (Eds.), (2014). *The Oxford handbook Asian business systems*. Oxford: Oxford University Press.

Wong, M., & Huang, P. (2015). Culturally embedded mechanism, guanxi in marketing. *Open Journal of Open Science, 3*, 154–158.

Woodward, J. (1965). *Industrial organisation*. Oxford: Oxford University Press.

Xin, K., & Pearce, J. L. (1996). Guanxi: Connections as substitutes for formal institutional support. *Academy of Management Journal, 39*(6), 1641–1658.

Yik, M. (2010). How unique is Chinese emotion? In M. H. Bond (Ed.), *The Oxford handbook of Chinese psychology* (pp. 205–220). New York: Oxford University Press.

Zhang, B. (2014). *Guanxi, network and knowledge transfer* (in Chinese). Beijing: Chinese Academy of Science. 张兵,关系、网络与知识流动.北京:中国社会科学出版社.

Zhang, J., & Keh, H. T. (2010). Inter-organizational exchanges in China: Organizational forms and governance mechanisms. *Management and Organization Review, 6*(1), 123–147.

Zhang, T., & Schwartz, B. (1997). Confucius and the cultural revolution: A study in collective memory. *International Journal of Politics, Culture and Society, 11*(2), 189–212.

Zhang, Y., & Zhang, Z. (2006). Guanxi and organizational dynamics in China: A link between levels individual. *Journal of Business Ethics, 67*(4), 375–392.

Zheng, Y. & Tok, S.K. (2007). "Harmonious Society" and "Harmonious World": China's Policy Discourse under Hu Jintao, Briefing Series. Issue 26 44(0). China Policy Institute, the University of Nottingham.

Zhou, K. X. (1996). *How the farmers changed China: Power of the people*. Boulder, CA: Westview Press.

CHAPTER 6

The Networking Strategies of the Jebsens and Chinese Merchants in the Late 19th and the Early 20th Centuries

W.L. So
University of London, London, United Kingdom

6.1 INTRODUCTION

Business networks may be thought of as the collective outcome of actors' strategic response to risks in interdependent relationships. Although a common logic of cooperation permeates networking strategies across business contexts, the institutional configuration of these interorganisational activities tends to diversify (Cook & Witmeyer, 1992, pp. 109–127). In some instances, actors try to consolidate old partnerships and create new ones through marriages and friendships, but in other situations the terms and conditions of cooperation are specified contractually. Since institutional analysis of business networks explains developmental processes and economic outcomes in a variety of historical settings (Padgett & Ansell, 1993, pp. 1259–1319), this chapter introduces the concept of networks to the research about the evolution of business institutions in China from the 19th century through the early 20th century, seeking to offer a context of significant socioeconomic transitions as members in these networks experimented with a mix of new and traditional practices to contain the risks associated with interdependencies in business activities. In a similar way to both Chapters 2 and 9 in this volume, this chapter seeks to show the central importance of understanding East Asian business networks in a historical perspective and through cross-national comparison.

In the final decade of late Qing China, exchanges between foreign and Chinese merchants experienced rapid change, set against the background of Western economic encroachment and the onset of the new policy ('*xinzheng*') of reform. The Chinese government was mired in crisis, inspiring

Business Networks in East Asian Capitalisms
http://dx.doi.org/10.1016/B978-0-08-100639-9.00004-9

different schools of thought in political economy, among which the notion of fighting Western imperialism by enriching the nation with Western military and industrial practices became popularised (Zhu & Zhang, 1958, p. 4830). It created a negotiating space that significantly transformed business life and practices, with the options of preserving traditional values or adapting Western practices, or a mix of both. In this process, both Chinese and Western merchants adapted new network strategies, according to how the values embedded in their traditional commercial institutions were interpreted and translated by both parties, enabling interaction and cooperation between them, and thus the building of formal and informal networks.

Recognising this, the late Qing era witnessed a turbulent time in both Chinese and global economic history. Chinese and foreign merchants chose one mode of networks over the other, revealing the ways in which they adapted to the clash of local traditions and foreign influences strategically. It is particularly true that when Sino-foreign trade necessitated interactions between both Chinese and foreign merchants, both informal and formal networks offered effective solutions to commitment problems subject to circumstances, all increasing the range of choices in facilitating networking decisions. Borrowing Williamson's concept of transaction costs in economic organisations (1989), the hypothesis we propose is that institutional choice in business networks functionally depended on payoffs of commitment, which in turn were contingent on task complexity and the attendant costs of transaction. Other context-specific factors, such as traditions and values, shaped the cultural form of cooperation.

This chapter is concerned with the institutional choice between formal and informal networks as a means to managing problems of commitment in business cooperation. Formal networks offer an institutionalised solution, and under this arrangement the injured party can exact damages and impose penalties according to contractual terms, when a partner reneges on its promise (Mellewigt, Madhok, & Weibel, 2007). Strong contract enforcement thus creates powerful incentives for commitment as the expected gains from defection are kept low. In informal networks, however, commitment issues are managed differently in the absence of comparable institutional supports for third-party intervention against defection (Mellewigt et al., 2007). Since cooperation is not based on formal contracts but private trust, network members can withdraw business from disreputable merchants. The withdrawing of social networks becomes an effective sanctioning mechanism for defection (Greif, 2006; Homans, 1961; Peng, 2004, p. 1061).

This chapter places discussions of formal and informal networks in Sino-Western trade in the context of East Asian capitalism, with a theoretical focus on how task environment shapes the institutional choice between these two options. It compares the networking strategies of Chinese merchants with the establishment and development of a German business in Hong Kong and Qingdao operated by the Jebsen family and their close friends. As a contemporary marketing and distribution group headquartered in Hong Kong since 1895, the Jebsen family joined with local business friends who followed North German shipping tradition and managed family shipping business in Aabenraa (now in Denmark but at the time part of Imperial Germany) and in their neighbourhood. Their Asian counterpart, interested in increasing trade and exchange with Western merchants, formed by the consolidation of existing unions of Chinese merchants based on their respective clans, later favouring the Chinese government to regulate business activities through institutionalising the organisation of informal Chinese networks. In this chapter, we also seek to establish the payoffs of commitment for Chinese businesses and the Jebsens. China ruled the choice of networking strategies, in correspondence with the requirements for managing commitment issues in different conditions.

6.2 FORMAL AND INFORMAL NETWORKS: MECHANISMS AND LIMITS

We define formal networks to be the interaction between merchants who use written contracts to specify the terms and conditions of cooperation, as well as provisions for sanction against failure to deliver (Mellewigt et al., 2007, p. 833). Informal networks, on the other hand, refer to merchants who have family ties or established friendships (Stiglitz, 2000). Any defection would cause an undesirable breach of trust, thus serving to ensure monitoring and compliance within the network.

The transacting parties choose to cooperate under contractual constraints when incentives to withdraw cooperation are not trivial. In collective action, such incentives are greatest when unilateral defection is better rewarded than mutual cooperation, exchange is nonrepetitive, and the exclusion of free-riders is unfeasible (Hardin, 1968, pp. 1243–1248). For formal networks to function properly against collective action failure, effective conflict resolution and sanctioning mechanisms must be available inexpensively (Bradach & Eccles, 1989; Ostrom, 2014). If the costs of organising effective sanctions against defection exceed any potential gains in cooperation, formal networks are more likely to emerge as a solution to monitoring and enforcement performed by a third party. Even so, they may offer insights on the role of self-organisation in network formation where third-party supports are nonexistent. Thus, a condition critical to growth in formal networks is the presence of effective mechanisms to monitor transactions and sanction defection (Ostrom, 2014). Because the provision of monitoring and sanctioning defection is scalable, the widespread inclusion of community members contributes to the decline in the average cost of sustaining institutions (Ostrom, Burger, Field, Norgaard, & Policansky, 1999).

In contrast, the growth and expansion of informal networks is limited by transaction costs, which prevents actors from generalising trust to others not sufficiently integrated into the network through marital, familial, and other private relations (Rothstein & Stolle, 2008), displaying a lower degree of openness to outsiders than in the case of formal networks. That means that informal networks are constrained by huge initial investment to include new actors in the same way formal networks do. Yet at the same time, informal networks mean even lower monitoring costs. This in effect encourages more concentrated form of capital organisation within personal and family networks who then are jointly invested and set a price to protect their own investments. Given these considerations, we hypothesise that tasks with an unusually high risk of defection are better managed in informal networks than arrangements that rely on third-party regulation in the formal settings (Wicks, Berman, & Jones, 1999, p. 110). Assuming networking decisions are all motivated by economic rationality, defection still can happen when the cost of monitoring becomes too high for the institutions to be economically sustainable, or when the benefit of defection becomes too strong an incentive despite the risk of being punished. These incentives regulate institutional choice undertaken by late Qing business actors to contain and manage risks attendant to their particular business settings.

Western merchants active in late Qing China, such as the Jebsens, collaborated with regional business interests to influence the market, with or without government support. Simultaneously, contractual agreements, including statutes of chamber of commerce, memoranda and articles of associations, as well as other contract establishment agreements, dominated their business endeavours. In comparison, their Chinese counterparts strengthened their own networks with others to broker long-distance trade, sometimes under the auspices of local government. As the Chinese government introduced new economic policies, Chinese merchants adopted new approaches to both Western and traditional Chinese networking practices, altering their business environment, proving that behaviour change within networks over time is an important factor shaping institutions.

Whether in informal or formal networks, the costs and rewards of collective actions are always looked at in light of the underlying principle of reasoning the choice of networking strategies. In the case of the Jebsens and their business friends, the level of trust is a decisive factor in affecting the risk level in partnership, exchange and transactions. In comparison, uniting Chinese merchants according to their family ties, clans and place of birth offered the highest network strengths in facilitating trade and exchange through collective actions. It favoured active participation in regulating the economy as a force of institutionalising the organisation of Chinese merchants. Both cases confirm how costs and risks in exchange rule the forms and levels of interactions between groups and the resulting dynamic developed from intragroup interactions in a different scale. In the social structure theory, exchange enabling collective actions of enough people can alter social structures and institutions over time (Cook & Witmeyer, 1992, p. 111), and the definition of exchange is not exclusive of monetary terms but also culture sharing. Thus, the social exchange theory serves to explain the economic rationale of applying different networking strategies in exchange, such as the building of formal and informal networks, and its role in shaping institutions and social structure.

As we will discuss later, personal networks offer an alternative to formal networks. Where exchange is repetitive, communication between actors is unobstructed (Ostrom, 2015, p. 51), and trust is high and generalisable, personal networks can reach a high level of effectiveness. It is also a superior mode of cooperation to formal networks for complex tasks, comparing with informal networks, because to gather and consolidate information in this case will incur significant transaction costs (Miller, 1996; Wicks et al., 1999, p. 108). But constraints on personal networks often are present in the business setting. First, informal networks are dominated by homogenous groups and often overlap with the identities of actors who share some fundamental values and beliefs (McPherson, Smith-Lovin, & Cook, 2001). As a result, they have limited potential for sustainable expansion beyond these groups. Second, unlike formal networks, there is no effective or centralised authority to punish defections. They share similar values and beliefs, cultivating a deep consensus in joint decisions. Then, personal networks offer limited flexibility for coordination and task delegation (Gargiulo & Benassi, 2000).

In the cases of both Chinese and Western merchants, the level of trust varied, affected by factors such as family and kinship links, or sharing a common surname or an ancestral home. These factors served the key role of increasing private trust in the building of informal and personal networks. Because of similar cultural backgrounds, they shared similar values and beliefs, building a deep consensus on joint decision-making. Also, the high transaction costs involved in personal networks offer limited flexibility for coordination and task delegation, despite the fact that repeating deals might lower information cost and thus the risk of defection (Williamson, 1989). In comparison with formal networks, informal or personal networks enable actors to structure cooperation at a low cost, largely because of their persisting trust, as well as similar values and beliefs (Wicks et al., 1999, p. 110). Practicing comparable levels of cooperation in a formal network would entail prohibitive costs in information and term specification, enabling effective third-party sanctions (Bendor & Mookherjee, 1990). However, the drawback is that contractual specification of terms of cooperation and codes of practice are confined to operational undertakings and repeated deals lower information costs, all increasing the substitutability of cooperation of partners in times of unsatisfactory performance. Unlike informal networks, whose relationship terms are too abstract to define, formal networks restrict the broader use of a contractual agreement to lowering the risks in impersonal networks. Considering these facts, the organisation of formal networks is relatively independent and less interdependent, as compared with personal networks.

6.3 INFORMAL NETWORKS: THE JEBSENS

The Jebsen Group, known as Jiecheng yanghang 捷成洋行 in Chinese, was a German trading house with its headquarters in Hong Kong since 1895. The two partners of the company, Jacob Jebsen and Johann Heinrich Jessen, both came from the part of North Schleswig, when it belonged to Germany between 1864 and 1919. As a result of the decision made in the Paris Peace Conference of 1920, the two partners became Danish in nationality overnight. The Jebsen Company in Hong Kong was actively involved in shipping and trade in East Asia. The two families both inherited a family tradition in shipping, and in 1898, they established another partnership with a prominent businessman from Kiel Heinrich Diederichsen from Kiel. Existing only for one decade, the partnership of Diederichsen and Jebsen chiefly managed shipping and government businesses for the German colony of Qingdao. After the two world wars, the Jebsen Group continues to transform their China business and has become a prominent marketing and distribution group in Hong Kong.

In the development of the Jebsen Group in Hong Kong and China, cooperation is built upon private trust in informal networks, with ongoing personal relations creating possibilities of sharing unique resources in entrepreneurial activities at a low risk. Michael Jebsen, for example, owned his own steamship company, M. Jebsen, in Aabenraa (now in Denmark, formerly part of Imperial Germany), and encouraged his son Jacob to enter a partnership business with his cousin, Heinrich Jessen (von Haenisch, 1970, pp. 32–33; also Hieke, 1953). This decision to establish a company on 1 Mar. 1895 was prompted partly by Michael's disapproval and mistrust of shipbrokers, and he consequently favoured his son Jacob's personal supervision of his vessel fleet in East Asia (So, 2014, p. 136). The young partners thus served as the local agents for M. Jebsen in East Asia, deploying family resources and receiving a steady income from ship agency fees that was reinvested in commodity trade.

Organising a father–son coinvestment and business partnership with a cousin is an example of how personal ties may ensure a high level of trust, to an extent that limited the possibility of giving preferential treatment beyond these closed groups. In Jul. 1895, for example, two shipping agencies, Yuen Cheong Lee and Yuen Fat Lee, reached an agreement with the Jebsens to operate a regular shipping line between Hong Kong, Pak hoi and Hoi how at their own expense, in return for Jebsen offering a commission for any profit generated from this shipping line (von Haenisch, 1970, p. 47; see also von Hassel, 1953). Their terms of business were clearly specified in the form of contractual agreements cosigned between the two parties, which was different from the more casual verbal and unspoken arrangements made between M. Jebsen and the Jebsen Company in Hong Kong, and similarly between the two cousins. The example of Yuen Cheong Lee and Yuen Fat Lee reveals how a lower level of trust in nonfamilial ties necessitated contractual arrangements against defections.

The two cousins built their commodity brokerage division for their company in Hong Kong and facilitated venture development, based on a good understanding between the partners. Because that established trust increased the tolerance for defection, their company had a low transaction cost that could have potentially induced this because of the challenges of monitoring partners' activities. During the process by which the young partners negotiated the terms and possibilities of founding a company in Hong Kong, the personal friendship between Michael Jebsen and Jacob 'Amigo' Diederichsen came into play. Amigo's nephews, Carl and Gustav Diederichsen, took into consideration the long-term friendship between the two families, and proceeded to offer Jacob Jebsen and Heinrich Jessen a business loan worth 20,000 German marks (von Haenisch, 1970, p. 54). The fact that both families owned a family shipping business in North Germany, and were actively involved in the advent of steamship navigation in their locale, all showed their overlapping identities built on their similar family and industrial background, and a common experience because of a local historical event. Michael Jebsen was based at Aabenraa, while the parent company, H. Diederichsen Steamship Company, was in in Kiel. The latter was managed by Heinrich Diederichsen, the youngest brother of Carl and Gustav Diederichsen (Seibel, 1970, p. 126).

Joint businesses and past business transactions recorded past reputation, determining the strength of a personal network, and thus the risk level of any business transaction. In this case, the Diederichsen family actively subscribed to the shipshares for Jebsen's steamers, in return for annual dividends from the Jebsens, building up a good business reputation that sustained the long-term business friendship between the two families (Hieke, 1953, pp. 28–41). The reward for the past good reputation of the Jebsens was that their credentials lowered the risk of Carl and Gustav offering Jacob Jebsen a short-term business loan that contributed to the founding fund of the Jebsen Company in 1895. Any failed repayment of loans, or any other failings, would destroy the friendship established between the two families. The consequence of risking defects was thus undesirably high, forcing both parties to comply strictly with their terms of understanding without putting in actual contractual terms to monitor their transactions.

As long-term business cooperation laid the foundation of building up trust between the two families, they shared a common source of information and resources, opening up the possibilities of collaborating in a variety of joint investments in China. In 1897, the German Navy occupied Jiaozhou, followed by diplomatic negotiations between China and German on recognising Jiaozhou Bay as a German-leased territory in China. And in Apr. 1898, Heinrich Diederichsen, the youngest brother of Carl and Gustav Diederichsen, was offered a contract with the German Navy to transport 6000 tons of briquettes to Qingdao (Diederichsen, 1898; Seibel, 1970). Simultaneously, he agreed with the Rheinisch–Westphalian Coal Syndicate for another agency contract for coal shipments and supplies to the new colony (Diederichsen & Jebsen, 1898). At a similar time, Michael Jebsen reached an agreement with the German postal office to run a bi-weekly steamer service in North China between Qingdao, Shanghai, Yantai, Tianjin and Taku, largely because of his influence in the Berlin government, as well as his shipping experience in China (Diederichsen, 1898; Gieseke,

1897; Imperial Post Office, 1896, 1897–1900, 1898; Jebsen, 1898a, 1898b, see also Becker, 2009). Jebsen had been a member of the budget commission that dealt with a new subsidy bill (Jebsen, 1898a, 1898b). Their access to government authorities created a common information and resource pool and inspired joint efforts in building a new segment of government business. All were important factors leading up to the decision to set up a new partnership company called Diederichsen, Jebsen & Company in Qingdao. Heinrich Diederichsen owned half of its company shares, with the remainder shared equally between Jacob Jebsen and Heinrich Jessen. From 1898 to 1908, Diederichsen and Jebsen opened new branches in North China and along the Yangzi Rivers (von Haenisch, 1970, pp. 104–107).

This partnership of Diederichsen and Jebsen illustrates how personal networks created possibilities for entrepreneurial activities at a low risk. As a result, the two families diversified their transaction types, which were not confined to ship finance investment. They further broadened the scope of their venture expansion by strategising the investments of a business group as a whole. The members included other shipping families from the same region in Imperial Germany, who were also family friends like Jebsen and Diederichsen. For example, Howaldt operated one of the biggest shipyards in Kiel, and because of family ties with Diederichsen, the two elder brothers in the Diederichsen family became prominent decision-makers in Howaldt (Ostersehlte, 2004, pp. 54 and 67), whereas the youngest brother inherited his father's shipping business H. Diederichsen, giving him access to business information from Howaldt and the Jebsens. All three families of Jebsen, Howaldt and Diederichsen had different sources of access to information from different government authorities, and in effect, Diederichsen and Jebsen specialised in government businesses in Qingdao and had the potential to monopolise the supply of bricks in North China (Diederichsen and Jebsen and the Imperial Naval Office, 1899–1901). To exchange information, they circulated personal correspondence and dispatched telegrams. They build a common resource network, all lowering risks in investment while reducing micromanagement, time spent and other costs arising from negotiations. By being in the same network, they jointly entered bids for government outsourcing projects, exemplified by the construction of the major harbour in Qingdao (Imperial Naval Office, 1902). Fig. 6.1 shows a family genealogy of Diederichsen, showing intermarriages between families Diederichsen, Howaldt and Jebsen. Fig. 6.2 shows the family genealogy of the Jebsens, showing intermarriage of the families Jebsen and Jessen.

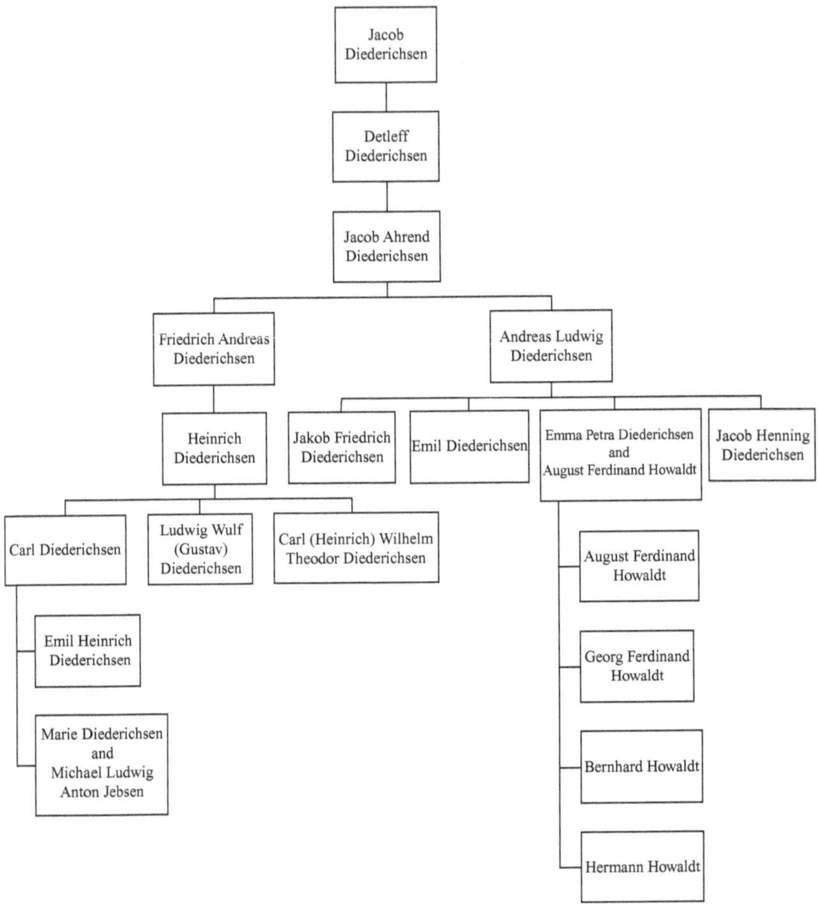

Fig. 6.1 Family genealogy of Diederichsen, showing intermarriages between families Diederichsen, Howaldt and Jebsen (Grönhoff, 1948; Sievers, 2005, pp. 123–156).

There was a trend in organised capitalism in Imperial Germany in which economic concentration inspired the development of new methods of capital organisation and networking for the North German shipping industry. The family networks of Jebsen, Jessen, Diederichsen and Howaldt, for example, linked to form bigger capital, facilitating investments across the sectors of shipbuilding, coastal trade and finance, and coal transportation. In the case of the steamer Vorwärts, Jessen acquired 20 shares, while Jacob Diederichsen and the Howaldt brothers from the Howaldtswerke had 14 shares each (Held, 1938). The investments of these family business friends and relatives of Jebsen made up 53% of the total shares issued, with Michael Jebsen owning eight shares and his contacts from Krupp the remaining

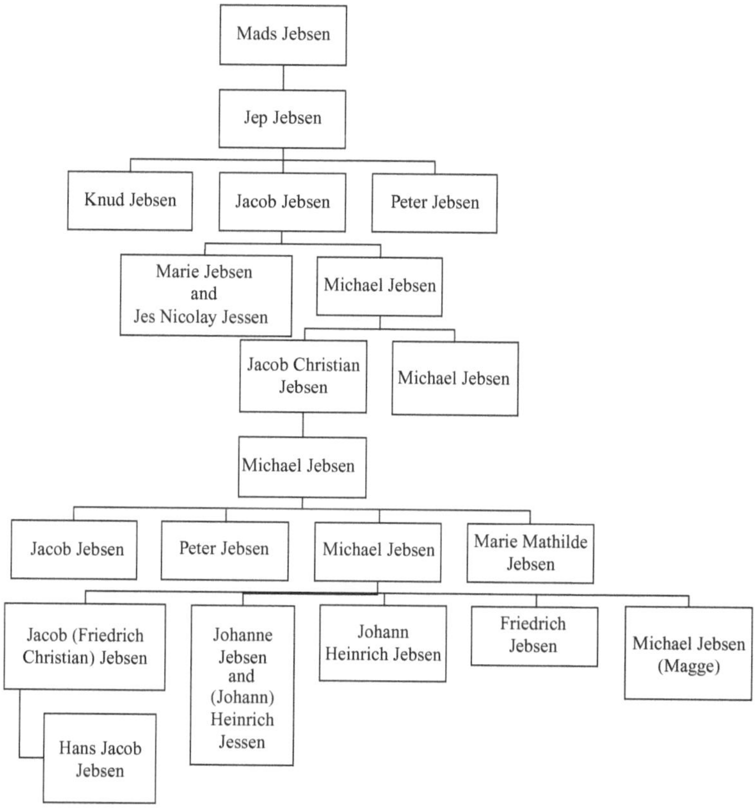

Fig. 6.2 Family genealogy of Jebsen, showing intermarriage of the families Jebsen and Jessen (Hieke, 1953; von Haenisch, 1970).

shares. Between 1879 and 1910, Howaldt built steamships in the shipyard at Kiel and invested in seven of the steamers they built for the Jebsens. Heinrich Diederichsen also had five steamers built in the Howaldtswerke (Hieke, 1953, pp. 221–231). In effect, through this new form of capital organisation, these family networks dominated the private steamship sector, jointly expanding overseas markets while applying cartelisation, clearly as a response to increased government regulation of the economy (Hardach, 2003, p. 65; also Lash and Urry, 1987).

Evaluated in terms of the chances of joint venture success, the Jebsen Company of Hong Kong was a joint venture between family members, whereas Diederichsen and Jebsen was an example of marriage after a business startup. The two partners in Hong Kong showed a higher level of trust and efficiency in joint decision-making, whereas in the case of

Diederichsen, the two partners in Hong Kong made frequent complaints about the dominance of Diederichsen in business decisions. They reported also on the branch manager being in line with Diederichsen's stance against the colonial administrators in Qingdao, and so remained both sceptical and doubtful about how this stance would benefit their government businesses (Jebsen, 1899). The two partners in Hong Kong shared a different level of trust, in comparing with Diederichsen, showing how geographical distance in networks may weaken commitment in informal networks.

Trust in personal networks plays a substantial role in ruling the quality of personal and business unions in the way that certain parties will be left vulnerable when trust breaks down. As seen from the example of the Diederichsen–Jebsen network that existed from 1898 to 1908, the partnership dissolution agreement was reached after all partners confirmed details of arrangements with contractual arrangements made to clearly define the division of business areas between the partners (Diederichsen, Jebsen, & Jessen, 1908). A consequence of this was that when cooperation was discontinued, family ties and private trust failed to ensure all parties' interests. For instance, the Hong Kong partners remained active in South China, whereas Diederichsen continued to operate his other branches in North China, and within the Yangzi River region (Imperial Naval Office, 1909). Marriages occurred among all these families, having the effect of increasing their trust level. The two partners from the Jebsen Company had direct family ties, whereas Heinrich Diederichsen had only distant family links with the Jebsen family, but a closer bound with the Howaldt family (Ostersehlte, 2004, p. 54). Judging from the fact that the partnership company in Qingdao existed only for 10 years, while the Jebsen Company in Hong Kong continues to exist today, family ties had primary importance over kinship links, ie relating be marriage in ruling the content of relations between members within the same network, and thus the process of making business decisions.

The Jebsen family and their business friends is an example of an informal network and shows that family ties and personal friendship encourage a high level of private trust to develop within the network. Strong family ties, for example, through marriages between business families, or sharing a common kin are factors for increasing trust and keeping outsiders from sharing the same level of trust. The Jebsen networks shared unique resources and information that favoured venture development and economic concentration. They jointly invested in East Asia, with the goal of protecting their capital. As the cost of risking defections was undesirably high, upholding network integrity was a powerful tool, comparing with contractual arrangements, in ensuring compliance. An exception is that distance in networks may weaken commitment. When no formal written contract rules how business is done, informal networks leave certain parties vulnerable when trust breaks down. As shown in the case of Diederichsen and Jebsen, they opted for a formal company dissolution agreement, showing how task environment shapes the institutional choice between the two networking strategies.

6.4 INSTITUTIONALISING SEMIFORMAL ASSOCIATIONS OF CHINESE MERCHANTS

As a prerequisite to institutionalising Chinese networks, domestic trade necessitated the development of commercial institutions, creating spheres where the organisation of mutual interest groups became formalised and institutionalised over time. During this process, Chinese merchants engaging in interregional trade enabled intragroup interactions and exchange between merchants sharing a common clan and ancestry. To ensure collective actions within the entire network and safeguard collective interests of the entire clan, they built semiformal commercial institutions to supervise the activities of its members. *Shangbang* 商幫, for example, was one typical form of Chinese commercial organisation that has a strong tie to geographical place and thus could be identified through its place origins. Generally speaking, *shangbang* did not involve the formation of any official institution, nor were there any statutes ruling merchants' conduct in interregional trade. Distinguished by their birthplace, *shangbang* is a loose organisation of merchants with strong economic influence, and in a very restricted sense, they flourished according to the political administrative significance of places. So for example, since the 17th century, economic prosperity was to be found in regions such as Shanxi, Huizhou, Longyou, Ningbo, Dongting, Jiangxi, Shaanxi, Shandong, Chaozhou and Guangdong. These regions emerged as the 10 most influential *shangbang* of China.

Based on the organisation of 10 prominent *shangbang*, Chinese merchants further developed their trade specialisms in their locality. Industrial guilds were organised only in places where a certain commodity had substantial market share. Since the beginning of early Qing rule, for example, some prominent Shanxi merchants had been appointed 'imperial merchants' and were granted the lucrative contract of managing government salt administration and other government-related financial operations, thus becoming the most influential merchant guilds in major commercial towns in North China. As a result, the term 'Shanxi-bang' is generally understood as the banking guild. The straw-braid production that developed in the Shandong Shahe region is another example of how industrial guilds were named after the place where they had substantial market share. The industrial guild for straw-braiders (who made hats, baskets and so on), was named the Shahe *bang* representing the interests of merchants who were engaged in this trade (Brown, 1996, p. 228). Within the industrial guild, Chinese merchants from *xiangbang* 鄉幫 and *waibang* 外幫 always presented diverging interests, showing that clans affected the shaping of collective values and actions among Chinese merchants. *Waibang* was the guild for merchants from places other than where the guild was active, whereas *xiangbang* formed by native merchants.

As early as 1803, foreign observers had pointed out that it was the natural tendency of the Chinese people to crystallise into associations (Brown, 1996). The existence of associations dominated Chinese life. The associations stimulated activities to 'quicken the vitality of the mass' (Brown, 1996). This 'natural' habit of association well described religious groups or literati elites, and merchants who banded together to make profits through price controls and increasing market share, especially when trade increased. Industrial and trade guilds existed not only to unite merchants with similar business interests, but they also set out industrial regulations to safeguard or secure the collective interests of the guild as a whole, in both politics and commerce, resulting in the development of more formal networks among the *shangbang*. As reported in the Tsingtauer Neueste Nachrichten (1909), in the 1905 and 1908 anti-American and anti-German boycotts, Guangdong merchants refrained from joining, resulting in collective antagonistic actions by all other Chinese merchants against Guangdong merchants. In other words, the organisation of clans laid the foundation of unity among Chinese merchants in the form of *shangbang*, creating common interests and values between them, and at times of disagreement between Chinese merchants, collective actions served to punish defection. As a result, informal networks developed common interests and values shared among Chinese merchants and they built trust to lower risks, all contributing to creating more permanent and official institutions for Chinese merchants.

As the organisation of Chinese *shangbang* gradually became institutionalised, *huiguan* started to be established as permanent institutions promoting clan interests in all major commercial towns of China. *Huiguan* 會館 was a term referring to the hostels that came into existence in the Ming dynasty in Beijing and in some provincial cities, and which provided lodging for candidates from the same native place taking the examinations for the 'civil service' Brown, 1996, p. 213). From the 18th century, *huiguan* became the unions of merchants of the same origin who engaged in the same trade, and generally were founded in major commercial towns. Where analyses are made of the diverse forms of Chinese associations that include religious sects, interregional trade networks, native place associations and private literati elites, *huiguan* falls into the category of native place commercial associations. As Skinner and Baker (1977) suggests, for trade to happen, commercial institutions and related occupations must be established, as well as the flow of raw materials that would encourage processing, resulting in a reduction in bulk while enhancing preservation (Skinner & Baker, 1977). Then, as the volume of extraregional trade increased, commercialisation would take place in regional trading centres and the hinterland. Based on these observations, Skinner develops an analysis of China's physiographic macroregions—a model that illustrates the relationship among trade, commercial institutions and markets in the Chinese interregional trading systems. This process of integrating Chinese merchants to form semiformal commercial networks that had an influence on crossregional trade was evidence of institutionalising informal networks based on their birthplace, clan and occupation.

Similarly, Pomeranz (1993) evaluates the coreness of Chinese networks as indicative of network strength in Chinese commercial networks in the Shandong and Hebei regions. Taking into consideration factors such as participation in long-distance trade and the number of trade fairs in specialised products, he concludes that the facctors implied a higher centrality in the trading network (Pomeranz, 1993, p. 279). By definition, Chinese commercial networks were a form of informal social bond, with its identity conferred by common geographical origin, and as Chinese merchants founded their respective *huiguan* to support trade and business, they drew up their own regulations, with reputable leaders arbitrating disputes between guild members, all serving to make *huiguan* an official institution for Chinese merchants.

In Jining, for example, six families dominated the export of tobacco from the 1820s, while other important handicraft industries included oil pressing, winemaking, leather, paper, bamboo products, copper and iron utensils, timber products, and silk. All these trades had their own streets and their own independent guild regulations, exemplifying how personal bonds of Chinese merchants from the same place origin became tightened through mass participation in long-distance trade and trade fairs while institutionalising the union of these merchant-networks into permanent interest groups. In Yantai, Ningbo merchants transported balls of paper, cotton wool, porcelain and Chinese furniture from Fuzhou to the port south of Jiaozhou, and exported oil, noodles, walnuts, cabbages and Shandong ham from Yantai and Shanghai in return for foreign goods from South China. They lived near the walls of the town of Jiaozhou and had their own warehouse at the coast where goods were loaded by horses, donkey and cart, as reported in a German newspaper in 1898. Foreign trade at Jiaozhou was relatively unimportant compared with Yantai and Shanghai, as a German newpaper Deutsch-Asiatische Warte (1898) reported, despite the fact that Chinese merchants from Shanghai and Yantai published advertisements for foreign goods on the street, on behalf of foreign merchants. In this port, Guangdong merchants became active from 1862. Amongst them, Fucheng 福诚 and Hengjucheng 恒聚成 were prominent in the export of peanuts and cotton at Jinan. Fujian, Guangdong, and Ningpo merchants made up 30% of Chinese merchants in Yantai. Despite the fact that Chinese merchants from Guangdong, Ningbo and Sanjiang had strong commercial interests in Yantai, only Fujian merchants founded their own *huiguan* in 1884, showing the way in which their choice of formal commercial institutions that could better support their business operations contrasted with other Chinese merchants in the same port.

Within Chinese networks, Pomeranz refers to horizontal relationships in society, and the network core is a position in another set of connections that had less to do with bureaucratic channels of commands (Pomeranz, 1993, p. 279). This implies a hybrid of informal and formal networks in traditional Chinese networks that served a key role in trade and commerce, with less to do with government politics. Other cross-cultural studies of trade guilds also put a strong emphasis on the relations between *huiguan* members and local governments, suggesting that Chinese guildsmen were apathetic about cooperating with officialdom in comparison with the much closer relations between guildsmen and the government in mediaeval Europe (Pomeranz, 1993, p. 209). Thus, *huiguan* was an institutional choice that offered low transaction costs for Chinese merchants to conduct trade independently from the government.

As the government became involved in regulating economic activities, the interests of Chinese merchants became more intertwined with that of politicians. Such change took place in two phases; the first witnessed the building of government-business joint ventures in heavy industries from the 1860s, while the second phase, beginning after 1895, concerned new forms of commercial organisation for governance (Reynolds, 1995). In the first phase, Chinese merchants sought government recognition to improve their social status and made capital investment available for government projects (Brown, 1996). The government-business joint ventures evolved initially from *guandu shangxiao* (official supervision and merchant sales) and *guandu shangyun* (official supervision and merchant transport), and later into *guandu shangban* (official supervision and merchant management) and *guan-shang heban* (joint management by officials and merchants), all reflecting the rising importance of merchants. Then, merchant organisations started being legitimised 'through a wider movement to mobilise society and formalise the participation of local elites in the formation and execution of policy which directly affected their areas' (Brown, 1996, p. 235).

Another trend of institutionalisation of Chinese merchant-networks began after the 1880s, when more Chinese merchants obtained official posts in the government, as a reward for their financial contributions to state commercial and industrial projects. In Shandong, some Chinese salt merchants and other general merchants echoed the initiative of a merchant-official named Sheng Xuanhuai 盛宣懷, from the beginning of the 1890s, joining forces to dredge the Xiaoqing River 小清河 through managing government-business joint ventures (Buck, 1978, p. 32). This project greatly improved stream navigation from the provincial capital at Jinan through northwest Shandong to Hebei, resulting in a boost to trade in eastern Shandong, and thus was evidence of closer relations between merchants and officials.

In 1898, Qingdao was declared a German colony. Yuan Shi-kai, who at the time was the governor of Shandong, took advantage of the German presence in Shandong to consolidate his power in the province, as well as on the Board of Commerce. He urged the founding of the local chambers of commerce in the major commercial towns in Jinan, Weixian and Zhoucun. In Qingdao, the German government appointed the members of the Chinese committees who later founded their native *huiguan*, ie *Qiyan Huiguan* 齊燕會館, Sanjiang Huiguan 三江會館 and Guangdong Huiguan 廣東會館. In 1905, the native trustee of the Chinese Committee, Fu Bingzhao, took the lead in uniting all the native merchant-networks from Huangxian **黃縣**, Jimo **即墨** and Yexian **掖縣** and building the guild hall for Shandong merchants in Qingdao (Zhang, 2006, pp. 578–579). Then he operated closely with the provincial bank to monopolise the exchange market in Qingdao, with the purpose of replacing the credit market that was dominated by the treaty port traders from Guangdong, Shanghai and Ningbo. In 1906,

Gu Chengzhang founded the guild hall representing Guangdong merchants, while Ding Jingchen, a merchant from Jiangsu, followed the following year. The move of the trustee members of the Chinese Committee to set up their respective guild halls was evidence for weakening bonds among the trustees in the Committee, symbolising further division between the native and nonnative merchants in Qingdao.

Shandong merchants in Qingdao became members of their respective local chambers of commerce simultaneously through direct government measures that turned the merchants into the economic agents of the Shandong provincial government (So, 2014). The significance was that Chinese merchant-networks that were organised according to their clans and birthplace became institutionalised, transforming government administrative structures while extending government supervision of the economy. This new economic setting empowered Shandong merchants whose commercial activities became politically related because of the involvement of local officials. Guangdong merchants in Shandong, despite their established transactional and trade relations with foreign merchants, faced intensifying economic competition with the former. As economic competition between Chinese merchants became politicised, in 1908, Shandong merchants caused jeopardy by provoking an anti-German boycott in Qingdao, pressuring the German government to seal deals with only native Shandong Chinese merchants (Truppel, 1908; Huang, 1999, p. 107). The German government remarked that the anti-German boycott was driven by a clash of commercial interests between nonnative and native Chinese merchants in the colony (Schrameier 1914, pp. 117–118). The institutionalisation of Chinese merchant-networks dramatically increased the importance of politics in regulating the mechanism of merchants, largely outweighing the importance of clans in the organisation of Chinese merchant-networks.

The case of Chinese merchants does not present as strong a case as the Jebsens about how task environment shapes the institutional choice of using different networking strategies. Instead, family ties and local values built strong collective interests over self-interests in affecting the calculation of cost–risk relations of a business venture. As a result, informal networks became formalised into semiformal and formal associations that favoured government supervision. To a large extent, the social exchange theory applies, proving how the evolutionary process of institutionalising informal networks gave shape to Chinese society. In this case, increasing government participation in the economy accelerated this process of formalising Chinese networks in the scene of trade and commerce.

6.5 CONCLUSION

In conclusion, a model of cooperation between German and Chinese merchants in late Qing China can be discerned from the selected cases and illustrates the institutional response to different levels of the risk of defection created by delegated decision-making, monitoring of costs, and regulatory mechanisms. Substantively, this chapter seeks to make sense of the diversity of networking modes in the business communities in Qing China where local norms and practices varied from one community to another, and where foreign business culture became increasingly widespread as trade with the West grew. In the case of the Jebsens and their business community, trust within the network rules the quality of personal and business unions, influencing their business endeavours in East Asia. At the same time, informal ties established between families through marriage and shared culture enabled more extensive delegation without incurring significant moral hazard because of the lack of effective monitoring. This in turn increased the possibility of joint venture success, with the likelihood of building a common pool of resources, information and capital at a low risk. However, communication between collaborating parties could be made difficult because of distance, resulting in weakening commitment.

On the other hand, Chinese merchants developed formal networks over time to regulate mercantile activities. This process of formalising networks justifies the social exchange theory that rules how collective actions of enough people can alter social structures and institutions. In this case, government's direct intervention in the economy, as well as political competition in the government acted as the force of changing social norms and behaviours of Chinese merchants. As Chinese informal networks became institutionalised according to their respective bases of clan and birthplace, they enhanced administrative efficiency while confirming rules and governance of the Chinese government. With written rules specifying treatment for undesirable behaviour, these organisations ensure compliance among members who otherwise lacked personal trust in conducting business. The arrangement expanded the network of trade by lowering the risk between participating members.

REFERENCES

Becker, B. (2009). German colony of Kiaochow and its postal steamer service. *International Journal of Maritime History*, *XXI*(1), 201–238.

Bendor, J., & Mookherjee, D. (1990). Norms, third-party sanctions, and cooperation. *Journal of Law, Economics, and Organization*, *6*(1), 33–63.

Bradach, J. L., & Eccles, R. G. (1989). Price, authority, and trust: From ideal types to plural forms. *Annual Review of Sociology*, *15*, 97–118.

Brown, R. A. (1996). *Chinese business enterprise* (vol. II). London: Routledge.

Buck, D. D. (1978). *Urban change in China: Politics and development in Tsinan, Shantung, 1890–1949*. Madison: University of Wisconsin Press.

Cook, K. S., & Witmeyer, J. M. (1992). Two approaches to social structure: Exchange theory and network analysis. *Annual Review of Sociology*, *18*, 109–127.

Deutsch-Asiatische Warte. (1898). *Kiautschou in 1898*. 17 December.

Diederichsen and Jebsen and the Imperial Naval Office. (1899-1901). *Correspondences between the German Navy and Diederichsen, Jebsen & Company*. [manuscript] Collection BArch-MA-RM3-6737, Freiburg: Bundes-Militaerarchiv.

Diederichsen, H., & Jebsen, M. (1898). *Correspondences with the Imperial Naval Office*. [manuscript] Collection 205 and A01-02-0009, Aabenraa: Jebsen & Jessen Historical Archives.

Diederichsen, H. (1898). *A letter to Michael Jebsen*. [manuscript] Collection 205, Aabenraa: Jebsen & Jessen Historical Archives.

Diederichsen, H., Jebsen, J., & Jessen, H. (1908). *Partnership dissolution agreement*. [manuscript] Collection 208, Aabenraa: Jebsen & Jessen Historical Archives.

Gargiulo, M., & Benassi, M. (2000). Trapped in your own net? Network cohesion, structural holes, and the adaptation of social capital. *Organization Science*, *11*(2), 183–196.

Gieseke, A. (1897). *Letter from the imperial post office to Michael Jebsen*. [manuscript] Collection A01-02-0013, Aabenraa: Jebsen & Jessen Historical Archives.

Greif, A. (2006). *Institutions and the path to the modern economy: Lessons from Medieval trade*. New York: Cambridge University Press.

Grönhoff, J. (1948). Kieler Bürgerbuch. *Mitteilungen der Gesellschaft für Kieler Stadtgeschichte*, (49).

von Haenisch, A. (1970). *Jebsen & Co. Hongkong—China-Handel im Wechsel der Zeiten 1895–1945*. Apenrade: Selbstverlag.

Hardach, G. (2003). Nation building in Germany: The economic dimension. In A. Teichova & H. Matis (Eds.), *Nation, state and the economy in history*. Cambridge: Cambridge University Press.

Hardin, G. (1968). The tragedy of the commons. *Science*, *162*(3859), 1243–1248.

von Hassel, E. (1953). *Michael Jebsen: Das Leben des Schiffsreeders und die Chronik seiner Vorfahren*. Apenrade: Selbstverlag.

Held, J. H. (1938). *Hundert Jahre Howaldt*. Kiel, Hamburg: Howaldtswerke A.G.

Hieke, E. (1953). *Die Reederei M. Jebsen A. G. Apenrade*. Hamburg: Hamburgische Bücherei.

Homans, G. C. (1961). *Social behavior: Its elementary forms*. New York, Harcourt: Brace & World.

Huang, F. D. (1999). *Qingdao: Chinesen under deutscher Herrschaft 1897–1914*. Bochum: Projekt.

Imperial Naval Office. (1902). *Project proposal for floating pontoon construction in Qingdao*. [manuscript] Collection BArch-MA-RM3-6934, Freiburg: Bundes-Militaerarchiv.

Imperial Naval Office. (1909). *Trade register of Qingdao in 1909*. Collection BArch-MA-RM3-6731, Freiburg: Bundes-Militaetarchiv.

Imperial Post Office. (1896). *Reichspostdampferlinie nach Ostasien, Australien (Unterhandlungen, Verträge)*. [manuscript] Collection BArchB-R4701-GA-1283, Berlin: Bundesarchiv.

Imperial Post Office. (1897-1900). *Letters concerning negotiations of postal steamer service*. [manuscript] Collection BArchB-R4701-GA-16239, Berlin: Bundesarchiv-Berlin.

Imperial Post Office. (1898). *Vertrag zwischen dem Reichskanzler und dem Schiffsreeder M. Jebsen in Apenrade über die Unterhaltung einer Post-Dampfschiffsverbindung zwischen Shanghai und Kiautschou*. [manuscript] Collection A01-02-0020, Aabenraa: Jebsen & Jessen Historical Archives.

Jebsen, J. 1898a. *A letter to Jacob Jebsen*. [manuscript] Collection A01-01-205, Aabenraa: Jebsen & Jessen Historical Archives.

Jebsen, J. (1899). *A letter to Heinrich Jessen*. [manuscript] Collection A01-01-294, Aabenraa: Jebsen & Jessen Historical Archives.
Jebsen, M. 1898b. *Letters to Jacob Jebsen*. [manuscript] Collection A01-01-314, Aabenraa: Jebsen & Jessen Historical Archives.
Lash, S., Urry, J. (1987). *The end of organized capitalism*. Madison, WI: University of Wisconsin Press.
McPherson, M., Smith-Lovin, L., & Cook, J. M. (2001). Birds of a feather: Homophily in social networks. *Annual Review of Sociology*, 415–444.
Mellewigt, T., Madhok, A., & Weibel, A. (2007). Trust and formal contracts in interorganizational relationships: Substitutes and complements. *Managerial and Decision Economics, 28*(8), 833–847.
Miller, J. H. (1996). The coevolution of automata in the repeated prisoner's dilemma. *Journal of Economic Behavior and Organization, 29*(1), 87–112.
Ostersehlte, C. (2004). *Von Howaldt zu HDW: 165 Jahre Entwicklung von einer Kieler Eisengießerei zum weltweit operierenden Schiffbau- und Technologiekonzern*. Kiel/Hamburg: Howaldtswerke-Deutsche Werft AG/Koehler.
Ostrom, E. (2014). Collective action and the evolution of social norms. *Journal of Natural Resources Policy Research, 6*(4), 235–252.
Ostrom, E. (2015). *Governing the commons*. Cambridge: Cambridge University Press.
Ostrom, E., Burger, J., Field, C. B., Norgaard, R. B., & Policansky, D. (1999). Revisiting the commons: Local lessons, global challenges. *Science, 284*(5412), 278–282.
Padgett, J. F., & Ansell, C. K. (1993). Robust action and the rise of the Medici, 1400–1434. *American Journal of Sociology*, 1259–1319.
Peng, Y. S. (2004). Kinship networks and entrepreneurs in China's transitional economy. *American Journal of Sociology, 109*(5), 1045–1074.
Pomeranz, K. (1993). *The making of a hinterland: State, society, and economy in inland North China, 1853–1937*. Berkeley: University of California Press.
Reynolds, D. R. (1995). *China, 1895–1912: State-sponsored reforms and China's late-Qing revolution: Selected essays from Zhongguo Jindaishi*. Armonk, NY: M.E. Sharpe.
Rothstein, B., & Stolle, D. (2008). The state and social capital: An institutional theory of generalized trust. *Comparative Politics*, 441–459.
Schrameier, L.W. (1914). *Aus kiautschous Verwaltung: die Land-, Steuer- und Zollpolitik des Kiautschougebietes*. Jean: G. Fischer.
Seibel, H. (1970). Diederichsen, Carl Heinrich Wilhelm Theodor. In O. Klose (Ed.), *Schleswig-Holsteinisches Biographisches Lexikon* (vol. 1). Wachholz: Neumünster.
Sievers, K. D. (2005). Heinrich und Thea Diederichsen und der Diederichsenpark. *Mitteilungen der Gesellschaft für Kieler Stadtgeschichte*, (82/83), 123–156.
Skinner, G. W., & Baker, H. D. R. (1977). *The city in Imperial China*. Stanford, CA: Stanford University Press.
So, W.L. (2014). Navigating protectionism—Diederichsen, Jebsen & Company in German Qingdao and the World, 1898–1908. Ph.D. SOAS.
Stiglitz, J. E. (2000). Formal and informal institutions. In P. Dasgupta & I. Serageldin (Eds.), *Social capital: A multifaceted perspective* (pp. 59–68). World Bank: Washington.
Truppel, V. O. (1908). *A letter to the State Secretary of the Navy*. [manuscript] Collection BArch-MA-RM3-6761, Freiburg: Bundes-Militaerarchiv.
Tsingtauer Neueste Nachrichten. (1909). *Die chinesische Handelskammer in Tsingtau*. 12 October.
Wicks, A. C., Berman, S. L., & Jones, T. M. (1999). The structure of optimal trust: Moral and strategic implications. *The Academy of Management Review, 24*(1), 99–116.
Williamson, O. E. (1989). Transaction cost economics. In R. Schmalensee & R. Willig (Eds.), *Handbook of industrial organization* (pp. 136–182). Amsterdam: Elsevier.

Zhang, S. F. (2006). Jindai Qingdao de sanda huiguan yu Qingdao shanghui 近代青島的三大會館與青島商會. In C. L. Li & Y. H. Zuo, *Jindai zhongguo de chengshi yu xiangcun 近代中國的城市與鄉村*. Beijing: Shehui kexue wenxian chubanshe.
Zhu, S. P., & Zhang, J. L. (1958). *Guangxuchao donghualu 光緒朝東華錄*. Beijing: Zhonghua shuju.

PART 2

Business Networks in Japan and Korea

CHAPTER 7

Business Networks in Japan: The Impact of Exposure to Overseas Markets

K. Jackson*, S. Matsumoto†
*SOAS, University of London & Doshisha University, Kyoto, Japan
†Doshisha University, Kyoto, Japan

7.1 INTRODUCTION

For the purpose of this discussion, we draw on Ford, Gadde, Håkansson, and Snehota (2011) along with Håkansson and Ford (2002) to define a 'business network' as traceable patterns of formalised relationships and other business-specific linkages that are negotiated and sustained between individual organisations.[1] Adopting a network perspective means recognizing that each organisation identifies problems in its particular business environment and seeks strategic solutions to these problems through interaction with other organisations to which it develops formalised networked relationships. Adopting this view further implies that managers and other stakeholders in each organisation recognise limitations to their own discretion and powers for action and thus, a discernible degree of interdependency with other organisations in the network. Correspondingly, the strategic thinking of managers in each networked organisation is influenced by the recognition that their organisation is 'incomplete' (Ford et al., 2011): managers recognise that their strategic knowledge and experience are insufficient towards resourcing solutions to the problems and opportunities they identify in their organisation's strategic business environment.

As with the other Asian economies discussed in this book, the manner in which Japanese business networks appear to respond to the dynamics of their respective business environments can appear both divergent and convergence. Divergence appears on account of history and of the institutional structures that appear to both facilitate and constrain network development (cf. Boisot & Child, 1996; Hamilton, 1996; Lechevalier, 2014a;

[1]As we later specify distinctively Japanese forms of 'firm' or 'company', we use the generic term 'organisation' in this introductory section.

Business Networks in East Asian Capitalisms
http://dx.doi.org/10.1016/B978-0-08-100639-9.00007-4

Tung & Worm, 2001). Specific to Asian contexts, patterns of convergence might appear when emphasising (for example) the still vibrant stream of social and cultural references shared by business networks in China, South Korea, Japan, and Vietnam as expressed in Confucian values and rituals (cf. Hasegawa & Noronha, 2009; Redding, 1990, 2014; Warner, 2003, 2011, 2013; Whitley, 1990). In this discussion, we explore the influence of history and Japan-specific institutions in relation to how Japanese business networks appear to be developing, and especially as they invest in overseas markets.

Specifically, we attempt to:

- Illustrate salient features of Japanese capitalism as context for the development of business networks in Japan.
- Illustrate distinctive features of business networks in Japan.
- Identify what appear to be enduring trends in how business networks in Japan operate.
- Identify emerging patterns of business network activities in Japan.

In pursuit of these objectives, we focus attention on *keiretsu* inter-firm relationships that continue to shape and influence the strategic thinking and decision-making evident in Japanese business (cf. Bird, 2002; Gerlach, 1993; Plath, 2002; Witt, 2014). We identify trends and patterns in the development of selected *keiretsu* as they become exposed to overseas markets. Generalising from these examples, we suggest that one enduring trend is the resource of performance strength drawn from maintaining embedded and vertically integrated network relationships. Looking ahead, we identify emerging patterns of development towards a more horizontal form of organisation as Japanese business networks seek to further develop competitive positions in overseas markets. However, before reaching these conclusions we outline contexts for the distinctive development of business networks in Japan, highlighting the extent to which these networks appear to be geographically, historically, socially, and institutionally embedded.

7.2 CONTEXTS: THE DEVELOPMENT OF JAPANESE CAPITALISM

The Merriam-Webster (2015) defines 'capitalism' as an economic system characterised by private or corporate ownership of capital goods, by investments that are determined by private decision, and by prices, production, and the distribution of goods that are determined mainly by competition in a free market. Capitalism as a system of social and economic organisation emerged initially during the Industrial Revolution, which, in Western economies, gained momentum during the late 18th century (Thompson,

1963). As a discernible pattern of social and economic activity, it is possible to identify 'pre-capitalist' antecedents to this form of organisation—a state of capitalistic development attributed by Western observers to pre-industrialised societies in Asia (cf. Weber, 1978). Taking this perspective as our premise, we attempt now to outline the historical development of Japanese capitalism in relation to distinctive forms of social and economic organisation.

7.2.1 Geography

Geographically, Japan is an archipelago of over seven thousand islets and islands. The four most populated islands support a mountainous and forested terrain that offers little in terms of natural resources to support human society or economic activity. With few navigable rivers or canals, Japan can also be defined geographically by the oceans that surround it and which, over time, have provided its people a major source of nutrition and, militarily, a defence against invasion (McKinstry, 2002). As European voyagers sought to improve the accuracy of their maps and simultaneously extend colonial networks into East Asia, Japan was described as a 'closed' or even 'hermetically sealed' society (cf. Walker, 2015), much as non-insiders might perceive North Korea today. During its early industrialisation period, Japan became conceptualised as part of 'The Orient' in American and European minds (Said, 1978). Unlike North Korea, this exotic imagery acquired more concrete form during the 1870s when artefacts of *japonisme* such as *ukiyo-ē* ('floating world picture') woodblock prints were exported *en masse* to 'The West' (Lambourne, 2005).

Imaging Japan as 'Land of the Rising Sun'—in Japanese, *nihon/nippon* (日本, 'sun origin')—makes enduring sense from an eastwards-looking and, by definition, 'Western' perspective. Correspondingly, the notion of a politically and culturally homogenous Japanese 'nation' or 'state' and thus, as a 'variety of capitalism' (Hall & Soskice, 2001) is biased by European diplomatic thinking from the nineteenth century and, more recently, under blanket occupation by United States forces after World War II (cf. Lechevalier, 2014b). Offering an emic ('insider-looking-in') perspective, Sugimoto (2014) prefers to describe Japan as 'a conglomerate of sub-nations' and thus a reflection of its geographical and climatic diversity.

7.2.2 History

An island nation, Japan systematically repelled any substantive foreign incursion until the arrival in 1853 of Commodore Matthew Perry of the fledgling American navy. Anchored in Edo (now Tokyo) Bay, Perry and his 'black ships' caused the then Japanese military command (*shogun*) to recognise their technological deficit and, after some resistance, concede the opening of ports in Japan to foreigners. According to Huffman (2010), it was Perry's gift of a 'quarter-scale model train' that appeared to impact most on popular memory. The concessions and close interaction with foreigners heralded, from 1868 onwards, the era of 'Meiji Restoration', wherein Japan rapidly transformed to an industrialised, urbanised and—during the early twentieth century—militarised nation state. From a global perspective, this historic transformation was highlighted by events such as the 1905 defeat of an Imperial Russian navy at Tsushima Straits. As a consequence of its remarkable economic recovery from defeat in the Second World War, Japan became Asia's only member of the Organization for Economic Cooperation and Development (OECD) in 1965.

It is tempting to explain specific patterns of government policy-making or strategic management behaviour with reference to Japan's island status. However, this can be misleading. To illustrate, in another comparable 'island economy' (the United Kingdom), the government recently commissioned the building of a nuclear power station by a Chinese state-owned enterprise (SOE)—a policy decision that remains incredible in other nationally defined capitalist economies such as France, Germany, the United States, or Japan.

7.2.3 Society

Giddens and Sutton define 'society' as 'a system of structured social and institutional relationships within a boundaried territory' (2013, p. 1071). Over time and within geographical boundaries, societies appear as voluntary self-gatherings or communities of people and may number from dozens to millions, according to how boundaries are physically drawn or perceived, (Giddens, 2006; Giddens & Sutton, 2013). Perceptions of urgency influence the intensity with which communities gather and bond—a process that is much more enduring, perhaps, when people are exposed to regular threats of extinction. For, only 30,000 years ago, the main Japanese islands were attached to what is today Mainland China. The Japanese archipelago continues to stretch away from this continental anchor, creating a society constantly threatened by natural disasters such as volcanoes, earthquakes, and tsunami. One metaphor commonly associated with how Japanese business networks endure is *unmei kyodotai* or 'community of fate' (cf. Debroux, 2003).

In describing social and economic contexts for the development of Japanese capitalism, it is useful to invoke general definitions of 'organisation'.

Echoing Senior and Swailes (2010, p. 4), 'at the simplest level' organisations can be interpreted as physical spaces in which people routinely work and interact with each other. In the Japanese context, the rice field (田) suggests a microcosm of Japanese society and work culture. Apart from warriors (*samurai*), most Japanese of the pre-Meiji era remained tied to the land, to labour, and the community of their birth—a social system recognisable as feudal. Markets for produced goods were predominantly local; distribution commonly stopped at the point of tribute payments to the local landowner. Although merchants also wandered freely, they were accorded little social status: 'doing business' was deemed of little social worth—an embedded social perception that might explain why Japanese researchers continue to interpret management concepts such as 'corporate social responsibility' (CSR) as 'foreign imports' (cf. Debroux, 2014).

Developing on the 田 analogy, one approach towards understanding fundamental forms of Japanese society and, by extension, of pre-capitalistic organisation, is 町, where the rice field is attached to a specified length of pathway that becomes the street or ward—a unit of social organisation fundamental to the evolutionary design of Japanese towns. In relation to rice cultivation, McKinstry (2002) makes the interesting observation that communities in pre-capitalist Japan failed to develop sophisticated animal-pulled agricultural machinery. The cultivation of rice remains a seasonal, location-specific, and labour-intensive activity. Consequently, until the introduction of 'Western' knowledge and technologies during the Meiji era, early Japanese capitalism was essentially subsistent, demanding long-term and (euphemistically speaking) 'back-breaking' commitment of its community members—a commitment discernible even today in the work ethic of Japanese employees (cf. Dore & Sako, 1998; Jackson & Tomioka, 2004).

7.2.4 Cultures

To this early industrial form of social organisation, we can apply common definitions of business organisations (cf. Butler, 1991; Daft, 1989; Senior & Swailes, 2010). These definitions tend to describe organisations as social, economic, legal, and technological entities that express purpose and offer discernible boundaries—actual and/or perceived. Within defined boundaries, researchers can observe patterns of activity among organisational insiders that, when generalised, might be perceived to form distinctive organisational structures, cultures and sub-cultures. Over generations, cultures become distinct and often exclusive through the sharing of codes of language and other patterns of socially expected or 'normal' behaviours, as individuals identify themselves collectively as 'in-groups', setting (by definition) boundaries to 'outsiders' (Jandt, 2010). Working together on the basis of shared knowledge and expectation facilitates efficiency of communication. Sharing perceptions of familiarity and mutual interest supports social cohesion and thus, facilitates future planning: if the behaviour of each community member appears reliably predictable then plans can be made for future harvests of rice. As we shall see, a reiteration of 'insider' status occurs when defining the boundaries of business networks such as *zaibatsu* and *keiretsu*. For now, we can recognise how one enduring impact of such distinctively Japanese processes of socialisation on Japanese employment practices: for example, the expectations of lifetime employment shared by male (*salaryman*) employees who, in return for loyal commitment to one employer, expect their 'insider' status to secure a 'job for life' (cf. Debroux, 2003).

7.2.5 Identity

According to Giddens (2006), social identity is commonly expressed in terms of gender, age, ethnicity, social class, and education, each in relation to a specified reference group. Until the introduction of formal systems of citizen registration, only Japanese of the aristocratic warrior class referred to family names: given names sufficed for common people (cf. Sugimoto, 2014). As mentioned previously, the transformation of Japanese capitalism proceeded rapidly. In 1900, the population of Japan was approximately 45 million, giving a population density of 115/km^2. By 1940, this had become 70 million with a density of 188 (MIAC, 2016). As during the combined processes of industrialisation and urbanisation that shaped Western capitalisms, people who migrate from 'home' communities to larger social organisations such as factories and cities, and who are then subsequently induced to work and share social and economic goals with relative strangers, experience opportunities for more complex expressions of individual and social identities than previous generations experienced, or perhaps even imagined (Giddens, 1991).

In Western contexts for employment, one standard and socially identifying question is 'who do you work for?' (Senior & Swailes, 2010, p. 4). In Japan, the answer is likely to be an offer to exchange business cards (*meishi*) as an expression of organisational citizenship: an enduring statement of an individual's social status and identity in Japan. Perhaps on grounds of ethnic identity, non-Japanese employees might feel excluded from such normal expressions of social identity (cf. Jackson & Tomioka, 2004; Yoshimura & Anderson, 1997).

7.3 THE ROLE OF INSTITUTIONS

Barley and Tobert (1997, p. 94) define 'institutions' as 'socially constructed templates for action, generated and maintained through ongoing interactions'. As such, institutions can be seen to overlap with the generic definition of organisations presented earlier. In contrast to organisations, however, institutions such as government and legal agencies appear more embedded in social and historical contexts—an observation that, according to Boyer (2014), is commonly underestimated when Western analysts seek to contrast and compare 'Asian' and 'non-Asian' capitalisms. Throughout this discussion, we attempt to balance etic ('outsider-looking-in') research approaches with emic ('insider-looking-in') perspectives. Consequently, we look beyond relatively static analytical models that have been conceptualised and theorised in application to Western contexts for capitalistic development before being generalised to Asian contexts. Accordingly, rather than invoking generalised notions of 'national culture', we instead echo Boyer (2014) and highlight the role of institutions towards shaping the development of Japanese capitalism and, thus, contexts for assessing the relative performance of Japanese business networks.

7.3.1 i-e

The first Japan-specific institution we focus on is 家 (*i-e,* pronounced 'ee-eh'), commonly translated into English as 'house' or 'home' (O'Neill, 1991, p. 45). The pictogram (Japanese *kanji*) depicts a pig under a roof, which suggests a 'home' acting as a combined social and economic entity. As a focal point for localised trading and bartering in a society where money still lay in the hands of relatively few people, 家 gave structure to the interactions and obligations of feudal community-based life (Smith & Musumi, 1994). When interpreted as a 'household', 家 represents a legal entity, for it is the named 'householder' who still today in Japanese society acts as the person registered as being responsible for the people and their activities brought under one roof. When 家 is interpreted as 'family', the line of household responsibility generally follows Confucian tradition and traces a patriarchal line (Sugimoto, 2014).

Senior and Swailes emphasise how institutions 'once created' commonly 'restrict actions within them' (2012, p. 99). Drawing on institutional theory and social–psychological concepts, such as embeddedness and path-dependency, the implication is that patterns of ritual and routine developed within institutional contexts become, over time, accepted by members as norms and reiterated uncritically. In relation to 家, this becomes strategically vital where the household is also the seat of a commercial enterprise: for example, a restaurant or shop run as a 'family business'. Unlike in (for example) Korea, Vietnam, or China, succession in relation to who leads the family business in Japan might or might not follow a consistent blood line (cf. Jackson & Tomioka, 2004). Rather, non-family members might be adopted into a 'quasi-kinship' or 'functional' linkage if this is believed to better serve the household's chances of economic survival or prosperity, or enhance family reputation within existing social and business networks (Sugimoto, 2014). In this sense, business ownership and stewardship in Japan is relatively flexible and can be extended beyond immediate family boundaries in order to leverage strategic convenience or competitive advantage—a pragmatic calculation we examine later in relation to the performance of Japanese business networks exposed to overseas markets.

7.3.2 Zaibatsu

In business and management research, topics such as ownership, leadership succession, and social interaction oriented towards confirming mutual obligations are commonly associated with family businesses (cf. Melin, Nordqvist, & Sharma, 2013), and with family businesses in Asia, specifically (cf. Amman & Jaussaud, 2012; Fletcher & von Staden, 2012; Redding, 1990). Networks of enterprising family-owned businesses can drive capitalistic development to remarkable and enduring effect: for example, as when migrating families bring 'the spirit of Chinese capitalism' to Singapore and other Asian and non-Asian economies (Redding, 1990). As with the overseas Chinese example, the enduring integrity of trust/obligation-based networks, such as *guanxì*, facilitates return flows of investment to 'home' markets.

Correspondingly, our discussion of technologically 'modern' and—with regard to their overseas impact—large-scale Japanese business networks begins with *zaibatsu*. These (usually) family-owned business conglomerates are not unique to Japan: equivalent business network types exist in Taiwan, Mainland China, and (for direct comparison) in South Korea, with the powerful and globally extended *chaebol* (Hemmert, 2014). The common translation of *chaebol* as 'wealth clan' applies also to *zaibatsu*. Gerlach (2002) talks of a 'financial clique', given that each pre-World War II *zaibatsu* was founded around a bank or other source of reliable 'in-house' credit or 'patient capital' (Redding, 2014). This emphasis on financial security is important: for, as Gerlach (2002) highlights, the type of 'public' (stock-/share-holding) equity markets that emerged to finance fledgling businesses in early Western capitalisms were not available in Japan until after the Second World War.

Consequently, when Japan began its own rapid 'catch-up' path towards industrialisation during the Meiji Restoration, the central and regional governments and institutions lacked the necessary human, technological, and (above all) capital resources to advance the nation. Consequently, large family-owned *zaibatsu* such as Mitsubishi, Sumitomo, Mitsui, and Fuyo were called to (for example) sponsor the emissaries sent to developed western economies, manage return transfer of the technological knowledge gained, import Western experts, invest in infrastructure relevant to applying new knowledge, develop strategic industries such as mining, steel production, shipbuilding, chemical processing, pharmaceuticals, transportation, and telecommunications (Aoki & Patrick, 1994; Gerlach, 2002).

A further transformational role played by *zaibatsu* in the development of Japanese capitalism appears as social and political perceptions of 'business' became oriented towards nationally development and social responsibility. To illustrate, in addition to building infrastructure that soon enabled Japan to compete as a global economy, *zaibatsu* were accorded responsibility for employing and training newly urbanised populations (cf. Witt, 2014). Furthermore, being arranged as vertically integrated networks allowed *zaibatsu* to set ever higher standards for the efficient management of supply lines, while the financial security afforded by arrangement around 'patient' or low-rent seeking capital sources allowed for the effective recruitment, training, and long-term retention of core human resources. As an employer investing heavily in training employees, the return on this investment became institutionalised as a social expectation of 'lifetime employment'—for Japanese males, at least (Jackson & Tomioka, 2004). This expectation logically extended during the 1940s towards the provision of pension, insurance, and other social welfare arrangements, initiated tentatively in partnership between government and *zaibatsu* employers (Estévez-Abe, 2008). This social expectation endures, albeit with diminishing degrees of certainty (Sueki, 2016).

As mentioned previously, Japan lacks many of the natural resources necessary to develop a heavily industrialised model of capitalist economy. Even today, Japan needs to import food and other vital resources, meaning that the integration of supply chains connecting to Japan's business networks requires international reach: for example, to neighbouring Asian economies (cf. Staples, 2014). This overseas resource-seeking activity took on a sinister aspect when the strategies of *zaibatsu* and a military government were combined during the Asia Pacific War (1931–45). This led to the occupation of territory in China (the Korean peninsula had been colonised since 1910) and subsequently, of other countries and territories across East and Southeast Asia—a legacy that impacts on foreign investment policy and international diplomacy to this day.

The role played by *zaibatsu* in producing military and technological assets ensured that they were targeted for dismemberment during the American occupation from 1945. Some *zaibatsu* were allowed to reform (several under new names) in the early 1950s, one reason being to offer non-military support to America and United Nations forces fighting the Korean War. However, by this time, the imposition of a democratic Constitution coupled with a systematic reform of the education system in Japan meant that the people and institutions supporting *zaibatsu* business networks were 'modern' in the sense that they were able to compete without sanction in the type of 'open' and 'free' markets that American-led capitalism worked globally to secure.

7.3.3 Employer Networks

In 2015 it was announced that the Australian government planned to upgrade its fleet of navy submarines. Mitsubishi Heavy Industries of Japan was invited to put in a bid. The Australian government then decided to solicit further bids from France and Germany. According to media sources, Mitsubishi was encouraged by the Japanese government to reduce its price estimate and target securing the deal ahead of forecasting a profit from the business (Nikkei, 2016; The Australian, 2015). Echoing Hall and Soskice (2001), such events appear to distinguish Japanese capitalism as supporting a 'co-ordinated market economy' in contrast to the type of 'liberal market economy' evident in (for example) the current UK government's invitation to Chinese suppliers of nuclear energy technology.

Attempting to compare and explain such high-profile business and diplomatic events encourages us to highlight a further consequence of the role *zaibatsu* has played in the development of Japanese capitalism: namely, the institutionalisation of relationships between national and regional governments and 'big business' or large-scale employers in Japan. As we have seen, successive Japanese governments relied on resource-laden and socially-embedded *zaibatsu* networks to further agendas for national development, while senior representatives of *zaibatsu* formed their own cross-industry networks ('Presidents' Clubs') in order to minimise any negative impact that government law-making and policies might have on their capacity to do business. The 'Japanese Federation of Economic Organizations' (*keidanren*) is a prime example of this form of institutionalised network for channelling influence, and because *keidanren* meets in Tokyo, for centralising networks designed to influence the business and industrial policies of national governments (Amyx, 2002). According to Sugimoto (2014, p. 322), *keidanren* members even extend their influence towards determining policies related to nuclear energy generation in Japan and for export to other Asian economies such as Vietnam, South Korea, and Russia.[2] This reflection leads us to echo the question posed by Stockwin (2008) as to 'who' actually 'runs Japan'. It also highlights another enduring legacy from the rise to prominence and influence in Japan of *zaibatsu*-type business networks and one that is at the core of our subsequent discussion linking the relationships that define Japanese business networks and the influence these relationships appear to have on business performance.

Finally for now, the enduring and (from an outsider perspective) commonly opaque influence of institutions such as *keidanren* illustrates the extent to which Japanese capitalism appears internally 'co-ordinated' when compared to the 'open market' style capitalism evident in (for example) the United Kingdom (Hall & Soskice, 2001; Lechevalier, 2014b).

7.3.4 Keiretsu

We defined society as 'a system of structured social and institutional relationships within a boundaried territory' formed by 'voluntary self-gatherings or communities of people' (Giddens, 2006; Giddens & Sutton, 2013) Applying the terminology of general systems theory (Von Bertalanffy, 1968), it can be argued that any form of social organisation represents an attempt by people collectively to achieve 'equilibrium', which, in hostile and/or competitive environments might be measured on a scale from bare survival to sustainable prosperity. Invoking capitalism as an ideologically driven economic system suggests an ontological premise that uncertainty is a given.[3]

When human perceptions of uncertainty are calculated in expressions of risk and probability, uncertainty appears to become manageable (cf. Gigerenzer, 2002). In response, managers can begin to formulate strategies designed to secure opportunities, while simultaneously minimising threats: for example, through the creation of and affiliation with patterns of

[2]We provide the semantic emphasis on 'even' here, being mindful of the enduring impact of the Great East Japan Earthquake and subsequent tsunami of 11th Mar. 2011, along with the enduring effects of the 'Fukushima' nuclear disaster.

[3]Having taken the combined ontological and business analytical position that uncertainty is a given, we recognise that research measures such as 'uncertainty avoidance'—when applied to comparative cultural analysis—express an academic conceit.

formalised relationships we refer to here as 'business networks' (Ford et al., 2011). As the strategic environment for business networks becomes more global—and more globally 'social'—the environment for strategic thinking among managers becomes simultaneously more complex (cf. Beck, 1992), and not least, when seeking competitive advantage beyond the shores of relative familiarity (Hemmert & Jackson, 2016). As a consequence, established social and business systems in Asia, as elsewhere, are prompted to become systematically more permeable in relation to the diversity of perspectives they might engage when calculating strategic risk and business opportunity (cf. Jackson, 2013). Against this background, we focus our discussion on another distinctive form of Japanese business network: *keiretsu*.

Since Japan began to challenge the economic dominance of Western and, above all, American business across global markets during the 1980s, numerous attempts have been made to explain how and why Japanese business networks could achieve such spectacular and durable success over such a short period of time (cf. Ouchi, 1981; Jackson & Debroux, 2009b). Consequently, and as with the 'floating' imagery of the aforementioned *ukiyo-e* block prints of the late nineteenth century, numerous 'exotic' Japanese-origin terms entered the global discourse of international business: *kaizen, JIT, kanban, keiretsu*. Loosely translated as 'succession' or 'linkage' (cf. Aoki & Lennerfors, 2013) and even 'headless combine' (The Economist, 2009) and commonly visualised as a spider's web (cf. Collinson & Morgan, 2009), *keiretsu* have been conceptualised as representing distinct patterns of 'inter-firm networks' (cf. Hall & Soskice, 2001) or 'close inter-firm relationships' (Gerlach, 1993). Again, it would be an overstatement to claim that *keiretsu* networks are 'unique' to Japan: for example, parallel functionality and strategic purpose might be observed in the 'information architecture' associated with what Kay denoted in Western business contexts as a 'co-operative ethic' (Kay, 1993). Before the global image of Japanese business philosophies and practices became mired during the so-called Lost Decade, there was talk of exporting the *keiretsu* concept to established American manufacturers such as Chrysler (Dyer, 1996). Once again, it is the institutional embeddedness of the network that lends *keiretsu* a distinctive Japanese identity. To illustrate, Plath (2002) conceptualises *keiretsu* as 'industrial groups' representing 'a post-war reincarnation of the pre-war *zaibatsu*' and being similarly distinguished by interlinked systems facilitating 'succession'. On this basis, Plath (2002) lists four *keiretsu* types:

(i) Financial group: similar to the aforementioned *zaibatsu*, these are centred around and integrated horizontally around a central bank.

(ii) Enterprise group: centred around and integrated vertically with one large enterprise.
(iii) Subcontracting group: networked organisations arranged (often with a high degree of business dependency) to supply one main enterprise.
(iv) Marketing group: networked organisations arranged (often with a high degree of business dependency) to distribute on behalf of one main enterprise.

Given the extent and depth of cross-shareholding and long-term loans serving to bond the 'spider's web' together and lend long-term resilience, one key governance feature is that opportunistic behaviour by managers in any one affiliate organisation is effectively tempered (cf. Lincoln, Kerbo, & Wittenhagen, 1995). However, when encountering the routine expressions of such 'in-group' business values and strategic rituals (cf. Jandt, 2010), a network member perceived by influential others as a subcultural 'outsider' might struggle to discern where key organisational variables, such as financial ownership and, by extension, financial, or legal accountability might lie (cf. Woodford, 2013). According to Plath (2002, p. 191), 'the clearest evidence of affiliation is appearance on the roster of monthly "Presidents' Club" meetings'. As with the aforementioned *keidanren*, these are likely to be held in Tokyo.

Overall, *keiretsu* appear to offer a distinctive form of response to business uncertainty and risk: for example, in that they are designed to embed social relationships and mutual obligations and long-term trust into a coherent structure. Taking a systems view, *keiretsu* endure and continue to demonstrate impressive equilibrium, as we discuss subsequently in relation to Toyota Motor Corporation. And although questions about the effectiveness and relative agility of the *keiretsu* model has been challenged in the wake of Japan's so-called Lost Decade between 1992 and 2004 (cf. Boyer, 2014; Porter, Takeuchi, & Sakakibara, 2000), it remains common to see reference to *keiretsu* as a 'classic' Japanese-specific form of business organisation: for example, in terms of ownership structure, management culture, and long-term strategic orientation (Witt, 2014). As such, *keiretsu* are commonly invoked in order to offer a direct contrast to American-style business organisations: 'J-Firm' versus 'A-Firm' (cf. Lechevalier, 2014b). We address this bi-polar approach to comparison in our concluding comments.

7.3.5 Sogo-shosha

Before moving on to identify what appear to be enduring trends and emerging patterns in the performance of selected *keiretsu*, we should consider the role of other distinctive players in the evolving global chain of Japanese business networks: general trading companies or *sogo-shosha*. Rudlin (2002, p. 165) defines these as 'integrated international trading enterprises engaged in importing and exporting a wide range of merchandise'. Conceptualised thus, *sogo-shosha* should not appear to be uniquely Japanese. International trading and logistics companies outside Japan are on hand to supply Japan-based business networks with (for example) raw materials from distant sources, 'inside knowledge' about particular targets for outward foreign direct investment (FDI), and the provision of 'contacts' to local politicians and other influential groups that might help secure a more reliable return on this FDI. Increasingly, multi- and transnational enterprises and corporations (MNEs, TNCs) have the resources to keep each of these services 'in house' (cf. Ietto-Gillies, 2012).

According to Redding (2014), *sogo-shosha* function as *keiretsu*, but with a strategic business focus on trading, rather than on manufacturing. Adopting a systems approach, Redding identifies the strategic role of *sogo-shosha* to be 'the co-ordination or economic exchange and control' (2014, p. 24) of Japanese business networks. The strategic comparison to *keiretsu* is telling: for, in Japanese business contexts *sogo-shosha* can appear as voluntary and perhaps even short-term affiliates in the 'spider's web' of Japanese networks. To illustrate, representatives of *sogo-shosha* might advise government officials about business trends and international risk assessments (cf. Yonekawa, 1990).

Correspondingly, another distinguishing feature of *sogo-shosha* is the social role they continue to play as attractors of internationally minded employees in Japan's domestic market for talent recruitment and retention (cf. Rudlin, 2002). Comparing across international and (not least) other Asian markets for 'talent' (Jackson, 2011), Japanese managers appear generally to lack cross-cultural competence or what today is increasingly referred to as a 'global mind-set', evinced most obviously in the general lack of competence or confidence in communicating through the medium of international English (Jackson & Debroux, 2009a). Consequently, in domestic markets for employment, *sogo-shosha* can appear pioneering in respect of the 'diversity of perspectives' they bring to their responses to the aforementioned growing complexity of global business environments: for example, in the career opportunities afforded to talented women managers in Japan (cf. Jackson & Tomioka, 2004).

Reconnecting with our theme of 'island nation', all international business activities sourced in Japan suggest a physical and conceptual relocation 'overseas' of 'tried-and-tested' domestic market solutions. Consequently, taking the example of *keiretsu* investing in Mainland China, and (for illustration) conceptualising through the medium of Ownership, Locational and Internalisation (OLI) advantages (Dunning, 1977, 1980), we can envisage the strategic role of *sogo-shosha* to be one that combines the effective assessment of OLI advantages: Joint venture? Wholly-owned subsidiary? Brownfield site in Shanghai or Greenfield site in Western China? Hire local Chinese managers, or multi-lingual Chinese nationals already working in Japan? We can further envisage the impact towards mediating FDI risk that networked *sogo-shosha* might play supporting *keiretsu* that are seeking access to fossil fuel resources in (for example) Mozambique. Here we can invoke concepts such as 'psychic distance', defined by Johanson and Vahlne (1977, p. 24) as 'the sum of factors preventing the flow of information from and to the market. Examples are differences in language, education, business practices, culture, and industrial development'. Drawing on experience from across global contexts for business, members of *sogo-shosha* can provide such wide-ranging services to *keiretsu* competing across business sectors.

The role of *sogo-shosha* as an integral network supporting the export success of *keiretsu* and other Japanese business networks has long been recognised by insiders as a key and dynamic element distinguishing Japanese capitalism (cf. Yoshihara, 1982): less so, perhaps, outside of Japan. Against this background, we consider now how selected *keiretsu* have performed when exposed to overseas markets, and with or without the affiliation of *sogo-shosha* business networks.

7.4 BUSINESS NETWORKS IN JAPAN: ENDURING TRENDS

Before highlighting and comparing specific examples of *keiretsu* business performance, it is timely to invoke the conceptualisation formulated by Gerlach (1993) that these networks represent a 'state of mind'. Echoing Ohmae (1982), it is possible already to imagine how strategic decision-makers at *keiretsu* formulating strategies for internationalisation might at first appear hesitant, seeking the support and agency of known networks such as *sogo-shosha* before venturing too far into unfamiliar waters. Drawing on Hemmert and Jackson (2016), a key question here is the extent to which strategies and network relationships that appear to have performed effectively in established markets might fare when investing in so-called emerging markets: for example, in Mainland China.

7.4.1 Toyota Motor Corporation

We begin with Toyota Motor Corporation (henceforth, Toyota). It was founded in 1937 and continues to carry the owning family name: in English, Toyoda. The philosophy of its founders was to produce vehicles of high quality with optimal efficiency and minimal waste, a system that became operationalised and emulated worldwide as the Toyota Production System (TPS), adopted into other industrial sectors as 'lean production'. As Liker (2004) maintains, beyond the investment in production and other business related techniques and tools, it is the consistency of its 'in-house' philosophy and vision that distinguishes Toyota from global rivals: the current CEO is Akio Toyoda, a direct descendant of the founder, Kiichiro Toyoda.

7.4.2 Vertical Integration

The Toyota *keiretsu* can be conceptualised as an 'enterprise group', whereby networked organisations (suppliers, distributors, and so on) are centred around and integrated vertically with one large enterprise (Plath, 2002). To illustrate, in 1939 the founder set up a 'suppliers association', whereby suppliers were invited to share technological information and subsequently be educated about developments in the TPS (Aoki & Lennerfors, 2013). Reflecting our earlier discussion, we can identify several other key relationships defining the Toyota *keiretsu*. Toyota maintains major shareholdings in Denso, a supplier of air conditioning equipment along with other electrical appliances, in Aisin Seki, a supplier of drive train, brake, and chassis, and engine components, and Jtekt, a supplier of machine tools. A more visible stake is held in in Toyoda Gosei, a supplier of rubber, plastic, and urethane products and in Toyoda Boshoku, a supplier of vehicle interiors such as fabrics and filters. Recalling Japan's early industrialisation, Toyota also holds shares in Aichi Steel, a supplier of both speciality steel and electromagnetic parts. The list of *keiretsu* cross-shareholdings goes on: however, already these examples serve to highlight the extent and depth of Toyota's vertical integration.

7.4.3 Toyota in China

Toyota has approximately 340,000 employees worldwide and currently sells around nine million vehicles each year. Although other China-based automobile manufacturers currently produce more units each year, Toyota remains the world's largest single producer by volume of sales (STATISTA, 2015). Toyota first exported vehicles to China in the late 1930s—as mentioned previously, a controversial era in China-Japan relations. Recently, Toyota agreed a comprehensive manufacturing, distribution, and sales relationship with China FAW Group Corp, a Chinese SOE, in 2002. Drawing on the success of this initial venture, Toyota subsequently formed a joint venture in 2004 with the much smaller GAC Group, primarily to assemble and supply engines for the *Camry* label—a vehicle targeting the middle-income segment in China (Toyota, 2015). Listed now as GAC Toyota Motor Co., Ltd., GAC and Toyota each hold 50% share ownership. China remains one of Toyota's main overseas markets, selling 1.03 million units in 2014, up 12.5% from 2013 (Reuters, 2015). Toyota's investment in mid-range vehicle production, distribution, and sales looks set to continue. For example, Toyota recently announced a multi-billion dollar investment in new facilities in the Chinese city of Guangzhou, targeting production of 100,000 units annually of the mid-range Toyota *Yaris* (in China, *Vitz*) from 2018 (Japan Times, 2015).

7.4.4 Impact on Performance

Despite its long history of exposure to Chinese markets together with its continuing strength across global markets generally, Toyota still ranks only sixth among global automakers in China and sells less than one-third as many vehicles as its two main rivals in that market, Volkswagen and General Motors. To illustrate further, Toyota introduced the *Lexus* luxury brand to market in the United States in 1989 and continues to enjoy high status there and in Japan. However, Toyota has hesitated to transfer any *Lexus* production to China (Bloomberg, 2011). Sales of the *Lexus* brand in China remain far below those for rivals Audi, BMW, and Daimler (Mercedes). One explanation for this apparent underperformance might be the relative maturity of the North American and Japanese markets compared to China (Bloomberg, 2011). Another explanation might lie in recent political and diplomatic tensions between the current Chinese and Japanese governments (Reuters, 2014)—a course of events and effects that a global player such as Toyota is likely to attract ahead of Japanese manufacturers of less socially visible products in China.

Independently of the exposure to Chinese markets, the performance of some long-established *keiretsu* affiliates in Japan have caused problems, resulting (for example) in the 2015 recall of millions of vehicles worldwide after faults had been found in brake installations and passenger air bags. These components had been manufactured by trusted Toyota suppliers and, given the speed of global news and social media flow, the story soon attached with the Toyota brand in China, as elsewhere. Consequently, it is possible to discern some loss of return on Toyota's 'internalisation' processes (cf. Dunning, 1977)—processes that Ietto-Gillies (2012, p. 103) defines as 'those benefits that derive from producing internally', enabling global manufacturers 'to bypass external markets and the transaction costs associated with them'. Of specific relevance to internalisation in enterprise group *keiretsu* such as Toyota are the potential internalisation 'benefits' generated by 'operating within hierarchies rather than markets' Ietto-Gillies (2012, p. 103). According to Aoki and Lennerfors (2013), Toyota has already begun to renegotiate selected long-established *keiretsu* relationships with suppliers by orienting strategic decisions more towards emerging supplier 'markets', rather than rely on established 'hierarchies'.

Toyota's aforementioned intention to invest heavily in transferring production of the *Yaris* (*Vitz*) to China appears to replicate previous investments in the China market: for example, the focus on mid-range vehicles and with a proposition of hybrid technology that is no longer 'unique' to any one manufacturer: The suggestion by Gerlach (1993) that *keiretsu* might be conceived as a 'state of mind' could appear in this case to stretch beyond 'enduring' (innovatory) strength to 'path dependent' lack of (strategic) agility (cf. Storz, 2009). However, and beyond academic argument, a decisive challenge to strategic decision-makers and family members at Toyota is likely to arise from shareholders in Japan demanding a higher return on their hitherto 'patient' investment. To illustrate, the return to Toyota shareholder investments in Chinese markets has been equated to a multiple of 4.52, as compared to an industry-wide 5-year average of 18.57 (Reuters, 2015).

7.4.5 For Comparison: Sony in China

Sony Corporation (henceforth, Sony) is the electronics business unit of the larger Sony Group, which maintains global investments in electronics (including mobile phone handsets, digital communications, computers, gaming consoles), entertainment media (including film studios and distribution channels), and financial services, including life insurance. Sony was founded (literally) among the ashes of post-World War II Japan when in 1946 two entrepreneurs, Akito Morita and Masaru Ibuka, opened an electronics store in Tokyo specializing in recycling components of radios and other electronic equipment discarded by the American military. From these humble beginnings, Sony has become one of the most recognised Japanese brand names, gaining a reputation for innovative miniaturised high-quality products such as the TR63 radio, the Sony Walkman, the Sony Discman, and today's PlayStation game console.

Sony (China) Limited was established in 1996 as a wholly-owned subsidiary and has been headed consistently by Japanese CEOs. Consequently, Sony Corp's appointment of a non-Japanese CEO (Sir Howard Stringer) in 2005 appeared to herald a new era of corporate governance in Japanese MNCs (Japan Times, 2005). However, an alliance forged during this period between Sony and Swedish Ericsson for the manufacture of mobile phone handsets proved a failure. The impact in this sector continues to be felt, as Sony's market share in the Chinese handset market has fallen from 4.1% (ranked 6th) in 2013 to 3.1% (ranked 10th) in 2015 (Trendforce, 2015). Increasingly, business researchers have been asking whether Sony's exposure to Chinese markets has damaged the brand such that their global market share in PC manufacture is also failing in response to the 'next generation' of Chinese rivals, such as Lenovo (Nguyen, Okrend, & Tan, 2013).

In China as elsewhere, Sony's attempts to refocus strategy and restructure production and distribution can appear surprisingly clumsy for a business that was founded on nimbleness and innovation. For example, the recent decision to sell off its VAIO PC line to Lenovo is expected to generate a net loss of over JPY100 billion (Bloomberg, 2015a). Sony explains this divestment with reference to the resources it can reallocate to a rapidly expanding gaming market, a move prompted by the Chinese government's lifting of a ban on non-domestic games consoles in 2014 (Technobuffalo, 2015). Correspondingly, Sony entered a 49:51 share joint venture with Shanghai Oriental Pearl in Jan. 2015. However, the planned Jan. 2015 launch of Sony's PS4 console was delayed for undisclosed reasons: suggestions include Sony's need to reassess the existing 'black' and 'grey' markets for gaming software in China before releasing its authentic version (Bloomberg, 2015a).

7.4.6 A Failure of Succession?

We mentioned earlier how *keiretsu* might be translated roughly as 'succession', suggesting, line of strategic coherence and continuity of business relationships that might adapt to and withstand exposure to various environmental pressures. According to Dzever, Jaussaud, and Androsso-O'Callaghan (2008, p. 98), Sony is unusual in being a globally recognised Japanese brand that began its life with 'few *keiretsu* relationships'. This relative looseness of the network—or, by another interpretation—its dilution through global strategic overreach—might help explain how and why Sony performed so inconsistently in response to technological advances, changes to the legal environment for doing business in China, social, demographic, and economic shifts in China and other so-called emerging markets. To this, we can see a demographic shift in Japan itself, where the number of young people who might be motivated to buy Sony gaming products continues to fall. Presented in a harsh light, the Sony case might add credence to the claim by Backman (1999, p. 149) that *keiretsu* represents 'a fancy name for a stale concept'. In a Japanese business context, Sony's relatively young history and maverick beginnings perhaps led the network to underestimate the value that the institutional embeddedness nurtured by *keiretsu*, such as Toyota have been able to learn and otherwise benefit from (cf. Lechevalier, 2014b).

Correspondingly, we can ask at this point whether one of the enduring trends in the development of Japanese business networks is that *keiretsu* such as Toyota continues to perform by any global comparison resolutely and impressively owing to the extent of their tightly and vertically integrated organisation. To illustrate, after an abrupt loss of sales and thus, market share, Toyota managed to restore its global supply lines and achieve expected levels of output remarkably quickly after the Great Eastern Japan Earthquake of 2011 (Cukier, 2012). In the longer term, rival non-Japanese automobile manufacturers have fared worse in some aspects, both in the aftermath of the disaster and across global markets today, where Toyota continues to play a leading role.

7.5 BUSINESS NETWORKS IN JAPAN: EMERGING PATTERNS

Since the early 1990s, the Japanese automobile sector has been dominated by Toyota. Prior to this period, the sector was more deregulated and several automobile manufacturers competed fiercely and on more equal terms in both domestic and overseas markets: Honda, Mazda, Mitsubishi, and Nissan (Lechevalier, 2014b). One competitive response to an institutionally supported 'primus inter pares' situation is to seek partners from outside existing networks. Founded in 1933, Nissan Motor Company Ltd (henceforth, Nissan) invited France's Renault to become a principal (43.4%) shareholder in 1999, while Nissan received 15%, but with no voting rights (Nissan Global, 2016). As Tiberghien (2014) explains, the then Japanese government 'verbally' supported the alliance, not only in view of Nissan's financial difficulties at the time, but also in the wake of prior measures towards business regulatory reform: notably, 'a softening of the ban on holding companies and liberalisation of all transactions in the currency markets for individuals and for firms' (Tiberghien, 2014, p. 42). As the economic stagnation associated with Japan's 'Lost Decade' appeared relentless, the government similarly 'supported' the restructuring plan proposed for Nissan by Renault's incoming CEO and now President and CEO, Carlos Ghosn—an allowance that echoes the aforementioned pragmatism with regard to succession in Japanese family businesses.

Apart from being 'innovative' in a Japanese organisational context, the restructuring at Nissan had implications across the whole landscape of *keiretsu* relationships, including financial ownership, strategic control, and management cultures (Lechevalier, 2014b; Tiberghien, 2014). Although a minority shareholder, Renault bought shares in Nissan suppliers and sold them on to non-*keiretsu* members, including overseas investors and suppliers. This led to the introduction of new 'global' standards for supply network activity, made feasible by reducing the total number of suppliers from over 1000 in 1999 to nearly 600 in 2002 (Lechevalier, 2014c).

A new purchasing network was created and named Renault Nissan Purchasing Company (RNPC)—interestingly, the name of the cultural 'outsider' coming first. RNBC started to buy more components from foreign suppliers, especially for their overseas assembly operations—decisions that initially put at risk the internalisation of technological innovation and adaptation from local markets to the parent company (cf. Lechevalier, 2014c). Correspondingly, Renault Nissan terminated Nissan's prior distribution agreements with Marubeni Corporation, a powerful *sogo-shosha* with a market capitalisation value approaching JPY 300 billion (James & Graham, 2014). Instead, Nissan sought 'OLI'-type internationalisation solutions (cf. Dunning, 1977) independently and as a joint venture with Renault, and especially in emerging markets (Deloitte, 2009).

Similar restructuring was introduced internally at Nissan as the established employee identity system was scrapped, meaning it was no longer apparent from an employee's ID number how long s/he had worked at Nissan and thus, what status they should expect in the seniority promotion and rewards systems—a major undertaking across a network with over 150,000 employees (cf. Jackson & Tomioka, 2004; The Economist, 1999). As performance-based rewards systems become perceived as 'normal' or even desirable across business sectors and (over time) across Japanese society, the impact on employment expectations among mid-career and older workers becomes especially uncertain; conversely, the boundaries of career certainty for younger employees become less clear (Jackson & Debroux, 2016; Sako, 2006).

Today, Nissan is the sixth largest producer globally in terms of unit sales (5.3 million in 2014), while Renault Nissan combined are the fourth largest after Toyota, Volkswagen, and General Motors (STATISTA, 2015).

In terms of current performance, the inbound alliance model represented by the Renault Nissan alliance has shown the success of diversification among business networks in Japan, and suggests that the closed and deeply embedded network model represented by market rival Toyota is not the only effective model for this sector.

7.5.1 Horizontal Integration

In terms of FDI, inflows during FY 2014 to Japan amounted to US$2.1 billion. In stark contrast, outflows totalled approximately US$114 billion, a net fall of around 25 billion from 2013 and a third of the total for the United States. It appears that Japanese sourced FDI is decreasing in net value terms, influenced by consistent falls in the exchange rate of the Japanese Yen. However, there is evidence that outward FDI sourced in Japan is being targeted more astutely (UNCTAD, 2016). Current government policy to maintain a 'weak' Yen in support of major exporters has rendered many Japanese companies 'cash rich' (Bloomberg, 2015b) and thus in a position of relatively strong strategic control. The continuing policy of 'quantitative easing' by the Bank of Japan (BOJ) is encouraging Japanese companies to seek greater returns overseas—an influence of institutional policy path dependency (and, perhaps, even perceived dysfunctionality?) that appears to be prompting diverse strategic responses from established business networks (cf. Bloomberg, 2015b; Sako & Kohsakam, 2012). As a consequence, one clearly emerging pattern among Japanese business networks is to look beyond 'patient' investments and 'vertical' cross-shareholding arrangements domestically and instead, extend their relationships overseas—a process of network development that might be termed 'horizontalisation' (Matsumoto, 2014).

The emerging pattern here is towards outbound FDI or overseas acquisitions. To illustrate, in 2015, the total value of Japanese overseas acquisitions exceeded JPY10 trillion (Nikkei, 2015). This figure includes landmark transactions between Japan and the United Kingdom, such as the *Nihon Keizei Shinbun* (henceforth, Nikkei) purchase of the Financial Times newspaper, the acquisition of Amlin by Mitsui Sumitomo Insurance, and Japan Tabaco's acquisition of (the United Kingdom) Gallagher in 2007—the largest of recent overseas acquisitions in terms of value (JPY2.5 trillion). Although this global horizontal network development by acquisition sounds like a fine move, Japan has been facing challenges in managing operation after the acquisitions. Longitudinal research since 1985 on major Japanese outbound acquisitions (transactions above US$ 100 million) demonstrates that around half of Japan-sourced overseas business investments have failed, leading either to a sell off or other forms of divestment (Matsumoto, 2014). The emerging pattern of current outward FDI is still in a stage of early development; however, it is possible to discern already that established Japanese business networks are seeking competitive advantage by extending their investments and simultaneously their networks 'horizontally' overseas.

7.6 CONCLUSIONS: IMPLICATIONS FOR FUTURE RESEARCH

In this discussion we have attempted to illustrate salient features of Japanese capitalism as context for the development of business networks in Japan. We have furthermore illustrated distinctive features of how Japanese business networks have developed, focussing on the example of *keiretsu*. Specifically, we have attempted to highlight the impact on these networks of exposure to overseas markets and in this way identify what appear to be enduring trends and emerging patterns in how Japanese business networks (including *keiretsu*) currently perform.

From an overall assessment, we can offer two key observations. Firstly, there is evidence to suggest that the institutional embeddedness of Japanese business networks appears to become reinforced in response to overseas exposure. For example, both Toyota (tightly networked, resilient business performance) and Sony (loosely networked, erratic business performance) illustrate the enduring strength and potential for global competitive advantage of being institutionally embedded in the domestic (Japanese) environment. Secondly, there is evidence to suggest that selected Japanese business networks are becoming more horizontally integrated as they seek to stretch strategically and develop competitive positions in overseas markets by, for example, establishing international alliances (Nissan-Renault) or by making large-scale and/or high profile overseas acquisitions: Mitsui Sumitomo Insurance, Japan Tobacco, and Nikkei in the United Kingdom.

On this basis, we can suggest a number of topics relevant to future research in the combined fields of Japanese, Asian and international business. These include:

(i) As a fundamental research approach, looking beyond established 'either/or' analytic frameworks. As the chapters in this book amply demonstrate, relying on bi-polar conceptualisations such as 'A-Firm' versus 'J-Firm', 'collectivistic' versus 'individualistic' national cultures is unlikely to capture the richness evident in narratives where (for example) Taiwan-based businesses invest in Mainland China, Korean MNCs invest in Southeast Asia, or Chinese SOEs invest in Africa.

Correspondingly, we recommend adopting a 'networked' research approach whereby cross-cultural teams of researchers combine to bring etic and emic insights to the research questions being addressed.

(ii) Following from (i), a re-conceptualisation and reassessment of the boundaries commonly used to define and compare societies, organisations, cultures, and business networks. For example, working within established research paradigms for defining and comparing business networks in Japan, we propose analysing their overseas investments within a conceptualisation of 'horizontalisation' in order to challenge embedded notions of vertical integration when researching selected *keiretsu*. This could entail comparing examples of performance strength anchored in vertical embeddedness with those emerging patterns demonstrating a more overtly horizontal strategic orientation.

(iii) Following from (ii), a re-assessment of what constitutes 'business performance'. Without making detailed reference to 'profit' or 'growth', we considered (albeit, briefly) a number of possible performance measures such as: (network) resilience, agility, social impact, sustainability, and succession.

(iv) Following from (iii), an extension of research into models of family businesses in Asia, globally, and across business sectors: for example, by attempting to apply measures of business 'success' commonly applied to small and medium-sized enterprises (SMEs) in respect of MNCs and TNCs, and especially across Asia. (Our experience as MBA professors suggests that analytical frameworks standardised through large-scale reiteration tend to be applied to smaller scale contexts rather than vice-versa.)

A final comment: it is remarkable to witness how networks originally 'Made in Japan' and developed under successive adaptations—and impositions—of Western capitalism have enabled an 'island economy' supporting a (still, largely) 'closed' set of overlapping social and political systems to create a source of global business activity and enduring global influence. We hope that the discussion presented here, together with the proposed research topics, will encourage more in-depth research into the unfolding shape of business networks in Japan and Asia.

REFERENCES

Amman, B., & Jaussaud, J. (2012). In Fletcher, M.III, & P.W. von Staden (Eds.), *Family and non-family business resilience in an economic downturn* (pp. 203–223).

Amyx, J. (2002). In A. Bird (Ed.), *Japan federation of economic organizations* (pp. 217–222).

Aoki, K., & Lennerfors, T. T. (2013). The new, improved keiretsu. *Harvard Business Review*, 109–113.

Aoki, M., & Patrick, H. (Eds.), (1994). *The Japanese main bank system*. Oxford: Oxford University Press.

Backman, M. (1999). *Asian eclipse: Exposing the dark side of business in Asia*. Singapore: John Wiley.

Barley, S. R., & Tobert, P. S. (1997). Institutionalisation and structuration: Studying the links between action and institution. *Organization Studies*, *18*(1), 93–117.

Beck, U. (1992). *Risk society: Towards a new modernity*. Los Angeles: Sage.

Bird, A. (Ed.), (2002). *Encyclopedia of Japanese business and management*. New York: Routledge.

Bloomberg. (2011). *Why Lexus doesn't lead the pack in China*. Available at: www.bloomberg.com/bw/magazine/content/(11_14/b4222032202135.htm. Accessed 14.05.15.

Bloomberg. (2015a). *China's video-game smugglers are helping Sony's PS4*. Available at: www.bloomberg.com/news/articles/(20(15-04-(27/china-s-video-game-smugglers-are-helping-sony-s-ps4. Accessed 04.06.15.

Bloomberg. (2015b). *Cash-rich Japanese companies aren't investing at home: They aren't buying into Abenomics*. Available at: www.bloomberg.com/news/articles/2015-03-09/cash-rich-japanese-companies-aren-t-investing-at-home. Accessed 10.02.16.

Boisot, M., & Child, J. (1996). From fiefs to clans and network capitalism: Explaining China's economic order. *Administrative Science Quarterly*, *41*(4), 600–628.

Boyer, R. (2014). In S. Lechevalier (Ed.), *Foreword: From 'Japanophilia' to indifference? Three decades of research on contemporary, Japan* (pp. xiii–xxv).

Butler, R. (1991). *Designing organizations: A decision-making perspective*. London: Routledge.

Collinson, S. & Morgan, G. (Eds.), (2009). *Images of the multinational firm*. Chichester: Wiley.

Cukier, K. N. (2012). In J. Kingston (Ed.), *The economic fallout: Japan's post-3/11 challenges* (pp. 223–236).

Daft, R. L. (1989). *Organization theory and design* (2nd ed.). St. Paul, MN: West Publishing.

Debroux, P. (2003). In M. Warner (Ed.), *Culture and management in Japan* (pp. 99–114).

Debroux, P. (2014). In H. Hasegawa & C. Noronha (Eds.), *Corporate social responsibility and sustainable development in Asia* (pp. 139–158).

Deloitte. (2009). *A new era: Accelerating toward 2020—An automotive industry transformed* Available at: www2.deloitte.com/content/dam/Deloitte/pt/Documents/manufacturing/pt(en)_dc_accelaratingtoward2020_05112009.pdf. Accessed 05.02.16.

Dore, R., & Sako, M. (1998). *How the Japanese learn to work*. London: Routledge.

Dunning, J. H. (1977). In B. Ohlin, P.O. Hesselborn & P.M. Wijkman (Eds.), *Trade, location of economic activity and the MNDE: A search for an eclectic approach* (pp. 395–431).

Dunning, J. H. (1980). Explaining changing patterns of international production: In defense of the eclectic theory. *Oxford Bulletin of Economics and Statistics*, *41*(4), 269–295.

Dyer, J. H. (1996). How Chrysler created an American keiretsu. *Harvard Business Review, July–August*, 42–56.

Dzever, S., Jaussaud, J., & Androsso-O'Callaghan, B. (2008). *Evolving corporate structures and cultures in Asia: Impact of globalization*. New York: John Wiley.

Estévez-Abe, M. (2008). *Welfare and capitalism in Postwar Japan*. Cambridge: Cambridge University Press.

Fletcher, M., III, & von Staden, P. W. (Eds.), (2012). 'Lost Decade': causes, legacies, and issues of transformative change. In *Asia Pacific Business Review, 18*(2).

Ford, D., Gadde, L.-E., Håkansson, H., & Snehota, I. (2011). *Managing business relationships* (3rd ed.). New York: Wiley.

Gerlach, M. (1993). *Alliance capitalism: The social organization of Japanese business*. Berkley, CA: University of California Press.

Gerlach, M. (2002). In A. Bird (Ed.), *Zaibatsu* (pp. 479–482).

Giddens, A. (1991). *Modernity and self-identity*. Cambridge: Polity Press.

Giddens, A. (2006). *Sociology*. Cambridge: Polity Press.

Giddens, A., & Sutton, P.W. (2013). *Sociology* (7th ed.). Cambridge: Polity Press.
Gigerenzer, G. (2002). *Reckoning with risk: Learning to live with Uncertainty*. London: Penguin.
Håkansson, H., & Ford, D. (2002). How should companies interact in business networks? *Journal of Business Research*, *55*, 133–139.
Hall, P.A. & Soskice, D. (Eds.), (2001). *Varieties of capitalism: The institutional foundations of comparative advantage*. Oxford: Oxford University Press.
Hamilton, G. G. (Ed.), (1996). *Asian business networks*. Berlin: de Gruyter.
Hasegawa, H. & Noronha, C. (Eds.), (2009). *Asian business and management: Theory, practice and perspectives*. London: Palgrave Macmillan.
Hemmert, M. (2014). In H. Hasegawa & C. Noronha (Eds.), *The business system of Korea* (pp. 219–238).
Hemmert, M., & Jackson, K. (2016). Is there an East Asian model of MNC internationalization? A comparative analysis of Japanese and Korean firms. In R. Fitzgerald & C. Rowley (Eds.), *Internationalization patterns and the evolution of multinational companies: Comparing Japan, Korea, China and India* (pp. 567–594).
Huffman, J. L. (2010). *Japan in world history*. Oxford: Oxford University Press.
Ietto-Gillies, G. (2012). *Transnational corporations and international production: Concepts, theories and effects* (2nd ed.). Cheltenham: Edward Elgar.
Jackson, K. (2011). In C. Rowley & K. Jackson (Eds.), *Talent management* (pp. 206–213).
Jackson, K. (2013). In M. Warner (Ed.), *East Asian management: An overview* (pp. 49–63).
Jackson, K. & Debroux, P. (Eds.), (2009a). *Emerging patterns and enduring myths of innovation in Japan: Concluding thoughts* (pp. 461–467).
Jackson, K. & Debroux, P. (Eds.), (2009b). *Innovation in Japan: Emerging patterns. Enduring Myths*. London: Routledge.
Jackson, K. & Debroux, P. (Eds.), (2016). *Ageing societies: Comparing HRM responses in Germany and Japan. Management Revue 27 1/2*. Meringen: Rainer Hampp. Available at: www.management-revue.org/current.php.
Jackson, K., & Tomioka, M. (2004). *The changing face of Japanese management*. London: Routledge.
James, S. & Graham, R. J. (Eds.), (2014). *Major companies of Asia and Australasia*. Andover: Cengage.
Jandt, F. E. (2010). *An introduction to intercultural communication: Identities in a global community*. Thousand Oaks, CA: Sage.
Japan Times. (2005). *Foreign CEO signifies a more globalized Japan*. Available at: www.japantimes.co.jp/news/(2005/03/(10/business/foreign-ceo-signifies-a-more-globalized-japan/#.VaYjd3qD79B. Accessed 20.05.15.
Japan Times. (2015). *Toyota to build new plants in China, Mexico*. Available at: www.japantimes.co.jp/news/2015/04/03/business/corporate-business/toyota-build-new-plants-china-mexico/#.VZDF_XqD75Y. Accessed 16.06.15.
Johanson, J., & Vahlne, J. E. (1977). The internationalization process of the firm: A model of knowledge development and increasing foreign market commitments. *Journal of International Business Studies*, *8*(1), 23–32.
Kay, J. (1993). *Foundations of corporate success*. Oxford: Oxford University Press.
Lambourne, L. (2005). *Japonisme: Cultural crossings between Japan and the West*. London: Phaidon.
Lechevalier, S. (Ed.), (2014a). *The great transformation of Japanese capitalism*. Abingdon: Routledge.
Lechevalier, S. (Ed.), (2014b). *Is this the end of the J-model of the firm?* (pp. 56–72).
Lechevalier, S. (Ed.), (2014c). *Is Japanese capitalism still co-ordinated?* (pp. 73–85).
Liker, J. K. (2004). *The Toyota way*. New York: McGraw-Hill.
Lincoln, J. R., Kerbo, H., & Wittenhagen, E. (1995). Japanese companies in Germany: A study in cross-cultural management. *Journal of Industrial Relations*, *25*, 123–139.
Matsumoto, S. (2014). 海外企業買収　失敗の本質　戦略的アプローチ *[Japanese foreign acquisitions: Why do they fail?]*. Tokyo: Toyo Keizai.

McKinstry, A. (2002). In Bird, A. (Ed.), *Geography* (pp. 168–169).
Melin, L., Nordqvist, M., & Sharma, P. (2013). *The Sage handbook of family business*. London: Sage.
Merriam-Webster. (2015). *Capitalism. Merriam-Webster dictionary online*. Available at: www.merriam-webster.com/dictionary/capitalism. Accessed 15.09.15.
MIAC. (2016). *Statistics bureau, MIAC—Ministry of Internal Affairs and Communications. 2015. Statistics, Japan*Available at: www.stat.go.jp/data/nenkan/index1.htm. Accessed 18.01.16.
Nguyen, K., Okrend, M., & Tan, L. (2013). Are Chinese companies the next generation of multinational companies? Lenovo versus Sony in the global PC industry. *American International Journal of Contemporary Research*, *3*(2), 1–10.
Nikkei. (2015). Japanese companies' foreign acquisitions hit record 10tn Yen. *The Nikkei Asia Review, 10*.
Nikkei. (2016). *Mitsubishi heavy willing to build subs down under. The Nikkei Asia Review* Available at: http://asia.nikkei.com/Business/Companies/Mitsubishi-Heavy-willing-to-build-subs-Down-Under. Accessed 12.02.16.
Nissan Global. (2016). *Nissan Motor Corporation corporate information*. Available at: www.nissan-global.com/EN/COMPANY/PROFILE/ALLIANCE/RENAULT03. Accessed 05.02.16.
O'Neill, P. G. (1991). *Essential Kanji*. New York: Weatherhill.
Ohmae, K. (1982). *The mind of the strategist: The art of Japanese business*. New York: McGraw-Hill.
Ouchi, W. G. (1981). *Theory Z: How American management can meet the Japanese challenge*. Reading, MA: Addison Wesley.
Plath, D. (2002). In Bird, A. (Ed.), *Industrial groups* (pp. 190–193).
Porter, M. E., Takeuchi, H., & Sakakibara, M. (2000). *Can Japan compete?* Cambridge, MA: Perseus.
Redding, S. G. (1990). *The spirit of Chinese capitalism*. Berlin: Walter de Gruyter.
Redding, S. G. (2014). In H. Hasegawa & C. Noronha (Eds.), *The business systems of Asia* (pp. 15–35).
Reuters. (2014). *Toyota to miss China 2014 sales goal of over 1.1 million vehicles: Executives*. Available at: www.reuters.com/article/(2014/12/30/us-china-autos-toyota-idUSKBN0K806R20141230. Accessed 02.05.15.
Reuters. (2015). *Exclusive: Toyota ends freeze on expansion, looks at three new plants*. Available at: www.reuters.com/article/(2015/01/12/us-autoshow-toyota-idUSKBN0KL2EU20150112. Accessed 04.07.15.
Rudlin, P. (2002). In Bird, A. (Ed.), *General trading companies* (pp. 165–168).
Said, E. W. (1978). *Orientalism: Western conceptions of the orient*. Harmondsworth: Penguin.
Sako, M. (2006). *Shifting boundaries of the firm: Japanese Company-Japanese labour*. Oxford: Oxford University Press.
Sako, M., & Kohsakam, M. (2012). In C. Lane & G. Wood (Eds.), *Institutional change and organizational diversity in Japan* (pp. 132–157).
Senior, B., & Swailes, S. (2010). *Organizational change* (4th ed.). London: FT/Prentice Hall.
Smith, P. B., & Musumi, J. (1994). In D. Hickson (Ed.), *Japanese management: A sun rising in the west?* (pp. 117–157).
Staples, A. (2014). In H. Hasegawa & C. Noronha (Eds.), *Regionalism and production networks in Asia* (pp. 117–137).
STATISTA. (2015). *Leading automobile manufacturers worldwide in 2014, based on vehicle sales (in million units)*. Available at: www.statista.com/statistics/271608/. Accessed 18.01.16.
Stockwin, J. A. A. (2008). *Governing Japan: Divided politics in a resurgent economy*. Oxford: Blackwell.
Storz, C. (2009). In K. Jackson & P. Debroux (Eds.), *Innovation, institutions and entrepreneurs: The case of 'cool Japan'* (pp. 401–424).
Sueki, N. (2016). In K. Jackson & P. Debroux (Eds.), *Ageing society and evolving wage systems in Japan*. Available at: www.management-revue.org/current.php.

Sugimoto, Y. (2014). *An introduction to Japanese society*. Cambridge: Cambridge University Press.

Technobuffalo. (2015). *Sony considers exit from phone, TV markets to focus on Playstation*. Available at: www.technobuffalo.com/(2015/02/18/sony-considers-exit-from-phone-tv-markets-to-focus-on-playstation/. Accessed 02.07.15.

The Australian. (2015). Submarines bill falls $5 billion as nations compete. In *The Australian, 26th December*. Available at: www.theaustralian.com.au/national-affairs/defence/submarines-bill-falls-5bn-as-nations-compete/news-story/14113935b80fae5078f4506ff3624188. Accessed 25.12.15.

The Economist. (1999). *Restructuring Nissan: o-hayo gozaimasu, mon ami*. Available at: www.economist.com/node/325904. Accessed 05.02.16.

The Economist. (2009). *Keiretsu*. Available at: www.economist.com/node/14299720. Accessed 04.01.16.

Thompson, E. P. (1963). *The making of the English working class*. London: Random House.

Tiberghien, Y. (2014). In S. Lechevalier (Ed.), *Thirty years of neo-liberal reform in Japan* (pp. 26–55).

Toyota. (2015). *Financial Results FY 2015*. Available at: www.toyota-global.com/investors/financial_result. Accessed 03.05.15.

Trendforce. (2015). *Top ten smartphone vendors based on market share*. Available at: it.sohu.com/20150121n407947218.shtml. Accessed 12.06.15.

Tung, R., & Worm, W. (2001). Network capitalism: The role of human resources in penetrating the China market. *International Journal of Human Resource Management, 12*(44), 517–534.

UNCTAD. (2016). *United Nations Conference on Trade and Development (UNCTAD)—World Investment Report 2015*. Available at: unctad.org/en/Pages/DIAE/World%20Investment%20Report/Annex-Tables.aspx. Accessed 07.02.16.

Von Bertalanffy, L. (1968). *General system theory: Foundations, development, applications*. New York: Brazilier.

Walker, B. L. (2015). *A concise history of Japan*. Cambridge: Cambridge University Press.

Warner, M. (Ed.), (2003). *Culture and management in Asia*. London: Routledge.

Warner, M. (Ed.), (2011). *Confucian HRM in greater China: Theory and practice*. London: Routledge.

Warner, M. (Ed.), (2013). *Managing across diverse cultures: Issues and challenges in a changing globalized world*. Abingdon: Routledge.

Weber, M. (1978). *Economy and society*. Berkeley: University of California Press.

Whitley, D. (1990). Eastern Asian enterprise structures and comparative analysis of forms of business organizations. *Organisation Studies, 11*(1), 47–74.

Witt, M. (2014). In H. Hasegawa & C. Noronha (Eds.), *The business system of Japan* (pp. 61–78).

Woodford, M. (2013). *Exposure: From President to Whistleblower at Olympus: Silenced, threatened, time to fight back*. Harmondsworth: Portfolio Penguin.

Yonekawa, S. (Ed.), (1990). *General trading companies: A comparative and historical study*. Tokyo: United Nations University.

Yoshihara, K. (1982). *Sogo Shosha: The vanguard of the Japanese economy*. Tokyo: Oxford University Press.

Yoshimura, N., & Anderson, P. (1997). *Inside the Kaisha: Demystifying Japanese business behavior*. Cambridge, MA: Harvard Business School Press.

CHAPTER 8

Can Informal Networks Positively Influence Economic Growth and Development? The Case of South Korean Yongo Networks

K. Restel*, S. Horak†
*University of Duisburg-Essen, Duisburg, Germany
†St. John's University, New York, NY, USA

8.1 INTRODUCTION

Informal networks, a certain type of informal institution, are usually perceived as being counterproductive to the economic development of a nation. Even though the definition of informal institutions is elusive, it is usually understood to include values, norms of behavior, or ethics and morals. Informal networks, however, are often linked to phenomena such as corruption or Mafia-like clubs, and even considered a threat to the stability of political governance mechanisms in general (Helmke & Levitsky, 2004; Ledeneva, 2006), especially in environments in which formal institutions are nonexistent or ineffective (North, 1990; Peng, Pinkham, Sun, & Chen, 2009). Nee (1998, p. 86) notes that informal networks have tended to "act in the shadow of the state, often at odds with the goals formulated by rulers." Prominent examples of the negative influence that informal networks can exert on a country's economy are the Mafia in Italy or in Russia. In the former case, hierarchically strong organized networks, which had existed for 150 years, were constructed as a means to provide protection and trust in an area that was confronted with a lack of social trust due to centuries of colonization by hostile powers (Gambetta, 1993). Formal institutions (formal rules, laws, courts) more or less lost their state power monopoly to these subcultural protection networks, unable to control their constant disregard for formal rules, drug trade, prostitution, racketeering, and so on. Due to the state's inability to deal with these networks and their criminal activities, but also due to the distrust created by those networks for personal gain (who needs protection when everybody is trustworthy?) and

Business Networks in East Asian Capitalisms
http://dx.doi.org/10.1016/B978-0-08-100639-9.00008-6

corruption, the south of Italy in particular never really managed to keep up with the prospering north, where the Mafia had not gained much of a foothold (Putnam, Leonardi, & Nanetti, 1993). A further case of economic development constrained by informal institutions is the *Blat* networks in Russia, which functioned as a means to circumvent redistribution problems by the Communist state and provide help, where money had little meaning. Those circular connections facilitated certain goods that were state-owned, not the generation of new goods, and thus upheld the status quo (Ledeneva, 1998). However, after the Communist regime had been replaced with new formal institutions and money started to play a significant role in economic transactions, *Blat* became an outlet for corrupt exchanges and thus, harmed economic development (Ledeneva, 2008).

Economies in transition are especially prone to being affected negatively by informal networks as they are usually equipped with ineffective formal institutions and are unable to control them. An example of this is the extensive body of literature dealing with the negative influence of Chinese *Guanxi* networks (Fan, 2002; Gu, Hung, & Tse, 2008; Li, 2011). Further discussion of the negative and positive consequences of *Guanxi* networks may be found in Chapters 4 and 5. Whereas *guanxi* is an old Chinese traditional informal institution that helped to maintain the status quo, even when formal institutions were ineffective or lacked certain capacities by facilitating goods and trust for those who needed them, and functioned rather well even under the Communist system, disadvantages started to appear when formal institutions started to change towards stricter rule enforcement and greater stability. On the negative side, *Guanxi* networks became safe havens for corrupt exchanges made possible by an increasingly free economy, involving powerful government officials with little money facing rather powerless entrepreneurs with lots of money (Fan, 2002; Luo, 2008; Yang, 1994). *Guanxi* was also attributed positive features, especially during China's economic transition (Taube, 2013; Taube & Schramm, 2003), by enabling trust to become essential to first economic business transactions when formal rules and regulations, ensuring the reciprocity of such transactions, had not yet been established.

Likewise, the informal *Yongo* networks (to be defined later) in Korea seem not to have had a negative effect on the country's rapid economic development, but rather contributed to it, compared with informal networks that hampered economic growth and effectively harmed a country's industry, like the Mafia (Ledeneva, 2008). Having experienced extreme poverty in the 1950s, Korea is today an economic powerhouse and an established democracy with effective and fully functioning formal institutions.

Whereas research has frequently pointed out the negative aspects of informal social networks, its positive aspects have often been ignored. This chapter thus suggests adopting a rather unconventional viewpoint and discussing the possible positive contributions of informal networks to economic development. We argue that informal coordination can actually have positive outcomes and can be beneficial for an economy. By introducing the Korean form of an informal social network to the literature, we outline the characteristics and antecedents of Korean *Yongo* networks that are assumed to have exerted a positive influence on Korea's economic rise.

8.2 THEORETICAL ANCHORAGE

8.2.1 The Washington Consensus and Its Discontents

To ignite economic development, certain measures have been assumed to be helpful. Those measures are, to a great extent, based on the so-called Washington Consensus, propagandizing a set of economic policy prescriptions issued by institutions based in Washington, such as the IMF and the World Bank. However, these policies have not always been successful or positively received (Stiglitz, 2002).

The Consensus reflects the conventional way in which Western international financial institutions have viewed developing countries and the way in which they need to be structured to achieve economic growth and development. The cure was perceived as consisting of neoliberal economic measures, such as privatization, the abolishment of subsidies, deregulation, and the removal of trade barriers, as well as the country's integration into the world economy. While those theoretical cure-alls were more or less successfully applied in the cases of Mexico and Poland, they yielded rather different results in other countries. These policies failed to take root in most of Latin America and Asia (Brown, 2009; Hutchison & Noy, 2003) and even harmed, rather than backed a sound recovery due to their neglect of the sociocultural structures and peculiarities of the respective country, for example South Korea (Bustello, 1998; Feldstein, 1998; IMF, 2003). These mixed results of the policies applied led to the question of why, on the one hand, they contributed to economic growth and development in some countries, but on the other hand, they failed to do so in others. In the same vein, it can be asked why certain countries, starting out the same and under similar circumstances, achieve rather mixed results.

The liberal economic policies represented by the Washington Consensus are, as argued by Fukuyama (2002), imperfect due to their disregard for the country-specific characteristics of the social capital, generated by informal institutions, which play a crucial role in the successful implementation of such measures. Not just the quality of the existing formal institutions (eg, rule of law, law enforcement, commercial courts) but even more, the nature of the hidden informal institutions and their relationship with each other need to be considered to be able to create effective economic policies (Fukuyama & Marwah, 2000; North, 1990). In this context, sociocultural factors, differing from country to country, come into focus, because social capital and trust are considered crucial factors for the composition, acceptance, and legitimization of institutions (Fukuyama, 2002; Putnam et al., 1993). Still, those factors have been largely neglected or not implicitly treated in mainstream economic theory (Coleman, 1988; Jones, 2006). Fukuyama, amongst others, points out in an early work the importance of trust as a feature of successful formal institutions and thus, the creation of wealth (Bourdieu, 1986; Coleman, 1988; Field, 2003; Fukuyama, 1995; Putnam et al., 1993; Woolcock, 1998). Especially in a society such as South Korea, which is considered low in general trust, informal institutions are an important factor for generating trust in social and economic exchanges (Fukuyama, 2000).

8.2.2 Economic Theory and Social Relations

Trust, as the precondition for economic exchange and the underlying social transactions based on reciprocity, has long been underrated in economic theory. The rationale of social relationships was regarded under the premises of a simple if-then logic by neoclassical thought: if a relationship maximizes profitability, then it will be upheld; otherwise, it will be discarded. It was only later that the influence of social relations was considered to be of interest, and new institutional economics provided an access opportunity for social and cultural phenomena into economic theory (Keefer & Knack, 2003). There is serious doubt about the universality of the explanatory power of rational choice theory, since rationality and human behavior are mainly influenced by network-related factors and thus are to be understood as culture-dependent (Fukuyama, 1995). Transaction cost economics proposes to regard economic actors as being only bounded rational and their behavior presumably moderated by the social structure in which they are embedded. Further, different types of economic transactions require different governance models. Proposed by Williamson (1996), different degrees of asset specificity require different monitoring and sanctioning systems for free riders and opportunistic behavior. Compared with formal (bureaucratic) control, informal networks can monitor and sanction free riding more effectively and more efficiently, that is, at a lower cost.

The efficiency and effectiveness of economic transactions have been studied within informal social networks. Compared with transactions with network external members, internal coordination and conciliation, informal peer pressure, and collective punishment are mechanisms to keep transaction costs low within an informal network (Buchanan, 1965; Sandler & Tschirhart, 1997). Once the network members are known, that is, once they possess a reputation for being norm abiding and reliable, the efficiency and effectiveness of transactions strengthen (Gulati, 1995; Li, 2007; Uzzi, 1997). Thus, the adherence to informal network norms becomes a self-enforcing mechanism to the benefit of low-cost transactions with network members in the future (Davis, 1995; Taube, 2013). Furthermore, to trigger transactions with thus far mutually unknown actors, research has pointed out that the general willingness to engage in a relationship at all is affected by social empathy, which usually occurs among people who share certain social traits and characteristics (Ibarra, 1992; Thomas, 1990). It is assumed that social empathy can happen without the individual knowing of the other individual's characteristics, as long as they belong to the same group or network (Farh, Tsui, Xin, & Cheng, 1998). If we take the Italian Mafia for example, simply belonging to this group implies to other individuals in this group that one can be trusted, since the newcomer is anticipated to have the same origin, to share the same values, and to abide by the same rules.

8.2.3 The Dark Side of Informal Networks

According to North, informal institutions are "humanly devised constraints that structure political and social interaction" (North, 1991, p. 97) or, in the case of economic exchange, they act as facilitators of the latter, as well as reducing transaction costs. Informal institutions are, contrary to formal institutions, mostly unwritten, and they are constructed, shared, and enforced outside of official channels. Many "rules of the game," which structure politics as well as economic interactions, are in fact, informal. The performance of formal institutions is crucially shaped and influenced by informal structures in an important and partially unpredictable way. The term informal institution has been applied in the past to Chinese *Guanxi* by, for instance, Wang (2000), who uses the expression for the phenomenon of social networks. As opposed to formal institutions, which are able to change rather rapidly, informal institutions are deeply shaped by cultural factors and are slow, if not impossible to change, since they are deeply embedded into a society's culture. Thus, newly established formal institutions can be influenced by informal ones long after they have been initiated. According to Helmke and Levitsky (2004), informal institutions can act *complementarily* to effective formal institutions when they pursue the same goals and can be *accommodating* when they do not. The latter indicates that official rules, made and enforced by formal institutions, are not violated but only slightly bent. However, when formal institutions are ineffective and unable to enforce fully the rules that they have created, informal rules and regulations can act substitutively when both have the same goals, but compete when they do not (Helmke & Levitsky, 2004).

Social relations can generate the background for cooperation, which leads to the combination and multiplication of individual resources, including the provision of information, a guarantee of trustworthiness, as well as sanctioning mechanisms (Lin, 2001, p. 18f). This safety background, however, also gives rise to the opportunity for corruption.

"Networks and associated norms of reciprocity are generally good for those inside the network, but the external effects of social capital are by no means always positive" (Putnam, 2000, pp. 21–22). Thus, networks cannot only produce good outcomes, but can also promote antisocial outcomes as well as economic inefficiencies. The normative systems developed and established by social networks are often not in compliance with the existing formal rules. A prominent case of this is the Italian Mafia (Della Porta & Vannucci, 1999, p. 255). On the other hand, especially societies with ineffective formal institutions face complications as a result of informal networks challenging their validity (Fan, 2007; Gu et al., 2008; Larsson, 2006; Li, 2011; Taube, 2013). Given the negative effect that informal institutions can have once the quality of the existing formal institutions differs, our first proposition is as follows.

Proposition 1 *Depending on the quality of formal institutions, informal networks can support corruption.*

8.2.4 The Case of Korea

Korea, now belonging to the Top 15 economically strongest countries (IMF, 2012), provides an excellent example of speedy economic development. Having suffered from heavy deprivation due to the Japanese occupation and the aftermath of a devastating war, Korea managed to develop rapidly and become an economic powerhouse within only 40 years. Korean firms such as Samsung, Hyundai, and LG belong to the global industry leaders today and represent benchmarks in segments such as semiconductor manufacturing, entertainment electronics, communication technology, automobile production, and so on.

Korea is now furthermore a stable democracy with fully functioning effective formal institutions (Agrast, Botero, Martinez, Ponce, & Pratt, 2013; EIU, 2010). The question arising in this context is how Korea was able to manage such an ascent in such a short time. Conventional arguments have put forward the role of a strong state (policy level), guided economic policies (investments), large firms (*Chaebol*) executing industrial development policies (business level), and export orientation (trade policy). However, the mechanisms orchestrating this mix of initiatives remain hidden. Still, as argued before, there have been several country cases in which effective formal institutions, as well as sensible economic policies were unable to achieve economic success, such as the case of Italy, so why was Korea successful? We will attempt to answer this question in the following by bringing the issue of Korean informal networks into the equation, addressing a third dimension, arguably an important factor in Korea's development (Lew, 2013).

8.2.5 Yongo: Informal Relations in Korea

Yongo (연고, sometimes referred to as *Yeon-gyeol*, *Yŏn'gyŏl*, or *Yŏn'go*), though considered the missing link in explaining Korea's rapid economic development (Lew, 2013), has so far been under-researched, especially when compared with the large number of studies conducted in the field of *Guanxi*. Lee defines *Yongo* "as a mutual patron-client network with a strong paternalistic tone" (Lee, 2000a, 2000b, p. 369). A *Yongo* network can serve its members as an informal platform for collective rent seeking. Horak (2014) describes *Yongo* as "the term for personal relationships in Korea that are attached to affiliation to an informally organized group. (...) *Yongo* derives its main cohesion power from strong particularistic ties, based on kin, educational institution (school/university), and region" (Horak, 2014, p. 87). The syllable "yon" can be translated into "tie," as it incorporates the concept of bonds by *affection* between individuals. The syllable "go" stands for the reason behind this particular bond, which is usually due to shared backgrounds in terms of kinship or blood ties (in Korean: *hyulyon*, 혈연), regional origin (*jiyon*, 지연), and alma mater or education-based ties (*hakyon*, 학연). All of these three tie bases are the foundation for a lifelong relationship and are predefined by birth in a certain region, to a certain family, and attending school in that region. Hence, they are cause-based. However, as students become more mobile and opt for universities outside their region, ties these days have become centered more on universities than on schools. *Yongo* is a natural, conventional, lifelong relationship and in principle, not purpose-based. Every Korean is a member of a *Yongo* network without much of a choice, which is sometimes perceived as a burden (Horak, 2014). *Yongo*-based ties, especially *hakyon* ties, are maintained for life. Those who share *Yongo* proactively help and support each other; graduates from schools and universities meet on a regular basis informally, sharing the costs of anniversary or wedding gifts, or obituaries, and so on. *Yongo* relations are immutable and irreversible. *Yongo* has the nature of an emotional pseudo-familistic tie. Whereas within a *Yongo* camp (based on *hakyon*, *jiyong*, or *hyulyon*) proactive cooperation, flexibility, mutual understanding, tolerance, loyalty, or trust prevails, relationships with a different *Yongo* camp are rather egalitarian to hostile. Scholars note that "outside the boundary, on the contrary, people are treated as "nonpersons" and there can be discrimination, and even hostility" (Kim, 2000, p. 179). Table 8.1 summarizes the main characteristics of *Yongo*.

Yongo-based fractionism in the Korean society is not a recent development. The earliest account of those networks was given as far back as the times of the Jeoson Dynasty (ca. 1392–1910), when the ruling *Yangban* class (elites promoting Confucian values as governance and societal ideal) "grouped itself into mutually exclusive factions and clans that engaged in fierce rivalry. The fragmentation of the Yanban society along the lines of scholarly association, kinship and region gave rise to purges and factional strife" (Sik, 2005, p. 84).

These phenomena can, at times, extend beyond institutional rules and formal instructions. However, these connections pose a hurdle to those who are not a member of the specific network (Yee, 2000). *Yongo* networks are rather closed and exclusive. Due to its preset nature, one cannot become a

Table 8.1 Summary—*Yongo*

Characteristics of *Yongo*
• Given by birth, partly preset (ie, exception today: *hakyon* ties)
• Immutable and irreversible
• Every Korean is a member of a *Yongo* network ("network society")
• Cannot be established, "it exists" (ie, cause-based)
• Strongly homogeneous and exclusive
• *Yongo* networks are often (not always) hostile towards each other and in competition
• Lifelong lasting relationships
• Not purpose-based, it is a conventional social relationship in Korea
• Sometimes perceived as a burden
• Used for (examples): job acquisition, career progression, information gathering, business-to-business, and business-to-government relations, etc.

member of a certain *Yongo* network. Certainly, one can establish deep and trustful relationships with others and with groups, but this would be rather a "normal" social network (in Korean named "*Inmaek*" [인맥]) and not *Yongo*. Whereas most scholars describe Korea as a typical collective society in which low general trust prevails between individuals, we suggest complementing this view by describing Korea as a relation-based or network society (Kim, 2000) consisting of different (large) *Yongo* circles in which a high level of trust prevails.

Yongo patterns are reflected in contemporary politics and the business world in Korea. For example, *Jiyon*- based (regional origin) ties are widespread in politics. Voting, for instance, is strongly influence by the regional origin of the candidate. "(...) many Koreans will vote for a political candidate, even if the person is less qualified, just because he or she attended the same school or came from the same region of the country (...)" (Shim, Kim, & Martin, 2008, p. 85). Of the ten presidents that Korea had between 1948 and 2013, 50% were born in the same region, the Kyungsang province (Table 8.2).

Table 8.2 Birth places of Korean presidents, 1948–2013

Name	Tenure	Place of birth (city, province)
Rhee, Syng-man	1948–1960	Pyongsan, Hwanghae
Yun, Bo-seon	1960–1962	Asan, Chungcheongnamdo
Park, Chung-hee	1963–1979	Kumi, *Kyungsang*
Choi, Kyu-ha	1979–1980	Wonju, Kangwon
Chun, Doo-hwan	1980–1988	Hapchon, *Kyungsang*
Roh, Tae-woo	1988–1993	Taegu, *Kyungsang*
Kim, Young-sam	1993–1998	Koje, *Kyungsang*
Kim, Dae-jung	1998–2003	Mokpo, Cholla
Roh, Moo-hyun	2003–2008	Gimhae, *Kyungsang*
Lee, Myung-bak[a]	2008–2013	Osaka (Japan)

[a]Succeeded by Park, Geun-hye (president elect as of Dec. 19, 2012), daughter of Park, Chung-hee (born in Kumi, Kyungsang).

Data from Horak, S. (2015). The multi-dimensional influence of informal social networks in Korea—Propositions for future management research. *Journal of General Management, 40*(2), 52; data derived from Encyclopaedia Britannica. (2012). Syngman Rhee, Quelle: http://www.britannica.com/ EBchecked/topic/501064/Syngman-Rhee, Yun Po Son, Quelle: http://www.britannica.com/EBchecked/topic/654928/Yun-Po-Son, Park Chung Hee, Quelle: http://www.britannica.com/EBchecked/topic/444035/Park-Chung-Hee, Choi Kyu Hah, Quelle: http://www.britannica.com/EBchecked/topic/113970/Choi-Kyu-Hah, Chun Doo Hwan, Quelle: http://www.britannica.com/EBchecked/topic/116919/Chun-Doo-Hwan, Roh Tae Woo, Quelle: http://www.britannica.com/EBchecked/topic/506868/Roh-Tae-Woo, Kim Young Sam, Quelle: http://www.britannica.com/EBchecked/topic/317907/Kim-Young-Sam, Kim Dae Jung, Quelle: http://www.britannica.com/EBchecked/topic/317874/Kim-Dae-Jung, Roh Moo Hyun, Quelle: http://www.britannica.com/EBchecked/topic/862048/Roh-Moo-Hyun, Lee Myung-Bak, Quelle: http://www.britannica.com/EBchecked/topic/1271389/Lee-Myung-Bak. Accessed 16.06.12.

Further, according to a study by Kim (2007), the vast majority (approx. 30%) of *Chaebol* founders, business executives, and government ministers were born in the same region, again, the Kyungsang province, in the southeast of Korea (Table 8.3).

Alma mater or education-based ties (*hakyon*) are said to represent the strongest *Yongo*-based tie in Korea. Today, Korea has 370 official higher education providers, including 179 private universities and 43 national universities (QS World University Rankings, 2015). However, selecting a university in which to study means at the same time selecting a community that can potentially provide a certain quality of *Yongo*, depending on the university's alumni base. A degree from prestigious universities could result in being on track for upward mobility through educational status and class by belonging to the "right" *Yongo* community. Prestigious universities with their alumni linkage or *hakyon* are better able to put their graduates in good positions. In fact, graduates from prestigious universities have better chances of being recruited by top firms, compared with graduates from the same cohort of other universities (Lee & Brinton, 1996a, 1996b). The most prestigious universities in Korea, and the ones providing potential access to high-quality *Yongo* networks, are Seoul National University, Korea University, and Yonsei University (commonly referred to as the SKY universities), with Seoul National University being the most preferred one. Unsurprisingly, the majority of the Korean business and political elite graduated from Seoul National University. According to Kim (2007), approximately 50% of ministers and senior officials, and more than 30% of business executives and national assembly members possess a degree acquired at Seoul National University (Table 8.4).

Family relations, unsurprisingly, represent an important pillar of *Yongo*, and extended Korean families can be quite large. One may assume that the *Chaebol* are in competition with each other, which in fact they are, but many of them are also connected with each other through marriage linkage. These marriage ties are a key mechanism to create ties among elites. Marriage should consolidate family ties and strengthen the financial and political situation. According to Kim (2007), 23 *Chaebol* families of the 30 largest *Chaebol* in Korea are connected with each other through intermarriage ties among the leader's family. Through cooptation in business, interests can be efficiently aligned.

Moreover, there is a high degree of career mobility from senior positions in the government towards private firms. The opposite direction is rather unpopular. As Kim notes: "The business community actively looks

Table 8.3 Regional backgrounds of *Chaebol* founders, business executives, and government ministers (1991/1995)

Region	*Chaebol* founders (in %)	Business executives (in %)	Government ministers (in %)
Seoul	7.2	34.4	15.9
Kyonggi	8.7	7.0	44.3
Kyungsang	31.7	34.6	32.0
Cholla	10.9	6.2	15.9
Chungchong	9.8	8.0	23.2
Kangwon	3.3	3.5	1.5
Others	28.4	6.3	7.2
Total number	92 (100)	96 (100)	60 (100)

Note: Circle: Kyungsang province.

Data from Kim, Y.T. (2007). Korean elites: Social networks and power. *Journal of Contemporary Asia*, *37*(1), 31.

Table 8.4 Alma mater of the *Chaebol* executives and government officials (1991/1996)

	Seoul National University (in %)	Korea University (in %)	Yonsei University (in %)	Military Academy (in %)	Other (in %)	Total (in %)
Executive (*Chaebol*)	37.2	8.9	10.9	1.4	41.6	100
Minister	52.5	7.3	–	10.1	30.1	
Senior official	53.8	13.4	6.7	–	26.1	
National Assembly member	32.1	10.3	3.0	3.6	51.0	

Data from Kim, Y.T. (2007). Korean elites: Social networks and power. *Journal of Contemporary Asia*, *37*(1), 31.

for retiring bureaucrats who have close personal connections within the relevant ministries" (Kim, 2007, p. 27). After retirement from government jobs, bureaucrats-turned-managers often receive positions as executives or affiliated consultants within business groups. This ensures a stronger voice towards the government to lobby for a business's interest whenever necessary.

As mentioned previously, Fukuyama (1995) describes Korea as being principally a low-trust society, which is supported by several scholars (Kim & Son, 1998; Lee, 2000a, 2000b); however, recent studies, such as the World Value Survey (2000) and the Korean General Social Surveys (Seok & Kim, 2004), suggest otherwise. In particular, Lee (2000a, 2000b) predicts that even though institutional trust is low, interpersonal trust facilitated by *Yongo* networks is exceptionally high. Further, interpersonal trust in Korea is said not to be lower than that in Japan or Denmark, for example (Yoo & Kim, 2002). The idea of regarding Korea per se as a low-trust society might be valid based on certain parameters of assessment applied. Ad hoc interpretation, however, can be misleading, as these parameters are likely not to capture the existence and distribution of networks and the level of network cohesion (through high trust) within *Yongo* networks on an aggregate level, and that could turn out to be exceptionally high in the case of Korea, as we speculate. Hence, we suggest the following propositions.

Proposition 2 *Cohesion within separate informal social networks (Yongo) is highly pronounced in Korea.*

Proposition 3 *Competition among separate Yongo networks spurred efforts to outperform the respective other network.*

Proposition 4 *Yongo served as an accelerator for efficient economic coordination and transactions.*

8.3 DISCUSSION

Many facets of the "miracle on the Han River" have been studied extensively (for an overview, see eg, Lew, 2013), but thus far the influence of informal networks has been largely neglected. However, Lew (2013) argues that those networks are vital for understanding not only the Korean society, but also its successful economic development. Certainly, its success can be partly explained by the favorable interplay of market forces, as well as strategic government intervention by means of well-calculated market-friendly policies; however, similar industrial policies, when applied to other countries, did not produce the same results (Lew, 2013). *Yongo* not only keeps the transaction costs at bay, but also contributes to firm-internal group cohesion and the free flow of information, as well as hedging firm-external relations.

Especially the ability to facilitate social cohesion and resulting trust is one of the most important aspects of *Yongo* networks. Even though networks may act in a hostile manner towards each other, the overall result is not destructive, but may rather be performance-oriented, as hostile networks compete to outperform each other, as proposed.

If countries with strong informal institutions are able to attain higher levels of economic development than those with weak ones (Williamson, 2009), it is thus appropriate to suggest that informal networks can contribute positively to the economic progress within a nation (Acemoglu & Johnson, 2005; Anderson & Hill, 1979; Benson, 1989; Pejovich, 2003).

This can also be partly explained by means of the framework suggested by Helmke and Levitsky (2004). For instance, in Korea's case, effective formal institutions meet informal institutions, which pursue the same goals and (unintentionally) support each other, thus generating a fruitful, safe environment for economic transactions with reduced costs. It is this interplay between informal and formal institutions that presumably helped to foster Korea's vast economic success. Lew (2013) mentions that in the case of Korea, a strong society is paired with a strong state. However, when we observe Korea's economic development, a strong connection between politics and *Chaebol* can be observed. When this thinking is applied to the model of Helmke and Levitsky (2004), it can thus be assumed that Korean informal institutions act complementarily to the formal institutions, pursuing the same goals, and consequently generate an outcome that results in economic progress.

When discussing informal institutions, the issue of culture also emerges (Tabellini, 2007; Williamson & Kerekes, 2008). In Korea's case, we are faced with a culture shaped by Confucian values, laying strong emphasis on hard work, education, and in principle, respect and obedience towards formal rules and regulations. However, when we focus our attention on China and its well-researched social institution of *Guanxi*, a different institutional interplay presents itself. In this case, ineffective, corrupt institutions with weak rules of law pair with strong competing informal institutions once used to generate interpersonal trust, as well as to distribute goods in a way in which the state was unable to, thus upholding certain stability. However, China is striving for stronger, more effective formal institutions to promote business, not only nationally, but internationally and is now struggling to transition to this desired state, as competing informal networks are trying to sabotage this development, as it is not congruent with their goals. It might be suggested that not only institutional effectiveness, but also stability may be an explanatory variable. In Eastern Europe, for example, the economic shock of a free market economy was combined with an abrupt break from communist formal institutions, whereas China was faced only with an economic shock and Korea with none of the above. It can thus be assumed that the positive influence of informal networks stands in strong connection to the nature of the formal institutions that they encounter as well as their stability.

8.4 CONCLUSION

When regarding the mixed outcomes of conventional industrial policies, such as those proposed by the Washington Consensus, several country cases prove that one size does not fit all. We thus propose the idea that industrial policies are not sufficient to explain economic success. Rather more informal institutions need to be taken into account to make formal policies effective in practice. In more detail, by using the case of Korea, we suggest that indigenous informal networks served as a platform to orchestrate a mix of political and economic initiatives in an informal and efficient way. We consider it important to understand this "platform" correctly. Further, as part of it, the way in which trust measures are currently defined may not reflect the diverse forms of trust precisely. Instead of regarding Korea as a low-trust society, we suggest shifting the focus to the group, instead of the individual level. This view proposes considering Korea as ranking high in group social cohesion, in which group-based trust is highly pronounced. However, the dark side of informal institutions cannot be left unmentioned. Exploiting informal institutions in a corrupt way may heavily depend on the quality and effectiveness of the existing formal institutions. What we mean to indicate here is that well-established rules of the game increase the costs of rent-seeking behavior as opposed to less stable environments. In Korea's case, successful economic development was possible because of a perfect interplay between informal networks and stable formal institutions striving for the same goal, thus greatly diminishing the negative influences of rent-seeking activities.

REFERENCES

Acemoglu, D., & Johnson, S. (2005). Unbundling institutions. *Journal of Political Economy*, *113*(5), 949–995.

Agrast, M., Botero, J., Martinez, J., Ponce, A., & Pratt, C. (2013). *World Justice Project (WJP) Rule of Law Index 2012–2013*. Washington, DC: The World Justice Project.

Anderson, T., & Hill, P. J. (1979). An American experiment in anarcho-capitalism: The not so wild, wild west. *Journal of Liberation Studies*, *3*(1), 9–29.

Benson, B. (1989). The spontaneous evolution of commercial law. *Southern Economic Journal, 55*(3), 644–661.
Bourdieu, P. (1986). The forms of capital. In J. Richardson (Ed.), *The Handbook of Theory and Research for the Sociology of Education* (pp. 241–258). New York: Greenwood.
Brown, C. (2009). Democracy's friend or Foe? The effects of recent IMF conditional lending in latin America. *International Political Science Review, 30*(4), 431–457.
Buchanan, J. M. (1965). An economic theory of clubs. *Economica, 32*, 1–14.
Bustello, P. (1998). The East Asian financial crisis: An analytical survey. ICEI Working Papers No. 10, Madrid: Complutense University of Madrid.
Coleman, J. S. (1988). Social capital in the creation of human capital. *American Journal of Sociology, 94*, 95–120.
Davis, H. (1995). Interpreting guanxi: The role of personal connections in a high context transitional economy. In H. Davies (Ed.), *China business: Context and issues* (pp. 155–169). Hong Kong: Longman.
Della Porta, D., & Vanucci, A. (1999). *Corrupt exchanges: Actors, resources and mechanisms of political corruption*. New York: de Gruyter.
EIU (Economist Intelligence Unit). (2010). *Democracy index 2010*. London: The Economist.
Fan, Y. (2002). Questioning guanxi: Definition, classification and implications. *International Business Review, 11*(5), 543–561.
Fan, Y. (2007). Guanxi's consequences: Personal gains at social cost. *Journal of Business Ethics, 38*(4), 371–380.
Farh, J., Tsui, A., Xin, K., & Cheng, B. (1998). The influence of relational demography and guanxi: The Chinese case. *Organization Science, 9*(4), 471–488.
Feldstein, M. (1998). Refocusing the IMF. *Foreign Affairs*, 77(2), 20–33.
Field, J. (2003). *Social capital*. New York: Routledge.
Fukuyama, F. (1995). *Trust: The social virtues and the creation of prosperity*. New York: The Free Press.
Fukuyama, F. (2000). Asian values, Korean values, and democratic consolidation. In L. Diamond & D. Chull Shin (Eds.), *Institutional reform and democratic consolidation in Korea* (pp. 305–334). Stanford, CA: Hoover Institution Press.
Fukuyama, F. (2002). Social capital and development: The coming agenda. *SAIS Review, XXI*(1), 23–37.
Fukuyama, F., & Marwah, S. (2000). Dimensions of development: Comparing East Asia and Latin America. *Journal of Democracy, 11*(4), 80–94.
Gambetta, D. (1993). *The Sicilian mafia: The business of private protection*. Cambridge: Harvard University Press.
Gu, F. F., Hung, K., & Tse, D. K. (2008). When does guanxi matter? Issues of capitalization and its dark sides. *Journal of Marketing*, 72(4), 12–28.
Gulati, R. (1995). Does familiarity breed trust? The implications of repeated ties for contractual choice in alliances. *Academy of Management Journal, 38*(1), 85–112.
Helmke, G., & Levitsky, S. (2004). Informal institutions and comparative politics: A research agenda. *Perspectives on Politics, 2*(4), 725–740.
Horak, S. (2014). Antecedents and characteristics of informal relation-based networks in Korea: Yongo, Yonjul and Inmaek. *Asia Pacific Business Review, 20*(1), 78–108.
Hutchison, M. M., & Noy, I. (2003). Macroeconomic effects of IMF-sponsored programs in Latin America: Output costs, program recidivism and the vicious cycle of failed stabilizations. *Journal of International Money and Finance, 22*(7), 991–1014.
Ibarra, H. (1992). Homophily and differential returns: Sex differences in network structure and access in an advertising firm. *Administrative Science Quarterly, 37*(3), 422.
IMF (International Monetary Fund). (2003). The IMF and recent capital account crisis—Indonesia, Korea, Brazil. Evaluation Report, Independent Evaluation Office. Washington, DC.

IMF (International Monetary Fund). (2012). World Economic Outlook Database, online, available at: http://www.imf.org/external/pubs/ft/weo/2012/01/weodata/download.aspx. Accessed 01.10.12.
Jones, E. L. (2006). *Cultures merging: A historical and economic critique of culture*. New Jersey: Princeton University Press.
Keefer, P., & Knack, S. (2003). Social capital, social norms and the New Institutional Economics. In C. Menard & M. M. Shirley (Eds.), *Handbook of New Institutional Economics* (pp. 701–726). Berlin, Heidelberg: Springer.
Kim, Y.-H. (2000). Emergence of the network society: Trends, new challenges, and an implication for network capitalism. *Korea Journal, 40*(3), 161–184.
Kim, Y. T. (2007). Korean elites: Social networks and power. *Journal of Contemporary Asia, 37*(1), 19–37.
Kim, Y., & Son, J. (1998). Trust, cooperation, and social risk: A cross-cultural comparison. *Korea Journal, 38*(1), 131–153.
Larsson, T. (2006). Reform, corruption, and growth: Why corruption is more devastating in Russia than in China. *Communist and Post-Communist Studies, 39*(2), 265–281.
Ledeneva, A. V. (1998). *Russia's economy of favours—Blat*. Cambridge: Networking and Informal Exchange.
Ledeneva, A. V. (2006). *How Russia really works: The informal practices that shaped post-Soviet politics and business*. Ithaca: Cornell University Press.
Ledeneva, A. V. (2008). Blat and Guanxi: Comparative analysis of informal practices in Russia and China. *Comparative Studies in Society and History, 50*(1), 118–141.
Lee, J. (2000a). Risk, trust, and externalities: A case of Korean civil society. *Sa-hoi Kwa-hak (Social Science), 39*(2), 97–135.
Lee, S. (2000b). Trust and civic participation in Korea. *International Studies Review, 3*(2), 59–77.
Lee, S., & Brinton, M. C. (1996a). Elite education and social capital: The case of South Korea. *Sociology of Education, 69*(3), 177–192.
Lee, S., & Brinton, M. C. (1996b). Elite education and social capital: The case of South Korea. *Sociology of Education, 89*, 180–183.
Lew, S.-C. (2013). *The Korean economic development path—Confucian tradition, affective network*. New York: Palgrave Macmillan.
Li, P. P. (2007). Social tie, social capital, and social behavior: Toward an integrative model of informal exchange. *Asia Pacific Journal of Management, 24*(2), 227–246.
Li, L. (2011). Performing Bribery in China: Guanxi-practice, corruption with a human face. *Journal of Contemporary China, 20*(68), 1–20.
Lin, N. (2001). *Social capital: A theory of social structure and action*. Cambridge: Cambridge University Press.
Luo, Y. (2008). The changing Chinese culture and business behavior: The perspective of intertwinement between guanxi and corruption. *International Business Review, 17*(2), 188–193.
Nee, V. (1998). Norms and networks in economic and organizational performance. *American Economic Review, 88*(2), 85–89.
North, D. C. (1990). *Institutions, institutional change and economic performance*. Cambridge: Cambridge University Press.
North, D. C. (1991). Institutions. *Journal of Economic Perspectives, 5*(1), 97–112.
Pejovich, S. (2003). Understanding the transaction costs of transition: It's the culture, stupid. *The Review of Austrian Economics, 16*(4), 347–361.
Peng, M. W., Pinkham, B., Sun, S. L., & Chen, H. (2009). The institution-based view as a third leg for a strategy tripod. *Academy of Management Perspectives, 23*(4), 63–81.
Putnam, R. D. (2000). *Bowling alone: The collapse and revival of American community*. New York: Simon & Schuster.
Putnam, R. D., Leonardi, R., & Nanetti, R. Y. (1993). *Making democracy work: Civic traditions in modern Italy*. Princeton, New Jersey: Princeton University Press.

QS World University Rankings. (2015): Country guides—Study in South Korea, source: http://www.topuniversities.com/where-to-study/asia/south-korea/guide. Accessed 15.08.15.

Sandler, T., & Tschirhart, J. (1997). Club theory: Thirty years later. *Public Choice*, *93*, 335–355.

Seok, H., & Kim, S. (2004). Korea general social survey. The data are available at the Korean Social Science Data Archive, Korean Social Science Library (http://www.kossda.or.kr).

Shim, T., Kim, M. S., & Martin, J. N. (2008). *Changing Korea: Understanding communication and culture*. New York: Harper Collins.

Sik, S. H. (2005). *A brief history of Korea. The spirit of Korean cultural roots*. Seoul: Ewha Womens University Press.

Stiglitz, J. E. (2002). *Globalization and its discontents*. New York: Norton.

Tabellini, G. (2007). Culture and institutions: Economic development in the regions of Europe. Mimeo.

Taube, M. (2013). Relational corruption in the PR China. Institutional foundations and its (Dys)-functionality for economic development and growth. *Comparative Governance and Politics*, 7(1), 89–116.

Taube, M., & Schramm, M. (2003). The institutional economics of legal institutions, Guanxi, and corruption in the PR China. In J. Kidd & F.-J. Richter (Eds.), *Fighting corruption in Asia. Causes, effects and remedies* (pp. 271–296). New Jersey: World Scientific.

Thomas, D. A. (1990). The impact of race on managers' experiences of developmental relationships (mentoring and sponsorship): An intra-organizational study. *Journal of Organizational Behavior*, *11*(6), 479–492.

Uzzi, B. (1997). Social structure and competition in interfirm networks: The paradox of embeddedness. *Administrative Science Quarterly*, *42*(1), 35–67.

Wang, H. (2000). Informal institutions and foreign investment in China. *Pacific Review*, *13*(4), 525–556.

Williamson, O. E. (1996). *The mechanisms of governance*. New York: Oxford University Press.

Williamson, C. (2009). Informal institutions rule: Institutional arrangements and economic performance. *Public Choice*, *139*, 371–387.

Williamson, C. R., & Kerekes, C. B. (2008). Securing private property: Formal versus informal institutions. Working Paper.

Woolcock, M. (1998). Social capital and economic development: Toward a theoretical synthesis and policy framework. *Theory and Society*, *27*(2), 151–208.

Yang, M. M. (1994). *Gifts, favors and banquets. The art of social relationships in China*. Ithaca, NY: Cornell University Press.

Yee, J. (2000). Too modern too soon? Dualism in civil society, everyday life, and social relations in contemporary Korea. *Korea Journal*, *40*(1), 282–284.

Yoo, K., & Kim, D. (2002). An analysis of changes in income distribution and impact of redistribution policy after the foreign currency crisis. Korea Development Institute. KDI Research Report 2002-08.

PART 3

Business Networks in South East Asia

CHAPTER 9

Chinese Capitalisms in Southeast Asia: Diverging Institutional Legacies of Southeast Asian Chinese Business Communities

H. Dahles
Griffith University, Nathan, QLD, Australia

9.1 INTRODUCTION

In the 1990s, scholars of diverse disciplinary backgrounds involving themselves with the study of Asian economies and societies, attempted to find plausible explanations for the spectacular rise of the "Tiger Economies" of East and Southeast Asia. Among the manifold explanations produced to address the "Asian Miracle" a prominent role was assigned to the business practices of the ethnic Chinese minority groups residing in these countries. The ethnic Chinese were viewed as endowed with exceptional entrepreneurial zest which—according to many scholars and business analysts—was rooted in Confucian culture that the ethnic Chinese brought along when migrating from China to Southeast Asia (Fukuyama, 1995; Redding, 1990). This "culturalist" approach has been criticized for essentializing culture as a constituting factor in ethnic Chinese business operations. The institutional approach, on the other hand, downplays the role of culture. While this approach does not deny that the Chinese establish business linkages with co-ethnics across borders, it does reject the proposition that these linkages constitute close-knit communities based on shared culture and identity. Instead, the ethnic Chinese "community" is viewed as an institutionally framed and loosely connected patchwork of partly converging and partly conflicting practices and principles (Hamilton, 2006; Yeung & Olds, 2000; Yen, 2014). The institutional approach views business ventures as embedded in ethnicity and culture as much as in economic dynamics and power relations. In this collection, similar themes are investigated in Chapters 7, 10, and 12.

Business Networks in East Asian Capitalisms
http://dx.doi.org/10.1016/B978-0-08-100639-9.00009-8

Upon China's reentry into the world economy, investments in countries with a substantial ethnic Chinese population, such as in Southeast Asia, were among the first steps taken in an international business environment (Bolt, 2000). Conversely, ethnic Chinese businesspeople from Southeast Asia, in particular Singapore, Malaysia, and Indonesia, were among the first who took their business to China in the 1990s (Bolt, 2000, p. 66). The ethnic Chinese in Southeast Asia soon realized their potential to act as a bridge between China and their respective countries of residence. The question is which considerations and expectations have been underlying this move to China? Capitalist reasoning in terms of factor advantages and market opportunities? Expectations of a smooth ride because of an alleged cultural advantage? Reminiscences of a common past and ancestral linkages? Loyalty to a pan-Chinese imagined community? Or manipulation by their state governments pushing them to capitalize on their Chinese background or rather to downplay it? In other words, the issue to be addressed is how do ethnic Chinese networks reflect economic integration into the Chinese dominated regional market and shape the particular variety of Chinese capitalism across Southeast Asia?

This chapter focuses in particular ethnic Chinese business communities in the Straits region comprised of Singapore, and parts of Malaysia and Indonesia. Once united in the Malay Union under British colonial rule, Malaysia and Singapore split into two separate nation states in 1957 due to ethnic disturbances between the Chinese and Malay populations. Singapore became a city-state and the only place outside of Greater China where the Chinese constitute the majority of population (Kian Woon, 1998, p. 200; Yen, 2014, p. 285). In Malaysia, the ethnic Chinese came to establish a substantial minority of 26 million people (24% of population) and major force in the Malaysian economy (Pek Koon, 1998, p. 172). In Indonesia, the ethnic classification scheme promoted by the Dutch colonial regime categorized the ethnic Chinese in terms of Foreign Orientals with far-reaching consequences for the c.5 million Chinese Indonesians until the present day (Heidhues, 1998, p. 151; Yen, 2014, p. 341). These three ethnic Chinese communities can be identified in terms of a common origin, a shared but diverse migration history, colonial legacy, and "diasporic" condition.

Based on a comparative review of literature addressing the emergence and operations of ethnic Chinese business networks, this chapter attempts to demonstrate that these ventures show both striking similarities and sharp differences among the ethnic Chinese business people from the three countries. Combined with the shared history on the one hand, and the diverging current position in three separate nation states on the other, the claim of a Chinese transnational (business) community based on ethnic affinity or common institutional frameworks will be challenged. Instead, it is proposed that it is not "culture" or "institutional support" in a narrow sense, but "context" in a wider sense, and more specifically "legacies of the past in the present," that provide a conceptual framework for explaining the diverse involvement of ethnic Chinese business people with China.

This chapter is structured as follows. In the next section, the theoretical underpinnings of this chapter are developed, discussing in particular, historical institutionalism. The empirical section compiles secondary data on ethnic Chinese businesses and their relationship with China in Singapore, Malaysia and Indonesia. These findings are then submitted to a cross-sectional comparative analysis, applying an historical institutionalist perspective. Finally, some concluding reflections are provided on the merits and restrictions of historic institutionalism for insights into the similarities and differences among Southeast Asian ethnic Chinese business ventures into China.

9.2 AN HISTORICAL INSTITUTIONAL APPROACH TO ETHNIC CHINESE BUSINESSES

9.2.1 Historical Institutionalism

The institutional approach to Chinese capitalism addresses the actor-structure relationship in its situational and contextual framework. Institutions are generally defined as "systems of established and prevalent social rules that structure social interactions" (Hodgson, 2006, p. 2; Scott, 2001, pp. 48–49). Or, as historical institutionalists would phrase it: "the formal or informal procedures, routines, norms, and conventions embedded in the organizational structure of the polity or political economy" (Hall & Taylor, 1996, p. 938). This historical institutionalist definition of institutions emphasizes the dimension of power that is intrinsic to rules, regulations, and conventions that shape the individual behavior and belief. Institutions understood in these terms provide "moral and cognitive templates for interpretation and action" (Hall & Taylor, 1996, p. 393). Moreover, institutions are characterized by a high degree of resilience which imposes constraints on human action that, at the same time, can open up new opportunities. Institutions are perpetuated because they represent accepted models *of* conduct while, at the same time, these models offer compelling guidelines *for* proper behavior and practice. While individual actors are born and raised within pre-existing institutions that "reside in the dispositions of other individuals"

(Hodgson, 2006, p. 8), it is human agency that enacts these institutions and thereby, both perpetuates and changes them. Despite their resilience, institutions are subject to processes of change (Scott, 2001, p. 48). In order to capture the simultaneously constraining and enabling impact of institutions on human action, historical institutional scholars reintroduced the concept of embeddedness as coined by Granovetter (1985) and elaborated by other economic sociologists (Portes, 2010). The significance of the concept of embeddedness for economic transactions has been elaborated by institutional scholars (Zukin & DiMaggio, 1990), arguing that embedded economic activities such as in business communities or business networks are useful institutional means of implementing cooperative strategies within and across national borders and enhancing "institutional thickness" in any business (Yeung & Olds, 2000).

In addition to "socializing" economic action, historical institutionalists also "historicize" human agency. A historical perspective enables scholars to understand the emergence and perpetuation of institutions, as "(h)istory provides the resources and constraints, in each case both material and cognitive, in which we think, act, and create" (Hodgson, 2006, p. 8). The concept of "institutional legacies" addresses societal transformations as a function of the social, cultural, and institutional structures created under past regimes that persist in the present period. In this view "the past casts a long shadow on the present, shapes the environment in which the battle to define and defend new institutions takes place..." (Crawford & Lijphart, 1997, p. 2). Proponents of this approach argue that dominant social, cultural, and political forces at work in the larger society are rooted in power struggles that evolved throughout history and currently shape the identity of new institutions (Crawford & Lijphart, 1997, p. 9). In order to capture the dynamics of such processes, individual and collective actors have to be viewed, not in terms of passive recipients of institutional resources, "but as actors involved in both the construction and reconstruction of such resources within and across national contexts" (Morgan & Quack, 2005, p. 1765). Actors that cross national borders have to deal with increasing diversity in both their organizational practice and institutional environment and may draw on "sleeping nearly forgotten institutional legacies as a resource for their institutional change projects" (Morgan & Quack, 2005, p. 1765).

The theoretical merit of historical institutionalism is that it brings together the individual actors, their structural embeddedness in environments characterized by unequal power relations, and a distinct view on history that postulates the path dependency of specific social configurations

(Hall & Taylor, 1996, p. 941). In this sense, historical institutionalism addresses both change and continuity. Historical institutionalism rejects the postulate of institutional economics as much as of sociological institutionalism that the same operative forces will generate the same results everywhere, in favor of the view that the effect of such forces will be mediated by the contextual features (embeddedness) of a given situation often inherited from the past (Nichols, 1998). Historical institutionalism then challenges the assumption that institutions simply reflect and articulate market logics or identities. Instead, it suggests that institutions also affect the very existence of markets and identities and create their social and political consequences. This position contributes to an understanding of how such configurations emerge, change, become socially and politically relevant, and are mobilized (Lecours, 2000, p. 511). As the remainder of this chapter will show, a comparative perspective on ethnic Chinese businesses in the Straits reveals the ways in which both long-standing and newly created institutional legacies are strategically employed, abandoned, even silenced and again revitalized in cross-border ventures under rapidly changing and ambivalent institutional regimes.

9.3 ETHNIC CHINESE ENTREPRENEURS VENTURING INTO CHINA

As implied by sociological institutionalists, ethnic Chinese businesses often show a strategic exploitation of personal "affinities," such as family ties and kin-like relations (such as lineage, hometown, dialect group, etc.). These allegedly "typical Chinese" strategies of employing social relations have been linked to the specific organization of centuries-long migration from China and the diasporic condition which positioned Chinese people in particular (labor) market niches in the colonial societies in the Straits (Kuhn, 2008; Yen, 2014). "Affinity groups" formed the social glue of the diverse Chinese communities in the Straits throughout colonial history, but underwent far-reaching changes as the former British and Dutch colonies in the Straits became independent nation states and participants in the globalizing economy. In the modern Southeast Asian nation states hosting large ethnic Chinese communities, new resources beyond the traditional affinity groups have emerged against the background of their increasing integration in the national and global economy. State-controlled institutions have gained importance, such as in the education sector (Dahles, 2004, 2005). In the economic domain, the emergence of Singapore, Kuala Lumpur, and Jakarta as regional centers of business services and high-tech industries brought about new business strategies such as subcontracting and other cooperative relations with either government-led (GLCs) or multinational corporations (MNCs). The strategic use of institutional resources for the advancement of business interests has come to supplement or even replace culture-based resources as institutional scholars claim. Conversely, sociological institutionalists argue in favor of the unrelenting reliance on culture-based resources or the persistent unreliability of institutions in particular for the ethnic Chinese. The data presented below identify the ways in which ethnic Chinese businesspeople deploy these resources when exploring business opportunities in China.

Regarding business opportunities in China mainland, ethnic Chinese entrepreneurs in Singapore, Malaysia, and Indonesia acknowledge the economic benefits as much as their sentimental ties with China, the practical advantages of having relatives in China, speaking the language, and their familiarity with and the pleasure taken in "Chinese ways of doing business." In the case of Singapore and Kuala Lumpur, many ethnic Chinese business people in Malaysia and Singapore hold on to the "family" discourse as a vehicle for business ventures (Dahles, 2010). A firm belief in the reliability of both cultural linkages and family ties exist among ethnic Chinese, irrelevant of how dormant the cultural affinity, or how distant the blood ties may have been. Conversely, such a dominant family-based discourse has not been identified among the Indonesian Chinese business people (Susanto, 2008; Koning, 2007; Koning & Susanto, 2008). In fact, maintaining and exploiting direct linkages with China has been discouraged by the New Order government and only slowly enters into current business practices of the majority of Chinese businesses in current Indonesia. While many are aware of business opportunities in China, they do not embark on business trips to China as massively as their Malaysian and Singaporean counterparts do. Instead, they prefer to work with (ethnic Chinese) agents in Jakarta who import goods from China to be sold in the numerous Chinese-owned shops across the country. This is in compliance with long-standing Chinese business practices that emerged during the colonial period as will be elaborated below.

Among young entrepreneurs in Singapore, Malaysia, and Indonesia, connections established during their education abroad (which implies that they are English-educated), with former employers and colleagues, and professional associations play a rather prominent role. These connections may provide a vehicle for launching business across the border into Southeast Asian,

China, and the Asia-Pacific, often with the ultimate aim to start a successful venture abroad. While many youngsters maintain an international network of peers which may be conducive for their careers, there is also a home-based source of such connections. For decades, the governments invited foreign multinational corporations to invest and locate their regional head offices in Singapore, Kuala Lumpur, and Jakarta. When the Singaporean government started to promote the establishment of an "external wing" of the domestic economy, these MNCs obtained the role of intermediary for introducing Singaporean entrepreneurs to foreign markets (Dahles, 2004, 2007, 2008). The preferred position of Singapore businessmen as subcontractors of foreign multinational corporations provided crucial assets to venture beyond Singapore. In Indonesia, a few large ethnic Chinese-owned corporations establish joint ventures with foreign companies with government backing, while smaller ethnic Chinese entrepreneurs require their patronage to enter foreign markets (Koning & Susanto, 2008). Malaysian entrepreneurs had to fend for themselves as their government has been keen on advancing *bumiputra* (ie, Malay) economic interests (Zwart, 2006). Such an ethnically biased economic policy also characterized the Indonesian government. In Singapore (Dahles, 2004, 2005, 2007, 2008), it was a risk-avoiding strategy that allowed small companies to ride the waves of the expansion drift of their main clients benefiting from their local knowledge, their networks, and contacts with the foreign state agencies. Many young Singaporeans enjoyed an education in the West, obtained an MBA degree, worked in foreign multinational companies and, therefore, make good partners for foreign MNCs in Singapore and beyond. The family still figures in ethnic Chinese business ventures in several ways, but its role is changing. For lack of credit facilities for SMEs, the family may provide start-up capital, but has lost its role as a provider of business training and networks in ways that the first-generation family firm had been. For third-generation Singaporeans, the establishment of a global network of college friends and professional connections, and some state patronage to reduce the risk of a cross-border venture has become the sine qua non of a successful business career. Their orientation is global and China figures among the opportunities that the global economy offers, but it does not take center stage. As has been observed by migration scholars in general, the close engagement with the "home-country" that is so characteristic of first and second generation migrants, usually subsides with the third generation (Tsuda, 2009). This is exemplified by the Singaporean case where third-generation Chinese could hardly be mobilized by the government to involve themselves with business investments in China (Dahles, 2004). Malaysian Chinese—although less privileged than their Singaporean counterparts—are catching up quickly in terms of overseas education and global professional networking. However, they are still disadvantaged as government support—such as scholarships and subsidized trade missions—is largely denied to the Chinese in Malaysia (Dahles, 2010).

In terms of government support, the young Chinese Indonesians may be even more disadvantaged than their Malaysian counterparts. However, they do feel particularly impressed by the rise of China. Some express a strong personal feeling of pride, whereas others mainly see China as a big hub for business opportunities (Koning, 2007; Koning & Susanto, 2008). Some embark on learning Mandarin as they envision great business or professional opportunities in China. The lack of government support available to Chinese Indonesians may also turn into an asset when it comes to successfully facing the unpredictable market conditions in China. Where Western and other business people from well-organized and developed economies fail because they cannot cope with Chinese officials, opaque rules and regulations, and unreliable business partners, Chinese Indonesian business people have been dealing with such conditions all their lives.

In summary, there are similarities and differences between Southeast Asian Chinese business people involving themselves with China. Generally, ethnic Chinese business people are aware of the manifold opportunities that China has to offer, and many develop strategies to enter this huge and unpredictable market while attempting to manage the risks involved. However, the resources available widely differ among them. Singaporean and Malaysian Chinese firms venture into China combining the strategic use of culture-based and state-based resources to pave the way for investments and business start-ups (cf. Dahles, 2004, 2005, 2007, 2008, 2010). They may enter in the slipstream of family visits, put trust in distant kin to take care of their business interests, build professional networks, and take part in government-sponsored trade missions. But whatever strategy they follow, kin and family-like relations as a binding factor constitute a persistent theme—either cherished by the ethnic Chinese businesspeople themselves or reproduced by their governments. As Chinese Indonesians face a severe lack of opportunities—family relations with China and Mandarin or dialect language proficiency have often not been maintained, government-sponsored missions are unavailable and professional networks are incremental—they depend more on their wits and skills to maneuver in unpredictable situations. As Susanto and Koning found in Yogyakarta, a city in central Java, only a few ethnic Chinese are directly involved in doing business in China (Susanto, 2008; Koning, 2007; Koning & Susanto, 2008). They leave this to Jakarta-based agents with the resources and knowledge to access the Chinese market. If they enter China at all, they come prepared, as they are used to opaque market conditions and know that they are viewed as foreigners. At home, they spread risk by investing in a large variety of businesses. Currently, Malaysian Chinese are encouraged by their government to increase their involvement in China. If they do so, they also come prepared and know how to weather the storm if setbacks occur. However, Malaysian Chinese develop a preference for investments in Commonwealth countries with a shared colonial legacy, in particular after experiencing failure in China or as a strategy of business diversification (Dahles, 2010). As a consequence, they may change from defining their identity as rooted in mainland China, to locating their roots in colonial Southeast Asia under British rule. The case of Indonesia differs from its neighbors due to the long marginalization of Chinese (Koning, 2007). Among Chinese Singaporean business people, the interest in China is fading. Many of them own a subsidiary in Malaysia and develop a preference for investments in the emerging economies in the global market (Dahles, 2008, 2010). The next section will make an attempt at shedding light on these similarities and differences by positioning them in the context of diverging legacies of the past.

9.4 CHINESE LEGACIES: A COMPARATIVE ANALYSIS

This section addresses the multilayered relationships of the three business communities of ethnic Chinese in Singapore, Malaysia, and Indonesia with their respective nation states from a historical institutionalist perspective. These relationships will be "historisized" in order to understand similarities and differences in the way both cultural and institutional resources are used for business relations. As the previous section has revealed, the current involvement in China of Chinese business people from the three countries shows a rather diverse pattern. In terms of the sociological institutionalist perspective, this diversity is disturbing as it conflicts with the idea of shared ethnicity as a unifying concept. In terms of an economic institutionalist approach, this diversity is simply related to diverging market conditions of the national economies in which the ethnic Chinese participate. However, in terms of the historical institutional approach, a critical analysis of the role of the nation state vis-à-vis its ethnic groups opens avenues for a better understanding of the diverging business strategies among Southeast Asian Chinese. The different national communities in Southeast

Asia provide widely diverging conditions for the ethnic Chinese to strategically utilize their multiple cultural repertoires for economic purposes, in particular when it comes to entering the China mainland market (cf. Kuhn, 2008). The ethnic Chinese in Singapore, Malaysia, and Indonesia maintain long-standing economic relationships with each other and with partners in China, which go back to colonial times when Chinese merchants played prominent roles in the colonial economies in the Peninsula of Malaya under British rule and the East Indies governed by the Dutch. The diverse legacies of the past will be at the basis of the following analysis of the ethnic Chinese and their relationship with China.

9.4.1 Colonial Legacies

The ways in which ethnic Chinese companies in the three countries organize their ventures into China are firmly rooted in the migration history of the ethnic Chinese in Southeast Asia and beyond. In the 17th century, Chinese merchants—and in their wake hundreds and thousands of countrymen—established themselves in the colonial port cities of Batavia (Jakarta), Penang, Singapore, and Malacca to act as the bridgeheads for Chinese migrants looking for work and opportunities outside of China (Pan, 1998, pp. 54–57). Under their leadership, the "overseas" Chinese organized themselves in associations based on affinity groups that traced their origin back to common regional descent distinguished by dialects, kinship, secret societies, and shared devotion to particular deity cults in China (Kuhn, 2008; Yen, 2014). Particular affinity groups identified with specific professions or economic activities in particular places, which explains the specialization—or "business involution" (Kuhn, 2008, p. 172)—of the Chinese in particular occupational sectors across Southeast Asia. Established Chinese business elites facilitated chain migration and return migration (sojourning), and recruited newcomers as laborers and employees through affinity groups and brokered relationships with the colonialists (Kuhn, 2008, p. 175).

Under British and Dutch rule, diverging legacies of colonialism evolved (Yen, 2014). The colonial regimes controlling Malaya on the one hand, and the East Indies on the other, practiced different forms of governance. In both locations, the Chinese were indispensible collaborators for the European administrators. With their language proficiency and cultural competences, the Chinese organized the trade with China, extracted wealth from the natives as tax farmers, collected taxes from Chinese traders, organized Chinese slave labor in the tin mines and on plantations, and serviced the colonial cities. In these "middlemen" positions, the Chinese enjoyed considerable privileges that enabled them to collect enormous wealth, but they were also hated by the native population and feared by the colonialists. However, the degree to which the Chinese elite held sway over the colonial society differed between Malaya and the East Indies.

In the East Indies, the Dutch—as early as the 17th century—established revenue farms run by Chinese under the "officer" system and bestowed titles and honors on their leaders, creating Chinese elite of intermediaries that formed a separate layer between the colonists and the indigenous population (Heidhues, 1998, pp. 155–156). Apart from their activities as tax farmers and intermediaries controlling the import of Chinese goods, these intermediaries also acted as rural tax collectors and money lenders, which gave them almost unlimited power over indigenous farmers. In the early 19th century, their wealth overshadowed that of the Europeans in the East Indies (Kuhn, 2008, p. 155). The deep historical roots and the economic dominance of the established Chinese society—called *peranakan*—gave it a distinct societal standing between the colonialists and the native population. In the course of the 19th century, the *peranakan* lost more and more of their economic privileges as the colonial regime found ways to degrade them to the status of "foreign Orientals" or even "natives" (Heidhues, 1998, pp. 156–157). However, the *peranakan* successfully resisted assimilation into the native society and, at the same time, distanced themselves from the new migrants arriving from China. Their proud identification with the resurgent Chinese state fueled the resentment among the native people (Kuhn, 2008, p. 291). The anti-Chinese riots that spring up in times of transition and crisis in modern Indonesia form a resonance of this legacy of the past.

In Malaya, the officer system was abolished by the British in the early 19th century in favor of a British-style judicial system, and the major ports were declared free trade zones. Singapore, where Chinese quickly became the majority population, emerged not only as the administrative center for the Straits Settlements, but also as the hub for the masses of Chinese migrants headed for the other destinations in Southeast Asia. The British encouraged the established Chinese to regulate the flow of new countrymen arriving from China. Like the Dutch in Java, the British in Malaya rewarded Chinese community leaders with honors and titles, a strategy that paid off in civic peace (Kuhn, 2008, p. 173). But in contrast to the Javanese *peranakan* who distanced themselves from their social environment, the Singapore *peranakan* showed themselves as more welcoming to new arrivals from China and found ways to promote shared cultural interests

(Kuhn, 2008, p. 178). The society that subsequently evolved capitalized on its hybridity. The Singapore Chinese represented themselves as intercultural broker-entrepreneurs (Kuhn, 2008, p. 179). This history is reflected in the current position of Singapore as the major Southeast Asian business hub.

9.4.2 Postcolonial Legacies

There are manifold relations among the Chinese across national borders in Southeast Asia. Among these ties are both close family and business linkages, and in many cases kinship and economic interests are closely intertwined. Equally important is the trust invested in institutional security. Many Chinese entrepreneurs quote the contract law based on the British legal system that survived decolonization in many former British colonies, as a significant advantage when doing business across borders (Dahles, 2010). Hence, the shared Commonwealth legacy has become conducive for business among countries with a British colonial past—an institutional legacy lying dormant underneath the Singaporean and Malaysian developmental state (Dahles, 2008). Conversely, the Dutch colonial heritage does not provide the Chinese Indonesians with the trust of being part of a Commonwealth that offers them institutional security where other institutions fail. This may partly explain why Chinese Indonesians are part of these "inter-ethnic" co-operative ties to a lesser extent. Chinese firms from Singapore and Malaysia maintain trade relations or establish subsidiaries in Indonesia. They do so to diversify their business, either as a response to failure in China, or as part of a global strategy to expand to emerging markets (Dahles, 2010). Undoubtedly, there are family ties between Singaporean/Malaysian and Indonesian Chinese. However, we found no evidence in Indonesia of family relations being closely intertwined with business interests across borders to the extent that they are intertwined between Malaysian and Singaporean Chinese. Indonesian Chinese business people do not maintain direct linkages with foreign partners as frequently and intensely as their counterparts from Singapore and Malaysia. In addition to diverse national legacies, it may also be for lack of resources (access to a sea port and business capital) that they have to rely on Chinese agents in Jakarta.

In terms of the strategic utilization of government support, the differences between Indonesian, Malaysian, and Singaporean Chinese are outstanding. These are based on the differential ways in which the Chinese are embedded in their respective post-colonial nation states. In Singapore, the government is the most important player when it comes to investments in China, building on the notion of a shared Chinese identity under their resinification program of the 1990s (Dahles, 2004, 2007). In fact, with this program, the Singapore government recreated the "imagined community" of the Chinese—after having destroyed it in the formative years of the city state. Upon independence in 1965, Singapore observed a distance towards China that lasted into the 1970s. The government formed by British-educated Lee Kuan Yew and his People's Action Party showed itself hostile to the non-English speaking Chinese of Singapore whom they felt were susceptible to China's communist propaganda and, therefore, a threat to the development of Singapore into a modern nation state. As a result, Singapore witnessed the emergence of a "Chinese Culture *Lite*" (Kuhn, 2008, p. 317) with a majority Chinese population developing a Singaporean national identity.

Reflecting the relative affluence of Singapore, many Singaporean pursue an academic or professional education overseas. This yields them a global network of peers who eventually may rise to positions of political or economic power. For Singaporean entrepreneurs ethnic and family ties—though not irrelevant—seemed to be less constitutive of the success they hoped to reap from their China venture. Business people can call on government funding for product development and expertise input, repeated government tenders, financial support under special programs, government scholarships, invitation for trade missions, and even government loans—provided they meet the strictly defined criteria that limit the eligibility. The vast majority of Singapore companies, however, have to be self-reliant in order to survive and prosper, whether at home or on cross-border ventures. This is what they share with their Malaysian Chinese counterparts (Dahles, 2010).

Malaysians and Singaporeans seem equally endowed with opportunities of entering China on the waves of foreign-owned companies. A number of our interviewees run a foreign-based subsidiary or branch office in Kuala Lumpur or Singapore and act as brokers for the owner in China. While only a decade ago, Singaporean businesses may have enjoyed an advantage in being eligible as broker, these days, Malaysia has caught up with Singapore as a Southeast Asian business hub. However, in Malaysia, only the English-educated Chinese entrepreneurial elite enjoy a comparable access to professional education and global networks. The SME-owners are usually Chinese-educated and have a more Malaysia-based radius of action (Lee, 2003, pp. 38-39). The Chinese SME owners experience an incongruity between their economic strength and their political weakness. Politically, the English-educated elites of Malay and Chinese descent have created "a Malay-weighted political formula in which all ethnic communities would enjoy equal political citizenship" (Kuhn, 2008, p. 305) which has managed to keep the civic peace in this multicultural country so far. Economically, the Malaysian Chinese have to vie for themselves. The New Economic Policy, which was installed in the 1970s to close the economic gap between the Chinese and the Malay population, did not break Chinese economic dominance (Ng, 1998, p. 180). However, the continued imbalance occurred against the background of economic growth which mitigates the effects of Chinese wealth for the Malay (Kuhn, 2008, p. 313). Nevertheless, the Malaysian Chinese businesspeople, in particular in the small- and medium-sized segment, suffered under the reverse affirmative actions of the NEP and were thrown back on their family-based resources because of lack of economic capital and patronage linkages with powerholders (Kahn, 1996, p. 69). Fuelled by the Chinese nationalists in their attempts to keep Chinese norms and values alive, these small entrepreneurs developed a strong sense of Chinese identity which facilitated their business venture into China once economic and political conditions were conducive to this move (Zwart, 2006).

In Indonesia, the small Chinese businesses cannot draw on government support or cross-border networks, afford to send their children to prestigious overseas educational programs, or capitalize on expert knowledge to act as brokers for foreign multinationals. The lack of institutional resources among the Chinese Indonesians originates from the explicit anti-Chinese policies that the Indonesian government conducted in the aftermath of the 1965 coup. The flourishing Chinese community in Indonesia was disrupted when, under the Assimilation Program, all institutions supporting this community were banned, and contacts with China were frozen (Hoon, 2006; Coppel, 2002; Yen, 2014). State bureaucracy has been one of the most important "variables, which has contributed to the 'separateness' of the Chinese in Indonesia, particularly in Java" (Suryadinata, 1993, p. 77). Despite the anti-Chinese sentiments making themselves felt in post-colonial Indonesia, the Chinese have strengthened their economic position. Under decolonization, a few ethnic Chinese took over some large firms left by the Dutch, while at the same time, the Indonesian government promoted the economic revitalization of indigenous Indonesian entrepreneurship. Under Suharto's New Order, a few Chinese became prominent players in new banking and manufacturing investments and entered joint ventures with foreign corporations. The top level of the Indonesian economy is formed by a number of hugely rich and well-connected business entrepreneurs of Chinese descent—not members of the old *peranakan* community but first-generation newcomers (Kuhn, 2008, p. 301). These Chinese share with their Malaysian Chinese counterparts a pattern of adaptation to unbalanced power relations in their country. Like Malaysian business tycoons, they co-opt people of power into the management of their enterprises, or become the client of a powerful government official (Kuhn, 2008, p. 302). Such patron-client relationships form a colonial legacy, in that they resemble the "officer system" in which Chinese leaders capitalized on their outsider position by obtaining lucrative intermediary positions between native and Chinese communities on the one hand, and the colonial power holders on the other.

9.5 CONCLUSIONS

In the late 1980s, when China re-entered the world economy, the ethnic Chinese in Southeast Asia realized their potential to act as bridge between China and their respective countries of residence. Singaporean, Malaysian, and Indonesian Chinese business communities were among the first who took their business to China. From a macroeconomic perspective, China is a very promising market due to sheer numbers (of both potential consumers and labor), but microeconomic experience often teaches otherwise. China is difficult to penetrate, as the multilayered state bureaucracy requires cautious handling. Ties based on cultural affinity were expected to facilitate a smooth entrance, but often seem to be part of the manifold obstacles that Chinese investors encounter in China. The strategic use of intermediaries to facilitate the entrance to this market (including the revitalization of dormant family relations) emerged as an adaptive strategy throughout the migratory history of the Chinese, and became institutionalized when Chinese merchants in the East Indies and Malaya turned intermediaries between the European colonists, then native communities, newly arriving Chinese migrants, and their home country. However, the Chinese merchant communities in the East Indies and Malaya positioned themselves differently vis-à-vis the native people and new arrivals from China and, by doing so, set out on different paths that have come to lead the way for generations of ethnic Chinese business people in the future. In the East Indies, under the "officer system," the *peranakan* Chinese created the revenue farm legacy which defined them as both separate and exploitative vis-à-vis native communities and cooperative towards the colonial regime, laying the foundation for in anti-sinicist sentiments among the Indonesian population after independence. In Malaya, on the other hand, the *peranakan* Chinese developed the intercultural broker-entrepreneur legacy, which is at the basis of the current position of both Singapore and Kuala Lumpur as major business and high-tech hubs in Southeast Asia.

The differences between the East Indies and Malaya find a historical continuity in the diverging post-colonial ethnic politics in the nation states that emerged after decolonization. The deconstruction of these politics involves an analysis of the role of state patronage towards ethnic groups, social engineering of majority and minority statuses, and the social construction of an imagined community. The Singapore government started its resinification policy by promoting the Singaporean entrepreneur as a cultural hybrid, versed in both Western and Asian cultural repertoires, and able to mediate between and benefit from both worlds. This self-presentation alluded to Singapore's colonial legacy of *peranakan* Chinese acting as intercultural broker-entrepreneur. However, the lesson learned by the Singaporean entrepreneurs was that Chinese identity represents a disadvantage rather than an advantage in China. This lesson has contributed to a relative loss of interest in China and a changing attitude towards the ethnic Chinese in Malaysia, their closest neighbors. Malaysia has come to represent a comfort zone to turn to in order to recover from business failures in mainland China and to reconsider business strategies for the future (Dahles, 2004, 2005, 2008).

In Malaysia, on the other hand, many entrepreneurs take pride in their alleged Chinese identity and management practices. Malaysian Chinese share this ethnic pride with many of their Indonesian counterparts. This attitude has to be understood against the background of their ambivalent position in the Malaysian respectively Indonesian nation state, a position that for decades forced them to develop their resilience in the face of political and economic hardship. Chinese SME-owners, used to bureaucratic adversity in their own country, were better prepared to face the challenges of mainland China's officialdom than were the Singaporeans. At the same time, they practice risk reduction by entertaining a diversity of business interests both at home, and in China instead of striving for specialization. In the face of crisis, they reconsider their assumption about their home market. Redefining Malaysia in terms of a post-colonial society with a British legal heritage, they came to focus their cross-border business activities on countries with a similar legal system (Dahles, 2010).

Among Chinese Indonesians, Chinese identity was a silenced legacy as a consequence of the assimilationist policies of the national government.

Doing business in China was either left to politically well-connected (Chinese) agents in Jakarta, or an individual venture that did not build on any kin or compatriot ties from the past. Reemerging pride in their Chinese heritage, coupled with high hopes for benefits coming their way from China's rise to power, is a new development manifest among the young generation with Chinese ancestry (Susanto, 2008; Koning & Susanto, 2008).

The organizational field of Chinese businesses in Southeast Asia is identified not in terms of shared ethnicity but in the situational and contextual terms of a common, but at the same time, disparate history which encompasses ancestral roots in China, a shared migratory past, and colonial experience that generated diverging legacies for the post-colonial nation states to build on. This aspect has not been acknowledged by current (economic and sociological) institutional theorists who attribute the success of Chinese businesses either to a culturally-based business zest or to ethnically organized mutual interests. A historical institutionalist perspective—without denying the role played by both culture and capitalist reasoning—adds one dimension to this framework, giving it historical depth and sensitivity to power relations, this dimension is the embeddedness of actors in institutional legacies based in the political economies of their nation states. The individual entrepreneurs in the different ethnic Chinese business communities in this chapter, spread across three different post-colonial states, draw on a multitude of resources when entering into China ventures. Such resources (family-based and ethnic-based networks, cultural competences derived from educational opportunities, government support emerging from patronage relations) are accessible to them to different degrees, depending on their structural embedding in horizontal and vertical linkages that may be conducive or restraining to business ventures in China. This structural embedding is path-dependent as it has been shaped by the migratory history of the first generation, the colonial governance system, and the role ascribed to Chinese minorities in colonial society, as much as their involvement in the struggle for independence and subsequent post-colonial political economy. Put simply, the more the ethnic Chinese were involved in the governance of both the colonial and post-colonial state, the more they established themselves as an independent economic and cultural force in the Southeast Asian region; the more the ethnic Chinese suffered discrimination and oppression in the colonial and post-colonial society, the more they lean towards China, seeking both economic benefits and cultural comfort. It is in a *liaison amoureuse* between institutional theory and history that a comparative historical perspective on the multiple embeddedness of current business communities can come to fruition (Verver & Dahles, 2013).

Such a perspective reveals how multilayered legacies of the past, shaped by interacting economic, political and cultural forces, become strategically employed, enforced, abandoned, even silenced and again revitalized under rapidly changing and ambivalent institutional regimes.

REFERENCES

Bolt, P. J. (2000). *China and Southeast Asia's ethnic Chinese. State and diaspora in contemporary Asia.* Westport, Conn./London: Praeger.

Coppel, C. (2002). The Indonesian Chinese: 'Foreign Orientals', Netherlands Subjects and Indonesian Citizens. In M. B. Hooker (Ed.), *Law and the Chinese in Southeast Asia* (pp. 131–149). Singapore: ISEAS.

Crawford, B., & Lijphart, A. (1997). Old legacies, new institutions: Explaining political and economic trajectories in post-communist regimes. In *Liberalization and Leninist legacies: Comparative perspectives on democratic transitions* (pp. 1–39). Berkeley: Global, Area, and International Archive (GAIA). Available at: http://escholarship.org/uc/item/)ds5j5ss.

Dahles, H. (2004). Venturing across borders. Investment strategies of Singapore-Chinese entrepreneurs in mainland China. *Asian Journal of Social Sciences, 32*, 19–41.

Dahles, H. (2005). Culture, capitalism and political entrepreneurship: Transnational business ventures of the Singapore-Chinese in China. *Culture and Organization, 11*(2), 45–58.

Dahles, H. (2007). Creating social capital as a competitive advantage in China. Singapore Chinese entrepreneurs venturing into China. In S. R. Clegg, Y. Wang, & M. Berrell (Eds.), *Business Networks and Strategic Alliances in China* (pp. 182–208). Cheltenham (UK) and Northhampton (MA, USA): Edward Elgar.

Dahles, H. (2008). Entrepreneurship and the legacies of a developmental state: Singapore enterprises venturing across national borders. *Journal of Developmental Entrepreneurship, 13*(4), 485–508.

Dahles, H. (2010). The multiple layers of a transnational 'imagined community': The notion and reality of the ethnic Chinese business community. In M.-L. Djelic & S. Quack (Eds.), *Transnational communities shaping global economic governance* (pp. 55–81). Cambridge: Cambridge University Press.

Fukuyama, F. (1995). *Trust: The social virtues and the creation of prosperity*. New York: Free Press.

Granovetter, M. (1985). Economic action and social structure: The problem of embeddedness. *The American Journal of Sociology, 91*(3), 481–510.

Hall, P. A., & Taylor, R. C. R. (1996). Political science and the three new institutionalisms. *Political Studies, XLIV*, 936–957.

Hamilton, G. G. (2006). *Commerce and capitalism in Chinese societies*. Milton Park/Abingdon: Routledge.

Heidhues, M. S. (1998). Indonesia. In L. Pan (Ed.), *The encyclopedia of the Chinese overseas* (pp. 151–168). Cambridge (Mass.): Harvard University Press.

Hodgson, G. M. (2006). What are institutions? *Journal of Economic Issues, XL*(1), 1–25.

Hoon, C.-Y. (2006). Assimilation, multiculturalism, hybridity: The dilemmas of the ethnic Chinese in post-Suharto Indonesia. *Asian Ethnicity*, 7(2), 149–166.

Kahn, J. S. (1996). Growth, economic transformation, culture and the middle classes in Malaysia. In R. Robison & D. S. G. Goodman (Eds.), *The new rich in Asia: Mobile phones, McDonald's and middle-class revolution*. London: Routledge.

Kian Woon, K. (1998). Singapore. In L. Pan (Ed.), *The encyclopedia of the Chinese overseas* (pp. 200–217). Cambridge (Mass.): Harvard University Press.

Koning, J. (2007). Chineseness and Chinese Indonesian business practices: A generational and discursive enquiry. *East Asia: An International Quarterly*, *24*(2), 129–152.
Koning, J., & Susanto, A. (2008). Chinese Indonesians and 'the Rise of China': From business opportunities to questions of identity. In E. Kok-Kheng Yeoh & J. Hoi-Lee Loh (Eds.), *China in the world: Contemporary issues and perspectives* (pp. 161–184). Kuala Lumpur: Institute of China Studies, University of Malaya.
Kuhn, P. A. (2008). *Chinese among others. Emigration in modern times*. Singapore: National University of Singapore Press.
Lecours, A. (2000). Theorizing cultural identities: Historical institutionalism as a challenge to the culturalists. *Canadian Journal of Political Science*, *XXXIII*(3), 499–522.
Lee, K. H. (2003). Political positions of the Chinese in post-independence Malaysia. In W. Ling-Chi & W. Gungwu (Eds.), Vol. II. *The Chinese diaspora. Selected essays* (pp. 36–65). Singapore: Eastern Universities Press.
Morgan, G., & Quack, S. (2005). Institutional legacies and firm dynamics: The growth and internationalization of British and German law firms. *Organization Studies*, *26*(12), 1765–1786.
Ng, B. K. (1998). The new economic policy (NEP) 1970-90. In L. Pan (Ed.), *The encyclopedia of the Chinese overseas* (p. 180). Cambridge (Mass.): Harvard University Press.
Nichols, P. M. (1998). Forgotten linkages—Historical institutionalism and sociological institutionalism and analysis of the World Trade Organization. *Journal of International Economic Law*, 19(Summer), 461–511.
Pan, L. (1998). Western expansion into China and Southeast Asia. In L. Pan (Ed.), *The encyclopedia of the Chinese overseas* (pp. 54–57). Cambridge (Mass.): Harvard University Press.
Pek Koon, H. (1998). Malaysia. In L. Pan (Ed.), *The encyclopedia of the Chinese overseas* (pp. 172–186). Cambridge (Mass.): Harvard University Press.
Portes, A. (2010). *Economic sociology. A systematic inquiry*. Princeton (NJ): Princeton University Press.
Redding, S. G. (1990). *The spirit of Chinese capitalism*. Berlin, New York: Walter de Gruyter.
Scott, W. R. (2001). *Institutions and organization* (2nd ed.). Thousand Oaks, London, New Delhi: Sage Publications.
Suryadinata, L. (1993). *Determinants of Indonesia's foreign policy in search of an explanation*. Singapore: National University of Singapore Press.
Susanto, A. (2008). *Under the umbrella of the sultan. Accommodation of the Chinese in Yogyakarta during Indonesia's New Order*. Dissertation, Radboud University, Nijmegen, the Netherlands.
Tsuda, T. (2009). Introduction: Diasporic return and migration studies. In T. Tsuda (Ed.), *Diasporic homecomings. Ethnic return migration in comparative perspective* (pp. 1–20). Stanford: Stanford University Press.
Verver, M. J., & Dahles, H. (2013). The anthropology of Chinese capitalism in Southeast Asia: From culture to institution? *Journal of Business Anthropology*, *1*(2), 93–114.
Yen, C. H. (2014). *Ethnic Chinese business in Asia. History, culture and business enterprise*. Singapore: World Scientific Publishing.
Yeung, H. W. C., & Olds, K. (2000). Globalizing Chinese business firms: Where are they coming from, where are they heading? In H. Wai C. Yeung & K. Olds (Eds.), *Globalization of Chinese business firms* (pp. 1–30). Houndmills, Basingstoke: Macmillan Press.
Zukin, S., & DiMaggio, P. (1990). *Structures of capital: The social organization of the economy*. New York: Cambridge University Press.
Zwart, E. (2006). *In pursuit of comfort. The transnationalisation process of Malaysian Chinese small and medium enterprises*. Dissertation, VU University Amsterdam, Amsterdam.

CHAPTER 10

Business Networks in Thailand: Import Substitution, Export Oriented, and Expansion in AEC

N. Wailerdsak*, S. Siengthai†
*Thammasat Business School, Bangkok, Thailand
†Asian Institute of Technology, Khlong Luang, Thailand

10.1 INTRODUCTION

It can be said that the socioeconomic development in Thailand since the 1960s is that of postdevelopmentalist capitalism which has been private-sector led. The State has its role to support in terms of infrastructure and reduction of risks due to business fluctuations in foreign exchange rates, energy cost, labour costs, etc. There is no direct state intervention as observed in the case of Japan or South Korea (Suehiro & Wailerdsak, 2014). This chapter aims to explain the characteristics of the Thai business networks, the relationships between the government and business, and some organizations that have played a significant role[1] in this process. It complements the discussions of Thai business networks presented in Chapters 11 and 12.

This chapter is divided into five sections. Section 10.1 provides the literature review on the role of the state and developmentalism perspective. Section 10.2 analyses the development of the Thai business networks from the beginning of industrialization of Thailand during the 1960s until the

[1]The Thai Chamber of Commerce (TCC) (http://www.thaichamber.org/), the Federation of Thai Industries (FTI) (http://www.fti.or.th), the Thai Bankers Association (TBA) (http://www.tba.or.th/), the Joint Foreign Chambers of Commerce in Thailand (JFCCT), the Thai Listed Companies Association (LCA), the Federation of Thai Capital Markets Organizations (FETCO)(http://www.fetco.or.th/), the Tourism Council of Thailand (http://www.thailandtourismcouncil.org/contact.php), the Thai Institute of Directors (IOD) (http://www.thai-iod.com/th/), the Thai National Shippers' Council (TNSC) (http://www.tnsc.com/html/), the Joint Public-Private Consultation Committee (JPPCC) (http://www.nesdb.go.th/Default.aspx%3Ftabid%3D378), and so on.

Business Networks in East Asian Capitalisms
http://dx.doi.org/10.1016/B978-0-08-100639-9.00010-4

current expansion of business into ASEAN countries[2] in the 2010s with the focus on Thailand's new development strategies. It will analyse the business network development in three dimensions: the fund raising in the money and capital markets, the accumulation of technology and marketing know-how, and the human resource development. Section 10.3 will review the Government investment policy (ie, Board of Investment Regulations) and other relevant business laws. In Section 10.4, we will explain the current anticorruption movement[3] of the private business sector and business ethics issues. In Section 10.5, we will suggest how the Thai business networks can be further developed within the ASEAN Economic Community (AEC) and globalization era.

10.2 LITERATURE REVIEW

A business group is defined as a collection of legally independent firms linked by multiple ties, including ownership, economic, and/or social (family, kinship, friendship) ties through which they coordinate to achieve mutual objectives (Khanna & Rivkin, 2001; Makino & Yiu, 2014). It is a prevalent organizational form that accounts for significant economic contributions in many Asian countries (Abbot, 2003; Claessens et al., 1999; Tipton, 2009).

Prominent political economy theories of business groups include the developmental state perspective (Amsden, 1989; Wade, 2010) and a variety of capitalism theories of competitive advantage (Schneider, 2009). Developmental state approaches emphasize the directive role of national states and policy processes that promote the accumulation of capital and the construction of firms with sufficient scale and scope to lead the process of industrial catch-up. The varieties of capitalism approach focus on the question of how states organize big business to build industrial capacity (Carney et al., 2009; Schneider, 2009).

[2]Some of the examples is Charoen Pokphand (CP) Group which jointly invested with Itochu (Japanese firm) to invest in China and ASEAN; Central Group with the SMEs to expand into ASEAN market; Ichi-tan Co. with Japanese and Indonesian company to expand green tea market in Indonesia; and Katana Entertainment Co. with two Japanese companies to aggressively expand its movies and content businesses in ASEAN; Ion Co. with Major Cineplex and some Thai SMEs to expand theaters and lifestyle businesses for middle class into ASEAN, etc.

[3]About 655 companies (as of January 2016) in the business sector have formed in late 2010 a nongovernment organisation to act as a watch dog against corruption, which is called 'Private Sector Collective Action Coalition Against Corruption (CAC)'.

Studies of the developmental state describe several modes of state-led industrialization. The general focus is upon political institutions and specific policy choices, such as selective protectionism, the development or suppression of private capital markets, promotion of main banks or state capital allocation, promotion of or restrictions on foreign direct investment (FDI), and joint-venture rules requiring substantial technology transfer as a condition of market entry (Guillen, 2000). Where the state is powerful, autonomous, and immune to interest-group pressure, it may co-opt and direct entrepreneurial elites toward favourable economic outcomes.

However, policy-induced groups can also emerge in the context of crony capitalism, where, due to private rent-seeking or public avarice, policy instruments are mishandled or combined in ways that impede firms from developing a sustainable competitive advantage. Under crony capitalism (see eg, Ip, 2007; Kang, 2003), business group scope is determined by the allocation of concessions to connected families and political supporters. Government policies restrict trade and foreign competition, but fail to monitor the technological and market achievements of domestic firms benefiting from protection. In these circumstances, the logic of business group diversification is driven by policy generated rents, rather than financial and technological achievements (Carney, 2014; Phongpaichit & Baker, 2009).

An alternative variety of capitalism that resonates in Asia is dependent market capitalism (Schneider, 2009). This concept suggests that economies can become permanently dependent upon foreign actors and institutions and reflects the growing importance of globalization and the growing market power of multinational corporations (MNCs) over domestic firms in emerging markets. As Asian economies have liberalized their trade and investment regimes over the past two decades, MNCs have increasingly penetrated their markets.

If the affiliates of business groups struggle to attain international competitiveness, they develop complementarities based on a division of labour between MNCs. For example, the MNCs provide technology, innovation, process production, and knowledge transfer, and its local partners provide commercial infrastructure and disciplined labour. MNCs require flexible and low-cost labour. They are unwilling to accept costly institutions, such as comprehensive collective agreements or cumbersome procedures for layoffs; consequently, labour is reluctant to invest, resulting in a low-skills trap (Carney, 2014; Yeung, 2006).

These perspectives also identify the potential effect of institutional inertia. Many middle- and low-income countries have been in an emerging condition for many years. They show few signs of catching up with more advanced economies. The development-state literature currently points to the problem of government failure and the growing risk of economies becoming enmeshed in a middle-income trap (Asia Development Bank, 2011; Chung & Hamilton, 2009; Wade, 2010).

The leading role of the state has been seen in the literature as the major characteristics of late industrialization in Latin America, Asia, and Africa.

Carney (2014) proposed that firms respond to global pressures, such as growing international trade and investment and transnational standards and regulatory norms. How? In the developmental states of East Asia, government officials' direct lending to industries is considered of strategic importance to lifting the nation up the rungs of the development ladder via export-oriented industrialization. In further refinements, the developmental state was seen as effective because of bureaucrats' autonomy from political pressure, while also retrieving information from the private sector via trade associations to make decisions. In the developmental state model, the state has more independent, or autonomous, political power, as well as more control over the economy. The argument from this perspective is that a government ministry can have the freedom to plan the economy and expect long-term national interests without having its economic policies disrupted by either corporate-class or working-class short-term or narrow interests (Hamiton, 1996; Suehiro, 2008; Whitley, 1992, 1999).

The implications for the business system are that there is an expectation that the financial system will be heavily reliant on banking, since over-borrowing and over-lending tend to be a crucial mechanism by which strategic industries are rapidly developed. As a consequence of the underdevelopment of the stock market as a source of external financing, corporate ownership will tend to remain concentrated, although this may be in the hands of families, the state, or through cross-shareholdings that form part of a business group, as with Japan's keiretsu (Suehiro, 2008; Wailerdsak, 2008b; Wailerdsak & Suehiro, 2010).

The state in China, Malaysia, and Thailand has played a developmental role, though perhaps less clearly so than in the other North-East Asian states (Carney & Witt, 2014).

10.3 EVOLUTION OF BUSINESS NETWORKS IN THAILAND

The empirical focal points of this section are changes that have occurred in Thailand in the past five decades (Table 10.1). Thailand has gone from being primarily an insulated manufacturing economy exhibiting distinctive organizational characteristics to a multisectored economy deeply integrated in regional and global economies. The service and, in particular, the retail sectors of Thailand are of particular concern. With continuing economic

Table 10.1 Evolution of business networks in Thailand: 1960–2010s

Period	1960– 1970s	1980– 1990s	2000–2010s
Strategy	Import-substitution industrialization	Export-oriented industrialization	Post-Asian financial crisis and expansion in AEC
Business networks	*Emerging business groups* Local capitalists Foreign MNCs (manufacturers) Government	*Diversified business groups* Local capitalists Foreign MNCs (manufacturers and trading partners) Government	*Regional expansion of business groups* Local capitalists Foreign MNCs (manufacturers and trading partners) SMEs Host countries' capitalists Government
Market	Domestic market	Domestic market and overseas markets (US, EU, Japan) M&A in domestic markets	Overseas markets (China, ASEAN, US, EU, Japan) and domestic market M&A in overseas and domestic markets
Finance	Loans from commercial banks Financial conglomerate	Loan from commercial banks Financial conglomerate Listed on the stock exchange (and pyramidal shareholding)	Listed on the stock exchange (and pyramidal shareholding) Corporate bond Infrastructure fund and property fund Loan from commercial banks
Technology	Joint ventures with foreign MNCs	Joint ventures with foreign MNCs	Owned technology and know-how Joint ventures with foreign MNCs
Human Resources	Personnel management Traditional human resource development	Human resource management Managerial education	Talent management International human resource management Global HR and global managers

crises around the world and falling demand for consumer products in the United States and Europe, Asian firms, as well as governments, have been trying to increase consumption in their domestic markets. This section primarily focuses on how Thailand has gone through major economic changes and has refocused on domestic consumer markets. Examining this issue tells us much about the ways firms and business groups integrate and structure the economies of which they are so much a part.

10.3.1 During the 1960–1970s: Building Domestic Manufacturing Networks for Import Substitution Industrialization

In the first section, we briefly describe the business network in Thailand in the period between the 1960s and 1970s, when Thailand developed its own distinctive domestic approach to import-substitution industrialization. The industrialization in Thailand began with the first National Economic Development in 1960. Currently, in 2015, it is under its 11th National Economic and Social Development Plan.

The strong-tie-based relationships with both business partners and government officials are pervasive in Thailand. (Suehiro, 1989; Phongpaichit & Baker, 1998).

10.3.2 During 1980–1990s: Building Domestic Manufacturing Networks for Export-Led Industrialization and Asian Financial Crisis

In the second section, we describe the confluence of events that occurred roughly from 1985 through the Asian Financial Crisis in 1997, and the effects of these events on Thailand. In this period, Thailand had received aggressive FDI and developed into export-oriented industrialization.

In the early 1980s, the more populous Asian countries adopted export-led manufacturing policies as a means of industrializing their economies (Deyo, 1987), which massively expanded the regions subcontracting capacity. At the same time, the less populous Asian economies began to encounter rising factor costs, so firms relocated their production activities to lower-cost newly industrializing states (Vogel, 1991). In successive Asian countries that turned to export-oriented development, the family business-controlled groups (FBGs) were able to utilize their governance advantage to mediate entry for foreign investors (Chung, 2013; Suehiro, 2006). The Plaza Accord of 1985 that brought a wave of labour and resource-seeking investment to the ASEAN region, again put FBGs into close contact with Japanese firms. In these ventures, FBGs mediated the entry of Japanese firms into the region in exchange for production and management technology (Siamwalla et al., 1997; Witt, 2014).

As the Thailand economy entered the 1980s, it was struggling to adjust to the same external shocks besieging much of the developing world at the time. Two oil shocks in the 1970s caused a severe deterioration in Thailand's terms of trade. The government of Mr. Prem Tinsulanonda (prime minister during 1980–88) responded by implementing costly, but needed policy reforms in several areas. The baht was also devalued, first in 1981 and then again in 1984. Independent central banks, currency boards, and independent regulatory agencies are examples of institutional tools created to help ensure that policy making and implementation are timely and free from interference by politicians and special interests (Hicken, 2001).

The fruit of the structural adjustment under Prem's government was a stable and restructured macro economy. This placed Thailand in a position to take advantage of the flood of FDI from East Asia during the late 1980s. As companies in Japan, Taiwan, and Hong Kong sought to move more production offshore in response to currency appreciation and rising labour costs after the Plaza Accord, Thailand's sound macro economy made it an attractive choice for investors. Thailand was able to enjoy high levels of foreign direct investment and economic growth (Hicken, 2001).

It can be said that in this period, Thailand started to build up its comparative advantages due to its successful economic expansion. When a country starts to develop, it will experience rapid economic growth because available factors of production will be utilized. These include natural resources, land, (cheap) labour, and capital which will be used to manufacture products and generate revenue, which lead to capital accumulation for further expansion in production. Thailand and other Asian countries all have gone through this journey in their economic development process (Doner, 2009; Hewison, 1989). Later on, Thailand would build up its competitive advantage which emphasized growth from improved manufacturing efficiency and productivity and FDI, especially that from Japan. This has enabled Thailand to improve its labour-intensive manufacturing to more of the upstream manufacturing of petrochemical-based products and achieved two-digit growth rates based mainly on its export-oriented strategy (Jestin, 2009; Wailerdsak, 2005). All these have been possible because of the successful exploration of natural gas in the Thai Gulf, which became the source of cheap energy resources, as well as an important petrochemical industry base. There also have been two rounds of government investment of industrial estates to support the Japanese FDI during the appreciation of Japanese Yen in 1985–90 and 2000–05. However, currently, the Japanese yen has depreciated and the remaining Thailand's natural gas will be available for less than 10 years (Phongpaichit & Baker, 1989; Suehiro, 1989).

The economic boom got its second wind as the financial sector was liberalized, a process that was completed by 1993 with the opening of the Bangkok International Banking Facility (BIBF). Financial liberalization brought a flood of new money into the Thai economy that fueled a stock market and real estate boom. Thailand's financial architecture and regulatory system needed to be adapted to manage the increased flow of foreign capital. However, the government failed to make the needed reforms. By the mid-1990s, the financial sector was in serious trouble. The lack of oversight had allowed cronyism and other imprudent lending practices to flourish as evidenced in the case of the Bangkok Bank of Commerce (BBC) scandal, which eventually went bankrupt and was force to close (Wailerdsak, 2006; 2008a).

The forms of capital campaign emphasized on commercial bank loans of which usually prime customers were preferred. Those from medium and small-sized customers are not their main source of revenue. However, after 1997, the banking institutions had to change their policies and strategies to focus more on the small and medium-sized companies. This is because the large corporations acquired their capital from the capital market or issued their own bonds. Europe and the United States did not encounter the financial crisis at the time. Thus, it was not difficult to solve the problems, because the Thai export markets in both Europe and the United States were still very good. The depreciation of Thai baht made the export sector the prime engine of Thailand's economic growth at the time. Thailand could substantially increase its payment of its international debts from 35% of its GDP in 1996 to 65% of its GDP in 2006. Later, Thailand's economic growth depended on increased foreign investment and ownership of financial and large corporations in the country (Suehiro, 2009; Pananond, 2011).

10.3.3 During 2000–2010s: ASEAN Economic Community and New Challenges

In this section, which is the main body of this chapter, we document the changes in economic structure in Thailand which occurred after the 1997 Asian Financial Crisis, the 2007 global financial crisis, and the ongoing integration of ASEAN Economic Community (AEC) to be completed by the end of 2015. Over this period and up to the present, Thailand has been deeply integrated in the Asian regional economy, which is now centred on China, and in the global economy, in which the Asian region plays an ever more prominent role. Leading firms in Thailand have also turned importantly towards ASEAN countries. Their strategies in doing so, however, remain distinct and quite differently organized. In this section, we pay special attention to new development strategies to cope with middle-income trap and the international expansion to ASEAN markets.

10.3.3.1 New Development Strategies and ASEAN Economic Community

10.3.3.1.1 New Normal

The economic growth of Thailand (GDP) was on average, 9% in 1990 and lowered to 5% per year in 2000. Followed by the political turbulence in the country during 2010–14, the economic growth became 3% per year. The export growth rate was also negative consecutively from 2012. Under the new normal of the economic conditions and growth, it is expected that the growth rate will be about 3% per year and the export growth rate will not be higher than 4% per year. This is due to the fact that many environmental factors are changing. Many of the main staple products such as rice, rubber, and palm oil have experienced a continuous decline in price. In addition, the EU has stopped the Generalized System of Preferences (GSP) privileges for Thailand as it has reached the expiration within the set time frame. In addition, Thai manufacturers or exporters have not ventured to other countries to make use of the GSP privileges that those countries could have offered. So, the problems must be solved by other means and mechanisms available in the country (Thailand Future Foundation Institute of Education, 2015; World Bank, 2015).

Thailand is currently faced with some significant problems, which contribute to the slow economic growth. The main problem is that the world trade has slowed down and its export growth rate is negative. From the expansion rate around 10% per year during 1998–2008, the growth rate of the export sector has gone down to 0.9% per year during 2011–13. Needless to say, part of this outcome was due to the world economic recession. But more importantly, Thailand's manufacturing sector, which is the foundation of the export sector and the source of wealth for the country, has been trapped and could not make a breakthrough from such a trap. It lacks technological advancement to compete in the international upper markets. At the same time, it could not come down to compete with China and Vietnam in the lower markets which utilizing cheap labour. This trap reflects the law of diminishing returns which is experienced when the economic opportunities and gains based on the utilization of local labour resources and foreign technology start to diminish (Siengthai et al., 2009). This necessitates the country increase its technological capacity with respect to production and labour productivity to build its production capacity and hence, competitiveness (Jestin, 2009; Suehiro, 2009). The second problem is the fierce competitive environment within the region itself. For example, the value of electronics products from Vietnam is much higher than that of Thailand (ie, about 40%). In spite of the fact that not many years ago (ie, in 2010), the value of electronics product export from Vietnam was only one in four times Thailand's export (IMD, 2014). In mid-2015, Samsung shut down its TV production base in Thailand and moved to set up a new manufacturing plant in Vietnam with about 90,000 mil. baht registered capital. The third problem issue for Thailand is that it is evident that Thailand is becoming an ageing society and the wage rates are increasing. The Thai population is rapidly ageing, while the active labour force is hardly increasing. The wage rates are increasing rapidly after the minimum wage policy was implemented in around 2010 which was above the labour productivity rate. This has decreased Thailand's competitiveness significantly when compared to its competitors in the global markets (IMD, 2014; Suehiro, 2009; World Economic Forum, 2014). In 2011, there was a great flood in Thailand, which led to the retrenched export sector, as many manufacturing plants had to close down and companies needed significant budgets to recover and renovate.

Under the 11th National Economic and Social Development Plan, the Thai economy, which earlier had depended on the manufacturing sector, is experiencing the saturation point. The export sector is declining. More and more emerging economies have entered into the manufacturing of basic needs products in competition directly with Thailand. Meanwhile, the upgrading to the production of high-technology products also demands time in development. The existing competitors are firmly controlling their market share. Thus, Thailand has come to a critical junction in its transition from a middle-level income to a high-level income and developed economy. The National Economic and Social Development Board (NESDB) has therefore established a strategy for the country that Thailand now is entering into the era in which the country growth will be based on innovation and creativity. Thailand has to transform from low-cost advantage manufacturing to the service sector which emphasizes 'Thainess'. In the 11th Plan, there is a clear indication about the development of industries which are knowledge-based. In the new BOI Investment Promotion Policy issued in January 2015, it is clearly stated that the government wants to create a competitive advantage in a Thai way by emphasizing the 'Thainess' as its strengths.

10.3.3.1.2 Trading Nation and Thailand Plus One Scheme

After the great floods in 2011 and the ongoing political turbulence in the country, the flow of FDI has declined. Much of the FDI flow went to other ASEAN countries such as Vietnam, the Philippines, Malaysia, Indonesia, etc.

The Thai government was required to prepare a long-term trade strategy to induce both domestic and foreign investment to mobilize the sustainable export sector. In the past, there was a clear strategy to develop the country to become a Detroit of Asia, where Thailand will be the regional centre for the world's automobile industry as well as to develop Thailand to become the World's Kitchen.

Currently in 2015, the policy that the government is pushing seriously to induce investors includes those such as the Special Economic Zones (SEZs), together with the border trade promotion, the Trading Nation policy, and the promotion for the private sector's investment in neighbouring countries, according to the Thailand+1 Scheme. All these are the government's effort to capitalize on the country's strengths to become the regional centre of AEC. They aim at mobilizing the foreign investment in Thailand and bridging the manufacturing supply chain in the AEC region to become the manufacturing bases of agricultural and semi-raw materials.

The Trading Nation policy, or the Trading Center policy will emphasize the export of services such as logistics, hotels, restaurants, wholesale and retail trade, product distribution centres, and tourism in combination with export. This will increase value-added rather than just export alone. In the past, Thailand has had to depend on the distribution channel and transport through foreign companies which lead to low profit margins for Thai companies as it had to compete in term of pricing mainly. The government has started to push more aggressively by providing support to the establishment of the international headquarters (IHQ) and international trading centres (ITCs). There is an emphasis for the private sector to observe the major principles of the Trading Nation Policy which is to be ready to 'move up and move out'. There are basically three steps in becoming the 'Trading Nation'. These are (1) exporting raw materials; (2) importing raw materials from sources that have lower costs than Thailand to be processed for more value added and then export; and (3) exporting services by capitalizing on the strengths of the country in term of its strategic location which is good as a regional centre (Thailand Future Foundation Institute of Education, 2015).

Thailand plus one refers to Thailand's future collaboration with each of its neighbouring countries.

10.3.3.1.3 Internationalization and ASEAN Economic Community

Currently, Thailand has invested overseas on a continuous basis. The investment volume has increased from about 3 trillion dollars before 2007 to about 6 trillion dollars per year. This is an increase in the last 8 years.

However, this is much lower when compared to that of Malaysia. In fact, the overseas investment of Thai companies is not new. Earlier, large corporations had already been able to expand their investment overseas. The promotion of the AEC integration in the last few years has made Thai corporations become more keen to invest overseas, especially in ASEAN countries (Table 10.2). FDI and technology are eagerly welcomed in these countries as the first stage of their economic development. Needless to say, one of the countries of interest to Thai investors is Myanmar. The industries that receive FDI from Thailand will tend to be those in the infrastructure development areas, such as construction, construction materials, energy and telecommunications. This includes some companies such as Millcon Steel Corp. Ltd. (Plc.), which established the construction materials plant and Toyo-Thai Corp. (Plc.) which participated in the bidding of Lignite-based Electricity Generating Plant.

Another country in which Thai companies are interested in investing is Laos PDR, especially in the renewable energy sector. These include CK Power Ltd. (Plc.), which will invest in the hydroelectricity generation plant at the Saiyaburi Dam, Banpu Co. Ltd. (Plc.) which will jointly invest with Ratchaburi Electricity Co. Ltd. (Plc.), and another local Laotian company to establish the Hongsa Electricity Generating Plant. Demco Co. Ltd. (Plc.), which will invest in the infrastructure in Lao PDR. Other than these, there will be some investment in other countries such as in Indonesia and Cambodia. For example, Siam Cement Co. Ltd. (Plc.) will invest in the cement plants in both countries, including those in Myanmar and Laos PDR. In addition, there is a Petrochemical Complex Project in Vietnam (Herzog et al., 2013). Ichitan Co. Ltd. (Plc.) started to distribute its beverage products in Indonesia and is anticipated to build a manufacturing plant in Indonesia if its sales volume is over 1000 million baht in the future. All these foreign investment initiatives support the market expansion of Thailand and cater to the needs of ASEAN customers.

The most important reason for the investment expansion in AEC region is to cater to the full launch of AEC integration in 2016. The free trade with 0% import tax rate is expected to promote the trading values among AEC member countries. This includes the border trade and the cross-border trade, which should increase the income of each country's labour force. It is also anticipated that the proportion of the middle-income strata of the population will increase in the future. This will enhance the investment opportunities in these countries. The most evident example is the case of Siam Cement Co. Ltd. (Plc.). The company has acquired various

Table 10.2 List of firms investing in AEC countries

Myanmar
Ratchaburi Electricity. Holdings—distributing gas, LNG gas, and hydro-electricity energy
Millcon Steel—construction materials
General Engineering—construction materials
Toyo-Thai Corp.—electricity generating plant
Italian-Thai—construction sub-contracting
Siam Cement—construction materials
Advanced Information Technology—communication systems set up
Thonburi Hospital—establishing hospital and healthcare facilities
Sahapatanapibul—garments, ready-made noodles, cosmetics
Modernform—establishing a furniture manufacturing plant

Indonesia
Ichitan—beverage
Siam Cement—construction materials
Plam B—advertising bilboards
Central—department store
Thai Summit Auto—automotive parts
Banpu—coal mining
Osotspa—groceries and related products
CP Charoen Pokphand—food processing

Singapore
Thai Beverage—alcohol and non-alcohol beverage
Minor Food Group—Thai Express restaurant
S&P—restaurant
Gunkul International—engineering procurement and construction

Lao PDR
Ratchaburi Electricity. Holdings—distributing gas, LNG gas, and hydro-electricity energy
Banpu—hydro-electricity generating plant
CK Power—hydro-electricity generating plant
Siam Cement—construction materials
Sor. Khonkaen Foods—food processing
Demco—infrastructure system
Major Cineplex—movie theater

Cambodia
Group Leasing—motorcycle leasing
CP Charoen Phokphand—food processing
Mega Life Sciences—manufacturing and distribution of drugs (medical) and health-related products
Major Cineplex—movie theater
Siam Cement—construction materials
Central—department store

Vietnam
CP Charoen Phokphand—food processing
M-Link Asia Corporation—telecommunications products
Oishi—food
Thonburi Hospital—salinated water, drug manufacturing plant, hospital
SriThai Superware—melamine factory, plastic packaging
Central—department store
Berli Jucker—trading, manufacturing

establishments in many ASEAN countries for its holding companies such as cement manufacturing, paper and pulp manufacturing, and petrochemical industries because it anticipates that the domestic demand in Thailand will become more limited (Herzog et al., 2013).

Another dimension of foreign investment is to ameliorate the problem of labour force scarcity in Thailand. This is one of the main obstacles for the company to increase its production capacity and revenue generation as planned (Jestin, 2009). For example, Sahapat Co. has about 100,000 employees in its holding group. It decided to invest in Myanmar which not only solved its problem of labour force scarcity, but also gained many benefits from its investment which follows, such as the GSP privileges to export to Europe, etc.

Moreover, some companies were faced with some business obstacles in Thailand on a continual basis. For example, the brewery industry was faced with legal constraints, banning its marketing strategies and advertising to control and reduce the population's consumption of alcohol-related beverages. In addition, the government has also recently been in the process of restructuring the tax structure for alcoholic beverages by calculating the tax from the final retail trade. This becomes a significant risk factor for these establishments' cost structure while the foreign market opportunities are still abundant. Thus, this industry also moves aggressively into the foreign markets.

There are both positives and negatives points of concerns for Thailand. On the positive side, Thailand has a unique advantage because of its location, in the centre of the region, as within 3 h, one can travel to almost every country in Asia. Infrastructure and logistics such as the East-West corridor, improved railway systems, a land-bridge connecting the Indian Ocean and Pacific Ocean would truly make Thailand a logistics hub for the region.

The negatives for Thailand could be the mobility of labour. The country today faces challenges dealing with the influx of workers and we may end up losing our best employees to Singapore because of higher salaries and standard of living.

10.3.3.1.4 New Challenges: International Politics and Foreign Investment

There are challenges faced by Thai investors other than fierce competition in international trade. These include international politics and international relations, which may become latent obstacles in the future. For example, Thailand is currently faced with the suspension notice that EU just gave for Thailand's fishery and rated Thailand as the country which lacks reporting and controlling of unregulated fishing (IUU—illegal unreported and unregulated fishing), and takes no action about illegal fishing.

This has negatively affected the fishery products, which are exported to the European Union. Thailand also had been moved to Tier 3 by the United States, which is the worst situation about trafficking in persons (TIP) report in 2015. Then, the country is also faced with the evaluation results by the International Civil Aviation Organization (ICAO), which reported the under-standard measures in the airlines industry in Thailand. Thus, this also negatively affected the Thai products to be transported by air.

Thailand's competitors such as Japan, Malaysia, and Vietnam have negotiated Trade Agreements with the United States within the Trans Pacific Partnership (TPP) Framework. There are, in total, 12 countries which have a combined GDP of about 30 trillion USD or about 40% of the majority is that of the United States and Japan, which is together about 22 trillion USD. South Korea also negotiated an open trade with the United States but Thailand has not yet joined this group. If this group successfully completes their negotiation rounds, we will observe the investment to set up manufacturing plants in Malaysia and Vietnam to serve as the production base for export to the United States, and Japan, as well as other members within the TPP. Thus, Thailand will be at a disadvantage in terms of getting entry to the markets in the United States, Japan, and other TPP countries.

Moreover, there are also laws that are obstacles to investing in foreign companies. These include the Act of Foreigner's Entrepreneurship. This Act prohibits foreigners from holding more than 49% of the ownership, especially in the service sector, which is considered the future of Thailand. However, if the country still continues to have its economy mobilized by the manufacturing sector, this will not be good for its future. Eventually, there will be a decline of the manufacturing sector.

10.4 GOVERNMENT INVESTMENT POLICY AND OTHER RELEVANT BUSINESS LAWS

Board of Investment (BOI) is an important government organization in developing countries like Thailand in promoting the investment in the country. Recently, there have been new investment policies. In the section below, we will describe and discuss these policies.

10.4.1 New BOI Investment Promotion Policy

Thailand's new BOI investment promotion policy is governed by the 'Seven-Year Investment Strategy' (2015–21), which came into effect on 1 Jan. 2015 (Table 10.3). This policy was aimed at moving Thailand into a

Table 10.3 BOI strategy in 2015 and its expected impact

BOI strategy—2015	Impact of the new BOI investment promotion scheme
'Broad-based' to 'focus and prioritized'	– Approximately 40 business activities (out of 240 activities) will no longer be promoted, eg, bread, green tea manufacturing – 40 activities which currently are eligible for tax incentives will be cut but will receive other incentives
'Sector-based' to 'section and merit-based'	– Basic tax incentives will be reduced – Other incentives will be granted if projects have merits to encourage competitiveness enhancement activities, eg, R&D, product and packaging design, advanced technological training and local supplier development or locate the projects in an industrial estate/zone
'Zones' to 'clusters' 'Tax incentives' to 'facilitation oriented' benefits	'Industrial clusters' will replace zones 1, 2, and 3. Instead of granting generous tax incentives to investors, the BOI will focus on – Nontax incentives and one stop services – Improving investment rules and regulations to reduce barriers and create a better investment environment – Promoting and coordinating human resource development – Packaging the support of various government agencies

higher level of development, focusing on competitiveness and value creation in the industrial sector.

The government has been continuously upgrading and improving its policies as stated by the BOI early in 2015. The significant turning point is that it is the first time BOI decided to stop promoting enterprises that are labour-intensive, such as textiles, garments, and sports shoes. This is because Thailand cannot compete with other countries especially its neighbouring countries in term of labour costs. The new investment promotion policy will give priority to investments that are beneficial to and supportive of the country's overall development strategy. These industries include high-tech and creative industries, service industries that support the development of a digital economy, and industries that utilize local resources. The BOI zoning system will be abolished under the new policy, although investment projects located in 20 lower-income provinces, as well as projects in industrial estates, will be offered special incentives. It also has changed the legal entity benefits from tax-exempt as well as the import tax of 7 years to the benefits in facilitating the benefits related to machinery, raw materials, and other benefits which are not related to tax. This has led to some protests from various business groups in the Federation of Industries as well as the Chamber of Commerce of Thailand, because they now are deprived of various benefits.

Promoting inbound and outbound investment is still included in the strategy. Whereas the BOI has primarily been focusing on inbound investment, the BOI will now promote overseas investment more actively to increase the competitiveness of Thai business.

In addition, the BOI will change the way it measures performance from the value of investment to the value of the project's outcome (ie, the value-added created by the promoted project in Thailand). The BOI will set clear KPIs to measure benefits and cost-effectiveness of investment promotion.

The new activities eligible for promotion under the new strategy will be divided into seven categories (similar to the existing scheme), but the BOI will have a stronger emphasis on industries with high technology, value-added creation, incorporating R&D or design, as well as being environmentally friendly. The eligible activities still include most activities, which are significant to the supply chain and have the potential to be strengthened. Eligible business activities are divided into two groups. Group A includes those that are important to support national economic restructuring. BOI offers corporate income tax exemption to encourage more investment and to enhance the country's competitiveness. Group B consists of activities that do not employ high technology, but still are important to the value chain. BOI will offer nontax incentives, as well as tax privileges related to machinery and raw materials.

In addition, the policy also promotes investment in special border areas. Investment projects located in the five special economic zones will receive an additional 3-year corporate income tax exemption on top of basic incentives. These special zones include areas within the five provinces, namely, Tak, Trad, Sa Kaeo, Songkhla, and Mukdahan.

10.5 ANTICORRUPTION MOVEMENT

Under the developmentalism capitalism, the State has a significant role in guiding or providing direction of national economic development. The investment by the government or public sector is expected to be one factor to boost the economic growth. This includes mega-projects which when the State invests, the private sector will follow suit. Moreover, the State will grant the concessionaries, or issue the license of enterprise for the entrepreneurs in many business sectors. Thus, this has made Thailand a patron–client system and a State-dependent economy. This also has led to the 'Corruption System Cycle'. That is, there is no fair play in business competition (Montreevet, 2006; Nikomborirak & Tawankul, 2006; Phongpaichit & Baker, 2009). There are some monopoly or oligopolistic power and some joint ventures between the government agencies and private sector enterprises. There is a limitation of access to resources and business opportunities. This boils down to inner circles of friends and acquaintances to agree on how to divide the cake (Suehiro & Wailerdsak, 2004, 2014). But eventually the responsibility falls onto the society. It destroys the constructive atmosphere of innovative products and services to compete in the market.

The reason that the business sector has given less attention and low importance to research and development is because there is a risk that the investment in R&D will not be successful. Or even when it is successful, firms still have a risk to compete with other competitors. It is not as effective to invest when compared to being involved in corruption, which is not a risk such as paying for some facilitation by the government agents, or to pay for convenience and expedite the transaction with the government offices. This way of thinking leads to the lack of R&D in the country and it is the main reason that has created inequality in the society. It also has led to the inefficiency in infrastructure management and it does not enhance the competitiveness of the country.

The corruption involved by politicians is another major reason which led to the protest of the former ousted Prime Minister Yingluck Shinawatr in 2013. The political turbulence has led to the coup d'état undertaken by the National Council for Peace and Order (NCPO) led by Prayut Chan-Ocha, the Commander in Chief of the Royal Thai Army, in 2014. This has led to the awareness and campaign in protest of corruption in the country.

Thailand's Private Sector Collective Action Coalition against Corruption (CAC, wwa.thai-cac.com) was initiated in 2010 with the aim of fostering awareness of corruption risks among the private sector and the need to resist and fight corruption through the implementation of policies and effective mechanisms to prevent corruption at the company and industry levels. The scope of CAC focuses specifically on the private sector and it works closely and in parallel with the government's National Anticorruption Commission (NACC) and the Anticorruption Organization of Thailand (ACT), which handles the civil society front.

The CAC was cofounded by the country's eight leading organizations in the private sector, including the Thai Chamber of Commerce, the Joint Foreign Chambers of Commerce in Thailand, the Thai Listed Companies Association, the Federation of Thai Industries, the Federation of Thai Capital Market Organizations, the Thai Bankers' Association, the Tourism Council of Thailand, and the Thai Institute of Directors Association, which also serves as its secretariat and takes a leading role in driving the program. The CAC's operations are sponsored by the US-based Center for Private Enterprise and the UK Prosperity Fund. Moreover, the CAC also exchanges anticorruption knowledge and experiences with international agencies regularly. It has joined the B20 Collective Action Hub and the ASEAN CSR Network.

Besides arranging regular training and education activities to promote establishing and implementing internal anticorruption policies and processes to executives and staffs of private companies, the CAC also gives certification to companies that have been externally verified for having put in place policy and compliance standards to prevent corruption as per criteria set by the CAC. This certification process is considerably more advanced than regional peers and many countries have expressed their keen interest to study the process and apply the concept with anticorruption initiatives in the respective countries.

The move is part of scaled-up government efforts led by Prime Minister Prayut Chan-Ocha to clamp down on corruption after Thailand's ranking on Transparency International's corruption perceptions index (CPI) slipped to 102nd out of 177 countries in 2013 from 88th in 2012. Private companies join the CAC voluntarily. As of end-2014, some 406 companies, including 212 listed companies, had joined—up by 138 companies from 268 at the end of 2013. Of the total, 78 companies have been certified by the CAC for having put in place policies and high compliance standards to prevent corruption, up from 22 companies at end-2013.

In the next phase, the CAC plans to increase the robustness of certification standards in order to make it more compatible with international standards, which will help facilitating Thai companies in dealing with foreign partners or trading counterparts on the issue of on anticorruption. The CAC plans a large increase in its member companies, focusing in particular on firms involved in public procurement.

Another factor that helped elevate corruption consciousness among the business sector was the Securities and Exchange Commission's (SEC) move to compile and disseminate an antigraft progress indicator. This records progress made by listed companies to put antigraft policies into action. This indicator will be another tool to help investors understand listed companies' profiles on anticorruption policies and commitments (SET, 2014).

In addition, there is a reform of the Anticorruption Act by the National Commission Against Corruption to be more strict against the corruption, and to be consistent with the Anti-Foreign Fraud Law by the Constitution Act III 2015 B.E. with respect to the Anticorruption Act is proclaimed in the Royal Gazette and effective since July 2015. In this Act, there is one issue that was revised, which is related to the private sector organizations. That is the establishment of the standards of crime, especially for the legal entity dealing with bribing the government officers.

10.6 CONCLUSION

In the last 10 years, Thai economy has achieved minimal growth rate (ie, about 3.8%) when compared to its neighbouring countries. In the last 3 years, especially, the country's economic growth rate is only 2.2%, when the world economic growth rate is about 3.3%, and no country is experiencing recession. If Thailand could not achieve the higher than 5% growth rate, it will move into what is considered 'new normal' at the 3–3.5% growth rate. The country has been fully utilising the available resources and is transitioning itself into an ageing society or 'getting older before getting rich' situation. It is expected that if the country is growing at the 3–3.5% per year, it would take Thailand about 32 more years to become a fully developed economy in 2047.

Based on the discussion above, one of the deep-rooted problems of Thailand is its patron–client system. Everyone demands the government to solve all problems. The economic growth that Thailand achieved in the past was due to the government's initiatives and efforts. Thus, this growth is not sustainable. What the country should do is to reduce the government's role and power. Thailand also has to reform in many areas: education, politics, and research and development, whose investment is only constantly about 0.2% of the GDP in the last 10 years. If the country's investment in R&D is increased to about or more than 1% of the GDP, it is likely that there will be some changes in innovation and advanced technology. In addition, this includes the reform of the state-owned enterprises which are significant assets of the country (ie, 12 trillion baht). But the returns on assets is less than 2%.

Moreover, there is a need to reform the laws of which many are outdated and have become a significant obstacle to business operations. The capital market also needs to be reformed so that there will be various services that would be more comprehensive and cost-effective. Finally, there is a need to reform, reduce, or do away with the corruption in the country.

In fact, currently, there is an alert in both the public and private sector due to the fact that the export sector has been growing at a negative rate in the past years. The effect of the fact that China's growth rate has been slowed down when China is Thailand's principal trading partner is evident. Thus, it is expected that Thailand should transform itself before it is forced to change. So, Thailand is preparing the 12th National Economic and Social Development Plan for 2017–21 to transform the country into the highest level of a middle-income country. This means that the per capita, or GNP would need to reach 8859 USD/year. So, this Plan is an important one that would facilitate the country to move out of the middle-income trap of Thailand, expected in the next 10 years.

The private sector needs to act by developing their business networks both within and outside of the country or by improving their network effectiveness in three ways: (1) there should be a network in technology and innovation to upgrade the productivity and brand of their products to be sold in the global markets. This is through promoting the design, research and development of products by emphasizing the Thai product groups that are ready; (2) developing the manufacturing network to expand the manufacturing supply chain and Thailand serves as the regional centre, according to the Thailand+1 Scheme. This can now be seen in industries such as the automotive and garment industries; (3) developing business networks for existing market development, as well as new market development, together with the communications technologies. In addition, the supporting roles of other institutions such as Federation of Industries, Chamber of Commerce, etc., are very crucial for the business expansion and network development of the firms in the future.

ACKNOWLEDGEMENT

The first author gratefully acknowledge the financial support provided by Thammasat University Research Fund under the TU New Research Scholar, 2559.

REFERENCES

Abbot, J. (2003). *Developmentalism and dependency in Southeast Asia: The case of the automotive industry*. New York: RoutledgeCurzon.

Amsden, A. H. (1989). *Asia's next giant: South Korea and late industrialization*. New York: Oxford University Press.

Asian Development Bank. (2011). *Asia 2050: Realizing the Asian century*. Manila: Asian Development Bank.
Carney, R. M. (2014). Business groups in Asia: An institutional perspective. In M. A. Witt & G. Redding (Eds.), *The Oxford handbook of Asian business systems* (pp. 309–331). New York: Oxford University Press (Chapter 15).
Carney, R. M., Gedajlovic, E., & Yang, X. (2009). Varieties of Asian capitalism: Toward an institutional theory of Asian enterprise. *Asia Pacific Journal of Management, 26*, 361–380.
Carney, R. M., & Witt, M. A. (2014). The role of the state in Asian business systems. In M. A. Witt & G. Redding (Eds.), *The Oxford handbook of Asian business systems* (pp. 538–560). New York: Oxford University Press (Chapter 24).
Chung, H. (2013). The role of family management and family ownership in diversification: The case of family business groups. *Asia Pacific Journal of Management, 30*, 871–891.
Chung, W., & Hamilton, G. G. (2009). Getting rich and staying connected: The organizational medium of Chinese capitalists. *Journal of Contemporary China, 18*(58), 47–67.
Claessens, S., Djankov, S., & Lang, L. H. (1999). *Who controls East Asian Corporations?* World Bank Policy research working paper no. 2054. Washington, DC: World Bank.
Deyo, F. C. (1987). *The political economy of the new Asian industrialism (Cornell Studies in Political Economy)*. New York: Cornell University Press.
Doner, R. F. (2009). *The politics of uneven development: Thailand's economic growth in comparative perspective*. New York: Cambridge University Press.
Guillen, M. F. (2000). Business groups in emerging economies: A resource-based view. *Academy of Management Journal, 43*(3), 362–380.
Hamilton, Gary G. (1996). *Asian business networks*. Berlin: De Gruyter.
Herzog, J. O., Munir, K. A., & Kattuman, P. (2013). The king and I: Monarchies and the performance of business groups. *Cambridge Journal of Economics, 37*, 171–185.
Hewison, K. (1989). Bankers and bureaucrats: Capital and state in Thailand. Southeast Asian Monograph 34. New Haven: Yale University.
Hicken, A. (2001). Governance and growth in Thailand. In J. E. Campos (Ed.), *Corruption: The boom and bust of East Asia*. Manila: Ateneo de Manila University Press.
IMD. (2014). *World competitiveness yearbook 2014*. Switzerland: IMD.
Ip, P.-K. (2007). Corporate social responsibility and crony capitalism in Taiwan. *Journal of Business Ethics, 79*, 167–177.
Jestin, B. (2009). Industrial upgrading and educational upgrading: Two critical issues for Thailand. In P. Intarakumnerd & Y. Lecler (Eds.), *Sustainability of Thailand's competitiveness* (pp. 78–125). Singapore: ISEAS.
Kang, D. C. (2003). Transaction costs and crony capitalism in East Asia. *Comparative Politics, 35*(4), 439–458.
Khanna, T., & Rivkin, J. W. (2001). Estimating the performance effects of business groups in emerging markets. *Strategic Management Journal, 22*(1), 45–74.
Makino, S., & Yiu, D. W. (2014). A survey of strategic behavior and firm performance in Asia. In M. A. Witt & G. Redding (Eds.), *The Oxford handbook of Asian business systems* (pp. 561–586). Oxford: Oxford University Press.
Montreevet, S. (Ed.), (2006). *Corporate governance in Thailand*. Singapore: ISEAS.
Nikomborirak, D., & Tawankul, S. (2006). Monopolies and politics. Paper presented at TDRI Academic conference, 9–10 December 2006. Thailand: Chonburi.
Pananond, P. (2011). The global value chains of Thai multinationals: Evidence from listed firms in Thailand. *Economics, Management, and Financial Markets, 6*(1), 84–141.
Phongpaichit, P., & Baker, C. (1998). *Thailand boom and bust*. Chiangmai: Silkworm Books.
Phongpaichit, P., & Baker, C. (2009). *Thaksin: The business of politics in Thailand* (2nd ed.). Chiangmai: Silkworm Books.
Schneider, B. R. (2009). A comparative political economy of diversified business groups, or how states organize big business. *Review of International Political Economy, 16*(2), 178–201.

SET. (2014). *Corporate governance report of Thai listed companies 2014*. Bangkok: Stock Exchange of Thailand.
Siamwalla, A., Vichyanond, P., & Christensen, S. (1997). *Thailand's boom and bust*. Bangkok: Thailand Development Research Institute.
Siengthai, S., Dechawatanapaisal, D., & Wailerdsak, N. (2009). Human resource management: Future trends. In T. G. Andrews & S. Siengthai (Eds.), *The changing face of management in Thailand* (pp. 115–145). London and New York: Routledge.
Suehiro, A. (1989). *Capital accumulation in Thailand 1855–1985*. Tokyo: UNESCO and Centre for East Asian Cultural Studies.
Suehiro, A. (2006). *A study of family business: Agents of late industrialization*. Nagoya: Nagoya University Press (in Japanese).
Suehiro, A. (2008). *Catch-Up industrialization: The trajectory and prospects of East Asian economies*. Singapore: National University of Singapore Press.
Suehiro, A. (2009). *Thailand: Challenge of middle income country*. Tokyo: Iwanami (in Japanese).
Suehiro, A., & Wailerdsak, N. (2004). Family business in Thailand: Its management, governance and future challenges. *ASEAN Economic Bulletin*, *21*(1), 81–93.
Suehiro, A., & Wailerdsak, N. (2014). Thailand: Post-developmentalist capitalism. In M. Witt & G. Redding (Eds.), *The Oxford handbook of Asian business systems* (pp. 260–282). New York: Oxford University Press.
Thailand Future Foundation Institute of Education. (2015). *Thailand 's economy in the context of new Thailand's new normal*. Bangkok: Thailand Institute of Future Studies Foundation.
Tipton, F. B. (2009). Southeast Asian capitalism: History, institutions, states, and firms. *Asia Pacific Journal of Management*, *26*, 401–434.
Vogel, E. F. (1991). *The four little dragons: The spread of industrialization in East Asia*. Cambridge, MA: Harvard University Press.
Wade, R. (2010). After the crisis: Industrial policy and the developmental state in low-income countries. *Global Policy*, *1*(2), 150–161.
Wailerdsak, N. (2005). *Managerial careers in Thailand and Japan*. Chiangmai: Silkworm Books.
Wailerdsak, N. (2006). *Business groups and family business in Thailand before and after the 1997 crisis*. BrandAge: Bangkok (in Thai).
Wailerdsak, N. (2008a). Companies in crisis. In P. Phongpaichit & C. Baker (Eds.), *Thai capital after the 1997 crisis* (pp. 17–57). Chiangmai: Silkworm Books.
Wailerdsak, N. (2008b). Family business in Thailand: Ownership structure and stock market. In V. Gupta, N. Levenburg, T. Schwarz, & L. Moore (Eds.), *Culturally-sensitive models of family business in Southern Asia* (pp. 108–133). Hyderabad: ICFAI University Press.
Wailerdsak, N., & Suehiro, A. (2010). Business groups in Thailand. In A. M. Colpan, T. Hikino, & J. R. Lincoln (Eds.), *Oxford handbook of business groups* (pp. 239–266). London and New York: Oxford University Press.
Wailerdsak, N., & Suehiro, A. (2014). Family business groups in Thailand: Coping with management critical points. *Asia Pacific Journal of Management*, *31*(4), 997–1018.
Whitley, R. D. (1992). *Business systems in East Asia*. Thousand Oaks: Sage.
Whitley, R. D. (1999). *Divergent capitalisms*. London and New York: Oxford University Press.
Witt, M. (2014). Japan: Coordinated capitalism between institutional change and structural inertia. In M. A. Witt & G. Redding (Eds.), *The Oxford handbook of Asian business systems* (pp. 100–122). Oxford: Oxford University Press.
World Bank. (2015). *Thailand economic monitor April 2015*. Bangkok: World Bank.
World Economic Forum. (2010). *Global competitiveness report 2010/2011*. Geneva: WEF.
Yeung, H. W. C. (2006). Change and continuity in Southeast Asian ethnic Chinese business. *Asia Pacific Journal of Management*, *23*, 229–254.

CHAPTER 11

Business Networks and Varieties of Capitalism in Thailand: Adding the Context of History, Political Structures, and Social and Cultural Values

V. Yukongdi*, C. Rowley†,‡,§,¶
*Asian Institute of Technology, Klong Luang, Thailand
†Korea University, Seoul, Korea
‡Griffith University, Nathan, QLD, Australia
§Nottingham University, Nottingham, United Kingdom
¶City University, London, United Kingdom

11.1 INTRODUCTION

Of relevance to business networks are their location within forms of capitalism. Attempts to model and theorise developments and trends in capitalism continue to be debated and critiqued. These include convergence theories and the re-emergence of its universalism, such as with Fordism, flexible specialisation, lean production, Japanisation, Toyotism, and globalisation (see Rowley, 1998), variegated and comparative capitalisms and business systems. One example, varieties of capitalism (VOC) analysis, lies within these and continues to generate interest across a range of academic areas, including politics, economics, sociology, industrial relations, organisation studies, management, international business, and business history (eg, Andriesse & van Westen, 2009; Blyth, 2003; Frenkel & Yu, 2014; Howell, 2003; Kelly & Hamann, 2008; Lallement, 2005; Peck & Theodore, 2007; Rowley & Quang, 2012; Rueda & Pontusson, 2000; Streeck, 2010; Witt & Redding, 2014).

Major criticisms of the VOC typology include its limited dynamism, narrow typology dichotomy, and limited geographical focus. It also underplays the role of context. Yet, historical and political background, social, cultural values and beliefs forge the 'playing surface' for business and capitalism, and so should be part of any analysis. Nevertheless, the VOC remains a powerful antidote to the naïve universalism mantra of too much research, especially in management, and it also provides a useful analytical framework.

Business Networks in East Asian Capitalisms
http://dx.doi.org/10.1016/B978-0-08-100639-9.00011-6

Therefore, we make several major contributions. We locate VOC in its historical and wider theoretical context. By using an example of a type of economy commonly ignored, we not only add to country-specific knowledge, we also push forward VOC's continuing usefulness and wider applicability, particularly to Asia by adding a missing 'sphere' to the VOC—the explicit influence of the context of history, political structures, and social and cultural values. The importance of investigating these factors is developed in many other chapters in this collection but especially in Chapters 2, 3 and 9.

11.2 LOCATING AND ANALYZING VOC

VOC can be located within earlier and broader theories and debates. These include universalism's convergence versus contingency's divergence. These are relevant to VOC's implicit (albeit binary) universalism. The central proposition of universal-type theories is of a world-wide tendency for political, social, economic, technological, and market forces to push national systems towards uniformity and convergence of practices assumed to be universally applicable and transferable. Such ideas have a long antecedence (eg, Kerr, Dunlop, Harbison, & Myers, 1962), are popular, and regularly re-emerge. Earlier ideas of 'the best way' at country level include France with indicative planning in the 1960s and Scandinavia with corporatism in the 1980s, and then the post-cold war (Fukuyama, 1992; Ohmae, 1990) literature, as well as at the practice level with the Excellence (Peters & Waterman, 1982), Lean Production, and Toyotism (Womack, Jones, & Roos, 1990) and Japanisation (Oliver & Wilkinson, 1992). Institutional Theory provides some explanation as adoption is not just because of 'effectiveness', but three specific social forces and factors. First, 'constraining' forces, as social constraints shift as ideas become interpreted positively and gain legitimacy. Second, 'cloning' forces pressurise firms to mimic actions of leading companies. Third, 'learning' forces, shaped through processes in educational institutions and professional associations. Together these forces push adoption of common institutional rules.

Linked to this are globalisation and the (re)emergence of 'A singular world view of market unification and institutional convergence…One world, one best way, no alternatives' (Peck & Theodore, 2007, p. 731). Theories from different subject areas seek to explain globalisation and Robinson (2007) reviews these grouped as: Global Capitalism, Network Society, Space and Place, Transnationality and Transnationalism, Modernity and Postmodernity to Global Culture and World-Systems. For example, World-Systems Theory (Wallerstein, 1974, 2004) is historical and multidisciplinary, emphasising: world-systems rather than nation-states; historical processes as they unfold over long time periods; and combining distinct bodies of knowledge. Thus, the world-system is a social reality comprised of interconnected firms, households, classes, and identity groups of all kinds with key moments significant in the development of the modern world-system, such as the 16th century development of a capitalist world economy. However, critics suggest world-systems collapse cultural forces into political systems and the independent influence of cultural forces cannot be reduced to different characteristics of political systems.

Commentators remain sceptical of universalistic theories, a literature again with a long lineage (see Lawrence & Lorsch, 1967; Woodward, 1965). Industrial sociology and industrial relations comparisons of the United Kingdom, including with Japan (Dore, 1974), often found national differences. Similarly, System, Society, and Dominance Theory (Smith & Meiksins, 1995) organised influences on work organisation in a triad of: modes of production; institutional patterns; best practice, or universal modernisation strategies generated (diffused by the dominant society). This argued societies were in a constant state of tension between divergence and convergence, which was not likely as structural pressures were conveyed through and conditioned by the histories and cultural contingencies of nations, which complicated convergence pressures. Indeed, for Sorge (2005), local actions were mediated through traditions at a national level, so '...successive rounds of institutional reinvention are layered up each other, resulting in place-specific "recombinant formations with distinctive properties"'(Peck & Theodore, 2007, p. 759).

Also, we can find evidence for both continuity and change simply because of their different research foci. Convergence studies concentrate on macro level variables, such as structure and technology, while divergence studies target micro level variables, such as the behaviour of people in organisations (Child, 1981).

Taking the above together, we see universalism constrained and diversity remaining for several reasons. Countries are at different stages of industrial and economic development and have distinctive political-economic frameworks, institutions and cultural features and value systems. Intranational heterogeneity exists via organisational decentralisation and flexibility and gaps between stated institutional frameworks and practice realities. The spread, take-up, operation, and configuration of technology, with alternative solutions to common problems, varies.

Other critiques of universalism as globalisation include the capitalist variety and comparative capitalism literature (Berger & Dore, 1996; Boyer, 2005; Coates, 2000; Crouch, 2005; Hollingswoth & Boyer, 1997; Kitschelt, Lange, Marks, & Stephens, 1999). These outline various capitalisms. Capitalisms were distinguished by: Dore (2000) as Stock Market (US, UK) or Welfare (smaller Europeans); Chandler (1990) as Competitive Managerial (US), Personal (UK) or Cooperative Managerial (Germany); Gerlach (1992) as Liberal (West) or Alliance (Japan); Albert (1993) as Neo-American or Rhinish (including Japan), Lazonick (1990, 1991, 1998) as Managerial (UK), Propriety (UK) or Collective (Japan). Amable (2003) used elements of product market, labour market, financial sector, social protection (welfare), and education to develop five models of capitalism: Market-based; Social-democratic; Continental European; South European; and Asian (but only based on Japan and Korea), characterised by 'governed' rather than regulated product market competition, regulated labour markets, bank-based financial systems, low level of social protection, and private tertiary-education systems.

There are few Asian-focused examples as exceptions. Boyer, Uemura, and Isogai (2012) used a Régulation Theory inspired approach to analyse Asia (Japan, China, Korea) by five basic institutional forms: competition and insertion into the world economy; labour market organisation; monetary and exchange rate regimes; style of state intervention via legislation, public spending and tax. Harada and Tohyama (2012) produced a five fold typology of Asian capitalism diversity using principal component and cluster analysis: City (Singapore, Hong Kong); Insular Semi-Agrarian (Indonesia, Philippines); Innovation-Led (Japan, Korea, Taiwan); Trade-Led Industrialising (Malaysia, Thailand); Continental Mixed (China). Similarly, these authors found institutional diversity produced five groups of Asian economies in terms of impacts on firm innovation activities (Tohyama & Harada, 2013) and four clusters of Asian welfare capitalisms (Tohyama, 2015).

However, the comparative capitalisms literature has been criticised for static analysis and bias towards predicting institutional stability rather than change, points made in earlier critiques of institutional pluralist industrial relations analysis and theory. So, Deeg and Jackson (2007) introduce change into comparative capitalism at three levels. First, micro, with less deterministic views incorporating greater understanding of how actors reshape institutions as both constraints and resources for new courses of action, incrementally changing institutions. Second, meso, to specify the linkages among institutions and institutional domains and how change in one affects the other. Third, macro, to incorporate views of national and international politics, and the impact of rule-breaking processes that govern institutional reform. Another alternative includes 'Variegated Capitalism' with its '...more expansive concern with the combined and uneven development of "always embedded" capitalism, and the polymorphic interdependence of its constituent regimes' (Peck & Theodore's, 2007, p. 733).

Other Asian-related models include business systems (Redding, 2005; Whitley, 2007, 2014), a framework '...consonant with many institutional analyses...' (Whitley, 1999, p. 5). Whitley (1992) used a three-fold framework of impacts from: Firms (management styles and structures, decision-making processes, owner-employee relations, patterns of growth and development); Markets (customer, supplier, and interfirm relations, financial sector and market and industry development); Societies (social influences on business evolution such as education, systems of power and status and family structures). This examined Japan, Korea, Taiwan and Hong Kong. Whitley (1999) detailed three types of North East Asian capitalism: Fragmented; State-organised; Collaborative.

Witt and Redding (2014) covered various Asian examples, not only the classics of Japan, Korea, Hong Kong, Singapore, Taiwan and now China, but also the less common ones of Malaysia, Thailand, Vietnam, and especially Indonesia, the Philippines, and Laos. Theories needed to incorporate '...social capital, culture, informality and 'multiplexity' and '...variations in the extent of informality in a business system and its interplay with formal institutions' (p. 686). By social capital, they meant 'trust', both interpersonal or relational; as well as institutionalised or system (with triple components: control; trust; morality) trust. Their framework includes the role of the state, financial system, ownership and corporate governance, internal structure of the firm, employment relations, education and skills formation, interfirm relations and social capital. This framework was used to organise the description of Thailand (Suehiro & Wailerdsak, 2014).

In sum, the VOC can be located within a context of other literatures and theories. Some of these preceded it, others followed in its wake. We argue comparative approaches should assume economic relationships and activities '...are socially constructed and institutionally variable...' and '...vary significantly between societal contexts...' (Whitley, 1999, p. 5).

11.3 VOC FRAMEWORK

VOC emphasised the role of the firm as a focal point of analysis and central actor in economic adjustment, focusing on the firm's relationship to five spheres of corporate governance: industrial relations, skills formation, interfirm relations, and employer-employee relations to resolve coordination problems. Firms are dependent on their ability to coordinate effectively with a range of other actors, including suppliers, clients, collaborators, stakeholders, trade unions, business associations, and governments.

Regarding corporate governance, firms encountered coordination problems accessing sources of funding and investors seeking assurances of returns on investments. Coordination issues also arise in industrial relations, where firms faced problems in coordinating bargaining over wages and working conditions with employees, labour organisations, and other employers. With skills formation, firms confronted problems in locating workers with appropriate skills, while employees needed to decide in what skills they should invest. Interfirm relations included suppliers and clients, as they seek to secure demand for products, access to supplies of inputs, and technology. Problems of coordination arise in the sharing of proprietary information and the risk of exploitation in joint ventures. In employer-employee relations, firms experienced problems in ensuring staff have the required skills and knowledge and work together to achieve objectives. While employees may have access to specialised information valuable to management, they could withhold such information. Information sharing, adverse selection, and moral hazards are some of the problems firms faced in this sphere.

The solutions to these problems affect the overall economy in terms of wages and productivity, unemployment, skill levels and competitiveness of the workforce, availability of finance, technological transfer and progress, firm competencies, and production systems. Economies differ in coordination problem resolution in two major ways, either: liberal market economy (LME), or coordinated market economy (CME), see the tables. LMEs are characterised by arm's-length exchange of goods and services, competitive relations, competition, formal contracting, and the operation of supply and demand based on price signalling. CMEs depended on nonmarket relations, collaboration, incomplete contracting, credible commitments, network monitoring and strategic interaction among firms, and other actors. Hence, in LMEs, market institutions are the means of coordination; while in CMEs firms rely on deliberative calculations. Firms will tend toward the mode of coordination for which there is institutional support (Tables 11.1 and 11.2).

Table 11.1 Liberal market economies (eg, Britain, United States, Australia, Canada, New Zealand, Ireland)

Financial system	• Access to capital linked to profitability • Pay attention to current earnings and share price • Investors depend on publicly available information to value the firm • Regulatory regimes tolerant of mergers and acquisitions and hostile takeovers • Large firms secure finance dependent on their valuation in equity markets • Compensation system reward top management for net earnings or share price increases
Internal structure of firm	• Top management unilateral control over firms • Fluid labour market, relatively easy to release or hire labour to take advantage of new opportunities • Less attractive to pursue production strategies based on long-term employment • Institutional features highly supportive of *radical innovation*[a] • High rates of labour mobility conducive to the development of new product lines as can hire in employees with requisite expertise who can be released if project proves unprofitable • Price increase passed on to consumers in order to maintain current profitability
Education and training	• Vocational training focuses on general skills • Loath to invest in apprenticeship schemes imparting industry-specific skills for fear of poaching by other firms not investing in training • Companies invest in substantial amount of in-house training • Employees face shorter job tenures and fluid labour markets • Firms encourage individuals to invest in general skills, transferable across firms • Career success depends on acquiring general skills transferable across firms
Industrial relations	• Firms under no obligation to establish representative bodies • Trade unions less powerful • Trade unions and employer associations less cohesive and encompassing • Economy-wide wage coordination difficult to secure and therefore depends more on macro-economic policy and market competition to control wages and inflation

Continued

Table 11.1 Liberal market economies (eg, Britain, United States, Australia, Canada, New Zealand, Ireland)—cont'd

Interfirm relations	• Competitive relationships, standard market relationships • Arm's-length exchange of goods and services • Formal contracting; strict interpretation of written contracts • Antitrust regulations to prevent companies from colluding to control price or markets • Firms run risk of being sued for damages under antitrust law • Relations based primarily on markets enhance firms' capacities to buy other, to poach their employees, to licence new products (ie, means of acquiring new technologies quickly) • Technology transfer secured through movement of scientists and engineers from one company to another that fluid labour markets facilitate • Firms rely heavily on licensing or sale of innovations

[a]*Radical innovation* entails substantial shifts in product lines, development of entirely new goods, or major changes to the production process.
Data from Hall, P. A., & Soskice, D. (2001). An introduction to varieties of capitalism. In *Varieties of capitalism: The institutional foundations of comparative advantage* (pp. 1–68). Oxford: Oxford University of Press.

Table 11.2 Coordinated market economies (eg, Germany, Japan, Switzerland, the Netherlands, Belgium, Sweden, Norway, Denmark)

Financial system	• Access to capital independent of current profitability • Access to capital not entirely dependent on publicly available information • Financial system provides capital on terms not sensitive to current profitability ('patient capital') so long-term employment more feasible • Possible to retain skilled workforce through economic downturns and invest in projects generating returns in long run • Finance not dependent on balance-sheet criteria so investors must have access to 'private' or 'inside' information about firm's operations • Close-knit corporate networks provide investors with inside information • Attentive to share price or current profitability to ensure access to finance or deter hostile takeovers

Table 11.2 Coordinated market economies (eg, Germany, Japan, Switzerland, the Netherlands, Belgium, Sweden, Norway, Denmark)—cont'd

Internal structure of firm	• Structural bias toward consensus decision-making • Production strategies based on long-term employment • Institutional features highly supportive of *incremental innovation*[a] • Lower rates of labour mobility conducive to development of product differentiation rather than intense product competition • Price increases not passed on to customers • Maintain prices and accept lower returns to preserve market share
Education and training	• Firms invest in substantial amount of in-house training in form of intensive apprenticeships • Intensive apprenticeships used to develop company-specific or industry-specific skills • Employees face longer tenures and less fluid labour markets • Firms encourage individuals to invest in company-specific skills • Career success for employees depend on acquiring highly specialised skills
Industrial relations	• Firms under no obligation to establish representative bodies • Strong trade unions • Powerful business or employer associations • Trade unions and employer associations cohesive and encompassing • Economy-wide wage coordination easier to secure (than in liberal market economies) • Long-term employment strategies as layoffs difficult
Inter-firm relations	• Nonmarket relationships, more collaborative relationships • More extensive relational contracting or incomplete contracting • Exchange of private information inside networks • Extensive networks of cross-shareholding • Legal or regulatory systems to facilitate information sharing and collaboration • Institutions provide capacity for monitoring of behaviour, network reputational monitoring • Extensive reputation building possible given dense business networks • Reputation for risk-taking or cutthroat competition rarely an asset in such networks

[a]*Incremental innovation* is marked by continuous but small-scale improvements to existing product lines and production processes.

Data from Hall, P.A., & Soskice, D. (2001). An introduction to varieties of capitalism. In *Varieties of capitalism: The institutional foundations of comparative advantage* (pp. 1–68). Oxford: Oxford University of Press.

11.4 CRITICISMS OF VOC

Along with the earlier criticisms of universalism, specific critiques of VOC emerged. Its division of capitalism into a neat polar dichotomy is a common target, as it lacks enough variety. Some countries fall between the typologies (Allen, 2004). It did not accommodate the diversity of capitalism at subnational, national, and transnational levels (Crouch, 2005; Hay, 2005; Howell, 2003; Thelen, 2004). Asian economies are at varying stages of development and hence, do not fit (Carney, Gedajlovic, & Yang, 2009). Studies are overly-focused on a small number of international firms (Collinson & Rugman, 2007). The VOC did not explain fundamental institutional change, referring only to the role of exogenous forces (Crouch, 2005; Howell, 2003; Streeck & Thelen, 2005), missing the importance of endogenous factors of incremental change and role of political coalitions, states and policy discourses (Culpepper, 2005; Mahoney & Thelen, 2010; Streeck, 2009). For Peck and Theodore (2007) the VOC was limited by: methodological nationalism, static analysis and institutional functionalism, inability to balance national specificity, and path-dependency with common underlying tendencies in capitalist restructuring. For Frenkel and Yu (2014), the VOC was too restrictive and had unrealistic key assumptions of: power parity among actors; synchronic developments across institutions and macro and micro levels; functional employee relations. Then there remains the too easily ignored issue of 'construct validity' in the VOC framework (Witt & Redding, 2014, p. 668; see also Cascio, 2012 more generally).

Furthermore, there was a limited and narrow geographical bias of the VOC's focus on advanced industrial societies (Walter & Zhang, 2012). Similarly, one extension of the VOC approach, the revised typology of capitalist varieties on the basis of state-economy relations and class-based interest organisation (Hancke, Rhodes, & Thatcher, 2007), did not include Asian economies in its four ideal types of coordination. With the exception of Japan, Asian economies have largely been overlooked and the VOC perspective underutilised in Asia (Steier, 2009).

Nevertheless, the VOC retains some usefulness as an analytical framework across a range of subjects not least as it established '...a plausible analytical counternarrative to the one-world visions of globalisation...' (Peck & Theodore, 2007, p. 765), calling attention to the historical embeddedness of economic systems and problematizing systemic institutional logics of a range of capitalisms. Indeed, while Witt and Redding (2014) started off arguing using the VOC was misguided, as systems could not be understood through categories identified in the West, their caveat was that it was not designed for Asia. We build on these ideas by taking the VOC forward as we add a sixth 'sphere' of context, recognising the crucial importance of historical, political, social, and cultural factors.

11.5 APPLICATION OF THE FRAMEWORK

We analyse Thailand using a VOC-type framework via: the financial system and corporate governance; internal structure of firms; industrial relations; education and skills formation and intercompany relations. We then add to this with another over-arching 'sphere' of context (historical and cultural).

11.5.1 Financial System and Corporate Governance

The financial system is comprised of: commercial banks; capital markets (including stock and bond markets); nonbank financial intermediaries (eg, finance, credit, life insurance, and various cooperative companies); and government-owned specialised financial institutions, such as Government Savings Bank, Government Housing Bank, the Bank for Agriculture and Agricultural Cooperatives (Disyatat & Nakornthab, 2003). Commercial banks dominated and still hold the largest share in the financial system, although the stock and bond markets have taken on a more important role (Rattanapintha, 2010; Satsanguan & Lewis, 2009). The growth in the equity and bond markets indicates the capital market and nonbank financial institutions as alternative sources of capital are emerging as important.

Family banks, which controlled corporate lending (Suehiro & Wailerdsak, 2014) continued to decline post-1997 and diversified to lending to individuals and small and medium-sized enterprises (SMEs), while companies diversified capital structures, and there was also the development of microfinance and the stock market for funds for medium and large firms (Suehiro & Wailerdsak, 2014). The government focused on the development of the capital market and fixed-income securities market in an attempt to reduce dependence on the banking sector (Rattanapintha, 2010).

At the organisational level, the principal source of capital was through commercial bank loans. Firms relied on financial institutions, mainly banks, as a source of capital and less on the bond market, which remained underdeveloped (Wiwattanakantang, 1999), but which was gaining a stronger presence (Jiraporn, Udomsirikul, & Jumreornvong, 2011).

In terms of corporate governance, accounting and auditing systems have improved and corporate governance given high priority, with increased awareness that corporate social responsibility can benefit companies

(Suehiro & Wailerdsak, 2014). However, the separation of ownership and control, particularly in family-owned businesses, remains an issue.

11.5.2 Internal Structure of Firms

There are professional and salaried managers in large businesses (Suehiro & Wailerdsak, 2014). However, owner-family networks continue, with concentration of control and centralised decision-making, and with controlling interests by families (Suehiro & Wailerdsak, 2014). Many firms are family-controlled and owned by a few families (Udomsirikul, Jumreornvong, & Jiraporn, 2011). Half of corporate assets are controlled by the largest ten families in Thailand (Claessens, Djankov, & Lang, 2000). Families own firms directly or indirectly through affiliates or subsidiaries (Wiwattanakantang, 1999). Family members also take part in managing the firms they own. The majority of family positions within business groups are occupied by the business group head and their brothers[1] (Bertrand, Johnson, Samphantharak, & Schoar, 2008).

One survey[2] found the following distribution of firms (Wiwattanakantang, 1999). First, single family-owned firms (34.8%) were classified into two groups: conglomerates, a group of companies with subsidiaries and affiliates in diversified industries, with 26 (9.6%) under the control of a single family through holding companies or affiliated companies; non-conglomerates (25.2%), directly owned by the founders and family members and less diversified. Second, were state-owned enterprises (SOEs), with two (0.7%) controlled by the government. While the government had holdings (25–50%) in four others, it was not a majority shareholder. Third, foreign firms (9.6%) of two types: financial institutions; multinational companies (MNCs), or individual investors that engaged in direct investment. Fourth, were firms that had more than one group of shareholders (54.8%).

Large firms tend to be centralised with tall hierarchies and structures (Aeimtitiwat, 2006). Many firms are family-styled businesses and management style is based on an obligation to look after employees in a manner similar to taking care of children (Komin, 1990; Niffenegger, Kulviwat, & Engchanil, 2006). Hence, decision-making tends to be concentrated at the top. Charismatic, team-oriented, and participative leadership were found to be the top three most effective (Gupta, Surie, Javidan, & Chhokar, 2002). Leadership styles were found to impact on organisational outcomes, with

[1] Of 70 of the largest business families in Thailand.

[2] Sample of 270 non-financial firms listed on the Stock Exchange of Thailand.

the most effective being transformational and transactional (Michie & Zumitzavan, 2012). One study[3] found transformational leadership styles adopted most frequently, transactional quite often and laissez-faire rarely, while transformational leadership yielded the most positive outcomes (Limsila & Ogunlana, 2007). In another study[4], leaders who had higher emotional intelligence scores tended to delegate work to others, were more proactive in attitudes, and used more open communication (Sunindijo, Hadikusumo, & Ogunlana, 2007). In another study, more democratic styles of leadership were preferred, with the most preferred style consultative, then participative, paternalistic, and autocratic (Yukongdi, 2010). However, while the largest proportion of employees perceived their managers to be consultative, it was followed by paternalistic, autocratic, and participative (Yukongdi, 2010).

11.5.3 Industrial Relations

The industrial relations system has been influenced and dominated by the state and the military-dominated regimes that frequently govern (Lawler & Suttawet, 2000). There is a pattern of unilateral control, domination by business elites, and weak employment relations institutions, resulting in very limited employee protection beyond that provided by customary values and norms (Frenkel & Yu, 2014). There are wide variations in industrial relations practices between types of firms (Frenkel & Yu, 2014).

In terms of trade unions, manufacturing industry growth produced a relatively stable urban working class to emerge, and legislation in 1975 allowed employees to join unions and collective bargaining (Frenkel & Yu, 2014). However, few are union members, although the main exception was the SOE sector, although while permitted to bargain over pay and conditions, they are not allowed to strike (Frenkel & Yu, 2014). Industrial restructuring also led to changes in labour force composition unfavourable to unionism, with women becoming the majority of the workforce and many employed in the informal sector (Frenkel & Yu, 2014).

Management committees (representing employees and employers) play some role (Suehiro & Wailerdsak, 2014). However, despite the intention of the 1975 legislation, tripartism is also limited, partly by the structure of unions and lack of desire by governments and businesses to consult. Weak unions means collective bargaining was virtually absent, although there have been some gains by unions linking up with NGOs in the form of a social movement and there are a few collective agreements (Frenkel & Yu, 2014).

[3]Of project managers in the construction industry in Thailand.
[4]Of Thai project managers and engineers.

Yet, individuals could not join workers from other provinces or from establishments having different working conditions. This policy served to hinder larger unions and promote enterprise unionism as the dominant form, with unions small and lacking funds. So, the labour movement, though tolerated, was kept relatively weak. Rather than a single, strong peak trade union organisation, there were several competing ones. Furthermore, national trade unionism was not stimulated or encouraged by employer developments or national collective bargaining (Yukongdi, 2008).

Overall, unions remain weak and fragmented, and even the formerly strong SOE unions were disbanded after the 1991 military coup. Private sector unions remain small and with very low rates of unionisation and limited unity. Union problems of finance, rivalry and training, remain prevalent and unions are weakened further by economic restructuring; financial market liberalization; labour market deregulation; employer tactics of sacking leaders, subcontracting, and casualisation of labour (Yukongdi, 2008). There has also been the importation of methods of union avoidance by MNCs (Lawler & Suttawet, 2000). Employers had relied on 'union suppression' strategies: discharging union supporters, using armed force, and colluding with government to foster state opposition.

There have been few labour disputes or strikes, with limited bargaining power, even at summit organisations. The number, types, and size of labour organisations and union membership post-2006 can be seen in the tables, as can the number of labour disputes, strikes, and lockouts (Tables 11.3 and 11.4).

Table 11.3 Labour organisations and labour union members

Labour organisation/year	2006	2007	2008	2010
Number of state enterprise unions	45	43	44	44
Member of state enterprise unions (no. of persons)	180,500	170,630	175,000	182,147
Number of labour union (private enterprises)	1313	1243	1229	1264
Member of labour union (private enterprises) (no. of persons)	335,600	331,250	341,520	349,501
Union density (total number of union members computed as a proportion of total employment[a])	1.4	1.35	1.37	1.37

NB: statistics are not available for 2009.

[a]Total employment figures are derived from the National Statistical Office Thailand.

Data from the Yearbook of Labour Protection and Welfare Statistics for various years, Labour Relations Bureau, Department of Labour Protection and Welfare.

Table 11.4 Labour disputes, strikes and lockouts

Labour organisation/year	2006	2007	2008	2009	2010
Labour disputes	80	100	57	119	77
Strikes	2	2	4	2	2
Lockouts	–	3	3	3	1

The Ministry of Labour provides definitions for the following terms as follows:
Strike: A temporary stoppage of work by a group of employees in order to express a grievance or to enforce a demand concerning changes in working conditions. Government statistics exclude all strikes lasting less than 1 day or involving fewer than six workers, and make no distinction between strikes and lockouts.
Lockout: A temporary withholding or shutting down of work by an employer, in protest against employee actions or to coerce them into accepting his terms.
Labour disputes: no definition available on the Ministry of Labour's website.
Data from the Yearbook of Labour Protection and Welfare Statistics for various years, Labour Relations Bureau, Department of Labour Protection and Welfare.

Legislation in 1998 encouraged welfare improvements by restricting working hours and hazardous work, stipulating overtime rates and holiday entitlements and regulating youth employment, although the implementation of labour laws is problematic, with many reported violations (Frenkel & Yu, 2014). Also, workers in the large informal sector are excluded from protective legislation, while in addition to pursuing cost-reductions, firms hired contract workers, often excluded from legislation (Frenkel & Yu, 2014).

In sum, for Frenkel and Yu (2014, p. 391), using micro and macro employee relations indicators (union density, tripartism, collective bargaining, pay determination, labour-employer cooperation, employment flexibility) Thailand's employee relations patterns are described as the most flexible (giving wide latitude to labour vis-à-vis labour) in Asia. Pay determination was decentralised and employment flexibility relatively high as employers, using contract labour and subcontracting to the informal sector, sought to reduce cost through numerical flexibility (Frenkel & Yu, 2014).

11.5.4 Education and Skills Formation

Comparatively large amounts are spent on public education. However, there remain problems of student quality, teacher academic credentials, and mismatch with labour market requirements (Suehiro & Wailerdsak, 2014). Education problems are in four interrelated areas of concern: low secondary enrollment; inadequate quality; lack of equity in access; financing and inappropriate subsidy (Khoman, 2005).

A World Bank study indicated that Thailand's traditional labour cost advantage was declining with fast-growing countries and currency appreciation (World Bank, 2008). Apart from political instability, skills shortages and education of available workers were perceived by the most (39%) firms to be major obstacles to doing business (World Bank, 2012). Employers face difficulties in filling job vacancies, specifically in manufacturing. Two main reasons for skilled labour shortages are the available workforce's: poor skills (skill shortage); and lack of the 'right' skills (skills mismatch) (World Bank, 2008).

Shortages of production, unskilled, semi-skilled, and skilled labour, as well as managers have been filled by migrants (Frenkel & Yu, 2014; Suehiro & Wailerdsak, 2014). The low-skilled labour force (primary school and lower) shrunk by almost 4 million since 1999 (Chalamwong & Archapiraj, 2011). Reasons for this include free education policies, compulsory education expansion, and demographics. Migrant workers from neighbouring countries have enabled labour intensive sectors to continue.

In terms of training and skills formation, Lawler, Siengthai, and Atmiyanandana (1998) usefully distinguish provision and forms of training (ie, focus, breadth, purpose, planning) by type of organisation (see Table 11.5).

Family enterprises—training is a problematic issue, as it is seen as cost with unclear future benefits and risk, although distinctions between family members and outsiders (not expected to move a great deal within the firm), so when training takes place it is: narrow, spontaneous, and short-term in focus and toward productivity rather than relational and quality of life issues.

Thai corporations—more pervasive training occurs as they are often in competition with foreign firms and so it can be more difficult to recruit, although more extensive training for managers than workers, and involves much management development activities, so long-term focus, planned, fairly broad, and concerned with both enhancing productivity and quality of work life, versus training workers that is more productivity enhancing and on-the-job and thus while planned, likely to be narrow and short-term focus.

Table 11.5 Skills and training in different types of firms in Thailand

	Type of firm			
Training	**Family enterprise**	**Thai corporation**	**Western subsidiary**	**Japanese subsidiary**
Focus	Short-term	Long-term	Mixed	Long-term
Breadth	Narrow	Broad	Mixed	Broad
Purpose	Productivity	Mixed	Mixed	Mixed
Planning	Spontaneous	Planned	Planned	Planned

Data from Lawler, J.J., Siengthai, S., & Atmiyanandana, V. (1998). Human resource management in Thailand: Eroding traditions. In C. Rowley (Ed.), *Human resource management in the Asia-Pacific region: Convergence questioned (Frank Cass, 1998)* (reprinted from Asia-Pacific Business Review).

Foreign-owned—Western—training is not a high priority as they buy-in skills rather than develop them internally, although there is more for management than workers (similar to Thai corporations in this respect), with training tending to be long-term, broad, and systematic, with an emphasis on both productivity and quality of work and some management development versus employee training that is on-the-job, relatively narrow, short-term and productivity-orientated, though planned.

Foreign-owned—Japanese—training at all levels is considerably more prevalent (consistent with Japanese practice) given the focus on internal development, tending to be long-term, broad and systematic, involving both productivity and quality of life issues (related to socialisation concerns), and employees as well as management, sent to Japan for extended training.

11.5.5 Inter-Company Relations

Interfirm relations pre-1997 were mostly via business groups in which families controlled ownership and management along with bank-led groups in which family-owned commercial banks served as core firms (Suehiro & Wailerdsak, 2014). Interfirm alliances are seen as becoming an increasingly attractive strategic option. Here firms establish various forms of strategic alliances, including joint ventures (JVs) (82.7%), and cooperation agreements to: carry out tasks with other firms (22.9%); gather information (13.5%); exchange information (13.3%); and other forms of alliances (0.2%) (Thechatakerng, 2006). Hence, JVs represent the most common form of interfirm alliance.

The majority in interfirm alliances are by medium and large enterprises. In terms of sectors,[5] over three-quarters (over 75%) in one study[6] (Thechatakerng, 2006) were in basic manufacturing (eg, textiles, vehicle supplies, heavy fabrics); 12% in natural resources (eg, feed mills, agricultural process products, wood processing); 6.4% in services (eg, wholesale/retail, lodging/entertainment); and 6.2% in high technology (electronic products, electronic supplies, telecommunication). The types of alliances include technology alliances relating to product R process R production, distribution, and purchaser-supplier relationships; export management; and marketing. The principal motivating factor for forming a strategic alliance was technological advancement. Over half (52.9%) entered into alliances

[5]On basis of the Standard Industrial Classification (SIC) and the Department of Industry classification in Thailand.

[6]Of 503 firms.

with a foreign partner, while the remainder (47.1%) established interfirm cooperation with Thai firms (Thechatakerng, 2006).

While technological advancement may be the main reason for forming strategic alliances, one survey (World Bank, 2008) found only a very few firms (just 1%) collaborated with universities and public institutions as a channel to acquire technological innovation. This finding emphasises the weak linkage between firms and institutions that are crucial for the generation of technological innovation (World Bank, 2008).

In terms of forming alliances with competing organisations, firms did not wish to establish interfirm alliances with competitors (Thechatakerng, 2006). One study[7] found entrepreneurs did not maintain close relationships with other entrepreneurs in the same sector and actually had cooperative relationships with other firms (Dulbeccoab & Vagneronab, 2001). Nearly one-half reported sharing orders with other firms, which occurred between firms that were located within close proximity, or were between entrepreneurs who knew each other.

While studies remain scarce, there is evidence suggesting that vertical and horizontal integration tend to be employed as a competitive strategy by larger firms in Thailand. Examples include firms in the agro-industry and food business (eg, Charoen Pokphand Group) (Charoen Pokphand, 2015); cargo transfer and barging industry (eg, S.P. Inter Marine); and tuna fishing industry (eg, Thai Union Group) (see Kuldilok, 2009). A case in point is a leading agro-industrial and food conglomerate in the Asia Pacific region, Charoen Pokphand, which operates vertically integrated businesses which incorporate the manufacturing of animal feed, animal breeding, and animal farming; meat processing, the manufacturing of semi-cooked meat and fully cooked meat; food products and ready meal products, as well as the meat and food retailer and restaurant businesses (Charoen Pokphand, 2015).

Interfirm relationships, for instance between 7 and 11 Thailand with suppliers, lean towards being cooperative rather than adversarial (Leelapanyalert, Wang, & Ghauri, 2012). Of the few available studies, there is a case study of vertical and horizontal linkages among ceramic firms in Lampang province that provides evidence that subcontracting appears to be initiated first on the basis of personal relations (Kamnungwut & Grey, 2007). Firms subcontract to manufacturers they know and trust, and contracts are on a verbal basis. In terms of horizontal cooperation, firms loosely cooperate through joint purchase of inputs and lending of machines. Firm owners meet quite

[7]Of the garment industry.

frequently at association meetings and for casual dinners. However, firm owners do not exchange detailed information about their business during such occasions. Interfirm cooperation among larger firms is relatively weak, because such firms are large enough to purchase large quantities without having to cooperate with other firms. In contrast, strong cooperation exists among firms having strong social ties of family linkages and friendship. Within such groups, firms share production knowledge, orders, joint purchase of raw materials, and also develop product and marketing strategy. In this study, it is suggested that trust based on friendship and personal relationships are key to sustaining long-term cooperation among ceramic firms (Kamnungwut & Grey, 2007).

Finally, the focus of mergers and acquisitions (M&A) in Thailand is on deals made by foreign investors acquiring Thai businesses, or investing in manufacturing facilities based in Thailand. In 2012, two notable outbound M&A transactions included Thai businesses investing overseas to diversify their business, such as the Charoen Pokphand group taking a stake in Ping An Insurance in China, and Thai Beverage completing a takeover bid for Fraser and Neave in Singapore in 2013. It has been suggested that hostile takeovers and M&A are not common among Thai firms (Weerawong et al., 2014).

11.5.6 Context

As noted earlier, the background and historical and cultural context is the final sphere we have added in our framework.

11.5.6.1 Geographical, Ethnic and Economic Backgrounds

Thailand borders Laos and Cambodia in the North and East, and Malaysia and the Gulf of Thailand in the South and has two distinct parts: the Chao Phraya River valley and the Korat Plateau, which form a compact area (Gullaprawit, 2002). The vast majority (95%) are Buddhists (Lawler & Suttawet, 2000) in this multiethnic country. Ethnic Thais form 82% of the population and although many speak different dialects, Bangkok's official Thai language is widespread. The Chinese are the largest ethnic group. Ethnic Malays are concentrated in the South and constitute a majority of the Muslim population in four of the 14 Southern provinces (out of 76 in total).

Thailand's post-1960s economic development emphasised agricultural development, then import substitution, with manufacturing replacing agriculture as the most important sector post-1980, with change into an export-orientated, industrialising economy. Prior to the 1997 Asian Financial Crisis, Thailand was one of the fastest growing economies in the world. Following the post-crisis collapse, Thailand's economy recovered and expanded by 7.8% in 2010 (BOT, n.d.a, n.d.b). This, in terms of GDP growth and proportions from agriculture, industry, services, can be seen in Table 11.6.

Recently, Thailand took steps to become a more knowledge-intensive economy and moving into producing higher value added products, developing into a manufacturer of processed foods, and not simply a supplier of raw materials, and in the auto industry employing more technologically advanced components to increase its production capacity and exports (BOI, 2012; Pantong, 2012).

11.5.6.2 Political and State Backgrounds

With respect to the state structure, there have been a series of coups and more democratic governments, mostly supportive of large, mainly family-based, business interests (Frenkel & Yu, 2014). The state is portrayed as '...predatory and developmental' with corruption and bribery and specification of manufacturing domestic content and shareholding (Suehiro & Wailerdsak, 2014, p. 261). The unitary administrative system has the government structured under a single hierarchy with ministries, departments, and divisions. At the top of the pyramid, is the prime minister, followed by the minister who oversees subdivisions within the ministry. Each ministry is broken down into departments, which are further divided into divisions. SOEs are attached to the ministries whose respective ministers have direct control over them. Ministers are also responsible for the appointment of SOE board members. It is through the appointment of the ministers' circle of friends and bureaucrats that SOEs, in effect, remain under a single hierarchy and are not operationally autonomous (Bowornwathana, 2006). Hence, in practice, all actors in this unitary system operate under a single hierarchy.

In the late 1990s, the government introduced a process of creating autonomous public organisations (APO). This implied the organisations created lay outside the single hierarchy. While SOEs can be considered as a form of APO, they have only limited autonomy and operate in a similar manner to departments. Three types of APOs exist. First, agency-type APOs (autonomisation through agencification), created through the (Autonomous) Public Organisations Act (1999), which perform a specific social function, for example in education, culture, sports, research training, science and technology, public health, and social welfare (Bowornwathana, 2004). Attached to

Table 11.6 GDP growth (annual %), agriculture, industry, services, value added (% of GDP)

Year	1987	1988	1990	1998	2000	2006	2007	2008	2009	2010	2011	2012
GDP growth	9.5	13.3	11.2	−10.5	4.8	5.1	5.0	2.5	−2.3	7.8	0.1	6.5
Agriculture	16	16	12	11	9	11	11	12	11	12	13	12
Industry	33	35	37	40	42	44	45	44	43	45	43	44
Services	51	49	50	50	49	45	45	44	45	43	44	44

Data from World Bank (1987–2013).

the ministries, these organisations are overseen by an APO board appointed by the respective minister. Second, APOs mandated by the Constitution (1997) to promote governance, transparency, and openness in government, and which are independent of the government's chain of command. Hence, these organisations are autonomous and are required to be neutral. Examples include the Ombudsmen, the National Human Rights Commission, and the National Counter Corruption Commission. Third, APOs created by the Constitution (1997) when government was required to allocate 35% of its annual budget to cover expenditures of local government. APOs, in practice, are not independent. This is because they operate within the conventional hierarchical structure of the government rather than autonomously, due to the politics of autonomisation that involves power struggles between: political executives and ministry bureaucrats in agency-type APOs; citizens versus political executives and bureaucrats in APOs mandated by the Constitution; and local government units and central government officials in local government APOs (Bowornwathana, 2006).

11.5.6.3 Organisational Backgrounds

Firms differ in terms of ownership structures, types, and size as shown in Table 11.7. Firms include locally owned companies (LOCs) categorised as large public (SOEs) and private (many single-family-owned), SMEs and MNCs, as well as foreign MNCs and those that are classified as foreign-invested enterprises and JVs. These organisations vary in terms of sector or product, labour or capital intensity, and low or high skills (see table).

Thai firms tend to be centralised and large organisations have tall structures, consistent with firms in high power distance countries (see Hofstede, 1980). Small and flat organisational structures are not significantly associated with large enterprises in Thailand (Aeimtitiwat, 2006). Managers appear to be adopting somewhat more participative styles of leadership, reflecting shifts in societal values (Yukongdi, 2010) and generational value differences (see Murphy, Mujtaba, Manyak, Sungkhawan, & Greenwood, 2010).

11.5.6.4 Cultural Background

National culture influences organisational culture and practices (see Hofstede, 1980, 1984). Thailand has the highest score on power distance practices and the least assertive societal values among other Asian countries (House, Hanges, Javidan, Dorfman, & Gupta, 2004). These cultural characteristics contribute to a relatively higher degree of centralization in decision-making and respect for individuals in supervisory positions at work

Table 11.7 Organisational; mediating impacts on VOC in Thailand

	Organisation type and size						
	LOC				FIE	JV	MNC
	Public	Private	SME	MNC	Partner	Partner	Parent nationality
Sector/product (primary-secondary-tertiary) (simplicity-complexity)	Spread across primary, secondary, tertiary	Spread across primary, secondary, tertiary	Spread across primary, secondary, tertiary	Spread across primary, secondary, tertiary	Leaning towards secondary, tertiary	Spread across primary, secondary, tertiary	Spread across primary, secondary, tertiary
Focus/intensity (labour versus capital)	Varies from labour to capital intensive	Varies from labour to capital intensive	Varies from labour to capital intensive	Varies from labour to capital intensive	Ranging from labour and leaning towards capital intensive	Varies from labour and leaning towards capital intensive	Varies from labour to capital intensive
Skills (low versus high)	Ranging from low to high	Ranging from low to high	Ranging from low to high	Ranging from low to high	Medium to high	Medium to high	Ranging from low to high

through paternalism and dependence (Niffenegger et al., 2006). Society is hierarchical and reflected in the management of organisations, such ordering of society supplemented by Buddhist doctrine—to accept one's station in life and work for a good 'next life', and Theravada Buddhism is personal and introspective and prone to social activism (Lawler & Suttawet, 2000). In terms of what Witt and Redding (2014) call 'social capital', Thai social values include the importance of family and kinship with interpersonal relations and Buddhism (Suehiro & Wailerdsak, 2014).

The importance of Buddhism to Thai society is reflected in the King's philosophy of the 'Sufficiency Economy' which reinforces the 'Buddhist concept of middle path as a way to conduct the life of the individual, family, community, and the nation' (Chalapati, 2008, p. 3). The philosophy emphasises the importance of economic self-reliance in conducting one's life and in overcoming poverty. Self-sufficiency stresses moderation of aspirations and a balance between success and fulfilment. Education and information technology are regarded as key factors in human capital development that can provide a link to alleviation of poverty. The Sufficiency Economy philosophy was incorporated into the National Economic and Social Development Plan (2006–2011) and integrated into education at school and university levels. Furthermore, the government has undertaken projects implementing the Sufficiency Economy in 75 provinces where villagers and farmers in rural areas are educated in the concept of economic self-reliance and the middle path as a means to solving social problems and alleviating poverty at the grass-roots level (Chalapati, 2008).

Also, while very much a collectivist culture, there is a lack of clear class consciousness and the centrality of Theravada Buddhism to Thai culture contributes to industrial relations (Lawler & Suttawet, 2000). In addition to the influence of the Sufficiency Economy, which embodies the Buddhist concept of middle way in conducting one's life as discussed earlier, the influence of Buddhism in the context of industrial relations is apparent. Industrial relations are underpinned by eight sets of Buddhist philosophy and principles identified as: (1) the six directions; (2) the divine abiding; (3) helpful integration; (4) of success; (5) the ten regal qualities; (6) the qualities of a good or genuine person; (7) collective responsibility; and (8) the principles for conducting oneself as a good citizen (Joungtrakul, 2005). Thai culture is also seen as having seven relevant concepts: (1) helping each other; (2) *Bunkhun*; (3) *Kreng Jai*; (4) face saving; (5) criticism avoidance; (6) sympathy; (7) compromising (Joungtrakul, 2005). The influence of religion and culture is taken to mean less social activism; with Buddhist (Theravada) doctrine to accept situations; hierarchical society, inequality in power and deference to authority figures (Yukongdi, 2008).

Further evidence of the influence of Thai culture can be observed in the sharing of orders among firms, which is based on reciprocity and reflects the Thai concept of *Bunkhun* or 'indebted goodness' (Niffenegger et al., 2006), implying an obligation to reciprocate favours. Firms also share information relating to potential business partners, production techniques, problems and solutions, including 'blacklists' of dishonest contractors. For example, the instability of the garment market renders it impossible for individual firms to be efficient. Hence, firms need to respond collectively to demand variability. A collective response among firms tends to create a community of interests and solidarity among firms that would, otherwise, be considered competitors (Dulbeccoab & Vagneronab, 2001). Structures that minimise risks tend to prevail (Vincent, 2005), as may be the case here.

11.6 DISCUSSION

Our analysis of Thailand using an enhanced VOC-type framework paints a mixed picture. This can be seen in the table. The financial system is bank-led and corporate governance provides firms with access to finance that is not entirely dependent on publicly available financial data or current returns. Hence, investors must be able to monitor company performance in order to ensure return on investments. To resolve this issue, investors need access to 'private' or 'inside' information on the firm's operations. In Thai society, this implies that who you know is often more critical than a written contract and newly formed business relationships. In such a culture, first and foremost, trust is based on personal relationships that are developed over time; the longer and more positive the relationship, the more trusting are the parties of each other. Such personal relationships tend to set up entry barriers for those who are not part of the network. Business networks are dense and joint membership in industry associations together enable the monitoring of company reputation. There are close relationships with major suppliers and clients and networks of cross-shareholding, hence hostile takeovers and acquisitions are rare. These features are characteristic of CMEs (Table 11.8).

On the other hand, the internal structure of firms tends towards top-down decision-making, which is characteristic of high power distance between managers and employees. This is somewhat similar to LMEs, but culturally specific to Thailand is its paternalistic leadership style, albeit with perhaps some hints of shifting towards somewhat more participative styles.

Table 11.8 Thailand in context

Financial system	• Corporate governance provides access to finance not entirely dependent on publicly available financial data or current returns • Access to 'private' or 'inside' information about firm's operations • Dense business networks • Network reputational monitoring • Close relationships with major suppliers and clients • Networks of cross-share holding • Hostile takeovers and acquisitions are rare • Joint membership in industry associations
Internal structure of the firm	• Top-down decision making • Paternalistic leadership shifting towards somewhat more participative styles
Education and skills formation	• Rely on general skills (as opposed to highly skilled labour and industry-specific skills) • Skills mismatch, low-skilled shortage • Poaching of skilled workers by other firms and from the government
Industrial relations	• Powerful employers • Weak labour unions • Among the lowest union density in the world
Inter-company relations	• Emphasis on relational contract as the basis for interfirm collaboration • Tendency to rely on informal rules and understanding • Formal contracts are inadequate to sustain interfirm relationships • Monitoring of behaviours of other actors • Network reputational monitoring • Joint ventures motivated by technological advancement • Vertical and horizontal integration employed by larger organisations
Context	• History o Dates back thousands of years o Modern history began with founding of the Kingdom of Sukhothai in the 13th and 14th centuries o Constitutional monarchy, currently overseen by Head of State, King Bumibol Adulyadej (1946–present) • Culture o Smooth interpersonal relationships, non-confrontation, face-saving, *Kreng jai*, *Bunkhun* concept o Uncertainty avoidance, high power distance, short-term orientation, feminine values o Respect for tradition • Religious beliefs o Theravada Buddhism is the official religion o 95% of Thais are Buddhists o Emphasise the middle path, the aim of which is the alleviation of suffering

Industrial relations are dominated by the state, while labour unions remain weak. The employees' position in high power distance cultures is low in the organisational hierarchy. Organised resistance is culturally incompatible among workers. Employees are not accustomed to direct confrontation with their supervisors and employers. Coupled with lower levels of educational attainment, low wages, the prospect of having employment terminated and becoming unemployed, there is little capacity for organised resistance (Frenkel & Yu, 2014; Morgan & Kristensen, 2006) and the power of the organisation over employees is strong. There is little governmental support for labour unions and the enforcement of laws and regulations remain weak, contributing to power imbalance as well. Furthermore, top-down decision making makes it less difficult for firms to release labour when faced with financial problems. This feature is similar to those found in LMEs as well.

Education and training skills formation rely on general skills. Thus, firms often have to conduct in-house training for firm-specific skills. Skills mismatch and low-skilled shortage exist as does the 'poaching' of skilled workers. This is also LME-like.

Intercompany relations emphasise relational contracts as the basis for inter-firm collaboration. Firms tend to rely on informal rules and understanding. Thus, formal contracts are inadequate to sustain interfirm relationships. Monitoring of behaviours of other actors and network reputational monitoring occur via informal channels, similar to CMEs.

Finally, while Thai culture emphasises smooth interpersonal relationships and a non-confrontational approach (Komin, 1990), there has been civil unrest in recent years. One of the authors has had informal discussions with university academics and part-time graduate students who work full-time in private and public sector organisations. One observation from the discussions suggests that there are generational differences, with 'Generation Y' expressing more liberal attitudes towards equality and are more open to changes, while the Baby Boomers and 'Generation X' are more conservative in their views (see Murphy et al., 2010). Second, regardless of generational differences, what emerges from discussions is that, consistent with Thai culture that is moderately strong on uncertainty avoidance (Hofstede, 1984), divergent political views that have polarised the nation are not tolerated well, and Thais find it very difficult to accept such growing divisions and polarisation in politics. When there is no shared middle ground, conciliation, compromise and consensus are not part of the solution, leaving street protests as the last resort. Third, social media, such as Facebook and Twitter (with many users remaining anonymous), have been utilised as tools to deepen differences and have had a dividing impact rather than a unifying one. In a democratising society, such as Thailand, it is argued social media has produced polarising effects, hence there is a need for greater transparency and user accountability (see Pongsudhirak, 2014). The evidence may also be reflective of a nation on the path to becoming a more democratic society. Finally, it should be noted that a national culture that emphasises smooth interpersonal relationships and non-confrontation does not necessarily imply that people in such society will not use confrontation as a means to resolve problems—this depends on the context as well.

Thailand has three elements (internal structure, education and training skills formation, industrial relations) found in LMEs and two (financial system and governance, interfirm relations) in CMEs. Of particular importance is our context sphere, the role of cultural values and religious beliefs, and their influence on actors in the economy. We argue that cultural values are inextricably linked to historical, social, and political structures. Therefore, it would not be possible to exclude the role that national culture and religious beliefs play in the analysis of a country and is a crucial element in VOC analysis.

We also went further and rather than being firm-centred, we see firms, employees, business systems, financial and labour markets interacting (Walter & Zhang, 2012). We stress the interlocking nature of VOC spheres with results for forms and types of competitive advantage. For example, we can see VOC spheres as interlocking and impacting on particular forms of comparative advantage and competition, price-based versus innovation strategies of firms (see others, such as Whitley, 1999), that is, underpinned by the use of cheap, largely uneducated and unorganised labour, producing simple, low value-added goods, requiring commensurate forms of control, education and skills. This configuration in turn encourages forms of competition which trigger further wage pressures. For example, responses to competitive pressures can involve wage and benefit reductions, outsourcing and temporary workers, as happened in Thailand (Lawler et al., 1998) or more innovative, value-added responses, which in turn would need to be underpinned by labour up-skilling strategies.

Our analysis demonstrates that the VOC approach can provide us with a useful basic framework for understanding system coordination and institutional complementarities in a country. However, our result underscores the limitation of its broad categories that are not able to sufficiently capture the differences that exist among Asian countries with varying stages of development, and especially cultural values. Diversity exists within Asian nations and different models may be needed to explain those differences.

11.7 CONCLUSION

Our analysis locating business networks in Thailand using an amended VOC framework indicates the following. First, in terms of the financial system and governance, it is bank-centred. Commercial bank loans represent the main source of financing for firms, but the capital and bond markets and nonfinancial institutions are becoming important alternative sources of capital. Corporate governance is relatively weak with top-down decision-making, but which has undergone some regulatory reform, although the separation of ownership and control, particularly in family-owned businesses, may not be truly independent. Second, in terms of the internal structure of firms, there is a high degree of ownership concentration. Large firms have relatively tall hierarchies and centralised organisation structures, while management style is shifting somewhat, moving from autocratic towards more participative styles, while paternalism remains the key characteristic. Third, in terms of education and training skills, there is a labour market mismatch, with shortages of semi-skilled labour (ie, vocational graduates) and over supply of university graduates. Fourth, industrial relations are dominated by a strong state, trade unions are weak, and employer organisations have a limited role. Fifth, interfirm relations exist in the form of JVs driven by technological advancement and on an informal basis in some industries (ie, garments), interfirm alliances involve the sharing of information and workers. Both vertical and horizontal integration are employed as strategies in large firms and relationships among firms are more cooperative rather than adversarial, and very much depend on trust and personal relationships. Sixth, taking account of context, of history and culture, provides a better explanation for the case.

We have a few final thoughts about Thailand's future trajectory. First, the interlocking nature of spheres in forms of capitalism remains. Industrial strategy and structure result in the use of cheap, unskilled labour strategy requiring an unorganised workforce and weak trade unions with promotion of FDI via industrial estates, which in turn leads to union avoidance. Breaking out of this 'race to the bottom' type of competition is a challenge, especially in the context where the influence of Buddhism and practices in the 'Middle Way', with Thai cultural influences, with norms and social values emphasising harmonious social relations and consideration of others, remains significantly salient. These all have implications for business networks.

REFERENCES

Aeimtitiwat, P. (2006). Corporate entrepreneurship characteristics and organisational innovativeness of large enterprises in Thailand. Unpublished Ph.D. thesis, Bangkok University.

Albert, M. (1993). *Capitalism against capitalism*. London: Whurr.

Allen, M. (2004). The varieties of capitalism paradigm: Not enough variety? *Socio-Economic Review*, *2*, 87–108.

Amable, B. (2003). *The diversity of modern capitalism*. Oxford: Oxford University Press.

Andriesse, E., & van Westen, G. (2009). Unsustainable varities of capitalism along the Thailand-Malaysia border: The role of institutional complementarities in regional development'. *Asia Pacific Journal of Management*, *26*, 59–79.

Berger, S., & Dore, R. (Eds.), (1996). *National diversity and global capitalism*. Ithaca, NY: Cornell University Press.

Bertrand, M., Johnson, S., Samphantharak, K., & Schoar, A. (2008). Mixing family with business: A study of Thai business groups and the families behind them. *Journal of Financial Economics*, *88*, 466–498.

Blyth, M. (2003). Same as it ever was: Temporality and typologies in the varieties of capitalism. *Comparative European Politics*, *1*, 215–225.

BOI (The Board of Investment of Thailand). (2012). Thailand to become knowledge-based economy. Thailand Investment Review. http://www.boi.go.th/tir/issue/201204_22_4/211.htm. Accessed 02.12.12.

BOT (Bank of Thailand). (n.d.). EC_EI_027 Thailand's Macro Economic Indicators. http://www2.bot.or.th/statistics/BOTWEBSTAT.aspx?reportID=409andlanguage=ENG. Accessed 15.04.11.

BOT (Bank of Thailand). (n.d.). Table 17: Population, labour force and wage. http://www.bot.or.th/English/Statistics/Indicators/Pages/index.aspx. Accessed 08.08.12.

Bowornwathana, B. (2004). Putting new public management to good use: Autonomous public organisations in Thailand'. In C. Pollitt & C. Talbot (Eds.), *Unbundled Government: A critical analysis of the global trend to agencies, quangos and contractualisation*. London/New York: Routledge, Taylor and Francis Group.

Bowornwathana, B. (2006). Autonomisation of the Thai state: Some observations. *Public Administration and Development*, *26*, 27–34.

Boyer, R. (2005). How and why capitalisms differ. *Economy and Society*, *34*, 509–557.

Boyer, R., Uemura, H., & Isogai, A. (Eds.), *Diversity and transformations in Asian capitalisms*. (2012). London: Routledge.

Carney, M., Gedajlovic, E., & Yang, X. (2009). Varieties of Asian capitalism: Toward an institutional theory of Asian enterprise. *Asia Pacific Journal of Management*, *26*, 361–380.

Cascio, W. (2012). Methodological issues in international HR management research. *International Journal of Human Resource Management*, *23*(12), 2532–2545.

Chalamwong, Y., & Archapiraj, S. (2011). Shortage of low-skilled labour in Thailand has reached a critical point. The Nation, 14th June.

Chalapati, S. (2008). Sufficiency economy as a response to the problem of poverty in Thailand. *Asian Social Science*, *4*(7), 3–6.

Chandler, A. (1990). *The invisible hand: The managerial revolution in American business*. Cambridge, MA: Belknap Press.

Charoen Pokphand. (2015). Operations in brief. Charoen Pokphand Foods PCL. Available at http://www.cpfworldwide.com/en/about/. Accessed 05.03.15.

Child. (1981). Culture, contingency and capitalism in the cross-national study of organizations. In L. L. Cummings & B. M. Staw (Eds.), *Research in organisational behaviour*. Greenwich, CT: JAI Publishers.

Claessens, S., Djankov, S., & Lang, L. (2000). The separation of ownership and control in East Asian corporations'. *Journal of Financial Economics*, *58*, 81–112.

Coates, D. (2000). *Models of capitalism: Growth and stagnation in the modern era*. Cambridge: Cambridge University Press.

Collinson, S. C., & Rugman, A. M. (2007). The regional character of Asian multinational enterprises. *Asia Pacific Journal of Management, 24*, 429–446.

Crouch, C. (2005). *Capitalist diversity and change: Recombinant governance and institutional entrepreneurs*. Oxford: Oxford University Press.

Culpepper, P. D. (2005). Institutional change in contemporary capitalism: Coordinated financial systems since 1990. *World Politics, 57*, 173–199.

Deeg, R., & Jackson, D. (2007). Towards a more dynamic theory of capitalist development. *Socio-Economic Review, 5*(1), 149–179.

Disyatat, P., & Nakornthab, D. (2003). The changing nature of financial structure in Thailand and implications for policy. Bank of Thailand Discussion Paper, pp. 1–34.

Dore, R. (1974). *British Factory-Japanese Factory: The origins of national diversity in industrial relations*. London: Allen and Unwin.

Dore, R. (2000). *Stock market capitalism: Welfare capitalism: Japan and Germany versus the Anglo-Saxons*. Oxford: OUP.

Dulbeccoab, P., & Vagneronab, I. (2001). Competition, co-operation and subcontracting: Lessons from the clothing industry in Thailand. *The European Journal of Development Research, 13*(2), 58–80.

Frenkel, S., & Yu, K.-H. (2014). Employment relations and HRM in Asia: Explaining patterns in Asian societies. In M. Witt & G. Redding (Eds.), *The Oxford handbook Asian business systems* (pp. 383–418). Oxford: Oxford University Press.

Fukuyama, F. (1992). *The end of history and the last man*. New York: Free Press.

Gerlach, M. (1992). *Alliance capitalism: The social organization of Japanese business*. London: University of California Press.

Gullaprawit, C. (2002). Thailand. In M. Zanko (Ed.), *The handbook of HRM policies and practices in Asia-Pacific economies* (Vol. 1). Cheltenham: Edward Elgar.

Gupta, V., Surie, G., Javidan, M., & Chhokar, J. (2002). Southern Asia cluster: Where the old meets the new? *Journal of World Business, 37*, 16–27.

Hancke, B., Rhodes, M., & Thatcher, M. (2007). Introduction. In B. Hancke, M. Rhodes, & M. Thatcher (Eds.), *Beyond varieties of capitalism: Conflict, contradictions, and complementarities in the European economy*. Oxford: Oxford University Press.

Harada, Y., & Tohyama, H. (2012). Asian capitalisms: Institutional configuration and firm heterogeneity. In R. Boyer, H. Uemura, & A. Isogai (Eds.), *Directions and transformations in Asian capitalisms* (pp. 243–263). London: Routledge.

Hay, C. (2005). Two can play at that game… or can they? In D. Coates (Ed.), *Varieties of capitalism, varieties of approaches* (pp. 106–121). Houndmills: Palgrave.

Hofstede, G. (1980). *Culture's consequences: International differences in work-related values*. Beverly Hills, CA: Sage.

Hofstede, G. (1984). *Culture's consequences: International differences in work-related values* (Abridged ed.). Beverly Hills: Sage.

Hollingswoth, J. P., & Boyer, R. (1997). *Contemporary capitalism: The embeddedness of institutions*. Cambridge: Cambridge University Press.

House, R. J., Hanges, P. J., Javidan, M., Dorfman, P. W., & Gupta, V. (2004). *Culture, leadership, and organizations: The GLOBE study of 62 societies*. Thousand Oaks, CA: Sage.

Howell, C. (2003). Varieties of capitalism—And then there was one? *Comparative Politics, 36*, 103–124.

Jiraporn, P., Udomsirikul, P., & Jumreornvong, S. (2011). Stock liquidity and capital structure: Evidence from Thailand. Proceedings of the 51stSouthwestern Finance Association Annual Meeting, 9–12 March. http://www.southwesternfinance.org/conf-2011/swfa2011_submission_7.pdf. Accessed 22.04.11.

Joungtrakul, J. (2005). Industrial democracy and best practice in Thailand: A Stakeholder study. DBA Thesis, Curtin University of Technology.

Kamnungwut, W., & Grey, F. (2007). Varieties of co-operation in an SME cluster: Ceramic tableware in Lampang, Thailand. In *DRUID Winter Conference, Denmark, 15 January*.

Kelly, J., & Hamann, K. (2008). Varieties of capitalism and industrial relations. In P. Blyton, N. Bacon, J. Fiorito, & E. Heery (Eds.), *Sage handbook of industrial relations*. London: Sage.

Kerr, C., Dunlop, J., Harbison, F., & Myers, C. (1962). *Industrialism and industrial man*. London: Heinemann.

Khoman, C. (2005). Education: The key to long-term recovery? In P. Warr (Ed.), *Thailand beyond the crisis* (pp. 251–284). London: Routledge.

Kitschelt, S., Lange, P., Marks, G., & Stephens, J. (Eds.), (1999). *Continuity and change in contemporary capitalism*. Cambridge: Cambridge University Press.

Komin, S. (1990). Culture and work-related values in Thai organizations. *International Journal of Psychology*, *25*(5–6), 681–704.

Kuldilok, K. S. (2009). An economic analysis of the Thailand Tuna Fish industry. Ph.D. thesis, Newcastle University.

Lallement, S. (2005). Europe and the economic crisis: Forms of labour adjustment and varieties of capitalism. *Work, Employment and Society*, *25*(4), 627–641.

Lawler, J. J., Siengthai, S., & Atmiyanandana, V. (1998). Human resource management in Thailand: Eroding traditions. In C. Rowley (Ed.), *Human resource management in the Asia-Pacific region: Convergence questioned (Frank Cass, 1998)* (reprinted from Asia-Pacific Business Review).

Lawler, J. J., & Suttawet, C. (2000). Labour unions, globalization and deregulation in Thailand. *Asia Pacific Business Review*, *6*(3 & 4), 214–238.

Lawrence, P., & Lorsch, J. (1967). *Organisation and environment*. Cambridge, MA: Harvard University Press.

Lazonick, W. (1990). *Competitive advantage on the shopfloor*. Cambridge, MA: Harvard University Press.

Lazonick, W. (1991). *Business organization and the myth of the market economy*. New York: Cambridge University Press.

Lazonick, W. (1998). Organisational learning and international competition. In J. Michie & J. Grieve-Smith (Eds.), *Globalization, growth and governance* (pp. 204–238). Oxford: Oxford University Press.

Leelapanyalert, K., Wang, F., & Ghauri, P. (2012). The study of inter-firm market orientation in the retail industry: The case study of seven-eleven in Thailand. In *20th Consortium for international marketing research (CIMaR)*. Taipei, Taiwan: National Chengchi University.

Limsila, K., & Ogunlana, S. (2007). Performance and leadership outcome correlates of leadership styles and subordinate commitment. *Engineering Construction and Architectural Management*, *15*(2), 164–184.

Mahoney, J., & Thelen, K. (2010). A theory of gradual institutional change. In J. Mahoney & K. Thelen (Eds.), *Explaining institutional change: Ambiguity, agency, and power* (pp. 1–17). New York: Cambridge University Press.

Michie, J., & Zumitzavan, V. (2012). The impact of 'learning' and 'leadership' management styles on organisational outcomes: A study of tyre firms in Thailand. *Asia Pacific Business Review*, *18*(4).

Morgan, G., & Kristensen, P. H. (2006). The contested space of multinationals: Varieties of Institutionalism, varieties of capitalism. *Human Relations*, *59*, 1467–1490.

Murphy, E. F., Jr., Mujtaba, B. G., Manyak, T., Sungkhawan, J., & Greenwood, R. (2010). Generational value differences of baby boomers in Thailand. *Asia Pacific Business Review*, *16*(4), 545–566.

Niffenegger, P., Kulviwat, S., & Engchanil, N. (2006). Conflicting cultural imperatives in modern Thailand: Global perspectives. *Asia Pacific Business Review*, *12*(4), 403–420.

Ohmae, K. (1990). *The borderless world*. London: Harper Collins.
Oliver, B., & Wilkinson, A. (1992). *The Japanization of British industry*. Oxford: Blackwells.
Pantong, K. (2012). Golden year for auto industry. The Nation, November 30, 2012. http://www.nationmultimedia.com/business/Golden-year-for-auto-industry-30195275.html. Accessed 02.12.12.
Peck, J., & Theodore, N. (2007). Variegated capitalism. *Progress in Human Geography, 31*, 371–372.
Peters, T., & Waterman, R. (1982). *In search of excellence: Lessons from America's best run companies*. London: Harper and Row.
Pongsudhirak, T. (2014). The roots of Thailand's political polarization in comparative perspective. In *Annual conference on Taiwan democracy, Taiwan Democracy Project, 17–18 October, Stanford, CA, USA*.
Rattanapintha, S. (2010). Liquidity measurement and management in Thailand. *Liquidity measurement and management in SEACEN economies* (pp. 267–297). Kuala Lumpur, Malaysia: South East Asian Central Banks (SEACEN) Research and Training Centre. Chapter 9.
Redding, G. (2005). The thick description and comparison of societal systems of capitalism. *Journal of International Business, 36*, 123–155.
Robinson, W. (2007). Theories of globalization. In G. Ritzer (Ed.), *The Blackwell companion to globalization*. Oxford: Blackwell.
Rowley, C. (1998). *HRM in the Asia pacific region: Convergence questioned*. London: Frank Cass.
Rowley, C., & Quang, T. (2012). Vietnam. In M. DeWitt & G. Redding (Eds.), *Oxford handbook on Asian business systems*. Oxford: OUP.
Rueda, D., & Pontusson, J. (2000). Wage inequality and varieties of capitalism. *World Politics, 53*(3), 350–383.
Satsanguan, P., & Lewis, S. (2009). Thailand's financial and banking systems. Working paper, Faculty of Economics, Thammasat University. http://www.trf.or.th/TRFGallery/Upload/Gallery/Documents/Files/1000000014.pdf. Accessed 19.04.11.
Smith, C., & Meiksins, P. (1995). System, society and dominance effects in cross-national organisational analysis. *Work, Employment & Society, 9*, 241–267.
Sorge, A. (2005). *The global and the local: Understanding the dialectics of business systems*. Oxford: Oxford University Press.
Steier, L. P. (2009). Familial capitalism in global institutional contexts: Implications for corporate governance and entrepreneurship in East Asia. *Asia Pacific Journal of Management, 26*, 513–535.
Streeck, W. (2009). *Re-forming capitalism: Institutional change in the German political economy*. Oxford: Oxford University Press.
Streeck, W. (2010). E Pluribus Unum? Varieties and Commonalities of Capitalism. MPIfg Discussion Paper, 10/12, Max Plank Institute for the Study of Society, Cologne, Germany.
Streeck, W., & Thelen, K. (Eds.), (2005). *Beyond continuity: Institutional change in advanced political economies*. Oxford: Oxford University Press.
Suehiro, A., & Wailerdsak, N. (2014). Thailand: Post-development capitalism. In M. Witt & G. Redding (Eds.), *The Oxford handbook Asian business systems*. Oxford: Oxford University Press.
Sunindijo, R. Y., Hadikusumo, B. H. W., & Ogunlana, S. (2007). Emotional intelligence and leadership styles in construction project management. *Journal of Management in Engineering, 23*(4), 166–170.
Thechatakerng, S. (2006). Alone or ally? Strategic alliance use, partner behaviour and satisfaction in Thai businesses. In *Paper presented at The 3rd EDP Workshop 2006, Universidad Autonoma de Barcelona, Spain, April 6–8*. http://www.bablog.mju.ac.th/Pusanisa/wp-content/uploads/2010/11/Alone-or-Ally.pdf. Accessed 20.04.11.
Thelen, K. (2004). *How institutions evolve: The political economy of skills in Germany, Britain, the United States, and Japan*. New York: Cambridge University Press.

Tohyama, H. (2015). Varieties of Asian welfare capitalisms and the influence of globalization. *Journal of International and Comparative Social Policy, 31*(1), 51–73.

Tohyama, H., & Harada, Y. (2013). Effect of institutional configuration on innovation activities in East Asian firms: A study of the institutional diversity of Asian economies. *Asian Business and Information Management, 4*, 2.

Udomsirikul, P., Jumreornvong, S., & Jiraporn, P. (2011). Liquidity and capital structure: The case of Thailand. *Journal of Multinational Financial Management, 21*(2), 106–117.

Vincent, S. (2005). Really dealing: A critical perspective on inter-organizational exchange networks. *Work, Employment and Society, 19*(1), 47–65.

Wallerstein, I. (1974). *The modern world-system: Capitalist agriculture and the origins of the European world-economy in the sixteenth century*. New York: Academic Press.

Wallerstein, I. (2004). *World-systems analysis*. Durham: Duke University Press.

Walter, A., & Zhang, X. (2012). Debating Asian capitalism: Issues and themes. In A. Walter & X. Zhang (Eds.), *East Asian capitalism diversity, continuity, and change*. Oxford: Oxford University Press.

Weerawong, Chinnavat & Peangpanor. (2014). Q&A Country chapter: Thailand. Mergers & Acquisitions Law Guide 2013/14 from LexisNexis: The 1st Annual Guide to Practicing M&A Law in Asia. Available at http://www.weerawongcp.com/data/know/50.pdf. Accessed 06.03.15.

Whitley, R. (1992). *Business systems in East Asia: Firms, markets and societies*. London: Sage.

Whitley, R. (1999). *Divergent capitalisms: The social structuring and change of business systems*. Oxford: OUP.

Whitley, R. (2007). *Business systems and organizational capabilities*. Oxford: OUP.

Whitley, R. (2014). Change and continuity in East Asian business systems. In M. Witt & G. Redding (Eds.), *The Oxford handbook Asian business systems* (pp. 626–657). Oxford: Oxford University Press.

Witt, M., & Redding, G. (Eds.), (2014). *The Oxford handbook Asian business systems*. Oxford: Oxford University Press.

Wiwattanakantang, Y. (1999). An empirical study on the determinants of the capital structure of Thai Firms. *Pacific Basin Finance Journal*, 7, 352–371.

Womack, J., Jones, D., & Roos, D. (1990). *The machine that changed the world*. New York: Rawson Associates.

Woodward, J. (1965). *Industrial organisation*. Oxford: Oxford University Press.

World Bank. (2008). Thailand investment climate assessment update, Report No. 44248-TH, Poverty Reduction and Economic Management Sector Unit, East Asia and Pacific Region, World Bank. http://www-wds.worldbank.org/external/default/WDSContentServer/WDSP/IB/2009/07/30/000333038_20090730022419/Rendered/PDF/442480ESW0P1061C0disclosed071281091.pdf Accessed 29.03.12.

World Bank. (2012). *Leading with Ideas: Skills for growth and equity in Thailand*. Thailand: The World Bank. http://www-wds.worldbank.org/external/default/WDSContentServer/WDSP/IB/2012/03/16/000356161_20120316012916/Rendered/PDF/672040ESW0P1170hig0res0AW0for0print.pdf. Accessed 26.03.12.

Yukongdi, V. (2008). Trade unions in Thailand. In J. Benson & Y. Zhu (Eds.), *Trade unions in Asia: An economic and sociological analysis* (pp. 216–235). London: Routledge.

Yukongdi, V. (2010). A study of Thai employees' preferred leadership style. *Asia Pacific Business Review, 1–2*, 161–181.

CHAPTER 12

Social Capital and the Social Context of Business Networks: The Case of Thailand

P. Susomrith, Y. Suseno
Edith Cowan University, Perth, WA, Australia

12.1 INTRODUCTION

Business networking plays a crucial role in determining organisational performance and also, economic growth. The networks of social structures and relationships facilitate beneficial outcomes for the 'actors' (individuals, groups, businesses), creating a distinctive form of capital–social capital. Although Putnam's (1993, 1995) studies have been fundamental in acknowledging the central role of social capital for economic prosperity and social well-being, extant studies on social capital have primarily focused on individual outcomes (eg, Seibert, Kraimer, & Liden, 2001; Suseno, Pinnington, Gardner, & Shulman, 2006), and organisational outcomes (eg, Leana & Pil, 2006; Tsai & Ghoshal, 1998; Wu, 2008). Less attention has, in fact, been given to understanding the social context in which social capital can be developed, utilised, and maintained. This potentially limits our understanding of how business networking and social capital are used in different countries. As Redding (1990) noted, while several East Asian regions share a common grounding based on Confucian values, they indeed vary in networking practices and operations due to the differences in cultural values, as well as historical and political backgrounds of these countries. This important point has been demonstrated in other chapters in this collection which have focused on different countries, for example Chapter 6 on China, Chapter 8 on Korea and Chapter 14 on Vietnam.

Typically, business relationships in many Asian countries are closely interlinked with social life through complex social relations and networks. The extent of this interweaving of social and business networks creates social capital. Competing to attain a competitive advantage requires many of these firms to develop, utilise, and maintain their social capital derived from their informal social relations and formal business networks. However,

Business Networks in East Asian Capitalisms
http://dx.doi.org/10.1016/B978-0-08-100639-9.00012-8

as Witt and Redding (2013, pp. 266–267) highlighted, "the further away one moves from Japan, the less well understood the institutional structures and dynamics of business systems in Asia become". The limited literature on the social context of Asian economies means that we have not been able to understand how social capital is developed, utilised, and maintained in these countries. In particular, an understanding of the nature of social context that enables social capital is relevant in businesses operating in emerging Asian markets. Social capital is not created in vacuum. The outcomes enabled by social capital are only realised if there is social fabric and structure that enable such capital to be developed, utilised, and maintained.

In this chapter, we examine the features of the social context of Thailand—the social fabric that enables social capital to be developed, utilised, and maintained in the country. Thailand is a country that is largely influenced by Chinese (Confucian) culture, tradition, and values. It is also a country that is rich in natural resources, yet is recently plagued by turmoil, political instability, and civil unrest. Thailand has, however, managed to stay resilient from persistent crises over the past decade (Arnold, 2014). The economic boom of the 1980s saw Thailand developed as an economic force, particularly in the Southeast Asian regions. The country's per capita income tripled and Bangkok's skyline was rapidly transformed into a high-rise metropolis. Thailand's economy is the second largest in Southeast Asia, after Indonesia. With a population of 67 million, Thailand has become an economic powerhouse with its exports totalling more than 60% of its gross domestic product. After the Asian Financial Crisis, Thailand, in fact, emerged stronger than ever. Thai businesses experienced a phenomenal growth with many entrepreneurs striking it rich in a country that is still characterised by a wide segregation between the rich and the poor. The World Bank (2015) reported that Thailand has been known as one of the success stories of the Southeast Asian region, with persistent growth and improved rate of poverty reduction, making the country an upper-middle income economy in 2011.

Historically, Thailand has had numerous constitutional changes of government, creating constant instability to the country's political situation. During the periods 2006–10, Thailand went through political turmoil with the clash between protesters wearing the 'Yellow Shirts' who opposed the former Prime Minister Thaksin Shinawatra, and those wearing the 'Red Shirts' who supported Mr. Shinawatra (Rojanapanich, 2010). Despite attempts to restore democracy, the political crises did not end after 2010. In recent years, Thailand's military issued martial law in 2014 to put a stop to the country's deepening political crisis and riots (Quinn, 2014). As a result of Thailand's continuing political unrest, the tourism industry, Thailand's important economic sector, has suffered a major blow. Several reports have also warned of the country suffering a weak domestic demand and insufficient government spending to stimulate economic activity and growth (Arnold, 2014). Despite the army's political pledge to reestablish peace and political calm, Thailand's economic growth has been noted as the slowest among the developing nations (Pesek, 2015).

The chapter first highlights the aspect of social capital as an important theoretical background. We then focus on Thailand's social context that is underpinned by unique cultural characteristics of collectivism, Buddhism, particularism, reluctance to change, relationship orientation, and hierarchical or vertical system. Following this, we describe how networking in Thailand is socially constructed, relative to its cultural values, to create social capital for the economic growth of the country. Before concluding the chapter, we offer our views on the future prospect of Thailand—a country currently at the crossroads.

12.2 SOCIAL CAPITAL

Putnam's (1993) work provides a rich analysis of social capital in democratic societies or communities. In 'Making Democracy Work', Putnam (1993) argued that the extent of social capital in society is determined by the longstanding traditions of civic engagement (ie, the participation of citizens in activities like membership in sports and various voluntary organisations). Putnam (1993) conducted a comparative study of the north and south regions of Italy and found that features of social organisation, such as networks and norms, enable the building of trust and connections among people. In 'Bowling Alone', Putnam (2000) extensively documented the declining social capital in America, observed in terms of the diminishing rate of active membership in civic groups, religious organisations, as well as in informal social gatherings. Putnam (2000) argued that the once highly social activity (bowling) was no longer seen as a social activity, lesser and lesser community members participated in it. The lack of civic engagement, as observed by Putnam (2000), indicated that social capital is diminishing in the American society.

Similar to Putnam's (1993, 2000) findings, Fukuyama (1995) acknowledged that a society needs to have and build social capital in order to succeed. This capital cannot be acquired by an individual, but rather it is based on the social virtues of the society like loyalty, dependability, and honesty. Fukuyama (1995, p. 11) argued that "[l]aw, contract, and economic rationality provide a necessary but not sufficient basis for both the stability and prosperity of postindustrial societies; they must as well be leavened with reciprocity, moral obligation, duty toward community, and trust, which are based in habit rather than rational calculation".

Social capital has been viewed as both a private good and a public good. As a private good, social capital is used to benefit individuals who are able to access and use resources embedded in their social networks for instrumental outcomes (eg, finding better jobs) (Leana & Van Buren, 1999; Lin, 2001). On the other hand, scholars, such as Woolcock (2001), argue that social capital is a classic public good because of its nonexclusive nature, benefiting all members of the community. Being members in certain social circles may provide these members with many opportunities (Granovetter, 1973; Ibarra, 1993). Social capital as a public good is thus essentially viewed as providing benefits to both the 'creator' and the 'receiver' (Putnam, 2000).

In examining several European regions, Beugelsdijk and Smulders (2004) highlighted interesting insights. Participation in open networks that span different communities, according to Beugelsdijk and Smulders (2004), creates bridging social capital, which is found to be significant for economic growth. The finding is similar to Granovetter's (1973) study on the value of weak ties as important resource for opportunities, such as for finding a job. On the other hand, networks of family and friends, according to Beugelsdijk and Smulders (2004), create bonding social capital but interestingly, this was found to be negatively related to economic growth. Shideler and Kraybill (2003), using network centrality measures as proxies for social capital, indicated that social capital is positively related to per capita income growth and thus, is seen as an enabler for community economic growth. Communities or regions desiring to attain positive economic growth must therefore increase their commitment and coordination to obtain resources and information within their networks to propel such growth.

Although research has highlighted the link between social capital and economic growth, economists have paid little attention to understanding the social context that enables the development, utilisation, and maintenance of social capital. In this chapter, we focus on the social context of a country that underpins the cultural influences and societal life. It is only when we understand the social context of a country, would we be able to acknowledge the extent of social capital in promoting economic prosperity and growth of the country. In the majority of extant literature of social capital, this is depicted as trust (Esser, 2008; Redding, 2005). In this study, we consider three dimensions of social capital that were proposed by Nahapiet and Ghoshal (1998), and subsequently tested by Tsai and Ghoshal (1998). The three dimensions of social capital are structural, relational, and cognitive. The structural social capital describes the extent and frequency of communication, as well as the structure of networks where information and critical resources are shared. Research examining the structural social capital emphasises the positive impact a network structure has on the sharing of information and knowledge within and between organisations (Rowley, Behrens, & Krackhardt, 2000).

The second dimension of social capital, the relational social capital, refers to the outcomes of relationships that are underpinned by trust (Krackhardt, 2014). In such relationships, members are trustworthy, which subsequently enables a more effective flow of information between the group members (Nahapiet & Ghoshal, 1998; Tsai & Ghoshal, 1998). In the context of a country's well-being, its prosperity, its degree of democracy, and its ability to compete, Fukuyama (1995, p. 7) noted that all these are "conditioned by a single, pervasive cultural characteristic: the level of trust inherent in the society". The final dimension of social capital, the cognitive social capital, refers to the shared understanding developed through the interactions of members within the network structure, that promote cooperation, a sense of shared responsibility, and a collective action (Chen, Chang, & Hung, 2008; Inkpen & Tsang, 2005).

In the following section, we describe the social context of Thailand—a country with its distinctive cultural characteristics of collectivism, Buddhism, particularism, reluctance to change, relationship orientation, and hierarchical or vertical system.

12.2.1 Thailand's Cultural Characteristics

Thailand has welcomed trade and diplomacy with foreign countries since the Ayutthaya period (1350–1767), famously known as the great era of international trade for the country. For over 400 years, the kingdom of Ayutthaya was the dominant power in the region, with the city of Ayutthaya becoming the capital in 1350 when King Ramathibodi I founded the city. Thai society became rigorously hierarchical during this period, with the formation of classes within its society. The class system made a clear distinction of three groups of people: commoners were placed at the bottom of the hierarchy, officials occupied the middle rank of the hierarchy, and the King, together with the princes, was at the highest level of the hierarchy. Only the Buddhist monks were exempt from this class system.

Over time, Thailand established relationships with England, France, Portugal, Netherlands, Spain, and China during the 16th and 17th centuries, fuelling the economic prosperity of this country. Its relationships with China blossomed from these early years, with China eventually having a significant impact on Thailand's trade and commerce. Many Chinese migrated to Thailand, who would eventually become ethnic Thais. Indeed, the societal values and business orientation of the Chinese has led to the establishment of many conglomerates of Chinese descent in Thailand (Kantamara, 2009).

Thailand provides an attractive location for foreign investment. The Thai government hugely welcomes foreign investment, particularly those that are committed to substantial investment and trade liberalisation. Many businesses, especially those from within the Association of Southeast Asian Nations (ASEAN) and the Asia-Pacific Economic Cooperation (APEC) regions, were interested to invest the country (Kantamara, 2009). Among its Asian neighbours, Thailand boasts good infrastructure and efficient transport, well-priced real estate and construction costs, affordable labour costs, and a central Asian location (Kantamara, 2009). Thailand is known as the 'Land of Smiles', denoting Thai people as happy and carefree. The Lonely Planet guide, for example, praised Thailand as "friendly and fun-loving, exotic and tropical, cultured and historic" with its "glittering temples, and tropical beaches to the ever-comforting Thai smile" (Lonely Planet, 2015). A smiling and friendly persona is evident in many parts of Thailand as a result of the distinctive Thai's cultural characteristics.

12.2.2 Collectivism

Historically, Thai people lived in villages and tended the land. Village life was communal in nature where an individual's survival was entirely dependent on group cooperation, mutual assistance, and harmony. Obligation and loyalty to the group were considered crucial in determining whether one could remain as a member of a particular group. This brought rise to Thai's cultural characteristic of collectivism. The emphasis on obligation and loyalty leads to the importance of one's role to take care of, and provide for, others of a higher status.

Similar to China, Thailand scores 20 on Hofstede's (2015) cultural dimension of individualism. One of the key characteristics of a collectivistic society is the need for individuals to belong to a group. The group, in turn, would support and take care of its members in exchange for their loyalty. In a collectivistic culture, one is also subconsciously discouraged to deviate from the norm. To preserve harmony within the group, members are usually not confrontational. This action prevents members from 'losing face' should there be any disagreements. Group members think collectively in terms of what is best for the group, thus developing a 'we' mentality (Hofstede, 2015). There is also an implicit understanding in a collectivistic society that tasks are secondary to relationships. Friendships are somewhat predetermined; for example, in a workplace, coworkers, particularly those who share common backgrounds, instinctively become friends. These friendships often hold greater importance than the task or the job.

In essence, the high collectivism score of the Thai society signifies a propensity for group-dependence and a desire to attain social harmony through empathy for the needs of others (Pornpitakpan, 1999). Growing up in extended families, Thais are taught to think of themselves as part of a larger group, whether a family group, school group, or work group. Friendships are established with coworkers with the focus on retaining a harmonious work environment.

12.2.3 Buddhism

As noted by Rowley and Warner (2010), Thailand's main religion is Buddhism. Buddhism emphasises harmony among people, society, and environment (Morrison & Conaway, 2006; Scarborough, 1998). The Buddhist philosophy denotes the importance of travelling the Middle Way and avoiding the extremes. The Middle Way is taught as the 'path of wisdom' between the extremes of sensual indulgence and self-mortification. Buddhism also teaches karma—a fundamental doctrine that highlights a moral action and its consequences. It is a belief that if a person does good deeds, he/she will receive assistance, guidance, or help when such is needed. Similarly, a 'bad' deed resulting from hatred or jealousy, for example, will be paid back in the future. Based on these ideals, Thais consider people and events to be interrelated. The focus of any relationships is on the long-term harmony through compromises, where a less than favourable outcome will be compensated by the expectation of a favourable outcome in the future (Yeung & Tung, 1996).

The teachings of Buddhism also influence the feminine values of Thai people. In general, Thai people are not overtly ambitious or assertive. They place greater emphasis on the quality of life rather than chasing for material possessions and wealth. This explains Thailand's low masculinity score of 34 (Hofstede, 2015). The characteristics of a low masculinity culture are the display of tenderness and care by people of that culture. Compromises and negotiations are often used to resolve conflicts. They are considerate of others' feelings and situations, and generally display politeness and good manners. This behaviour is referred to as *kreng jai*. The reasons for *kreng jai* are various, for example because 'I don't want to bother them', 'I don't want to hurt their feelings or make them angry', 'I don't want to make them lose face', or 'I don't want to impose'. This perplexing phenomenon is noticeable particularly in situations involving seniority. Thai people place a huge importance on respecting the elders whether in terms of age, experiences, wealth, or those of higher positions in organisations. They have the tendency to think of their actions carefully and if these are more likely to lead to negative consequences for the elders or the more senior people, they will not do it. A certain degree of *kreng jai* is expected, and if practised socially, it demonstrates good manners.

12.2.4 Particularism

Particularism refers to the exclusive connection to a group. Group members treat insiders quite differently than outsiders of the group. Within the Thai society, insiders are devoted to assist members of the group. At the same time, they are more likely to reject people who are outside of the group. Insiders are provided with information and opportunities that encourage business relationships to develop. Ongoing particularistic behaviour supports and strengthens business relationships within that group. Outsiders, however, are unable to receive this same level of support, hindering any likelihood of establishing a business venture. This behaviour thus creates a stark difference in the treatment of people depending on their position within a group, such as the level of wealth or education. For Thai people to gain an advantage of being part of a group, they form close bonds with their family group, their ancestral village, and their community.

12.2.5 Reluctance to Change

Thai people are often anxious when faced with change. They see change as a threat as it gives rise to uncertainty. Indeed, Thailand scores 64 in the dimension of uncertainty avoidance (Hofstede, 2015), a score that is higher than the Asian average score of 58. This moderately high score indicates that Thai people are hesitant to change, be it for changing their employment, or using new products or technologies. The events of recent years however, indicate that Thai people also embrace change when change is required. Thus, we argue that the term 'avoidance' may not be entirely appropriate in the Thai context. Thai people are reluctant to change but they also welcome change if they perceive this as for their collective good.

Due to their reluctance to change, Thai people are rather conservative when making an investment. They seek security and have an emotional need for rules. Hallinger and Kantamara (2000, p. 207), for instance, found that "Thais are strongly socialised to conform to group norms, traditions, rules and regulations…[and] they find change more disruptive and disturbing than in 'lower uncertainty avoidance' cultures". Thus, in the Thai context, people tend to avoid risk as much as possible, preferring conformity and control over their environment.

12.2.6 Relationship Orientation

There is a strong Chinese influence on Thailand's way of life and values. Chinese account for approximately 14% of Thailand's population. Thailand and China have a long history of bilateral relations in various fields such as politics, economics, trade, education, science, and military. The immigration of the Chinese from mainland China brought rise to the growth of ethnic Chinese Thais. Many of these ethnic Chinese Thais are entrepreneurs and increasingly establish their businesses—this is a common feature of overseas Chinese business families often known as the 'bamboo network'. In fact, it is estimated that 80% of listed companies in Thailand are controlled by Chinese descents.

Although many of Thai businesses and conglomerates are run by ethnic Chinese Thais, the assimilation of the overseas Chinese with the indigenous Thai is different from those found in the neighbouring countries. In Indonesia, for example, assimilation between Chinese descents and the indigenous, or *pribumis*, has long been a thorny issue. With only about 1.2% of Indonesia's total population being ethnic Chinese (Franciska, 2014), the vast majority of businesses in the country is actually controlled by them. Even though Chinese descents attempt to assimilate with the indigenous Indonesians, there is always a feeling of segregation between the two groups. In fact, in a comprehensive study of overseas Chinese communities in a book called 'Sons of the Yellow Emperor' by Lynn Pan, it was quoted that "no country harbouring a Chinese minority possesses a blacker record of persecution and racial violence than Indonesia" (as quoted in Higgins, 2012). This eventually led to the May 1998 riots when more than 1000 Indonesian ethnic Chinese were tortured and killed by the rioters, and many Chinese women and girls were gang-raped (Franciska, 2014). Although the situation in Indonesia is improving, particularly with the election of the first ethnic Chinese, Basuki Tjahaja Purnama, to govern Indonesia's capital city from 2014 (Kwok, 2014; Roberts, 2014), racism is still evident for many Chinese Indonesians. The recent situation in Malaysia also highlights the deep-rooted feelings of wide segregation between Chinese descents and indigenous Malays, with protesters and rioters vowing to denounce ethnic Chinese community and leaders (ABC, 2015).

In Thailand, on the other hand, it is difficult to differentiate the Chinese descents and the indigenous Thais. Regardless of the different racial and ethnic backgrounds, Thais live in harmony with one another. In the neighbouring countries that are predominantly Muslims, the religions of many people of Chinese descent are mainly Buddhism or Christianity. The main religion in Thailand, however, is Buddhism which binds its people together. The Thai society is largely influenced by Confucianism that places an emphasis on social relationships, also known as 'Guanxi' (Chan, 2000; Chen, 1995). Guanxi is based upon two premises: a relational promised exchange, and trust. The relational promised exchange encompasses reciprocal favours (Leana & Pil, 2006). The trust component of Guanxi goes beyond just the current business transaction; it encapsulates the social, personal, and business relationship, strengthening the relationship over time. The Guanxi-relationship is based on the length and quality of the personal relationship (Perry, 1999; So & Walker, 2006; Zahra, George, & Garvis, 1999). Guanxi bonds two parties in a reciprocal obligation through ongoing cooperation and exchange of favours (Chen, 1995; Davies, 1995).

Buun Kuln is similar to the Chinese concept of Guanxi, where a relationship is based on reciprocal obligations from the continuous exchange of favours. Doing business together at the first get-go is not how the Chinese do business. Face-to-face contact is preferred, as it facilitates the feelings of obligation to maintain the relationship (Niffenegger, Kulviwat, & Engchanil, 2008). In a *Buun Kuln* relationship, there is a feeling of affection and obligation. Affection is the emotional attachment between members of the network, resulting in a sense of loyalty, solidarity, and willingness to support each other. Such an affective relationship is also often characterised by regular visits to one another's places, participating in regular common activities, paying respect to the elders, and maintaining a harmonious relationship with others.

In a *Buun Kuln* relationship, there is also a feeling of obligation, which is about *mutual obligation* and *reciprocity*. Mutual obligation is the motivation and willingness to provide assistance for the other party in a *Buun Kuln* relationship. The expectation that the other party will repay or provide a favour is the reciprocity component of the relationship.

This exchange of favours in both directions builds and strengthens the *Buun Kuln* relationship.

12.2.7 Hierarchical or Vertical System

Thai society is heavily based on a hierarchical structure as a result of traditional values being passed down for generations. As evidenced in the high score of 64 in power distance (Hofstede, 2015), the Thai society is characterised with an uneven distribution of power. Respect is assumed to be given to those who are in power or a position of seniority (Holmes & Tangtongtavy, 2003).

The hierarchical structure within the Thai society can be traced back to the era of King Trailok of Ayudhya, who in 1455, established a law that classified the population by ranks. The classification was based upon a person's authority and responsibility in the society, and the ranking inferred a person's position based on that hierarchical structure. The classification law also included *Sak Di Na* which was the grading for monks and religious men. This level of classification continued until the Thai King Chulalongkorn (1853–1910) abolished *Sak Di Na*. Despite this, the influence of the hierarchical or vertical system in the Thai society continues.

The hierarchical system in Thailand produces inequality in the society as evidenced by the existence of social classes based on wealth, education, position, family relation, and seniority. Respect for the hierarchical structure is considered natural. Thai children are taught to respect their elders, including parents, grandparents, teachers, and people more senior, or those in positions of authority. People respect monks regardless of whether they are young or old. For Thais, the concept of 'superior-inferior' is dominant in all Thai organisations (Thanasankit & Corbitt, 2000). As long as everyone behaves according to the hierarchical or vertical structure, social harmony is always attained. At the same time, as long as there is an atmosphere of sociability and friendliness, the hierarchical nature of the society is accepted (Mulder, 1994). As noted by Witt and Redding (2013), many Asian nations indeed display high hierarchy and place greater importance of groups. However, the recent events of dissent and protest in Thailand highlight that the concept of hierarchy is not necessarily institutionalised and permanent in all social systems in Thailand. Many Thais believe that the economic downturn the country experienced with weak consumer spending, low investment, and shrinking trade and tourism, indicate weak government leadership, which has to be changed. The military rule to run the country and the economy once again underlines the hierarchical or vertical structure in the Thai society.

12.3 THAILAND'S SOCIAL CONTEXT FOR THE CREATION, UTILISATION AND MAINTENANCE OF SOCIAL CAPITAL

Like many of its neighbouring countries, Thailand's businesses function in an environment dominated by complex networks encompassing social and business interactions. A number of researchers have highlighted the need to consider both the social and personal relations within business processes and practices in Thailand, due to the complexity of separating these different types of networks (Atmiyanandan & Lawler, 2003; Holmes & Tangtongtavy, 2003).

Thailand's business networks are shaped as a result of the nation's cultural characteristics, such as collectivism, Buddhism philosophy, particularism, reluctance to change, relationship orientation, and hierarchical structure. These cultural characteristics are based on Thai philosophies that shape the values and beliefs of Thai people, influencing the way they interact and undertake daily activities. The characteristics of Thai culture emphasises the importance of family and social relationships and this is carried through to business practices. Unlike Western cultures that base decisions on cost-benefit analysis, Thai businesses consider the interactions between organisations and family as interlinked (Mandel, 2001). This demonstrates the importance placed on social power within this context, as business ventures in Thailand are very much based on social relationships (de Alwis & Senathiraja, 2003). Thai managers do not perceive a difference between social and business relationships, although the social aspects must exist prior to the business being conducted (Bjorkman & Kock, 1995).

In terms of the structural social capital, network structure often provides beneficial outcomes to those operating within the structure. Parker and Vaidya (2001), for instance, noted that informal contact and relationships that continue over an extended period of time, result in the sharing of information and resources. The study by Patterson and Smith (2001) also highlighted a sense of belonging, recognition, friendship, and social support as other benefits of social networks. These benefits are then translated to business relationships, resulting in an improved efficiency and operations, as well as the opportunity to secure further contacts (Perry, 1999). Chittithaworn et al.'s (2011) study highlighted that social networks is one of the three main external factors influencing the success of small- to medium-sized organisations in Thailand, together with government support and conformity to legal framework. In addition, social structure and networks were found to offer a reduction in risks and transaction costs and access to knowledge, capital, and ideas. A study comprising of

339 One Tambon (meaning 'sub-district') One Product (OTOP) entrepreneurs within Bangkok and surroundings, found that entrepreneurial networks were the second highest predictor of organisational performance after work experience. These networks provide the access to additional resources not previously available to the entrepreneur, leading to an improved organisational performance (Pillai, 2012). As many of Thailand's big businesses are conglomerates, they are also often linked in networks that span across different industries and communities. Such networks restrain opportunistic behaviour and enable reputation to grow. Walker, Kogut, and Shan (1997), for instance, state that in such networks of closure, information about any deviant behaviour is disseminated quickly, and that individuals who 'misbehave' are quickly sanctioned by others in the network. The importance to social networks is further supported by research done by Tooksoon and Mohamad (2010), where networking, including the development and maintenance of relationships with financial institutions and business associates, has been found to have a strong correlation with organisational performance.

As with most countries in Asia, people from Thailand are relationship-focused and prefer to interact with family, friends, and 'insiders' who can be trusted (Gesteland & Seyk, 2002). Thai businesses rely on their social capital for referrals and social contacts. In fact, one of the few ways to build relational social capital in this country is to be introduced or referred by a trusted person or organisation. Without this referral, outsiders face significant difficulties, requiring extended periods of effort to build relationships and trust.

The concept of trust is very important and relevant as Thai people prefer to work with people they know and who can be trusted, as they are generally hesitant of change and uncertainty. Trust reduces fear and anxiety, and helps to build long-term relationships. Thai business relationships in Thailand are developed over long periods of time and based upon trust and confidentiality. Face-to-face meetings are preferred, which help to strengthen the relationships further and enhance the feelings of *Kreng Jai*, the consideration of other's feelings and the reluctance to impose on others. Such relationship is also characterised by *Buun Kuhn*, reciprocated favours between two parties that continue for some periods of time. Thai businesses place a high importance on the quality of relationships, illustrated by Crosby, Evans, and Cowles (1990) as the strength of ties, the frequency of interactions, trust, and the commitment in the relationship. Frequent relationships enable the development and maintenance of a harmonious relationship, characterised by close interactions, warmth, and enthusiasm.

In a highly collectivistic and group-oriented society, such as Thailand, social interactions and cooperation are considered a necessity in developing a business relationship (de Alwis & Senathiraja, 2003). During the establishment phase, businesses are most vulnerable and depend heavily on their structural and relational social capital for financial support, approvals from government, securing orders and resources. Similarly, processes and approvals may be accelerated by the influence of contacts in positions of authority. Formal procedures may be bypassed or reduced through the influence of social contacts, thereby providing competitive advantage to a business. Businesses may also receive information through social contacts, including advanced notice of competitors' product releases and performance. As Thailand is hierarchical in nature, business negotiations are often influenced by obligations and loyalties (Holmes & Tangtongtavy, 2003; Lasserre & Schutte, 1995; Patterson & Smith, 2001). Hewison (2002), for example, interestingly highlighted the role of wealth and business networks in electoral politics. Thai magnates are well-known for being able to mobilise their business networks to canvass and hand out money to secure opportunities that will give advantage to them. Once they hand out the substantial amount of funds, those who receive these favours are obligated to assist them in return.

The study by Fongtanakit (2013) illustrated the positive relationships between the three dimensions of social capital and organisational performance, with cognitive social capital and relational social capital having the greatest effect on performance. In the context of Thailand, cognitive social capital is important in any relationship. Shared interpretations and meanings among parties in the relationship are essential to ensure that social relationships can be nurtured to result in business relationships. Individuals and organisations share language and codes as well as shared narratives. This provides the basis of control, trust, and morality (Esser, 2008).

12.4 THAILAND'S SOCIAL CAPITAL: WHERE TO NOW?

Thailand's meteoric economic growth since emerging from the Asian financial crisis has built the wealth of many Thai individuals and organisations. Although there is an increasing population of the Thai middle class, the rich is also getting richer. There is, in fact, a widening inequality between the rich and the poor. Social capital in the country has been utilised by individuals and organisations at the top level of the hierarchy effectively, creating immense wealth and prosperity for owners of these organisations. Thai's larger firms are more effective in terms of their corporatist interest and network coalitions. Their economic interests encompass several industries, products, and services. The networks of many of the large Thai businesses (often controlled by ethnic Chinese Thais) also extend far beyond its domestic boundaries, creating a denser and more effective network structure that enables beneficial outcomes.

However, the stock of social capital appears limited or at least, ineffectively utilised, by those at the lower end of the hierarchy, and by smaller organisations in Thailand. They display a less effective and less successful network structure and have difficulty in building their relational and cognitive dimensions of social capital, particularly with those at the upper level of the social structure. As particularism is deemed as important by Thais, large and more successful businesses (and individuals) tend to be doing business with other successful businesses (and individuals). Those who do not fit in with the criteria of being rich and successful are considered as outsiders and therefore, are not 'invited' into that social circle. The country's economic growth is thus very much dependent on a small fraction of the economy.

The disparate distribution of social capital among the different sizes of organisations in Thailand is also evident in cases involving the Thai's rich and elite. For example, the incident in 2012 involving the hit-and-run accident of Vorayuth Yoovidhya, an heir to Thailand's Red Bull, the world's most popular energy drink company, sparked bitterness amongst Thai lower- and middle-class (Purnell, 2013). The Yoovidhyas are worth $9.6 billion, making them the fourth-richest family in Thailand (Forbes, 2015). The young Yoovidhya, 27 at the time, was allegedly speeding in his silver $1million Ferrari. He then crashed into a police officer on motorcycle patrol, killing the policeman, who died immediately on impact. The Yoovidhya family paid 3 million baht (roughly $100k) as a funeral fee to stop a civil lawsuit from the victim's family (Daily Mail, 2012). The date for a trial still has not been set, with ordinary citizens voicing their unhappiness and claiming that the rich and privileged often get away with crimes in Thailand.

Unlike the other neighbouring countries, Thailand has constantly undergone leadership changes. The event of May 2014 revealed the fragility of Thai's political and economic situations. The Constitutional court ordered Prime Minister Yingluck Shinawatra and several ministers to be removed from the office, and the army seized power in a coup to seize control of the government in May 2014. In March 2015, the army-appointed Prime Minister Prayut Chan-o-cha continued to rule the country by executive order, and ended martial law. In August 2015, a terrorist bomb at Hindu

Erawan shrine, Bangkok, killed 20 people, damaging the economy further (BBC, 2015). Although social capital and effective business networking in the past have benefited many individuals and corporations, the fragile situation in the country could no longer sustain economic growth. Interestingly, recent news has revealed that the Thai military has tried to build their social networks again to bring in former arch-enemy Thaksin Shinawatra, to promote growth and income of the country (Peel, 2015). Thailand, as a country, needs to formulate and implement policies and strategies at the upper government level, to bring about drastic changes in the economic and political situation. It is too early to predict the outcomes of such action, although it is evident in this case that business and social relationships often intermingle in the context of Thailand.

12.5 CONCLUSION

The chapter highlights the social context of Thailand that enables informal social relationships and formal business networks to flourish, creating social capital for the country's economic growth. Thailand, marked by events of political turmoil and civil unrest, however, needs to overcome structural inertia to bring the country to stability once again and progress to the next step of economic growth. An understanding of the social context within the Thai society is crucial for the reform of the country. The country has unique, and yet, complex cultural characteristics. Only by understanding the social context of the country, policies, and strategies can they then be formulated and implemented to create, maintain, and utilise social capital to enable Thailand's economic prosperity once again.

REFERENCES

ABC. (2015). Ethnic Malays openly denounce Chinese in rally organised by Malaysia's ruling party UMNO. *ABC News*. Available from http://www.abc.net.au/news/2015-09-16/ethnic-malays-openly-denounce-chinese-in-umno-rally/6781556. Accessed 15.09.15.

Arnold, M. S. (2014). Thailand's political unrest deals a blow to key tourism sector. *The Wall Street Journal*. Available from http://blogs.wsj.com/economics/2014/05/22/thailands-political-unrest-deals-a-blow-to-key-tourism-sector/. Accessed 01.09.15.

Atmiyanandan, V., & Lawler, J. (2003). Culture and management in Thailand. In M. Warne (Ed.), *Culture and management in Asia*. New York: Routledge Curzon.

BBC. (2015). Thailand profile: Timeline. *BBC News*. Available from http://www.bbc.com/news/world-asia-15641745. Accessed 01.10.15.

Beugelsdijk, S., & Smulders, S. (2004). Social capital and economic growth. Available from http://down.cenet.org.cn/upfile/51/200591785152126.pdf. Accessed 01.09.15.

Bjorkman, I., & Kock, S. (1995). Social relationships and business networks: The case of western companies in China. *International Business Review, 4*(4), 519–535.

Chan, R. (2000). Overseas Chinese management styles. In J. T. Li, A. S. Tsui, & E. Weldon (Eds.), *Management and organisations in the Chinese context* (pp. 325–337). London: Macmillan.

Chen, M. (1995). *Asian management systems: Chinese, Japanese, and Korean style of business.* London: International Thomson Business Press.

Chen, M. H., Chang, Y. C., & Hung, S. C. (2008). Social capital and creativity in R&D project teams. *R&D Management, 38*(1), 21–34.

Chittithaworn, C., Islan, M. A., Keawchana, T., & Yusuf, D. H. M. (2011). Factors affecting business success of small & medium enterprises (SMEs) in Thailand. *Asian Social Science,* 7(5), 180–190.

Crosby, L. A., Evans, K. R., & Cowles, D. (1990). Relationship quality services selling: An interpersonal influence perspective. *Journal of Marketing, 54*(3), 68–84.

Daily Mail. (2012). Family of Red Bull heir charged over crash which killed police officer pay victim's relatives $100k in bid to avoid civil lawsuit. *Daily Mail.* Available from http://www.dailymail.co.uk/news/article-2209219/Vorayuth-Yoovidhya-Family-Red-Bull-heir-charged-crash-killed-police-officer-pay-victims-family-100-000-bid-avoid-civil-lawsuit.html. Accessed 01.09.15.

Davies, H. (1995). Interpreting Guanxi: The role of personal connections in a high context transactional economy. In H. Davies (Ed.), *China business: Context and issues* (pp. 155–169). Hong Kong: Longman Asia.

de Alwis, W. P. G., & Senathiraja, R. (2003). The impact of socio-cultural background of the entrepreneur on management and business practices of selected small and medium scale business in Sri Lanka. In *Paper presented at 9th international conference on Sri Lanka studies, Matara, Sri Lanka.*

Esser, H. (2008). The two meanings of social capital. In D. Castiglione, J. W. van Deth, & G. Wolleb (Eds.), *The handbook of social capital* (pp. 22–49). Oxford: Oxford University Press.

Fongtanakit, K. (2013). *Social capital, knowledge sharing, and performance.* Unpublished doctoral dissertation. Bangkok, Thailand: National Institute of Development Administration

Forbes. (2015). Thailand's 50 richest. *Forbes Magazine.* Available from http://www.forbes.com/thailand-billionaires/list/. Accessed 15.09.15.

Franciska, C. (2014). New voting power of Chinese Indonesians. *BBC Indonesian.* Available from http://www.bbc.com/news/world-asia-27991754. Accessed 20.09.15.

Fukuyama, F. (1995). *Trust: The social virtues and the creation of prosperity.* New York: Free Press.

Gesteland, R., & Seyk, G. (2002). *Marketing across culture in Asia: A practical guide.* Denmark: Copenhagen Business School Press.

Granovetter, M. (1973). The strength of weak ties. *American Journal of Sociology, 78*(6), 1360–1380.

Hallinger, P., & Kantamara, P. (2000). Learning to lead global changes in local cultures, designing a computer-based simulation for Thai school leaders. *Journal of Educational Administration, 39*(3), 197–220.

Hewison, K. (2002). *Political change in Thailand: Democracy and participation.* New York: Routledge.

Higgins, A. (2012). In Indonesia, ethnic Chinese see a new future. *The Washington Post.* Available from https://www.washingtonpost.com/world/asia_pacific/in-indonesia-ethnic-chinese-see-a-new-future/2012/08/18/4befc374-e870-11e1-9739-eef99c5fb285_story.html. Accessed 12.09.15.

Hofstede, G. (2015). What about Thailand? *The Hofstede Centre: Strategy, culture and change.* Available from http://geert-hofstede.com/thailand.html. Accessed 15.08.15.

Holmes, H., & Tangtongtavy, S. (2003). *Working with the Thais: A guide to managing in Thailand* (2nd ed.). Thailand: White Lotus Press.

Ibarra, H. (1993). Network centrality, power, and innovation involvement: Determinants of technical and administrative roles. *Academy of Management Journal, 36*(3), 471–502.

Inkpen, A., & Tsang, E. W. K. (2005). Social capital networks, and knowledge transfer. *Academy of Management Review, 30*(1), 146–165.

Kantamara, P. (2009). Management in Thailand. In H. Hasegawa & C. Noronha (Eds.), *Asian business & management: Theory, practice and perspectives* (pp. 201–212). Hampshire, UK: Palgrave Macmillan.

Krackhardt, D. (2014). A preliminary look at accuracy in egonets. In D. J. Brass, G. (JOE) Labianca, A. Mehra, D. S. Halgin, & S. P. Borgatti (Eds.), *Volume 40. Contemporary perspectives on organizational social networks (Research in the sociology of organizations)* (pp. 277–293). Emerald Group Publishing Limited.

Kwok, Y. (2014). Indonesia reaches racial milestone with Chinese governor of Jakarta. *Time Magazine*. Available from http://time.com/3594125/indonesia-jakarta-chinese-christian-governor-joko-widodo-jokowi-ahok-basuki-purnama/. Accessed 15.08.15.

Lasserre, P., & Schutte, H. (1995). *Strategies for Asia pacific*. London: Palgrave Macmillan.

Leana, C. R., & Van Buren, H. J. (1999). Organisational social capital and employment practices. *Academy of Management Review, 24*(3), 538–555.

Leana, C. R., & Pil, F. K. (2006). Social capital and organizational performance: Evidence from urban public schools. *Organization Science, 17*(3), 353–366.

Lin, N. (2001). *Social capital: A theory of social structure and action*. New York: Cambridge University Press.

Lonely Planet. (2015). *Introducing Thailand*. Available from http://www.lonelyplanet.com/thailand. Accessed 10.08.15.

Mandel, D. R. (2001). Gain-loss framing and choice: Separating outcome formulations from descriptor formulations. *Organisational Behaviour and Human Decision Processes, 85*, 56–76.

Morrison, T., & Conaway, W. A. (2006). *Kiss, bow, or shake hands: The bestselling guide to doing business in more than 60 countries*. Massachusetts: Adams Media.

Mulder, N. (1994). *Inside Thai society: An interpretation of everyday life*. Bangkok, Thailand: Duangkamol Press.

Nahapiet, J., & Ghoshal, S. (1998). Social capital, intellectual capital, and the organizational advantage. *Academy of Management Review, 23*(2), 242–266.

Niffenegger, P., Kulviwat, S., & Engchanil, N. (2008). Conflicting cultural imperatives in modern Thailand: Global perspectives. In C. Rowley & M. Warner (Eds.), *Management in South-East Asia: Business culture, enterprises and human resources* (pp. 14–31). London: Routledge.

Parker, D., & Vaidya, K. (2001). An economic perspective on innovation networks. In O. Jones, S. Conway, & F. Steward (Eds.), *Social interaction and organisational change: Aston perspectives on innovation network*. London: Imperial College Press.

Patterson, P. G., & Smith, T. (2001). Relationship benefits in service industries: A replication in Southeast Asia context. *Journal of Service Marketing, 15*(6), 425–443.

Peel, M. (2015). Thailand economic tsar pumps in billions and hopes for hit sequel. *The Financial Times*. Available from http://www.ft.com/intl/cms/s/0/6ac7077c-6747-11e5-a155-02b6f8af6a62.html#axzz3ncediNvl. Accessed 04.10.15.

Perry, J. (1999). *Small firms and network economics*. London: Routledge.

Pesek, W. (2015). Thailand's generals don't have an economic plan. *Bloomberg View*. Available from http://www.bloombergview.com/articles/2015-08-04/thailand-s-generals-don-t-have-an-economic-plan. Accessed 05.09.15.

Pillai, A. (2012). *The Impact of ICT and networking on the business performance of One Tambon One Product enterprises in greater Bangkok and metropolitan areas*. Unpublished doctoral dissertation, National Institute of Development Administration. Available from http://libdcms.nida.ac.th/thesis6/2011/b171637.pdf. Accessed 05.09.15.

Pornpitakpan, C. (1999). The effects of cultural adaptation on business relationships: Americans selling to Japanese and Thais. *Journal of International Business Studies, 30*(2), 317–338.

Purnell, N. (2013). The Red Bull heir and inequality in Thailand. *The New Yorker*. Available from http://www.newyorker.com/business/currency/the-red-bull-heir-and-inequality-in-thailand. Accessed 10.09.15.

Putnam, R. D. (1993). *Making democracy work: Civic traditions in modern Italy*. Princeton, NJ: Princeton University Press.

Putnam, R. D. (1995). Bowling alone: America's declining social capital. *Journal of Democracy*, *6*(1), 65–78.

Putnam, R. (2000). *Bowling alone: The collapse and revival of American community*. New York: Simon & Shuster.

Quinn, B. (2014). Thailand's army declares martial law after six months of political unrest. *The Guardian*. Available from http://www.theguardian.com/world/2014/may/20/thai-army-declares-martial-law-amid-unrest. Accessed 01.10.15.

Redding, S. G. (1990). *The spirit of Chinese capitalism*. Berlin: Walter de Gruyter.

Redding, G. (2005). The thick description and comparison of societal systems of capitalism. *Journal of International Business Studies*, *36*(2), 123–155.

Roberts, G. (2014). Jakarta's first Chinese governor Basuki Tjahaja Purnama 'Ahok' sworn in, *ABC News*. Available from http://www.abc.net.au/news/2014-11-19/ahok-sworn-in-as-jakarta-governor/5904404. Accessed 02.09.15.

Rojanapanich, P. (2010). *The social imaginary in Thai society: Globalisation, cultural dimensions and education*. Unpublished doctoral dissertation. Australia: RMIT University. Available from https://researchbank.rmit.edu.au/eserv/rmit:15880/Rojanapanich.pdf. Accessed 01.09.15.

Rowley, T., Behrens, D., & Krackhardt, D. (2000). Redundant governance structures: An analysis of structural and relational embeddedness in the steel and semiconductor industries. *Strategic Management Journal*, *21*(3), 369–386.

Rowley, C., & Warner, M. (2010). Management in South-East Asia: Key findings, conclusions and prospects. *Asia Pacific Business Review*, *16*(1–2), 259–267.

Scarborough, J. (1998). Comparing Chinese and Western cultural roots: Why East is East and….". *Business Horizon*, *41*(6), 15–24.

Seibert, S. E., Kraimer, M. L., & Liden, R. C. (2001). A social capital theory of career success. *Academy of Management Journal*, *44*(2), 219–237.

Shideler, D. W., & Kraybill, D. S. (2003). Social networks, social capital and community economic growth. In *Paper presented at the American Agricultural Economics Association annual meeting, Montreal, Canada, July 27–30*.

So, Y. L., & Walker, A. (2006). *Explaining Guanxi: The Chinese business network*. New York: Routledge.

Suseno, Y., Pinnington, A. H., Gardner, J., & Shulman, A. D. (2006). Social capital and knowledge acquisition in professional-client relationships. *International Journal of the Legal Profession*, *13*(3), 273–295.

Thanasankit, T., & Corbitt, B. (2000). Cultural context and its impact on requirements elicitation in Thailand. *The Electronic Journal of Information Systems in Developing Countries*, *1*, 1–19.

The World Bank. (2015). *Thailand: Overview*. Available from http://www.worldbank.org/en/country/thailand/overview. Accessed 15.09.15.

Tooksoon, P., & Mohamad, O. (2010). Marketing capability and export performance: The moderating effect of export dependence. *The South East Asian Journal of Management*, *4*(1), 39–52.

Tsai, W., & Ghoshal, S. (1998). Social capital and value creation: The role of intrafirm networks. *Academy of Management Journal*, *41*(4), 464–476.

Walker, G., Kogut, B., & Shan, W. (1997). Social capital, structural holes and the formation of an industry network. *Organization Science*, *8*(2), 109–125.

Witt, M. A., & Redding, G. (2013). Asian business systems: Institutional comparison, clusters, and implications for varieties of capitalism and business systems theory. *Socio-Economic Review*, *11*(1), 265–300.

Woolcock, M. (2001). The place of social capital in the understanding of social and economic outcomes. *Canadian Journal of Policy Research, 2*, 11–17. Retrieved from, http://www.ebscohost.com.ezproxy.ecu.edu.au/academic/sportdiscus-with-full-text.

Wu, W. P. (2008). Dimensions of social capital and firm competitiveness improvement: The mediating role of information sharing. *Journal of Management Studies, 45*(1), 122–146.

Yeung, I. Y. M., & Tung, R. L. (1996). Achieving business success in Confucian societies: The importance of Guanxi (connections). *Organizational Dynamics, 25*(2), 54–65.

Zahra, S. A., George, G., & Garvis, D. M. (1999). Networks and entrepreneurship in Southeast Asia: The role of social capital and membership commitment. In F. J. Ritcher (Ed.), *Business networks in Asia: Promises, doubts, and perspectives* (pp. 39–60). Westport, CT: Quorum.

CHAPTER 13

Business Networks in Myanmar: *Kjei zu*, Corrosion and Reform

T.G. Andrews*, K.T. Htun†
*Thammasat University, Bangkok, Thailand
†Myanmar Womens Entrepreneurs' Association, Yangon, Myanmar

13.1 INTRODUCTION

With its turbulent, almost unprecedented recent history of isolation and oppression, Myanmar constitutes an apt example of an Asian nation which—while sharing a number of key norms and values widely shared across the sub-continent—at the same time embodies an institutional and cultural profile borne of its unique trajectory (Carney, Gedajlovic, & Yang, 2009). Having recently opened its border to foreign business and tourism, Myanmar has rapidly become the world's fourth fastest growing economy (World Bank Group, 2014), housing a 65 million-strong population and a critical geo-strategic location bordering both China and India. As such, Myanmar holds huge investment and tourism potential for local and foreign businesses alike. However, set against a backdrop of decades of military dictatorship and insularity, there is a marked gap in our knowledge of Myanmar, more than for any other Asian nation (O'Brien, 1991). Often described as insular, backward and 'set in aspic', for many years (Syrota, 2003) Myanmar has been gravely overlooked in Asian cultural and management research (Andrews, Htun, & Nimanandh, 2016). This paucity of work also extends to our understanding of the country's business system, as well as the role of commercial networks. In the small, largely journalistic body of work to date on Myanmar business culture, the importance and pervasiveness of networks and relationships is universally acknowledged (eg, Yin, 2013). If one Googles 'Myanmar business networks', this presents only surface level data, principally advertisements for brokers. There has been little done on exploring the underlying processes, of the nature and characteristics of networks, or their influence on the wider (micro) institutional (business) climate.

In this chapter, we explore in depth foundations, characteristics, evolution, and implications of business networks—*a hse a thwe*—in Myanmar. Our central proposition is that, though culturally grounded in norms expressing deeply held Buddhist principles, the common workings of business-related networks in Myanmar have been corrupted during the past generation of

Business Networks in East Asian Capitalisms
http://dx.doi.org/10.1016/B978-0-08-100639-9.00013-X

military control and repression which, indirectly, has profoundly shaped the particular variety of economic capitalism to have emerged. In recent times, however—spurred by economic reform, the easing of international sanctions and the NLD election victory in Nov. 2015—there are hopes this may trigger a reversion of sorts to more traditional Burmese values (*bamar hsan chinn*), in business practice, as well as in society at large.

Given Myanmar's unique status, rather than seeking to compare business networks in Myanmar with its Asian neighbours, we have instead pursued an internal, intranational investigation comparing *a hse a thwe* and its evolution over *time* (adopting the temporal take on the term 'comparative'). Through this emic ('from the inside') approach, our aim is to provide a more in-depth understanding of the specific cultural, religious, and political influences on the country's business networks and how the latter, in turn, have shaped which way business is conducted and efficiency is perceived. In approaching the topic in this way, we pick up on gathering calls in recent years for more indigenous, emic research in emerging economies (eg, Andrews & Chompusri, 2013; Holtbruegge, 2013) as a means of gaining a more refined, nuanced, and less judgmental understanding. Compared to the other countries investigated in this collection, both primary data and secondary literature are very restricted, nevertheless our analysis of the role of Buddhism in network development complements discussions in Chapters 11 and 12.

Structurally, this chapter is organized as follows: firstly, we explore traditional interpersonal relationship networks in Myanmar and how they express wider, deeper social norms, culturally grounded (ultimately) in Theravada Buddhist teachings. We then chart how these networks have shifted and evolved in the sphere of organizational processes and practices under the military regime from the 1980s and how, in turn, they have grown to shape and delimit what constitutes 'normal' business activity at both intra- and interorganizational levels (particularly government). In both sections, we flesh out our depiction of how business networks operate in Myanmar by drawing on rich, detailed accounts from 17 key participants from the realms of private business, the civil service, and academia situated in Yangon, Mandalay and Nay Pyi Taw. We wish to stress that the opinions and perspectives expressed in this chapter are those of our participants, not necessarily our own.

13.2 UNDERSTANDING BUSINESS NETWORKS IN MYANMAR

As is often observed about East Asian countries, the importance of socially derived networks in business in Myanmar cannot be overstated. A business enterprise can neither exist nor succeed without the 'right' individuals with the 'right' social relationships (eg, Sim, 2001). At the individual level, you can get a job—even pass an exam—easily if you or your relatives/friends possess good social connections. At the organizational level, contracts are won, licenses secured, and competition neutralized if one's network is sufficiently robust. Rules can be bent, broken, changed, and even created for you if you know the right people. Traditionally depicted as being synonymous with networks of interpersonal relationships, business networks in Myanmar are typically drawn from (extended) family, friends, and even working acquaintances (often along the lines of ethnicity, religion, social class, and politics). Within the wider cultural milieu, such networks serve as a 'bank of assistance' for survival and prosperity (Gesteland & Seyk, 2002). At the more practical level, dealing with those in your network is efficient. The trust that's both inherent and implicit here cuts down perceived risk, speed things up, cuts through bureaucratic and other obstacles, and makes outcomes more certain. Networks work in this way, grounded in the cultural import ascribed to harmonious relationships. Indebtedness, mutual assistance, and long-term reciprocity of kindness/favours represent pervasive and deeply held values, such that, broadly enacted, they extend to anyone within your patron's own network. Accordingly, it is quite acceptable that someone in a position of influence, a gatekeeper, agrees to your request for assistance on the grounds that eg, your grandfather assisted her younger brother years ago. These things are not forgotten. One is expected to reciprocate if needed and, moreover, happy to do so.

13.2.1 Cultural Foundations

A hse a thwe is, first and foremost, a *social* construction, rooted in a cultural environment where the personal side of business relationships traditionally takes precedence over the professional.

As one business owner put it:

> *before (the) military government social networks (were) not just for business, they (were) for all other things in daily life, all mixed together, so that you never think of other things as more important than (the) relationship…*

Culturally framed through the comparative dimensions of national culture (popularized since the 1980s by Hofstede, 1984; Trompenaars, 1993), Myanmar reads as a conservative, collectivist, conforming culture based around the extended family as the nucleus unit. As with Thailand and much of South and East Asia, the twin Myanmar cultural pillars can be seen in the shape of relationships and hierarchy, a particularist environment where relations will often override rules and regulations (see also House, Hanges, Javidan, Dorfman, & Gupta, 2004; Schwartz, 1999). However, to understand these issues with the appropriate degree of nuance necessitates delving deeper into an understanding of the *indigenous* cultural constructs that both shape and regulate Burmese social behaviour.

13.2.2 *A Hse A Thwe*, Buddhism and Right Conduct

The existence, the management, and the use of *a hse a thwe* (business/social networks) are both grounded in and indicative of wider, culturally congruent attitudes and behaviours (*si saun*) which govern Burmese social relations. As often stated, the culture and social structure of Myanmar is, in turn, almost inextricably intertwined with Buddhist values, standards, and morals. In a standard Burmese Buddhist text it is stated: "a person with a good heart cultivates noble practice...(of) 'right' attitude...(in which the)...mind must be clear...(and)...accompanied by a moral conscience..." (Htay & Tin, 2002, p. 17). Noble practice, right attitude, is held to be key toward 'progress with value' and is expressed through *goun thei kha* (integrity; dignity), and *a kjin za rei ta* (moral behaviour). These then thread through traditional notions of appropriate conduct (*si saun*) including, importantly, within the sphere of right livelihood and work relationships and processes.

A key construct in the Burmese societal culture is *sei da na* which broadly translates as 'goodwill', 'benevolence', *sei da na* embodies action with good grace, of doing something properly in and for itself rather than simply for what one may receive in return—except, perhaps, for the intrinsic value of *ku dhou* (benediction, merit, blessing). However, as a matter—originally—of courtesy, within one's 'network', the recipient of an act of kindness will acknowledge it through acts of reciprocated gratitude—often for as long as either party may live (and even after through descendants and offspring). Concerning the sense of indebtedness, *kjei zu hsa* denotes this repaying of an act of kindness, or doing something out of gratitude, even if one is very poor. The old Burmese saying, *ta lou sa hpu thu kjei zu*, states how even if you receive but one mouthful of food from the giver, you have to note down with a view to reciprocation when the opportunity presents itself. If this does not occur—for example, among the poor—the recipient may pay the benefactor visits from time to time bearing gifts, eg, vegetables from one's garden or some handmade product (Hla, 1985). Gift-giving is thus very much embedded in Myanmar social relationships, such that Myanmar is even often referred to as housing a 'gift-giving culture' (Gesteland & Seyk, 2002). No matter if the gift holds no monetary value, traditionally if you help someone with *sei da na*, it is said that they can actually feel this to be the case, they will benefit from the inherent goodwill. The notion of mutually reciprocated favours is traditionally pervasive in local business dealings, such that regulations would be bent or broken to protect friends and/or relatives, but in a 'good' way, with *si saun*. As one business owner explained it:

> *because our habit about* kjei zu *and* sei dana *and also* a na *(i.e. reticence based on consideration for another's feelings) means we cannot always work according to formal legal rules and laws, we'll work around these obstacles if necessary to help somebody back....*

This may often be the case with protecting related wrongdoers within the organization or even dismissing staff, as will be discussed in more detail below. Within the concept of *a hse a thwe*, simply being *known* implicitly as a 'member', may be enough to shape business dealings (ie, irrespective of issues of clear gratitude). This is clearly seen in the following quote from a participant describing how investing in an acquaintance's company is often, albeit tacitly, really a matter of helping them in a time of need:

> *We don't expect or want a contract to formalize/explicate the amount we give. The profit given to us, whether 1, 2, 5 or 10%, or even a loss, is something we don't question. That's how business was done in Burmese tradition to do with we trust each other. If we ask to sign the 'received' document to show money that's seen as being very rude....For me myself I assimilated that habit and even now I never use documents with my friends, and this means not only close friends but all friends, even acquaintances...for example, last year I loaned money for my father's former colleague doing business and they are giving me profit as interest every month. He told me that he will sign on paper and also give me the document for his land ownership as a guarantee. But I told him that, no, I don't want to keep and no need because I've known him since I was 10 years old...*

13.2.3 Corruption and Greed: The Monetization of *A Hse A Thwe*

Notwithstanding the deep cultural roots which undergird the traditional notion of *a tse a thwe* in Myanmar, there is a widespread perception that over the past generation (since around 1988) this system has become corroded—both in business and more widely—by what amounts to a 'military-industrial club' populated by all-powerful minsters and their business cronies (including entrepreneurs from the once marginalized immigrant Chinese community). According to our participants, this started around the time of Ne Win, the *ta ma do* commander widely (dis)credited with leading Myanmar down the path of autarky and repression (cf. 'the Burmese way to socialism'). It was under Ne Win's governance (1962–88) that the regulatory and education system was felt to be lowered in the process of his seeking a centralized, quasi-totalitarian form of state control. The regulatory system—such as it was—was also perceived as breaking down, and quickly lost much of its transparency, such that people quickly began losing faith in their ability to sue illegal activity with any success, due to the attendant loss of transparency (Table 13.1).

Against this backdrop, the military political system as a whole and the behaviours of many ministers, the perceived need for written documentation in commercial dealings has become commonplace, almost the norm. The effective breakdown in trust within and across networks which lies behind much of this shift shows that the efficiency inherent in the 'old way' has been eroded and devalued. The breakdown in traditional interpersonal networks in commerce can be illustrated from a number of interrelated vantage points. At what may be seen as its tangible periphery, the traditional giving of gifts and/or assistance is seen as having progressively been monetized, giving way to jewellery (relatively inconvertible), then bangles, then bars of solid gold (much more convertible), to the now almost ubiquitous US dollar. According to many of our participants, this custom changed also with the rise of the immigrant Chinese in Burmese commerce to consider. Without contacts, largely ignorant of the subtleties of Burmese cultural gift-giving and unwilling to give any more than they have to, the Chinese were forced to ask directly, 'how much will it cost to....?', or 'how much do we have to give to get...?'

Incrementally, the nature of *a hse a thwe* became more increasingly commercialized. According to our participants, nowadays there is now no need to have relationships with the director of an organization or department to get things done in the old way, you can give money to his/her admin personnel (eg, 500,000 kyat) so that your document, for example, may reach at least the table of the minister you wish to contact.

> *"Today", another of our participants bemoaned, "there are less and less people who behave like in Burmese culture, to bamar hsan chin, most give no thought to kjei zu or a nar de"*

Another factor behind the changing nature of *a hse a thwe* lies in the progressive and deliberate concentration and centralization of power in the hands of the Burmese military *ta ma do*, to the extent that these days, only family, relatives, and friends of the military are in good position and can get good projects, etc. In such circumstances, both the acquainted individual and his or her relatives/friends will also benefit from the connection and the rewards inherent in it. They are thus advantaged not on the grounds of

Table 13.1 Myanmar social relations/conduct: key indigenous constructs

Construct	Meaning(s)	Emergence/origins	Illustrations
Mje hna tha pei	Social assistance (doing or repaying a favour)	Theravada Buddhism: *Metta* – to get *ku tho* (blessing) (from Pali script)	Letting somebody off (eg, not firing them) for a mistake made as person is within your network, eg, his/her father is your benefactor
Ta lou sa hpu thu kjei zu	Social assistance (repaying kindness)	Wider preservation of harmony and mutual survival/prosperity	A close friend of the second author remembers referring her friend to jewellery shop of an acquaintance because she'd always been satisfied with the product and the service quality. She thought nothing of it until later on that same day the shop owner called her to give her quote of service, ie, a paid agent's commission. It wasn't necessary at all but constituted *kjei zu*
Sei da na	Goodwill/good grace	Pali Buddhist scripture/ teaching	Salaried employees put heart into their jobs, same as if own business Case: despite the fact that a minister who helped you has retired and has no power, when his second daughter holds a wedding you give her an expensive gift same as for first daughter. This means you do with *sei dana*, expecting nothing in return, from the goodness of your heart
Bamar hsan chin	The 'Myanmar way': personal network trust without need for contracts, etc.	Informal, emergent, collective self-image of being Burmese	Lending money to a friend without contact nor stipulation for any interest, not document, nor date of repayment
A na	Be embarrassed by feelings of respect; restrained for fear of offending/disturbing	Expressing the emergent norm of reticence borne of deference and compassion	Reticence to speak/act wherein potential for negative feeling or where one feels obligation or indebtedness to others Reluctance to disturb Acquiescence

qualifications, experience, or capability, but due exclusively to the connection. As one participant noted:

> *There is a saying in Burmese - sin phyu taw hmi kyan sou - which translates approximately as 'the one who has the elephant gets the sugar cane.' So if your relative is a minister so you can use his name to assist you in many respects, so the entire extended family can rely and depend on one minster, only need one so rest of family can keep well taken care of*

There are manifold illustrations of just how much influence is held among these higher echelons. One concerns the very highest levels of law enforcement. One participant told us:

> *...even if you are a police officer or a judge, you cannot do according to the laws and regulations...because you have to ask firstly who is the accused, you have to then ask whose son or how is he/she related and with whom? If you don't ask that questions and only make decisions according to rules and regulations then the next day you will lose your job. Because of this no one dares to take any action...*

Others, though 'smaller' on the face of it, are more pervasive and seen as just as insidious. One example recounted to us concerned the son of a prominent civil servant whose influence was such that he was able to pass a university exam despite an almost unbelievably low score by persuading the university authorities to lower the overall pass threshold score until it captured his own score, effectively serving to expand the number of passable papers to 100%. There are also countless, pervasive, and alas, sadly believable accounts of those with power bribing and or intimidating those with position in other areas of society—for example university professors. The feeling among all our participants was that as a result of the military regime from around 1988 onwards, the attitude of the Burmese people—you can say the culture—changed in that they care less and less about moral character and reputation and more and more about money. In a Burmese Buddhist text, in a section which discusses 'five occupations that should be avoided...', it is stated that, 'one should avoid giving or receiving bribes, kickbacks, unlawful presents, etc. so that true, pure *sila* and conscience may reign supreme in one's noble heart...' (Htay & Tin, 2002, p. 75). One participant, agreeing, referred to a related saying, *thu mja mou kha jei thau lai ma thau pa ne*, which translates roughly into 'don't drink bitter water even though others are doing so'. Nonetheless, as the same business owner continued:

> *...nowadays in people's minds the most important thing is money in life and if you have money you can get everything and you can buy even power and authority.... military kids and business crony kids even start getting married each other just to facilitate business....*

Another participant added:

> *...now if people get money from corruption, and cannot it back when forced to do so they don't care, they go to jail as they know they will be out again after 2-3 months...they care nothing about their behaviour or their reputation...*

The situation among the *ta ma do* is exacerbated in that even officers and ministers are bound by the inherent uncertainty of patronage from those on high. Accordingly the widespread perception is that, as one participant explained to us:

> *...the position is not permanent, so the individual feels he could be forced into retirement at any time, so everyday every second they worry and want to get max benefits while they have power, don't think about their longer-term reputation.*

Soldiers are generally very poor before their ascent within the military, such that they want to grab what they can for their futures, fearing the sink back into poverty. In this environment, the quote *mou jwa toun jei khan* is particularly apt. As one interviewee described it:

> *... this saying is about the value of perseverance when it rains even if night time or early morning you have to get up, keep/get water for future use. But now military people and most used that quote to squeeze money from others while they can, not doing in a fair way...*

The original meaning, in other words, has been perverted such that now it's more a question of 'make hay while the sun shines', or just 'get it while you can'.

13.3 ORGANIZATIONAL IMPLICATIONS: FROM THE INSIDE

Business organizations in Myanmar are predominantly business-to-business for any outfit much larger than a street noodle vendor, and this is the sector we thus focus on below. We centre our discussion on the evolving impact of *a hse a thwe* and how this has shaped the micro-institutional climate within organizations through the enabling of certain behaviours and the sanctioning of others. Within the porous boundaries that frame organizations in Myanmar, this is most clearly visible in key 'people-related' processes, practices, and norms surrounding sourcing and positioning, appraisal/evaluation, and retention/dismissal.

13.3.1 Sourcing and Positioning

In the early stages of formation and development, most organizations will be populated entirely by relatives and close friends, and others within the founders' networks. For this reason, there is typically very little need to advertise in newspapers and so forth. Network recruiting is perceived as beneficial for all parties involved. For the organization concerned, there is little need to look at professional qualifications, aptitude or track record, or education, nor with wasting time and resources going through a selection process. Rather, the company will just select individuals based on the trust intrinsic to network request/recommendations—eg, for the sensitive cashier role, there may be no concern for accountancy qualifications, so long as they are proficient in bookkeeping, or were even just numerically proficient at school.

This is both quick and effective, so much so that a boss may ask existing staff to ask around if they have a friend for that position they could refer. One organization we know has also recently taken to sourcing Myanmar engineers based in Singapore on the basis of offering a similar salary with lower living costs and 'home' residence. But it's not just any Burmese engineers being tapped, only from those within network of a close friend of the controlling family, somebody who had already recommended one individual from this groups and with whom the family were 'delighted' and anxious to secure additional recruits.

For the 'suppliers'—typically the parents or friends of the candidate concerned—it may also be beneficial in that it will help them in the uncertain period following graduation during when it may be difficult to find suitable employment. Unlike in Western culture, in Myanmar it is still traditional for parents to secure employment for their children. But if you know somebody senior at an organization, you can request them to appoint your children or relatives, or children of friends even. You can also, as one participant phrased it '…check your boss for your friend to get a job, because according to Burmese business culture, we must help each other even not your relatives…'. For the government/civil service sector, the importance of the right contacts here cannot be overstated. It has become commonplace for highly positioned military government officials people requested to appoint their children and relatives at the department of their liking. This has also, increasingly, spilled over into the private sector where they are often 'placed' inside a company.

Unsurprisingly, the company has to accept even if sure it does not have any suitable vacancy, no choice if they want to remain in business. An army chief may ask his son or daughter—or the son and daughter of an associate, or relative or such—what position they would like to get. And of course, the major consideration is one which will entail most benefits/power, even if there is no such position available, or in existence and it has to be created especially for the purpose. In this context 'western' notions of distributive or procedural justice are not only nonexistent, but almost unthinkable. This is not to say that among the individuals involved there will be none without the qualifications and attitude and—yes—contacts to succeed. But, at least according to our participants, there are very few cases like this and, more often than not, where qualifications and documents are required they tend to be fabricated. One respondent recounted that:

> *to get a government job my father asked and checked his friends and family. I had never heard of the position offered and I was told that this was because it was reserved or 'VIP kids' only. It was a good job in that there was no need to go anywhere else other than in head office in Rangoon, the perks were good and included several foreign trips and also there was not so much to do so that I could also study at the same time for my Master's entrance exam....*

Another spoke of a friend of hers who'd once been married to the son of a government minister. During the parent-arranged courtship the suitor:

> *...was working at one company as a Director, this is what his parents had told my parents, as well as me as well. After marriage I realized that the position was a fake one, that it had all been about adding to his nominal value as prospective husband, and also to look good on the wedding invitation card for his family's 'face'. This he finally confessed to when I asked him, and he added the reason of looking to get from that company as they owed a favour to his father for giving them a project in years gone by...I found out that though he would go there every day in actual fact he was not really working, just messing around all day, not even sure exactly what he was doing at office all day...I was shocked so I told him to quit that job and do something else instead because it was clearly just nonsense...*

13.3.2 Appraisal, Dismissal and Retention

Recent years have seen a shift in appraisal thinking in Western-based companies, away from the old tangible results-based, towards what can be described as 'person-based' or 'developmental'. This embodies a joint effort between employer–employee to help the individual realize his/her potential. In some ways this apparent 'person focus' has long been the norm in Myanmar in the sense of emphasizing the character behind the performance, not just what they've done. However, unlike in the West, the most important aspect is liable to be not attitude, not even loyalty, but back to whom they are and to whom they are connected. Across the civil service in Myanmar, the perception is that even if you try and systematize the standards of appraisal, there will still be a favouring for who you know or your connections, and they are always more likely to get reward or gift or bonus. One senior manager explained:

> *...usually there is no fixed standard, often not even a bonus and just like a family business where the staff gets like pocket money for special events such as New Year, Tha Din Gyut festival, Da Zaun Dain. Various managers might say 'ohhh he worked hard, we (family owners) should pay pocket money for him more this time.'*

This discretionary approach—all pervasive in Myanmar—can also work negatively against the individual. One participant cited a recent case where a faculty member at a big city university requested a leave of absence for a friend's wedding. On informing her boss, she was told this should be okay. But then on the planned day of her departure she was kept back another 24 h finishing off her tasks. So then after she finished, a friend of hers contacted the Dean through her father and subsequently the approach of the former changed markedly 'for the better'.

The same discretion also holds for situations where a dismissal incidence occurs. A traditional Burmese saying holds that 'we have to consider his face', as a reminder to remember the family connection concerned. Typically, this may mean taking stock of the father who has once done you a favour, the father whose son is now about to be fired for an organizational offence. In this context, the likelihood is that whatever the son has done, that it will be 'sorted out' internally due to such network loyalty, that the individual concerned would be highly unlikely to lose his job. In recent years, however, within the field of organizational life, even in private organizations, the values inherent in *si saun* and right conduct held to be breaking down, our participants all bemoaned what are felt to be a shift in attitudes and behaviours for the worse. One example is the growing tendency for the 'poaching' of staff and the lack of loyalty this both expresses and encourages. We were also told of several cases where government projects and private organizations overlap, with certain employees developing their own contacts with the *ta ma do* and harming their own employers in the process (see Table 13.2). At the organizational level in recent years, appraisal has begun to mean being evaluated by external accreditors (as progressively required to gain international accreditation from eg, ISO). But if within the accreditor's *a hse a thwe*, then the latter will go where you ask them to go, not necessarily where you are weakest. This is clearly held to be cheating or, as it's known in Burmese, *ka lein ka kji*.

13.4 INTERORGANIZATIONAL ILLUSTRATIONS

The external engagement of any business organization anywhere will typically be focused on a small cluster of stakeholders, usually customers and suppliers, along with business partners, government, media, NGOs, and even competitors. In Myanmar, such a list would be usually both smaller and more clearly defined, with the weighting massively skewed toward the military government: all powerful, irresistible, and unavoidable. Against this

Table 13.2 Eroding traditions: *A Hse A Thwe* under military rule (1988–2015)

Construct	(Literal) Meaning(s)	Illustrations and examples
Si ma saun	Failure to observe/adhere to social norms/principles of conduct	A director and family member of one business organization, started working his own personal side project during office hours. He also had his staff working on it, part of which involved building the house for one of the brothers-in-law of a high-ranking military officer, with whom he'd initiated a connection (*a hse a thwe*). When he was offered a lucrative project because of this connection, he continued to do this as a side project rather than quitting his job honourably as a direct competitor. Apparently he had known of the plans to award the said contract to the company, but he requested it be given him personally, which it was. This is an example of *si ma saun*, for which his uncle (the company chairman) fired him, only to now have his own nephew continuing to milk this connection and be a direct competitor to this day
Baun Kjo	'Crossing the line', 'going' over the limit(s) of 'admissible conduct'	'…nowadays it's not only high-ranking military personnel, but also managers who do *baun kjo* that before we never saw about using *a hse a thwe*'. This particular case concerns an individual in charge of a construction project, who asked her friend to make a 'ghost bid' to be the main contractor, and made sure this friend of hers won, not because he intends to have anything to do with the project, but simply that she would get the control she wants to profit from subsequent sub-contracting deals…'
Ka lein ka kji	To swindle, to cheat, to twist	Abusing one's networks is rife. In one reported case due to an individual's connections with the government she was chauffeur-driven along a route supposedly designed as a running track used for gauging the applicant's physical suitability.

backdrop, it's all but impossible to separate politics from business, from the wider interpersonal networks which weave through Burmese society. As with internal organizational concerns, engaging with external stakeholders also works on the basis of *a hse a thwe*. Where connections exist, then they will be favoured and drawn upon. If there are no preexisting connections to leverage, then they will need to be created on a gift-giving basis.

Where customers are concerned, the prevalence of networks can be illustrated using two common situations. The first concerns the organization's ability to reach customers through desirable retail space/locations. The simple fact is that if a business owner has a contact (connection) with the owner of a shopping centre, then he/she will get the space without needing to queue. Similarly, if a business has relatives with power or good contacts inside the military, then it will be given the space in an established mall when the first vacant lot becomes available, even if others are already queuing. Indeed, for 'captive' shopping areas such as the country's airports, it's often seen as impossible to get any space at all, for any reason, unless one holds the right connections. From the standpoint of the customer, as one participant put it:

> *there is no such thing as customer right in Myanmar. There are no fixed rules, even in a shopping center and supermarket. So, for example about ability to change faulty products within certain number of days, it not depend on receipt, it depend if you know the staff or owner, for whether you can change or get refund or not…*

Concerning partnerships and alliances for international companies now entering Myanmar, it has become common knowledge that a local partner is only 'good' in so far as they have a useful *a hse a thwe*—and this invariably means a partner (at the very least a 'crony') with good connections, at some level, with the ruling military regime (see BMW, the Accor group, KFC, and Carlsberg for recent examples). Essentially, however, these Western brands are only adhering to the traditional logic of combining West and East in terms of know-how with know-who, respectively. Such has always been the case when dealing with so-called relations-based cultures. The once critical concern with the ethical credentials of the partner in question—of entering Myanmar under military rule at all—is now one on the wane, as increasingly once blacklisted individuals and organizations are witnessing their statuses being revised and changed as Myanmar opens up for business. The other justification for working with military-connected partners in Myanmar is also the oft-cited preference for 'engagement' over 'isolation'. 'We can do more good from the inside than from nowhere' is the basic idea.

13.4.1 Government

Winning government tenders means often nothing more or less than being the favoured bidder from the outset, such that your bid will win whatever is being offered by others. In practice, once the sealed bids have all been opened, the preferred bidder would typically receive a call from the ministry to tell you how much the lowest bid submitted is, so that there is then time for the favoured to rush across and revise their own downward so they win. This doesn't mean to say that no money will change hands in the process—it will. And this will mean both at securement stage and also usually at the completion, launch, and/or opening stage of the project concerned. One company we deal with has a running account with the upmarket department stores in Bangkok where Louis Vuitton or Prada handbags are the desired gift of choice for the wives of military top brass involved. But it often goes further even than this. Increasingly government ministers have insisted that gifts should also be given for weddings of their family members, particularly children and grandchildren. In recent times, the value of what is being given also needs to be disclosed—ostensibly for precaution against future theft. As one participant put it: 'there is no thought for *kjei zu* at all now...'. Another added that:

> *...sometimes nowadays the government representative (is) asking so much kick-back for a flyover bridge project that all involved either lose or make next to nothing for themselves. So after this they use low-grade materials so bridge sometimes cracking even before or during opening ceremony...!*

Bidders who lose out will often nonetheless give gifts (gold, diamonds and money) to the decision-maker in the hope of being favoured and given generous concessions for the next project, a ploy that increasingly works where network loyalties and *kjei zu* seem to be declining against the might of cash money. In some situations, bidders wishing to secure a tender will propose a new project and are told explicitly how much they will need to give in order to be awarded the license. After the government has agreed and the confirmation announced to the

> *This is increasingly the case with lower level staff who nowadays want to show their power, so even though you paid your money then they may say 'I've no time today, come back tomorrow' or then you have to pay more...also they are not friendly. So now all are scared to go there...*

Some projects emanating from the government are never even tendered publicly at all—or indeed to anyone aside from the interested individual/ group of individuals involved. A lot of ministers' children are also now involved in business, setting them up being an especially common occurrence as the father may be about to retire and concerned about a possible loss of influence. Examples abound. One participant cited the case of Myanmar's first—and so far only—Internet provider. The license concerned was apparently given to the son of a previous senior civil servant without anybody knowing about it. Moreover, as soon as other potential providers/companies became aware that the Internet was now in existence, and also got interested in gaining rights to do so, nobody was allowed—so that no one was able to get a license/permit and no one has been able to compete.

The same is also true for other communications providers such as FM radio stations, where the majority are held by the sons or daughters of now retired minsters. Often, when approaching retirement—or even just in uncertain times—a sitting government agent with contacts in place will seek to ensure his children are as secure as possible for when or if things turn against them. On the other hand, there are many cases over the years where the father has lost his position in the regime for whatever reason, only to witness the subsequent closing down of his children's business as well, often with little or no warning or explanation.

Sometimes, even after retirement, they will seek to secure what are essentially government projects for their children, often going through a private organization. One recent case involved a chief engineer who had been in charge of a government road project. After retirement, he returned to visit one of the companies to whom he had previously awarded a bid and asked them to place his daughter as a subcontractor in charge of one particular portion of road—this being part of a new government project for which he now had no official involvement. Given the company's sense of debt to this individual they were obliging, although this will often not happen in the climate of business networks to have has evolved under the military Government ministers—often on behalf of their children—have also been turning to obliging some of Myanmar's larger private companies to become involved in projects they do not want to on the basis of 'we'll award you this project if you also do that project…'. Typically this will concern a high-ranking government official who has an idea for a new business, but little experience or know-how in how to set it up. Thus they wish, in essence, to exchange their know-who for know-how with a favoured company or crony. In essence, this works as a kind of 'bundle' agreement. So for example, it might be a case of 'yes will give you the license to open a department store/shopping mall in Nay Phi Taw, if you also agree to running this hotel project as well—even if you are hesitant' (it being outside your self-perceived area of core competence/expertise).

Indeed, all hotels are built and managed on a mandatory basis by the government. A recent example would be that of the beach project at Nge Saung. Though not far from Yangon, this beach area does not benefit from access by air—the only way being via a hazardous road trip—and so certain companies involved are only involved because it came as an unwanted enclave of a more attractive whole.

13.5 EMERGING CHANGE

In November 2015, during the composition of this chapter, the NLD, led by Aung San Suu Kyi won an election victory with a landslide majority. This in a sense represents the culmination of years of democratic campaigning on the one hand, and the progressive relaxation of strict political repression on the other. According to our participants—and in accordance with our own experience and observation—the huge turnout to vote and the overwhelming push for change is also indicative of a wider thirst for change across all sectors of Burmese society. It expresses the feelings of the vast majority of people who are weary of repression, confinement, corruption, a lack of transparency or fairness, and the wider erosion of what is seen as traditional societal values. Within the sphere of business and economics, the last few years have also witnessed many changes. Rules and regulations regarding business conduct, including for foreign businesses, are being relaxed (Cockett, 2015). A new generation of educated Burmese are being exposed to western business practices, norms, and management theories, as well as values. Many, based overseas, are now looking to come back to Myanmar after the recent changes and fuelled by the NLD electoral victory, and perceptions that the power of the military will be less. These come armed with their overseas business education, skills, and knowledge. Against this backdrop, the nature of 'networks' and how these have changed under military repression are increasingly being criticized. Within Myanmar's borders there is also a growing push for change, where even the so-called cronies are growing tired of increasing ministerial greed/demands. This is not to say they're tired of the advantages which their relations with the controlling military has afforded them, or tired of being able to send their children and grandchildren to the best schools (and so forth). But there is nonetheless a desire for change and renewal based on what are considered to be traditional Burmese concerns for moral character and reputation, where 'being Burmese' can extend beyond xenophobia, totalitarianism, and repression. Given the changes in the past generation, it's probably a little naïve to a wistful notion of 'Burmese-ness' in the way our business and economic and even social affairs are conducted. The rapidly rising influx of tourists means money through the door, but it also entails, of necessity, an increasing interaction/engagement with foreign ways. It is hoped that the 'monetization' of interpersonal dealings (*a hse a thwe*) in and across organizations will give way to a more decentralized, transparent, fairer system. To conclude we offer an observation by one of our participants:

> *Myanmar people easily forgive, they believe in kan or kan ma… so for the army who done the bad things to our country they will get bad things one day, so we don't need to punish and we don't want revenge… we just want to move forward, to be Burmese style, which is about using our a hse a thwe to help others, to be fair, not just greedy. I am hoping the new government can begin so that people can join together again so a hse a thwe is not a way to do corrupt thing but how to help in making strong and sustainable companies…*

REFERENCES

Andrews, T. G., & Chompusri, N. (2013). Understanding organizational practice adoption at the Thai subsidiary corporation: Antecedents and consequences of *kreng jai*. *Management International Review*, *53*(1), 61–82.

Andrews, T. G., Htun, K. T., & Nimanandh, K. (2016). Business system evolution and the indigenization of MNE practice transfers in Thailand & Myanmar: An 'emic' perspective. In R. Whitley & X. Zhang (Eds.), *Changing business systems in Asia: Globalisation, socio-political change, and economic organisations*. Oxford: OUP.

Carney, M., Gedajlovic, E., & Yang, X. (2009). Varieties of Asian capitalism: Towards an institutional theory of Asian enterprise. *Asia Pacific Journal of Management*, *36*(2), 361–380.

Cockett, R. (2015). *Blood, dreams & gold: The changing face of Burma*. New Haven: Yale University Press.

Gesteland, R. R., & Seyk, G. F. (2002). *Marketing across cultures in Asia: A practical guide*. Copenhagen: Copenhagen Business School Press.

Hla, P. (1985). *Burma: Literature, historiography, scholarship, language, life and Buddhism*. Singapore: Institute of Southeast Asian Studies.

Hofstede, G. (1984). *Culture's consequences: International differences in work-related values* (abridged ed.). Thousand Oaks: Sage.

Holtbruegge, D. (2013). Indigenous management research. *Management International Review*, *53*(1), 1–10.

House, R. J., Hanges, P. J., Javidan, M., Dorfman, P. W., & Gupta, V. (2004). *Culture, leadership, and organizations: The GLOBE study of 62 societies*. Thousand Oaks, CA: Sage.

Htay, U. H., & Tin, U. C. (2002). *How to be a Good Buddhist: Vol. 1*. Yangon, Myanmar: Department for the Promotion and Propagation of the Sasana.

O'Brien, H. (1991). *Forgotten land: A rediscovery of Burma*. London: Michael Joseph.

Schwartz, S. H. (1999). A theory of cultural values and some implications for work. *Applied Psychology: An International Review*, *48*(1), 23–47.

Sim, H. C. M. (2001). *Myanmar on my mind: A guide to living and doing business in Myanmar*. Singapore: Times Books International.

Syrota, T. (2003). *Welcome to Burma: And enjoy the totalitarian experience*. Bangkok: White Orchid Press.

Trompenaars, F. (1993). *Riding the waves of culture*. London: Nicholas Brealey Publishing.

World Bank Group. (2014). http://www.worldbank.org/2014/content/dam/Worldbank/document/EAP/Myanmar/WBG_SCD_Full_Report_English.pdf.

Yin, S. M. (2013). *Myanmar: A survival guide to customs and etiquette*. Singapore: Marshall.

CHAPTER 14

The Network-Based Economy in Vietnam: Business Networks in Context and Over Time

Q. Truong*, C. Rowley†,‡,§,¶
*Maastricht School of Management, Maastricht, The Netherlands
†Korea University, Seoul, Korea
‡Griffith University, Nathan, QLD, Australia
§Nottingham University, Nottingham, United Kingdom
¶City University, London, United Kingdom

14.1 INTRODUCTION

It is generally agreed that Vietnam has recently achieved significant economic growth with increases in people's living standards. During the first two decades after the introduction of the "*Doi moi*" reform in 1986, the country achieved a constant annual gross national product (GNP) growth of 7–8% and an overall reduction of poverty levels from 58% to 10% (Asian Development Bank, 2011; Vandemoortele & Bird, 2011). However, this development trend, once held as an "example for development," now needs to be revisited. The *Doi moi* policy saved the country from a total collapse as the result of the fall of the Communist bloc in Eastern Europe. It has generated some benefits for an economy growing from a low base, but will not help Vietnam realize its ambitious goal of becoming an industrialized country by 2020 or even to join the league of "emerging" economies in the region. Above all, economic performance has remained below potential and has often achieved development only with unjustifiably high externalities (Tran, 2015).

The "ideology versus reality" dilemma facing Vietnam today is generally held as the main block holding back the momentum *Doi moi* initially generated growth but has prevented the country jump-starting and accelerating economic growth toward a more qualitative and sustainable development phase. This is because of the Communist Party of Vietnam's (CPV) continued insistence on building "a market economy with socialist orientation" (Huynh, 2013; Nguyen, 2012b; Vu, 2013).

Business Networks in East Asian Capitalisms
http://dx.doi.org/10.1016/B978-0-08-100639-9.00014-1

The fact is that during the growth period of two decades after *Doi moi*, not much attention had been placed on building a supportive infrastructure, an innovative and dynamic capacity necessary to provide solid fundamentals for the economy to advance toward a less labor-intensive, manufacturing-based and to venture into greater value-added and high-tech industries with a well developed private sector, globally competitive value chains, and comparable productivity labor force—the development path that the "Asian Tigers" such as South Korea, Taiwan, Malaysia, and Thailand had followed earlier.

The "socialist" model of development, typically of a state capitalist or network-based economy, which favors state-owned enterprises (SOEs) as the "pillars" of the economy with all the privileges and protection attached to it, has drained the country's resources and prevented the private sector from joining the market and the development process on an equal footing. Instead, it has created and nurtured a breeding ground for corruption, cronyism, favoritism and nepotism (De Treglode, 2015; The Economist, 2013a, 2013b) that leaves little room for private innovation, efficient production and effective management so that Vietnamese products can compete and grow sustainably in international markets (Tran, 2015). In this collection, some of these themes were discussed in Chapter 3 which demonstrated how Chinese state-owned banks struggle to establish international credibility.

Against this backdrop, our chapter will first describe the political-economic situation in which a network-based, state-led capitalism economy in Vietnam has emerged and developed. This will be followed by an analysis of the roots and impacts of such economic anomaly. Finally, future development of the Vietnamese economy will be predicted and possible solutions suggested.

14.2 POLITICAL-ECONOMIC BACKGROUND

The two most dominant factors that determine the conditions and landscape of the Vietnamese economy are: the supreme role of the political party in power and the "market economy with socialist orientation" ambivalence.

14.2.1 The Supreme Role of the Political Party

Analogous to China, the political system in Vietnam is unusual in that supreme power rests, not with the government, but with a political party, the CPV, which has solely claimed its popular legitimacy since it came to power in 1945 in the North, and later in the whole of Vietnam in 1975. Maintaining this legacy requires the continuance of a stable political order as a precondition for improving people's living standards through economic growth (Witt & Redding, 2014, p. 13).

The CPV dominance and socialist principles, channeled through its controlled networks of mass organizations, including trade unions, influence all sectors of life and economic activities of the country. This provides privileges and monopolies to political and economic organizations under CPV control, and associated with the party, especially the SOEs.

The politburo (*bo chinh tri*) and the permanent secretariat (*ban bi thu*) are positioned at the top and oversee the daily activities of the CPV. The CPV central committee (*ban chap hanh trung uong dang*) is the all-important decision-making body, under which all local committees, constituted by CPV members, are located (Rowley & Truong, 2010a, 2010b). In this respect, the politburo has the absolute right in the nomination or appointment of top positions in the party as well as in the state organs, such as Chairman of the National Assembly, the State Chairman, the Prime Minister and his cabinet members.

In practice, The CPV leadership holds ultimate power in deliberating strategic issues and policy implementation at country and enterprise level, leaving only little room for bottom-up participation and grass-roots participation (Truong & Rowley, 2014). Socialist tenets, such as "dictatorship of the proletariat" (*chuyen chinh vo san*), "democratic centralism" (*dan chu tap trung*), and "collective leadership" (*lanh dao tap the*), in the form of "resolutions" (*nghi quyet*), are common practices in decision-making and execution process of the CPV. The dominance of the CPV and the rule of socialist principles still have strong influence on all activities of Vietnam (De Treglode, 2015).

14.3 SOCIO-CULTURAL BACKGROUND

In relative terms, Vietnam is considered to be part of the same cultural region under a common Confucian heritage influence as China, Japan, and Korea. These cultures tend to be more collectivist and hierarchical than Western cultures. Following Hofstede's (1997) typology, Vietnamese culture is typified as being high in "power distance" (acceptance of authority), "collectivism"(value group membership), and "context" (direct and indirect in expression) (Swierczek, 1994).

To begin with, the Confucian thought of a well-ordered universe in the procedures of a "mandarinate," characterized by relationships, respect for seniority, hierarchy and authority, patronage (mentor/protégé), collective responsibility, etc. (Thang, Quang, Rowley, & Warner, 2007) was extended by the French colonial bureaucracy administering the Napoleonic Code with more of an emphasis on prohibiting activities than encouraging independent actions (Truong & Swierczek, 2000).

Although contemporary Vietnam enjoys a more pluralistic blend of behaviors and practices as a result of the opening-up period, and the Vietnamese often insist on their own formula of "adaptation" instead of "adoptation" (*hoa nhap nhung khong hoa tan*) to preserve its "independent" cultural identity (Thang et al., 2007), both of these trends are compatible with the command and control orientation of present-day Vietnam (Truong & Swierczek, 2000).

The most illustrative example related to the development of network-based systems is that while *guanxi* (in Chinese) or *quan he* (in Vietnamese) could work out positively, especially in harnessing long-term mutual benefits, cultivate trust, and personal relationships (Yeung & Tung, 1996), it can evolve and develop into widespread corruption as a result of nepotism, favoritism, and cronyism in the absence of an effective legal system, good governance, and social control norms, conditions prevalent in Vietnam today. In other words, sharing the background (Confucianism and socialism) with its neighbor, the practice of *quan he* in Vietnam has developed in support of an incompetent and corrupt bureaucracy in the form of a widespread "*ban phat an hue*" or "*co che xin/cho*" (distributing favors) (Tran, 2010) and "culture of envelops" (*van hoa phong bi*), which has put heavy strain on the development endeavor of the country (Quynh, 2013; Tran, 2010).

14.3.1 The Market Economy With Socialist Orientation

Political conditions are essentially important to the evolving economic context in Vietnam. The level of party/state control and involvement in the economy has been evolutionary and conditioned to the socio-economic challenges facing the country at the time (Truong & Rowley, 2014). Table 14.1 summarizes the evolution of Vietnam economy after the reunification of the country in 1976.

Prior to 1986, Vietnam suffered a severe economic backlash in the 10-year postwar period as a consequence of a failed centrally planned system à-la the Soviet model in which the state held an absolute control over the whole economy. Under such a rigid system, individual interests were disregarded or ignored for the promotion of egalitarian and collective welfare. Economic development was not regarded as a relevant concern (Dang, 2012; Rowley & Truong, 2010a, 2010b).

Table 14.1 Vietnam political economy in distinct phases

Period	Phase characteristics	GNP growth %	Leverages/issues
1976–1985	Collectivist-socialism	NA	Low production Highly dependency on foreign aid & loans Shortages of foods & basic need products End of aid from socialist bloc Run-away inflation Economic system near total collapse Negative growth period
1986–1990	Socialist/capitalism (*doi moi*)	1985–1989: 4.5 1990–1994: 7.4	Multiple economic structure introduced SOEs restructuring Administrative decentralization/reform Growth period begins
1991–2005	State capitalism	1995–1999: 7.5 2000–2004: 6.7	US embargo lifted 1994 ASEAN membership and AFTA 1995 VN-US BTA signed 2000 FDI inflow/ODA funds 500,000 private enterprises registered High growth period Poverty rate reduced to 10% Anticorruption campaign intensified
2006–2015	Crony capitalism/ network-based	2005–2009: 6.5 2010–2014: 5.8	First stock exchange market setup (2000) WTO membership 2007 High public debts to GNP Widespread corruption Private SME bankruptcies Widening rich-poor gap Economic stagnation Declining growth period

Adapted from World Bank. (2015). GDP Growth (annual %),Vietnam; available at http://data.worldbank.org/indicator/NY.GDP.MKTP.KD.ZG. Accessed 14.08.15.

The dependency on foreign aid, the brutal liquidation of the "capitalist elements" (*tu san mai ban*), the forced immigration to the "new economic zones" (*khu kinh te moi*), the massive outflow of high-skilled professionals, run-away inflation in the wake of severe shortage of foods and articles for basic needs, etc., together contributed to the failure of the harsh collectivist policy imposed on the South after reunification of the country in 1976.

For a decade, Vietnam had practically been kept in the shadow of development in the region and was isolated from the world, until the dire situation compelled the leadership to take a break-through decision to rescue the country from a fully fledged economic crisis and imminent threat to political stability. To a large extent, *Doi moi*, which was launched in 1986, was patterned after the similar reactions for survival in China and in the Soviet Union some 10 years earlier. It primarily aimed at transforming the command economy into a more open and market-oriented system, albeit with "socialist characteristics." Essentially, its attempts included a centralization of some decision-making power to local SOEs, limited deregulation of market prices of agricultural products and allowance of some private activities with a focus on light industry, agriculture, and exports (Thoburn, 2009). As a result, the economy started to pick up for the first time, with an annual growth rate of 3.9% in the initial period (1986–1990), and entered a high growth phase of 7.5% between 1990 and 2000 (World Bank, 2015).

From an ideological point of view, the *Doi moi* campaign was the boldest decision ever taken by the CPV during its rule (Dang, 2012). In effect, *Doi moi* dramatically altered the economic landscape and brought about significant improvement in the living standards of the people to the extent that Vietnam has been expected to be another emerging economic "Tiger" of the region.

Nevertheless, the fact that economic policies were mostly half-way measures and still highly *dirigiste*, the intended scope of *Doi moi* and subsequent reform efforts with priority targets in economic growth and welfare, are believed only to have helped pull the country out of dire situation politically and economically. Vietnam always finds a justification to move slowly and inhibit reform (Truong & Swierczek, 2000) and stays loyal to its socialist ideology.

Thirty years *post-Doi moi*, Vietnam is at a crossroads again. The economy has stagnated for a long period, thwarted by rampant corruption, sky-high public debts, widening gaps between the rich and the poor, running out of natural resources, environmental depletion, and increasing social discontent. On a comparative basis, the country has lost its competitive advantages of an emerging economy and lacks solid, sustainable fundamentals that have trapped it in a bizarre system of its own creation.

In effect, the country is still in a transitional stage, having evolved from a Stalinist system toward a more developmental/welfare state (Masina, 2006) or neo-capitalist state (Le, 2011; Truong & Rowley, 2014) rather than a genuine a free market economy as possibly intended. Current developments of a network-based economy of the economy make it look like a rent-seeking state (Vuvinh, 2013).

In terms of the implications of the above for areas of management, leadership and teamworking see Rowley and Truong (2010a, 2010b); Thang et al. (2007); Truong, van der Heijden, and Rowley (2010); Vo, Hannif, and Rowley (2014); Luu and Rowley (2015); Collins, Chou, Rowley, and Warner (2016).

14.4 CRONY CAPITALISM OR NETWORK-BASED ECONOMY

Like in China, Vietnam today is a developmental state with distinct "predatory admixtures" (Witt & Redding, 2014, p. 13). The typical characteristics of this phenomenon can be found back in the ideological supremacy as the major influence guiding policy direction of the Vietnamese economy and a strong cultural background, traditionally favoring a crony capitalism or network-based system. Many of these symptoms can be found in parallel examples in socialist China or post-Soviet Russia.

14.4.1 Party/State/People Relationship

As described above, the state structure of Vietnam mirrors that of the CPV, often with the same personnel occupying parallel positions in both organizations, *horizontally* and *vertically*. This dualistic system is meant to ensure the political stability of the party in power, on which the material living conditions of the people can be improved by economic growth (Witt & Redding, 2014).

The governing formula based on the ideal, yet blurred tripartite relationship ("the People are the owners, the Party leads, the Government manages," *Dan lam chu, Dang lanh dao, Nha nuoc quan ly*) invented by the CPV in the 1960s (Ha, 2014) reinstates the CPV's absolute power in all affairs. The task of carrying out this arranged mechanism is entrusted to a close-knit network of approximately 4 million party members (representing 4% of the total population) and 45.000 local party cells (De Treglode, 2015), actively involved in all activities of the country.

Interestingly enough, it is reported that the national budget reserved for the operation of the CPV's central office amounts to VND1.925 billion (equivalent to about US $200 million) in 2014, much higher as compared to those allocated to the National Assembly (VND1.200 billion), the Office of the State Chairman (VND196 billion), the cabinet (VND1.290 billion), or the National University of Hanoi (VND709 billion) and of Ho Chi Minh City (VND833 billion) (Kinh, 2015).

14.4.2 Alliance of Interests

Like in China, predatory elements can be seen in personal enrichment by party officials, their families and friends (Witt & Redding, 2014). Together, they form an alliance of multichanneled network of vested interests spreading *vertically* from the top of the party/state hierarchy at the center down to the local lords (provinces, districts, and villages); and *horizontally* between ministries, SOEs, and their connected private businessmen.

In effect, the power-money relationship further expanded its arms-length and even-handed network through so-called Princelings and close relatives of the CPV leaders (central and local), to reach larger circles of large state-owned groups/corporations (*tap doan/tong cong ty*) or well-connected private companies in the areas of the stock exchange, banking, real estate, construction, and development projects, using their connections to maximize their influence for mutual benefits. In this context, ambitious individuals and opportunists attempt to join the CPV just to have access to building connections and improving their materialistic life (De Treglode, 2015).

The sponsor/protégé practice, which was characteristic in the feudal era, finds its way to revive and strive in growth in the absence of a well-developed and regulated environment. The merit system, which is used as the yardstick for appointment and promotion, is another driver to expanding the network-based system. Appointments can be bought, even for high positions. The appointment term (*nhiem ky*) as a condition attached to appointment, making the appointees loyal to their sponsors instead of the organizations they are to serve. The prices for these positions are believed to be unaffordable to most citizens (De Treglode, 2015).

Despite the high prices, candidates are keen to join the network and expand their own circle of influence to recover the costs of the appointments before the term's expiration. This makes the party/state organization impossible to control and coordinate toward achieving common goals, and sanction in case of abuse or deviation from the main course.

The party/state/business (SOEs) alliance, characterized by CPV dominance, concentration of power at the top and collective responsibility, are linked to quick decision-making, but also negatively affects the quality of policy implementation, such as favoritism, cronyism, red tape, and corruption (Truong & Rowley, 2014). Together with their family and associates, this group of privileged elites are believed to actually control the economy and amassed billions of dollars in personal wealth, siphoning off aid funds and through corrupt sales of natural resources, are believed to have the economy under their control.

It is estimated, for example, that the aggregated wealth of these well-connected "Red capitalists" (*tu san do*) amounted to VND22.127 billion (equivalent to US $10 billion) or 48.7% of the total value of the Vietnamese stock market are controlled by the top 20 richest stock holders in 2015 (Ngoc, 2015). Many of them are active in land-related businesses, such as real estate, project development, and banking. The leader of the list, Pham Nhat Vuong, is a well-connected *nouveau riche*, who has built his comparatively enormous wealth equivalent to US $1.59 billion and became the first-ever Vietnamese to enter the Forbes's List of World's Billionaires, ranked 1092th in 2014 (Forbes, 2015).

14.4.3 Collective Ownership and Land Management

In this context, economic decisions and regulations are intended to help facilitate the illegal appropriation of communal land or state property (which is in principle "collectively owned" by the people, *lam chu tap the*) for private benefit.

As land is "collectively owned by the people and managed by the state," the main source of mean of production of farmers (70% of the population still live and work in rural areas), becomes the target of the corrupted network. According to a recently published study (n = 3.648 farmer households in 12 provinces), 27% of the surveyed rural households lost their lands in 2014, an increase of 10% compared to the previous year. More than 98% of the appropriated land falls in the hands of the state (Giang, 2015) to be allocated to development projects, or simply distributed among the network members for real estate speculation. The same trend occurred in urban areas where "golden slots of land" (*khu dat vang*) were taken away from the people and given to well-connected "Red capitalists" (Davies, 2015). This land-grab process has led to large-scale continued (sometimes turning violent, eg, the case of Doan van Vuon in Tien Lang, Hai Phong province) protests of angered farmers in many provinces (The Economist, 2013a, 2013b). The most publicized cases are in the provinces of Thai Binh, Hai Phong, Ha Bac, Bac Ninh, Long An, etc. The abuse has become so out of proportion that land management was officially seen as the "gravely abused gravest area," with more than 700,000 petitions in 2008–2011; 70% of these complaints involved forced appropriation of productive lands to clear the ground (*giai phong mat bang*) for big projects and for personal interests (Bao, 2012; Le, 2012).

14.4.4 Collective Responsibility and Reform Process

In 2007, Vietnam entered into a new phase of development with deeper integration into the global economy that was marketed by its accession to the WTO. Efforts focused on further reducing the role of the state in the economy, encouraging private sector development, and improving the quality of public services. A state-dominated economy can easily open the way for corruption that effectively holds back the development/integration process. On this ground, the government proposed a privatization roadmap for the loss-making, ineffective SOEs. The optimistic view is that asset sales by SOEs, along with more graft-busting, may boost the country's sluggish economy (The Economist, 2014).

Strategically held as the backbone of the economy, SOEs enjoy favorable operating conditions and privileges, such as subsidies, preferred access to credit, land use, and markets. There were about (central and local) 12,500 SOEs in 1990, declining to 5600 in 2001 and 2100 in 2006 (World Bank, 2006) as a result of restructuring and equitization.

The equitization (the Vietnamese version of privatization) program aimed at further reducing the remaining SOEs to a more manageable number. A total of 950 SOEs were planned to be equitized in 2010, leaving 544 SOEs, including 26 large scale economic groups (*tap doan*) and corporations (*tong cong ty*). By 2010, there were still about 1473 SOEs (Do & Truong, 2010).

The planned reform of the remaining SOEs has been slow as they tried in many ways to keep their public ownership status. In many cases, the state continues its influence by holding majority shares in equitized enterprises (Brown, 2011), while many others reappear in the form of joint-stock enterprises (JSEs), which are still managed by the same individuals (often led by a party person), just as they were in the past (Bui & Nunoi, 2008; Masina, 2010; Sjoholm, 2006; Truong & Rowley, 2014).

SOEs can be characterized as bureaucratic with many layers, duplicated functions, and excessive staffing, especially the strategic groups and corporations (in energy, banking, transport, shipbuilding, telecommunications, oil, coal, etc.) operating on the Korean *chaebol* model (Do & Truong, 2010). The majority of SOEs lose money with heavy nonperforming debts and poor governance as a result of corruption, nepotism and mismanagement (Wright & Nguyen, 2000). Instead of becoming more competitive after reorganization, they further consolidated their monopolistic positions and expanded their areas of influence over to cover noncore businesses (hotel, import/export, finance, telecoms, etc.) to serve their own interest. The recently disclosed scandals involving the cases of Vinalines, Asian Development Bank, Ocean Bank, EVN (Electricity Vietnam), and PVN (Petro Vietnam) have shown the downsize of this practice (eg, Tuoi Tre News, 2015).

In parallel with the campaign to restructure collective ownership, the state launched a comprehensive program to reorganize itself into a development administration, shifting emphasis from bureaucracy-oriented to citizen-and market-oriented provider of public services (Do & Truong, 2010). Efforts focused on developing a more complete regulatory framework by introducing a decentralization program to delegate decision-making authority from central to local governments, for example, the FDI license approval process and finding ODA (Official Development Assistance) sources to finance local development projects). The campaign also attempted to reduce state subsidies by promoting the development of the private sector and involving related stakeholders (business and community) in providing services, especially in education and healthcare areas. However, these efforts to build a more effective, responsible, and accountable system have yet to materialize (Do & Truong, 2010).

One explanation is that while the party/state/business monolithic system may be an effective mechanism to push policy through quickly, it does not necessarily guarantee smooth and successful implementation. As decision-making is based on consensus, checks and balances occur *horizontally* (across ministries and departments), *vertically* (between central and local governments) and *geographically* (North, South, Middle, and remote areas) (Ohno, 2009). Under this typical decentralized, quasifederalist structure (Redding & Witt, 2007), any important decision requires lengthy negotiations, extensive compromises, and networks to satisfy the vested interests of stakeholders (Truong & Rowley, 2014).

Furthermore, the development and integration process led to greater "autonomization," in which the state is forced to gradually yield more latitude to local authorities and thus forms of "para-state" entities (eg, 64 provinces and 5 principal cities) have emerged (Painter, 2008). Under these circumstances, decentralization has given rise to localism (Nguyen, 2008) and cronyism (Roberts, 2010), notably the practice of "favor distribution" or "request-approval" (*co che xin-cho*) (Tran, 2010). An example of localism can be seen in the race among provinces/cities for "prestige" infrastructure projects. Many local CPV leaders also sit on the Party's Central Committee (the NA), or hold key ministerial positions in the cabinet (Truong & Rowley, 2014). The result of this intraparty lobby is a proliferation of airports, seaports, industrial/special economic zones, universities, monuments, golf courts, etc., many of them are close to each other in neighboring provinces and often left idle or underused (Truong & Rowley, 2014). Unfocused and uncoordinated delegation/decentralization thus allows corruption in the public sector, such as "facilitation fee," "under-the-table payments" (Le, Rowley, Truong, & Warner, 2007; Nguyen, 2010; Papin & Passicousset, 2010).

14.5 CORRUPTION AND NETWORK-BASED ECONOMY

14.5.1 Relationship Between Economic Growth and Corruption

Among the many disagreeable aspects of corruption is evidence that it slows economic growth through a wide range of channels. Related to this, corruption is seen as both the outcome and the symptom of weak governance (Anvig, 2004; Do & Truong, 2010, p. 197; Rose-Ackerman, 2004). According to a World Bank estimate, between US $1 trillion and US $1.6 trillion are lost globally each year to illegal activities (Nguyen, 2012a). Also, empirical evidence suggests that corruption lowers investment and reduces economic growth to a significant extent in several surveyed countries (Mauro, 1997). Studies on Vietnam have established the same relationship. For example, Brady (2013) argues that if the sole criteria for economic success were GDP growth, Vietnam's system was clearly effective and many ordinary citizens benefited. However, income inequality in the country also rose and the recent boom was accompanied by a wave of corruption scandals. Many cases involve bribery charges against officials or executives, or against journalists and activists accused of highlighting the problem. In the same vein, Bai, Jayachandran, and Malesky (2013) based their work on surveys of thousands of firms in Vietnam from 2006 to 2010 and came to the overall conclusion that countries might "grow" their way out of corruption. In this case, it may not be necessary to eliminate corruption to spur growth, but rather corruption might subside as a country grows. The key factor is secure and transferable property rights, which enhance firm mobility and thus allow them to put pressure on public officials.

It has only recently been that the CPV began to acknowledge and tackle the part hidden below the tip of the iceberg, which have been blamed for the country's ongoing economic malaise. Four critical challenges are listed in order of importance, of which the two most direct dangers to the economy are lagging behind (*tut hau*) and corruption and bureaucratism (*tham nhung va quan lieu*), besides deviation from socialism (*chech huong xa hoi chu nghia*) and "peaceful evolution" (ie, attempts to overthrow the party (Vu, 2015). Specifically, the multiple profile, scope and influence of the "money-power alliance," typical of the network-based economy, are identified and analyzed in detail, albeit with some ambiguity:

> *'Group benefits' (loi ich nhom) are the reasons leading to the forming of 'groups of interest' (nhom loi ich). The characters of the groups of interests is the combination of common interest objectives, acting collectively, sharing the benefits together among people who have lots of money and those who have the power in the government and in the party in power…Currently, 'group benefits' and activities of 'groups of interests' in our country has occurred and are happening in all important sectors, notably in the management of SOEs, investment projects, especially public investments, national budget, taxes, banks and financing institutions, capital resources and social investment projects, property, land, real estates, mineral resources, import/exports; in the management of (party) cadres and state public servants; in the management of issuing all types of licenses; including in the case handlings at tribunals (Vu, 2015).*

With this, the CPV's leading theorist admitted that the network-based system has expanded its scope and scale and hence has greatly damaged the country's resources and reduced the effectiveness of investments so that the economy could not accelerate its growth or even develop normally (Vu, 2015).

The CPV definition of the ongoing network-based system is not very far from that of the increasing crony capitalism in countries sharing the same conditions as Vietnam (Haber, 2002), which is generally accepted by the world development and financing institutions, only the measures proposed to cure it differ. For example, the Heritage Foundation describes how crony capitalism poses danger to economic freedom (Roberts, 2010):

> *Backroom deals between members of the governing class and their hand-picked cronies influence the legislative, executive, and regulatory actions of governments around the world…Government intrusions into the private sector as a partner, financier, or outright owner are not only morally hazardous, but toxic to economic freedom. Such special-interest arrangements directly contradict the principles of freedom, incentives, and opportunity detailed in The Heritage Foundation's Index of Economic Freedom.*

To highlight the damage of corruption brought about by the network-based economy to Vietnam, the Transparency Index ranked Vietnam 119th, making it one of the most corrupted among 175 countries surveyed (Transparency.org). The directionless in development strategy and low productivity level have further reduced the country's competitiveness stand globally. The 2014–2015 Global Economic Forum Report ranked Vietnam 68th of 144 countries worldwide, a position not much improved compared to previous years (eg, 65th of 183 countries in 2010–2012) (Schwab, 2015).

Against this background, it is suggested that with sluggish annual growth of 5–6% during 2010–2014, Vietnam in many aspects is "lagging behind" most of its ASEAN neighbors, including such emerging "new frontier markets" as Laos (8.1%), Cambodia (7.0%), and Myanmar (8.4% in 2013–2014) in the same period (Tran, 2015; World Bank, 2015). In another aspect, with a GDP per capita of US $2.052 in price parity (PPP) in 2014, notwithstanding that it is 21 times higher from the starting low base of US $98 in 1990, Vietnam is still trailing most of its ASEAN peer, being only 3/5 of Indonesia, 2/5 Thailand, 1/5 Malaysia and 1/27 of Singapore (Tu, 2015).

According to the country's economic think tank, this income per capita level will only match 75% that of China and 83% of Thailand with the ongoing growth rate of 5%/year in 2035 (Tu, 2015). To catch up with these countries, it will need a constant growth rate of 7%/year in the next 20 years (Huyen, 2015); a level that is perceived as not impossible given the total public debt of US $110 billion or 59.6% of GDP in 2015 (Economist, 2015, Huyen, 2015), averaging $1.200 for each citizen (Huyen, 2015). Added to this is the total ODA funds (Official Development Aids) of US $90 billion over the time span of 20 years for a relative level of economic achievements (Hai, 2015).

Five years before the deadline to become "an industrialized country," Vietnam entered a decline phase and finds itself at a crossroads again. To come out of the stalemate created by the corrupted network, the country badly needs another bold decision *à-la-doi-moi*.

14.5.2 Anti-Corruption Campaign

Corruption in Vietnam is so entrenched in the country that is not easy to root out. To be sure, corruption is seen as a direct product of the network of its own creation. On the other land, paying bribes is generally perceived as a normal "habit" of the Vietnamese (Do & Truong, 2010). However, recognizing corruption as a foremost danger (*ke noi thu*, internal enemy) and identifying its practices (including fraud, corruption, collusion, coercion, and obstructive practices) are necessary, but practical solutions are needed as well (Nguyen, 2012a), especially with regards to restore people's trust in the system.

To be sure, Vietnam has been stepping up its fight against corruption. In 2000 the National Assembly passed the Anti-Corruption Law to make sure the legal system is enhanced. Most recently, the CPV reestablished the Internal Affairs Committee (*Ban noi chinh trung uong*) in 2012 (CPV, 2012), to ensure state money would not go to anyone's pocket (CPV, 2015).

Nevertheless, given the scope and size of corruption and its network as perceived by the general public, the efforts of the party/state to battle "the number one enemy of the nation" seemingly touches only the tip of the iceberg (Do & Truong, 2010). One reason is that corruption remains so incurable that the victims are not willing to reveal it for fear of reprisals. Another reason is that in the absence of a complete and consistent legal framework, corrupt officials can make decisions on an ad hoc basis, making them in favor of those who are willing to pay bribes. This scenario is most common in the bidding process for construction projects using ODA funds (Do & Truong, 2010).

A recent survey ($n = 5460$) jointly undertaken by the State General Inspection and the World Bank in 2012, revealed that 75% of respondents (citizens, businessmen, and public servants) perceived that corruption is a serious matter. The four most corrupted areas in the public administration are identified, namely traffic police, land management, customs, and construction (Doan, 2012).

The World Bank Enterprise Survey published in 2011 ($n = 1.053$ firms with 5 employees and more, in 2009–2010), concluded a list of 15 obstacles to growth and performance measures. Accordingly, one-fourth of Vietnamese firms ranked access to finance as the biggest business environment obstacle, especially with high collateral requirements, up to 218% relative to loan amount. Corruption in Vietnam was also identified as one of the major constraints to their business as 52.5% of surveyed firms expected to pay informal fees to public officials, compared to 29.5% in 20 countries in the low-middle income category like Vietnam (World Bank, 2011).

Following this line, the CPV officially recognized that corruption as a result of expanding crony capitalism is one of the most serious challenges to the livelihood of the party and the nation, but stopped short of suggesting/taking concrete measures against it (Vu, 2015). In a similar vein, another World Bank study in 2004 shows that 71% of the residents in Hanoi and 67.5% in Ho Chi Minh City admitted they are willing to bribe "to get things done." Transparency International Report (2013) revealed that 30% of Vietnamese citizens admitted to have bribed public servants when dealing with them regarding public services; 55% agreed that corruption is on the increase and 38% did not believe that all the government efforts to combat corruption was effective. The same report highlights that 53% of urban Vietnamese disagree that ordinary people can make a difference against corruption, compared to only 33% in 2010. Some 79% of people said they would not report corruption because "it wouldn't make a difference" or because "they are afraid of the consequences." (Transparency International, 2013).

The impact of corruption is extremely damaging to private SMEs. A survey proved that it would cost an enterprise VND1.02 for a "facilitation fee" to generate VND1, which implies that if corruption was reduced by 50%, private enterprises could have earned 50% more income. It also explains the reason that private SMEs have reduced their size by a half in 2015 as compared to 10 years earlier and were financially incapable to reinvest for growth (Hai, 2015).

Also, although the top of the party/state leader remains an "off limit" protected area, at least some members of the Central Committee and ministers have been objects of public scrutiny and the media for their wrong-doings or sponsors of the network and consequently received heavy penalties in the recent anti-corruption campaign. The high-profile cases are the PMU 18 in the North and PCI in the South involving senior party/state officials and large-scale embezzlement from ODA funds from Japan in 2007 and 2009 respectively (Do & Truong, 2010). Recently, the links to the biggest graft cases (eg, Vinalines and Asia Commercial Bank) can be traced back to the very top of the party/state hierarchy (The Economist, 2014).

Vietnam's anti-graft campaigns over the past decade have been largely ineffective and seemingly only touched the tip of the iceberg. The vast majority of corruption trials ended with slaps on the wrists in the form of warnings or suspended sentences as Vietnamese elites are not in the habit of openly accusing party/state bigwigs of corruption (The Economist, 2014).

Corruption protesters and whistleblowers (eg, Le Hien Duc, a female retiree turned activist for the cause of corruption victims, who was granted the "Integrity Awards Winners" by Transparency International in 2007) are often harassed by the corrupted persons and their protection network, sometimes even being condemned to imprisonment terms for politics-related crimes (eg, land-grabbed protesters in Thai Binh, Hai Phong, Quang Nam, Bac Ninh, Long An, Dong Thap, etc.). This has forced the corruption and antiestablishment activists to air their grievances via informal channels, such as blogs and multimedia trying to escape the state setup firewall and security censorship (eg, boxitvn.com, lehienduc2013.blogspot.com, toidihoilo.com, xuandienhannom.blogspot.com, to mention a few).

As the 2013 Transparency International Report indicated Vietnamese citizens are the least willing out of all countries surveyed in South East Asia to report a case of corruption and the least likely to refuse to pay a bribe. Positive examples of successful challenges to systemic corruption can change this. Especially at a time when the level of corruption in Vietnam is perceived to be increasing and public confidence in government anticorruption efforts decreasing, it remains important to highlight success and call on the authorities to support, not attack those who seek to uncover wrongdoing (Transparency International, 2013).

14.5.3 Solutions for the Corruption Problems

An effective anticorruption strategy should help discourage corrupt behavior and identify those who are corrupt (World Bank, 2000). Legal and institutional frameworks aimed at curbing graft and bribery have been strengthened. The NA passed the Anticorruption Law in 2000 and began to monitor anticorruption initiatives. In recent years, the government has emphasized more positive, systematic approaches, including fostering transparency, minimizing bureaucracy and red tape, improving the accountability of government officials, etc.

However, the independence of institutions responsible for detecting and prosecuting corruption remains in question after the denouncement of the Head of the General Inspection Directorate that led to his immediate removal in 2014 (Khoa, 2014). The CPV also shows its determination to fight the "number 1 national enemy" by reestablishing the Central Committee for Internal Affairs (*ban noi chinh trung uong*) to effectively deal with corrupt party members, without an "off limit" zone as before. This new initiative has yet to deliver concrete results after some unexplainable incidents occurred to the head of the newly set up organization.

On the other hand, the continued negative impact of corruption on the economy have compelled world leading financing donors to Vietnam (eg, World Bank, ADB, IMF, JICA) to issue stark warnings and advise the country to take immediate actions to improve the situation. The main lines called for more transparency to help bring out a more efficient allocation of resources, build trust among citizens, and counter the "democratic deficit" in the current system (Deutscher & Fyson, 2008).

Nevertheless, up to now efforts to systematically curb the privileges of SOEs; vehemence over official corruption; poorly compensated land-grabs; new restrictions on online dissent; is a recognition that further economic reform is not just desirable, but essential. Hence, cleaning up the SOE sector, perhaps by starting to privatize the profitable businesses (eg, telecommunications, energy, brewing, etc.) and trimming the loss-makers (most of the rest), is believed to be a prerequisite for putting the country back on a fast-track growth path. It may also be essential if Vietnam succeeds in joining an American-led free-trade agreement, the Trans-Pacific Partnership (TPP). However, dismantling the state-led economic sector remains terrifying for many, not only are officials corrupt beneficiaries of business links, but it also helps to justify single-party rule, and the political legitimacy of the CPV (Thayer, 2009; The Economist, 2013a, 2013b).

In the final analysis, to be effective and not just pay lip service, measures aimed at anticipating and fighting corruption (aka, the network-based economy) requires first and above all radical measures to fix the "system defects" (*loi he thong*), typically of an almost feudalistic political system (London, 2015), with a clearer ideological stand on the ambivalence of "the socialism-capitalism" cohabitation, a long-term, realizable vision and a consistent, concrete implementation roadmap (Truong & Rowley, 2014), not the "muddle-through approach" (Du Venage, 2011) or the "damage control mode" (Cain, 2012) of current practice.

14.6 CONCLUSION

This chapter provides a comprehensive analysis of the anomaly network-based economy in Vietnam. It sheds light on the underlying part of the economy in a perato-rule like situation. Despite much upbeat talk about the "Vietnamese miracle" (eg, The Economist, 2008), the unknown face of the floating part of the iceberg begins to surface. Officially, published figures of a used-to-believed high-performing/emerging economy are doubtful at best as they are systematically manipulated for political purposes rather than for society benefits. Several structural defects have been detected and reasons analyzed, all geared to the incompetent, corrupt, and political maneuvering of the system, typical of a network-based economy. The economic achievements of the last three decades do not correspond to the available potential of the country and the costs attached to them. On balance, growth in quantitative terms does not match development in qualitative terms.

Since the CPV leadership firmly reinstated its full belief and unconditional dedication to the socialist dogma in the revised Constitution in 2014, one can predict that this type of network-based economy will continue to exist, even if no one, including the top party leadership, could be clear as to how and when such an ideal socialist society model could be realized (Nguyen, 2012b; Vu, 2013). Real-life evidence has shown that the 40 years of development model *à-la-socialisme* has resulted in the country's social-economic backwardness and stagnation, as compared to regional peers at the cost of political consolidation and abuse of power.

Vietnam is at a momentous juncture in its social and political development. Yet, a change in the existing economic system could occur only when the CPV faces an imminent "life-and-death" dilemma that necessitates a breakthrough *à-la Doi-moi*. This implies a priori an all out change in the political structure, meaning a definitive departure from socialism (Huynh, 2013). In this scenario, political transformation will clear the way and lay the favorable conditions for sustainable economic development and a participating society to follow, not vice versa as the PCV has hitherto firmly believed and made the world believe.

However, as long as corruption continues to be epidemic, the bureaucracy cumbersome, the banking system inefficient, the majority of the SOEs loss-making, and the private sector still discriminated against, the slogan currently exhorted by the party/state to break up the current stalemate to turn "Vietnam into an industrialized country" in 2020 remains lip-service and a mere illusion.

The experience gained in the last three decades has brought new realism and greater economic resilience and maturity that could help Vietnam to prosper. What Vietnam really needs to come out of the dire situation of today and to become more sustainable is a "development-oriented market economy" (*kinh te thi truong dinh huong chu nghia phat trien*) (Tran, 2015), not the impractical and unworkable "market economy with socialist orientation," if the country was to keep pace with development in the region, let alone in the world.

In more concrete terms, the next transformation should include a radical restructuring of the political system (London, 2015) and the development of a "grassroots capitalism" (Kotkin, 2011) that supports the building of a for-tax-payer-oriented public services, good governance at all levels (free of red tape, bureaucratism, and self-interest) to definitely break up the "comfort zone" currently enjoyed by the power-money alliance network as observed. Furthermore, a check-and-balance mechanism is needed to allow the participation of a more active civil society (eg, professional associations, trade unions, interest groups, popular ombudsmen, etc.) to counter the excessive abuse of power brought about by the corrupted network that has caused severe threats the economic sustainability of the country.

REFERENCES

Anvig, J. C. (2004). The challenge of poor governance and corruption. In B. Lomborg (Ed.), *Global crisis, global solutions* (pp. 1–13). Cambridge: Cambridge University Press.

Asian Development Bank. (2011). *Vietnam's poverty reduction, development: A regional success story*. Manila: Asian Development Bank.

Bai, J., Jayachandran, S., Malesky, E.J., & Olken, B.A. (2013). Does economic growth reduce corruption? Theory & evidence from Vietnam. aeaweb.org, 28-10-2014; available at https://www.aeaweb.org/aea/2015conference/program/retrieve.php%3Fpdfid%3D186+&cd=2&hl=nl&ct=clnk&gl=nl. Accessed 29.08.15.

Bao, C. (2012). Khieu nai to cao ve dat dai rat nghiem trong. Thanhnien Online, 19-09-2012.

Brady, B. (2013). The relationship between economic growth and corruption: The Case of Vietnam. Journalistresource.org; available at http://journalistsresource.org/studies/international/development/relationship-economic-growth-corruption-case-vietnam. Accessed 29.08.15.

Brown, D. (2011). Vietnam change courses. Asian Times, 12 April. Available at www.atimes.com/atimes/...Asia/MD12Ae01.htmlIn cache. Accessed 08.12.11.

Bui, X. H., & Nunoi, C. (2008). Corporate governance in Vietnam: A system in transition. *Hitotsubashi Journal of Commerce and Management, 42*(1), 45–65.

Cain, G. (2012). The end of the Vietnamese miracle: So much for the next Asian Success Story. Foreign Policy. 11-07-2012; http://foreignpolicy.com/2012/07/11/the-end-of-the-vietnamese-miracle. Accessed 03.09.15.

Collins, N., Chou, Y., Rowley, C., & Warner, M. (2016). Human factors in East Asian virtual teamwork: A comparative study of Indonesia, Taiwan and Vietnam. *International Journal of HRM, 27*, 1–24.

CPV. (2012). Ban noi chinh trung uong (The Central Committee of Internal Affairs). Available at http://noichinh.vn/gioi-thieu/ban-noi-chinh-trung-uong. Accessed 03.09.15.

CPV. (2015). Chong quan lieu, tham nhung, lang phi (Fighting Bureaucratism, Corruption, Waste). Bao dien tu dang Cong san Viet Nam, 17-06-2015.

Dang, P. (2012). Pha rao' trong kinh te vao dem truoc doi moi. Hanoi: Nha Xuat ban Tri thuc.

Davies, N. (2015). Vietnam 40 years on: How a communist victory gave way to capitalist corruption. Theguardian, 23-04-2015.

De Treglode, B. (2015). Viet Nam, le Parti, l'Armée et le Peuple: Maintenir l'Emprise Politique à l'Heure de l'Ouverture. In *Hérodote*, Les Enjeux Geopolitiques du Viet Nam, N. 157, 2015-2: 82–96. Paris: Editions La Découverte, 224 p.

Deutscher, E., & Fyson, S. (2008). Improving the effectiveness of aid. *International Monetary Fund, 45*(3).

Do, X. T., & Truong, Q. (2010). The changing face of public sector management in Vietnam. In C. Rowley & Q. Truong (Eds.), *The changing face of Vietnamese management* (pp. 187–220). New York: Routledge.

Doan, L. (2012). 4 ngành tham nhũng nhiều nhất. VNExpress, 20-11-2012.

Du Venage, G. (2011). Hasty Vietnam in a hurry to catch up with its neighbours. The National, 14-04-2011. Available at http://www.thenational.ae/business/industry-insights/economics/hasty-vietnam-in-a-hurry-to-catch-up-with-its-neighbours. Accessed 03.09.15.

Forbes. (2015). The World's Billionaires. www.Forbes.com/profile/phamnhatvuong. Accessed 28.08.15.

Giang, T. (2015). Ngheo doi van cao, dat dai roi vao tay nha nuoc tai nong thon VN. Thoi bao kinh te Sai Gon (The Saigon Times), 26-08-2015.

Ha, T. K. (2014). Tăng cường sự lãnh đạo của Đảng để nhân dân tham gia xây dựng Đảng, xây dựng chính quyền trong sạch, vững mạnh. Tap chi cong san, 18-06-2014.

Haber, S. (2002). *Crony capitalism and economic growth in Latin America: Theory and evidence*. Stanford, CA: Hoover Institution Press.

Hai, C. (2015). Việt Nam là mô hình kỳ lạ nhất thế giới: Nước... không chịu phát triển!. Infonet.vn, 19-08-2015; http://infonet.vn/viet-nam-la-mo-hinh-ky-la-nhat-the-gioi-nuoc-khong-chiu-phat-trien-post171047.info. Accessed 30.08.15.

Hofstede, G. (1997). *Cultures and organizations: Software of the mind*. New York: McGraw-Hill.

Huyen, T. (2015). Kinh te Viet Nam: mat 15 nam chi 'do da qua song'. VTC News, 29-08-2015.

Huynh, T. D. (2013). Luan giai ve kinh te thi truong dinh huong xa hoi chu nghia o Viet Nam (Dicussion on the market economy wit socialist orientation in Viet Nam). Thoi dai moi (New Era): 11-2013 (29), 3–80.

Khoa, C. (2014). Vietnam's embattled former anti-corruption czar slapped on wrist. Thanhnien News, 31-12-2014.

Kinh, H. (2015). Đảng cộng sản Việt nam xài ngân sách quốc gia như thế nào? (How does the CPV Use National Budget), Viet Nam thoi bao, 27-03-2015. Available at http://www.ijavn.org/2015/03/ang-cong-san-viet-nam-xai-ngan-sach.html.

Kotkin, J. (2011). Hanoi underground capitalism. Forbes, 29-03-2011.

Le, S. L. (2011). Vietnam's State Capitalism and the Rise of Southeast Asia. Bauer Global Study.

Le, K. (2012). Khieu nai dat dai rat 'nghiem trong'. Tuoitre Online, 19-09-2012.

Le, C. T., Rowley, C., Truong, Q., & Warner, W. (2007). To what extent can management practices be transferred between countries: Human resource management in Vietnam. *Journal of World Business*, *42*(1), 113–127.

London, J. D. (2015). Is Vietnam on the verge of change? Current History, 09-2015, 229–235.

Luu, T., & Rowley, C. (2015). From value-based human resource practices to ideosyncratic deals: Software companies in Vietnam. *Personnel Review*, *44*(1), 39–68.

Masina, P. (2006). *Vietnam's development strategies*. Oxford: Routledge.

Masina, P. (2010). Vietnam between Developmental State and Neoliberalism: The Case of the Industrial Sector. Working Paper 1007, Department of Social Sciences, University of Naples.

Mauro, P. (1997). The effects of corruption on growth, investment, and government expenditure. International Monetary Fund, Working Paper 96/98; available at https://www.imf.org/EXTERNAL/PUBS/FT/ISSUES6/INDEX.HTM. Accessed 29.08.

Ngoc, L. (2015). Giat minh truoc khoi tai san cua nguoi giau nhat Viet Nam. Nguoi dua tin, 04-03-2015.

Nguyen, D. C. (2008). *Corporate governance in Vietnam: Regulations, practices, and problems*. Hanoi: CIEM/GTZ.

Nguyen, M. S. (2010). Van hoa phong bi (The Envelop Culture). Sai Gon Tiep thi, 15-10-2010.

Nguyen, N. H. (2012a). Fighting corruption in Vietnam: The question is how, not why, 28-11-2012. http://blogs.worldbank.org/eastasiapacific/fighting-corruption-in-vietnam-the-question-is-how-not-why. Accessed 30.08.15.

Nguyen, P. T. (2012b). Socialism and the path to socialism:Vietnam's perspective. Political affaiirs, 30-12-2012, available at http://www.politicalaffairs.net/socialism-and-the-path-to-socialism-vietnam-s-perspective. Accessed 19.06.15.

Ohno, K. (2009). *Avoiding middle-income trap: Renovating industrial policy formulation in Vietnam*. Singapore: Institute of Southeast Asian Studies.

Painter, M. (2008). From command economy to hollow state? Decentralisation in Vietnam and China. *The Australian Journal of Public Administration, 67*(1), 79–88.

Papin, P., & Passicousset, L. (2010). Vivre avec les Vietnamiens. Paris. Editeur l'Archipel.

Quynh, H. (2013). Benh phong bi o Viet Nam tren bao Anh. VnExpress, 28-07-2013.

Redding, G., & Witt, M. A. (2007). *The future of Chinese capitalism: Choices and chances*. Oxford: Oxford University Press.

Roberts, J. M. (2010). Cronyism: Undermining economic freedom and prosperity around the world. The Heritage Foundation, 09-08-2010; available at http://www.heritage.org/research/reports/2010/08/cronyism-undermining-economic-freedom-and-prosperity-around-the-world. Accessed 05.04.15.

Rose-Ackerman, S. (2004). The challenge of poor governance and corruption. In B. Lomborg (Ed.), *Global crisis, global solutions* (pp. 1–62). Cambridge: Cambridge University Press.

Rowley, C., & Truong, Q. (2010a). *The changing face of Vietnamese management*. London: Routledge.

Rowley, C., & Truong, Q. (2010b). Setting the scene for the changing face of management in Vietnam. In C. Rowley & Q. Truong (Eds.), *The changing face of Vietnamese management* (pp. 1–23). New York: Routledge.

Schwab, K. (2015). The global competitiveness report 2014-2015. World Economic Forum.

Sjoholm, F. (2006). State-owned enterprises and equitization in Vietnam. EIJS Working Paper No. 228, Stockholm, European Institute of Japanese Studies, Stockholm School of Economics.

Swierczek, F. W. (1994). Cultures and conflicts in joint-venture in Asia. *International Journal of Project Management, 12*(1), 7.

Thang, L. C., Quang, T., Rowley, C., & Warner, M. (2007). To what extent can management practices be transferred between countries: HRM in Vietnam. *Journal of World Business, 42*(1), 113–127.

Thayer, A. C. (2009). Political legitimacy of Vietnam's one party-state: Challenges and responses. *Journal of Current Southeast Asian Affairs, 28*(4), 47–70.

The Economist. (2008). Asia's other miracle, 24-04-2008, available at http://www.economist.com/node/11089442. Accessed 03.09.15.

The Economist. (2013a). Land-grabs in Vietnam, losing the plot, anger rises over corrupt local officials. 14-03-2013.

The Economist. (2013b). Across the party wall, 26-10-2013; available at http://www.economist.com/news/asia/21588359-vietnams-communist-party-bit-mess-chinas-may-have-little-teach-it-across. Accessed 19.06.15.

The Economist. (2014). Graft-busting in Vietnam: Wrist-slapping, 27-06-2014.

The Economist. (2015). Land-grabs in Vietnam, losing the plot, anger rises over corrupt local officials, 14-03-2015.

Thoburn, J. T. (2009). Vietnam as a role model for development. United Nations University, World Institute for Development.

Tran, P. (2010). Ban ve co che xin-cho. VNEconomy, 18-01-2010.

Tran, V. T. (2015). Viet Nam 40 nam qua va nhung nam toi: can mot nen kinh te thi truong dinh huong phat trien (Vietnam in the past 40 years and the years to come: the need for a development-oriented economy). Thoi dai moi (New Era): 07-2015 (33), 13–64.

Transparency International. (2013). Vietnam: Citizens against corruption, 12-09-2013.

Tuoi Tre News. (2015). Former PetroVietnam chairman arrested for abusing power to appropriate assets. Available at http://tuoitrenews.vn/society/29359/former-petrovietnam-chairman-held-for-abusing-power-to-appropriate-assets. Accessed 03.09.15.

Truong, Q., & Rowley, C. (2014). Vietnam: Post-state capitalism. In M.A. Witt & G. Redding (Eds.), *The Oxford handbook of Asian business system* (pp. 283–305). New York: Oxford University Press.

Truong, Q., & Swierczek, F. (2000). Implications of the Asian crisis for official ideology and investments in Vietnam. In U. Haley (Ed.), *Strategic management in the pacific: Harnessing regional & organizational change for competitive advantage: 406-8* (pp. 585). Oxford: Butterworth-Heinemann.

Truong, Q., van der Heijden, B., & Rowley, C. (2010). Globalisation, competitiveness & HRM in transitional economy: Vietnam. *International Journal of Business Studies, 18*(1), 75–100.

Tu, G. (2015). Hon 50 nam nua moi bat kip Thai Lan ve nang suat lao dong. The Saigon Times, 26-08-2015.

Vandemoortele, M., & Bird, K. (2011). *Vietnam's progress on economic growth and poverty reduction: Impressive improvements*. London: Overseas Development Institute. 22 p.

Vo, A., Hannif, Z., & Rowley, C. (2014). Leadership styles & generational effects: The case of US companies in Vietnam. *International Journal of HRM, 25*(1), 1–22.

Vu, V. P. (2013). Special characteristics of socialist oriented market economy in Vietnam. Communist Review, 08-08-2015.

Vu. N. H. (2015). Lợi ích nhóm và 'chủ nghĩa tư bản thân hữu - cảnh báo nguy cơ. Tap chi cong san (Journal of Communism), 02-08-2015; http://www.tapchicongsan.org.vn/Home/Nghiencuu-Traodoi/2015/33662/Loi-ich-nhom-va-Chu-nghia-tu-ban-than-huu-canh.aspx. Accessed 29.08.15.

Vuvinh, A. L. (2013). Vietnam in 2012: A rent-seeking state on the verge of crisis. Southeast Asian Affairs, 05-06-2013: 324–347.

Witt, M. A., & Redding, G. (2014). China: Authoritarian capitalism. In M. A. Witt & G. Redding (Eds.), *The Oxford handbook of Asian business system* (pp. 11–32). New York: Oxford University Press.

World Bank. (2000). *Anti-corruption in transition*. New York.

World Bank. (2006). *Vietnam development report 2007 – Vietnam aiming high*. New York.

World Bank. (2011). Enterprise survey: Vietnam, Country note No. 13; available at www.enterprisesurveys.org. Accessed 21.07.15.

World Bank. (2015). GDP growth (annual %), Vietnam; available at http://data.worldbank.org/indicator/NY.GDP.MKTP.KD.ZG. Accessed 14.08.15.

Wright, C. P., & Nguyen, V. V. (2000). State-owned enterprises (SOEs) in Vietnam: Perceptions of strategic direction for a society in transition. *International Journal of Public Sector Management, 13*(2), 169–177.

Yeung, Y. M. I., & Tung, R. L. (1996). Achieving business success in confucian societies: The importance of *guanxi*. *Organizational Dynamics, 25*(2), 54–65.

CHAPTER 15

Conclusion: Making Sense of Enduring Trends and Emerging Patterns in Business Networks in East Asian Capitalisms

J. Nolan*, C. Rowley[†,‡,§,¶], M. Warner[//]
*Newnham College, Cambridge, United Kingdom
†Korea University, Seoul, Korea
‡Griffith University, Nathan, QLD, Australia
§Nottingham University, Nottingham, United Kingdom
¶City University, London, United Kingdom
//University of Cambridge, Cambridge, United Kingdom

In our collection, we have thoroughly examined the richness and diversity of business networks in East Asian capitalism. We have included studies of the conventional main players, such as China, Japan, and Korea, as well as introducing readers to developments in South East Asia, including Thailand, Myanmar, and Vietnam. We have also added a more general chapter on the historical development of East Asian business networks, as well as a review of the successes and failures of ethnic Chinese business communities in the Straits region, comprised of Singapore and parts of Malaysia and Indonesia.

International contributors from a range of disciplines and countries have adopted a variety of perspectives on business networks in these countries, including investigations of the influence of history, economics, politics, society, and culture.

In this conclusion, we sum up their contributions through reference to the comparative business systems approach, which we outlined in the introduction (Redding, 2005; Witt & Redding, 2013). To recap, Redding (2005) developed a comparative business systems approach that was concerned with investigating why business organization and economic action varies in different societies. This model integrates three levels of analysis: culture and meaning, institutional order, and firm coordination. It also examines the interaction between the three different levels and highlights the importance of developing an historical approach to understanding business systems, to examining the role of interest groups in motivating certain forms of economic action, and to mapping the complexities of the material and ideational 'logics' that are adopted by key actors.

Business Networks in East Asian Capitalisms
http://dx.doi.org/10.1016/B978-0-08-100639-9.00015-3

As outlined in the introduction, Witt and Redding (2013) adapted this model to investigate the different kinds of capitalist economies that have emerged in Asia. In doing so, they argued for the fundamental importance of identifying the influence of social capital, culture, informal relationships, and 'multiplexity'. These four concepts will be used to help us summarize and analyse the contributions which have been made to this volume. In addition, we add the role of historically embedded power relations and international markets. As Robert Fitzgerald notes in Chapter 2, it is important to understand cross-border influence in business networks in East Asia and not just assume they can be fully explained by sole references to national business systems and/or culture.

What we present below are our own reflections on the contributions to the volume. A number of the chapters do, in fact, straddle several, if not all, of the concepts. That said, space constraints dictate that we must focus on just the most salient and this necessitates a certain telescoping of the complex arguments developed by each author. Readers may, of course, draw differing conclusions having read the volume.

15.1 SOCIAL CAPITAL

Witt and Redding (2013) define social capital as trust, more particularly they make a distinction between interpersonal trust (often a dyadic relationship involving reciprocity between friends and family) and institutional trust (reliable social, legal and political systems). Levels of institutional trust influence the formation of business networks in a number of ways. *First*, low levels of institutional trust may encourage business owners to look to their close family and friends to carry out management functions, and it may also encourage high levels of family ownership and control. *Second*, clusters of business groups and networks emerge because of the relative effectiveness of peer group systems in enforcing contracts when legal frameworks are weak. While contributors to the volume may not specifically use the term 'social capital' as it is defined by Witt and Redding (2013) in their own work, the concept nevertheless resonates in a number of chapters. A few examples of this are described below.

David Mayer's investigation of the career trajectories of CEOs in the Bank of China International (Chapter 4) demonstrates that while CEO connections with the Chinese Communist Party may help create strong bonds with mainland Chinese firms, it also leads to a lack of trust among the bank's international peers. This lack of trust confers low status on the bank in relation to the international investment community. Wai Ling So's historical comparative study of German and Chinese merchants during the Qing dynasty (Chapter 6) shows the importance of interpersonal trust for both groups in developing networks when formal institutions are nascent, or indeed, closed to certain groups. In Chapter 8, Katja Restel and Sven Horak propose that we consider Korea as a country which actually ranks highly in terms of group social cohesion and that trust through *yongo* networks is decidedly pronounced. Rather than being framed as a low-trust society, they suggest that successful economic development in Korea was possible because of a well-balanced interplay between informal networks and stable formal institutions striving for the same goal. Pattanee Susomrith's and Yuliani Suseno's study of Thai business networks (Chapter 12) uses a more extensive definition of social capital than that adopted by Witt and Redding (2013) nevertheless, they also focus on the importance of relational social capital based on interpersonal trust. They argue that, in Thai business networks, one of the few ways to build relational social capital is to be introduced or referred by a trusted person or organization. Without this referral, outsiders face significant difficulties building business networks. In Chapter 13, Tim Andrews and Khin Thi Htun show that the military political system in Myanmar may have actually increased the perceived need for formal written documentation in commercial dealings. This demarche may be because of a breakdown in trust within and across traditional informal networks which had previously been seen as a more reliable and efficient means of reducing risk and cutting through bureaucratic obstacles.

15.2 CULTURE

Redding (2005) adopts a definition of culture which fully embraces the socially constructed 'meanings' that we attach to the world around us. This approach allows for a more holistic investigation of culture where the importance of interest groups, the influence of history, and the role of the state are not 'factored out' in the pursuit of highly decontextualized results (see also Child, 2009). That said, the concept of 'culture' remains a controversial and contested concept across many disciplines including business and management studies due, in large part, to its connection with reductionist, essentialist modes of explanation which are based on a highly restrictive positivist methodology (McSweeney, 2002; Nolan, 2011). With these caveats in mind, there is, nevertheless, a large body of evidence which indicates that culture is important for understanding variation in business networks and economic organization (eg, Bond et al., 2004; Gu & Nolan, 2015; Hofstede, 2001; House, Hanges, Javidan, Dorfman, & Gupta, 2004). Culture influences important networking characteristics, such as the interpretation and allocation of authority, definitions of identity and group belonging, as well as the development of interpersonal trust and the formation of institutions.

Our contributors vary in the degree of importance they place on culture in developing business networks, but none entirely dismiss its influence. In Chapter 5, Barbara Wang and Chris Rowley investigate the way in which Confucian ethics of the 'rule of man', rather than the 'rule of law' permeates business practice in China. Keith Jackson and Shigeru Matsumoto (Chapter 7) draw attention to the importance of 'insider status' in defining the boundaries of Japanese business networks such as *zaibatsu* and *keiretsu*. A number of authors have drawn attention to the important cultural influences of both Buddhism and Confucianism in South East Asia (Rowley & Abdul-Rahman, 2008; Rowley & Warner, 2011). Cultural characteristics that influence business networks include not just collectivism, particularism, relationship orientation, and a preference for hierarchical or vertical systems, but also a reluctance to change and an acceptance of the status quo (Vimolwan Yukongdi and Chris Rowley, Chapter 11; Pattanee Susomrith and Yuliani Suseno, Chapter 12). Interestingly, Tim Andrews and Khin Thi Htun (Chapter 13) note that while the culture and social structure of Myanmar has historically been deeply intertwined with Buddhist values, their participants perceived that, as a result of the military regime from around 1988 onwards, 'attitudes' or 'culture' has shifted away from concerns with moral character towards more worldly and materialistic priorities.

15.3 INFORMALITY

Informality, in turn, refers to the pervasiveness of informal institutions in a society, including the influence of social conventions, acceptable modes of behaviour and uncodifed norms (North, 1990; Witt & Redding, 2013). The degree of informality in a society may undermine the effectiveness of formal institutions. For example, formal rules may simply be ignored if they diverge too much from the expectations of more well-established informal conventions, especially when enforcement mechanisms are weak. Where informal business networks, both at the interpersonal and interfirm level, are well-established and based on, for example, seniority principles or reciprocity within a closed network, then formal institutions aimed at greater transparency and meritocracy may struggle to gain a foothold. There is a distinction, then, between the way in which the formal institution of law may define rules and the informal day-to-day realities of actual behaviour (Aoki, Jackson, & Miyajima, 2007; Witt & Redding, 2013). Informality is more likely to be found in societies where institutional trust is low. At the same time, historically and culturally embedded informal institutions are unlikely to encourage the development of reliable formal institutions. Witt and Redding (2013) note that this will tend to be linked to cultural factors, in that informal institutions are more likely to emerge in collectivist societies with higher levels of group-conformity pressures (Hofstede, 2001). Our authors offer differing interpretations on the consequences of informality in East Asian business networks. For example, Katja Restel and Sven Horak (Chapter 8) argue that the assumption that economies in transition are especially prone to being negatively affected by informal networks need not always apply. They suggest that, in the Korean case, *yongo* networks may in fact contribute to in-group cohesion within each network, as well as to improving competitive efforts between different networks. They argue that informality has, in fact, had a positive impact on Korean economic development.

Other authors are less optimistic. For Natenapha Wailerdsak and Sununta Siengthai (Chapter 10), the existence of an informal patron-client system in Thailand has, in their words, led to the 'corruption system cycle', where market competition is distorted and access to resources and business opportunities are confined to elite networks. Consequently, the development of innovative products and services has been severely hindered. Ultimately, the cost of this situation has been borne by Thai society at large, in terms of restricted growth opportunities. Similarly, in Chapter 14, Quang Truong and Chris Rowley have shown that while the informal networks of *quan he* in Vietnam could work out positively for business, especially in terms of harnessing long- term mutual benefits and cultivating trust, in the absence of an effective legal system and good governance, it has evolved into corruption and cronyism.

15.4 MULTIPLEXITY

The prevalence of informal institutions is likely to encourage the development of 'multiplexity', in that it is quite possible to have different sets of informal rules for different sectors (Witt & Redding, 2013). In other words, it is possible to identify the existence of multiple forms of business systems within the same economy. In many instances, it does not make sense to talk about a single, homogenous, nation-state based business systems. A very obvious example of this is China, where there is a clear co-existence of state-owned and private sectors, each operating its own 'rules of the game'. Acknowledging multiplexity means that asking broader questions about change over time and institutional convergence towards Western models become redundant. There may or may not be a degree of convergence depending on the particular system, or element of the system, that is under investigation (Almond et al., 2005; Rowley, 1998; Rowley & Benson, 2004).

Examples in this collection include Chapter 5, where Barbara Wang and Chris Rowley identify the duality of state-led capitalism juxtaposed with entrepreneurial *guanxi* capitalism in China with key players interacting across a dynamic web. Again, Shaoyu Zhao and Stephen Morgan (Chapter 3) identify the differential roles played by local government connections and distant government ties for Chinese private entrepreneurs. Keith Jackson and Shigeru Matsumoto (Chapter 7), note that, in the case of Japan, an analytical focus on 'individualistic' national cultures is unlikely to capture the richness evident in the contemporary Japanese organization. They argue for the need for an analytical framework which examines such business networks in relation to their overseas investments. This means developing a conceptualization of 'horizontalization' in order to challenge embedded notions of vertical integration when researching selected *keiretsu*.

15.5 HISTORICALLY EMBEDDED POWER RELATIONS AND THE ROLE OF INTERNATIONAL MARKETS

Robert Fitzgerald (Chapter 2) and Heidi Dahles (Chapter 9) use historical analysis to show that a variety of business networking outcomes have emerged in East Asia, each of which is dependent on power relations, both within the region and between the region and global players, more generally. Fitzgerald notes that while government policy in the region has historically encouraged the establishment of networks between international and local business, at the end of colonialism and with the founding of new nation states, a significant shift occurred, whereby indigenous business groups were often given preferential treatment and special status. Dahles shows that whether or not ethnic Chinese in the Straits region became involved in China's economic development depended on the degree of discrimination and oppression they experienced in the colonial and postcolonial societies in which they were based. In other words, their migratory history, their experience of colonial governance systems, the roles which were allowable to them in colonial society, and their involvement in independence movements and the postcolonial political economy, generated very different outcomes. These cannot be fully explained by reference to their 'entrepreneurial spirit' or assumed long-standing 'connections' with the Mainland. Their relative successes and failures were also enmeshed in long-standing power relations which are best understood through historical analysis.

15.6 CONCLUSIONS: ENDURING TRENDS AND EMERGING PATTERNS

Explanations for the emergence of East Asian capitalisms have tended to focus on looking for *differences* in relation to Western models of economic development (Hamilton, 1996; Hamilton & Shin, 2015). East Asia is all too often turned into a 'negative case', with the emphasis placed on what the region *lacks* in relation to 'normal' Western economies (Sachs, 2006). This typical Anglo-American ethnocentrism and bias results in narrowness and inflexibility of thought and analysis. In relation to business networks, a common theme has been that the importance of interpersonal networks in businesses endures largely as a consequence of weak legal and regulatory institutions that emerged in particular historical, political, and economic contexts (Guthrie, 1998; Sachs, 2006). The assumption has been that the competitive pressures of market economies would, over time, modify the influence of interpersonal networks to an extent where they would be broadly equivalent to those found in the West. Underlying this assumption was the belief that networks have an inherently corrosive effect on organization and society, and would necessarily decline as modernization continues. In other words, global convergence on an Anglo-Saxon free market structure was considered an inevitability (Redding & Witt, 2015), as seen in the now discredited 'end of history' type assertions.

Time has now shown that these assumptions were incorrect. More nuanced views have emphasized the need to focus on the *continuity* of 'civilizational' and cultural norms in various capitalist economies (Hamilton & Shin, 2015; Warner, 2014). Others have underscored the enduring influence of power relations at the level of the individual, the group, the state and in international relations (Walter & Zhang, 2012). There is now a tendency to shy away from the usual theoretical practice of understanding modernity in terms of 'breaks with the past' and to emphasize that East Asian civilizations, while diverse in many ways, are based on a set of philosophies and principles which prioritise natural harmonies and hierarchies in relationships (Hamilton, 2006) Consequently, while interpersonal relationships in business may well be concerned with establishing and maintaining networks that are ultimately concerned with material advancement, they may, nevertheless, still retain an affective base. However, as noted earlier, there is a distinction between culturally rooted (and fairly ubiquitous) favour-seeking, reciprocity based networks and institutionally driven rent-seeking political networks, which are more likely to be concentrated among powerful elites. The ethics of interpersonal networks in business become a 'problem' when they affect the collective interests of society at large. It is the use of public resources for personal advancement (most often associated with the link between political and business networks) that violate ethical rules and should be defined as corruption. While business to business networks can bring economic benefits, the effects of political networks can be more ambiguous in that while they may provide short term advantages, they can constitute a serious risk over the long-term.

There are, then, problems with the 'teleological' assumptions of Modernization Theory which assume that markets must inevitably create 'fairer' competition and more efficient organizations both of which, in turn, will allegedly lead to a decline in the importance of interpersonal networks in business (Barro, 2012; Guthrie, 2012). As we have seen in our volume, the influence of interpersonal networks endures. In many instances, economic reforms and marketization actually led to a commodification of local bureaucratic power and influence, rather than to a retreat of the state. There is a world of difference between the informality of relationships among small market-traders and those of entrenched political and elite networks which have created in some parts of the region, as they have in many other parts of the world, including the West, widening income gaps, endemic corruption, poor governance, and slow growth (Walter & Zhang, 2012). Moreover, an historical perspective draws our attention to the need to investigate the importance of international and cross-border factors in studying business networks. Consequently, we need to develop our understanding of the relationships between international markets, multinational business organizations and national business networks. Similarly, a detailed focus on the position of actors (at both the individual, organizational, and national level) in the international political economy draws close attention to 'who gets what' in terms of resources.

Finally, we conclude that business networks are necessarily enmeshed in power relations which, in turn, should be investigated using a broader range of theoretical and disciplinary perspectives and methodologies than those currently favoured in conventional business research. Such a move can only enrich our understanding of business networks in East Asia and beyond.

Table 15.1 provides a summary of the key points made in each chapter and highlights the enduring trends and emerging patterns identified.

Table 15.1 Chapter summaries

Chapter	Coverage of business networks	Country(s)	Key points	Enduring trends and emerging patterns
2	Historical overview of the region	East Asia	• Multinational trading companies operated through complex networks of international and local alliances, repeat contracting, trust relationships, kinship ties and shared partners and personnel, in which personal contacts, market intelligence, and deal-making were critical competitive tools • European multinationals and local enterprises adopted similar forms of organization and operation and the market and policy circumstances of developing and commodity-exporting economies were more determinant than the cultural or the institutional • Links with colonial administrations were as important to the rise of Chinese businesses in South East Asia as the later contacts they forged with independent governments. Government policy encouraged international and local business networks and end of colonialism and founding of new nations marked important trend in which indigenous business groups were favoured	• Highlights the importance of international or cross-border factors in shaping business networks and the impossibility of considering national or cultural issues in isolation

(Continued)

Table 15.1 Chapter summaries—cont'd

Chapter	Coverage of business networks	Country(s)	Key points	Enduring trends and emerging patterns
3	Social status and network access in investments banks	China	• Draws on an extensive analysis of the career paths of BOCI's CEOs who are educated elite. Their social status and integration into elite investment banking networks offers an important perspective on the network position of BOCI as an organization • Outlines the financial reforms that were needed to incorporate the Bank of China International (BOCI) as an investment bank in Hong Kong in 1998 • As a wholly-owned subsidiary of Bank of China (Beijing), the government continues to hold ownership through various entities. BOCI remains directly subject to central government policy which has led to mixed outcomes • BOCI has high social status within China precisely because it is a subsidiary of Bank of China (Beijing). However, these same factors mean that BOCI has low social status within the global investment banking hub of Hong Kong	• Central government remains in control of a key Chinese investment bank indicating a resistance to adopting existing business norms that such entities should operate freely from government policy

4	Business to government networks in resource acquisition	China	• Entrepreneurs emphasize importance of local government connections in accessing financial resources, while both local and distant government connections helped them acquire technology • Connections with local government assisted in obtaining subsidies and government support in R&D. Distant government connections enabled application of technology through speeding up approval process and providing information about technologies developed by others • Demonstrates the important role government played in resource allocation • The rule of reciprocity in culture also motivated people to cultivate personal relationships and hold future-orientation towards potential benefits that might accrue from maintenance of personal connections	• Although new policies improved market and institutional environment and circumscribed conduct of government officials, they still influenced allocation of resources, especially in local government
5	*Guanxi* capitalism	China	• Features of economic systems are embedded deeply in cultural-social-political environment • Consequently, a form of *guanxi* capitalism emerged, evolved, and dominated the economic system	• Illustrates the enduring role of *guanxi* as the 'invisible hand' in the Chinese economy

(Continued)

Table 15.1 Chapter summaries—cont'd

Chapter	Coverage of business networks	Country(s)	Key points	Enduring trends and emerging patterns
			• Review of business history helps understand attitudes towards business and elaborated the 'five classified relationships' ('*Wulun*') of Confucian ethics • Develops conceptual framework of the '*guanxi* capitalism structure' building on 'differential mode of association' ('*Chaxugeju*'), 'central managed capitalism', 'network of *guanxi* circles', and *guanxi* knot and *guanxi* web	
6	Formal and informal networks in used in Sino-Western trade	China	• Compares and contrasts models of cooperation used by German and Chinese merchants in late Qing era, where local norms and practices varied as foreign business culture spread and trade with the West grew • Informal ties established between German families through marriage enabled more extensive delegation without moral hazard. Chinese Merchants developed formal networks to regulate mercantile activities as the result of direct intervention by the government in the economy, as well as political competition within the government • Written rules specified treatment for undesirable behaviour so organizations ensured compliance among members who otherwise lacked personal trust in conducting business. This arrangement expanded the network of trade by lowering the risk between participating members	• Identifies, historically, a variety of networking styles in different business communities which, counter to common cultural assumptions, provides evidence of the use of informal networks among Western traders, as well as the development of formal networks among Chinese merchants

7	Impact of exposure to overseas markets on business networks	Japan	• Identifies the salient features of Japanese capitalism as a context for the development of business networks • Institutional embeddedness of business networks become reinforced in response to overseas exposure. However, some business networks became more horizontally integrated as they sought to stretch strategically and develop competitive positions in overseas markets by establishing international alliances or large-scale and/or high profile overseas acquisitions • Highlights the impact on business networks of exposure to overseas markets and identifies enduring trends and emerging patterns in business networks. Enduring trends are that *keiretsu* (eg, Toyota) continue to perform impressively owing to the extent of their tightly and vertically integrated organization. Emerging patterns are towards outbound FDI or overseas acquisitions (eg, the Nikkei purchase of the Financial Times newspaper, the acquisition of Amlin by Mitsui Sumitomo Insurance, and Japan Tabaco's acquisition of Gallagher), though there are varying degrees of success in managing postacquisition operations	• Traditional *Keiretsu* continue to perform well in a large part because of their vertically integrated network structures, however, there are indicators of the development of horizontal networking through outbound FDI and overseas acquisitions

(Continued)

Table 15.1 Chapter summaries—cont'd

Chapter	Coverage of business networks	Country(s)	Key points	Enduring trends and emerging patterns
8	Informal networks and economic development via *yongo* networks	Korea	• Social network theory often assumes that some kinds of informal networks, under certain circumstances, may undermine and/or circumvent the rule of law • In Korea, *Yongo* networks are informal networks which derive their cohesiveness from strong particularistic ties, based on kin, educational institution (school/university), and region • A strong connection between politics and *Chaebol* can be observed which may indicate that Korean informal institutions act in a way which is complementarily to formal institutions, pursuing the same goals, and consequently, generate an outcome that results in economic progress • One size does not fit all in relation to both theoretical work and industrial policy on the assumed influence of informal networks	• There are diverse forms of trust. If the focus is shifted to trust at the group level, rather than the individual level, then Korea can be viewed as a high-trust society not a low-trust society, as is currently assumed
9	Institutional legacies of Asian Chinese business communities	Malaysia, Indonesia, Singapore	• Comparative historical perspective on the multiple embeddedness of business communities reveals how multilayered legacies of the past are shaped by interacting economic, political, and cultural forces and became strategically employed, enforced, abandoned, and revitalized under changing institutional regimes • Challenges claims of a Chinese business community in the Straits region which are based on ethnic affinity or common institutional frameworks in the narrow sense	• A common, but disparate, history encompassing shared roots, migratory past, and colonial experience generates diverging legacies for Asian Chinese business communities in the Straits region to build on

10	Strong tie-based relationships between government, state, and significant businesses	Thailand	• Investigates the networks that have evolved between state, government, and significant businesses over time. Explores the role of the state and the developmentalism perspective, beginning with industrialization in the 1960s • Shows how business network development can be understood through three dimensions: fund raising in money and capital markets; accumulation of technology and marketing know-how; human resource development • Considers the development of the anticorruption movement in the private business sector and business ethics issues and how Thai business networks can be further developed within the ASEAN Economic Community and the globalization era more generally	• Thailand is its patron-client system and economic activity is dominated by 'inner circles' of friends and acquaintances. The private sector needs to improve business network effectiveness by ensuring they are based on developing business efficiencies, such as R&D, supply chains, and communications
11	Varieties of capitalism in context	Thailand	• Locates the VOC model within a wider historical context, comparing with other theories and critiques. Develops the model and demonstrates its enduring utility by introducing an additional explanatory sphere defined as 'context'. This includes the incorporation of a nation's historical and political background, as well as its social, cultural values, and beliefs	• Both vertical and horizontal integration are employed as strategies in large firms and relationships among firms are more cooperative rather than adversarial, and very much depend on trust and personal relationships

(Continued)

Table 15.1 Chapter summaries—cont'd

Chapter	Coverage of business networks	Country(s)	Key points	Enduring trends and emerging patterns
			• Notes that in Thai society trust is based on personal relationships that are developed over time. Such personal relationships tend to set up entry barriers for those who are not part of the network. Business networks are dense and joint membership in industry associations together enable the monitoring of company reputation. There are close relationships with major suppliers and clients and networks of cross-shareholding, hence hostile takeovers and acquisitions are rare	
12	Social capital and the social context	Thailand	• Investigates how the nature of social context influences the development, utilization, and maintenance of social (structural, relational, and cognitive) capital. Business networks are socially constructed and shaped by cultural characteristics of: collectivism, Buddhism, particularism, reluctance to change, relationship orientation, and hierarchical system • Social capital is concentrated in individuals and organizations at the top level of the hierarchy effectively, creating immense wealth and prosperity for owners of these organizations. Social capital appears limited or at least, ineffectively utilized, by those at the lower end of the hierarchy, and by smaller organizations in Thailand • As particularism is deemed as important by Thais, large and more successful businesses (and individuals) tend to be doing business with other successful businesses (and individuals)	• Those who do not fit in with the criteria of being rich and successful are considered as outsiders and therefore, are not 'invited' into that social circle. The country's economic growth is thus very much dependent on a small fraction of the economy. There is a widening inequality between the rich and the poor

13	Characteristics, evolution, and implications of *a hse a thwe* (business networks)	Myanmar	• While culturally grounded in social norms based on Theravada Buddhist principles, the common workings of *a hse a thwe* were corrupted during military control and repression • Shows how network practices shifted under the military regime, demonstrating changes in what constitutes 'normal' business activity at both intra- and inter-organizational levels (particularly government) • The nature of change in business networks under military repression is increasingly being criticized by both overseas Burmese looking to return, as well as business people already working in the country • Many are weary of repression, confinement, corruption, a lack of transparency or fairness, and the wider erosion of what is seen as traditional societal values • Adopts an emic ('from the inside') qualitative approach to concept development drawing on the perceptions of 17 participants	• Spurred by economic reform, the easing of international sanctions and the election in 2015, there may be a reversion to more traditional values in business networking practices and society at large

(Continued)

Table 15.1 Chapter summaries—cont'd

Chapter	Coverage of business networks	Country(s)	Key points	Enduring trends and emerging patterns
14	State-led crony capitalism and *quan he* networks	Vietnam	• *Doi moi*, the 'socialist' model of development, favoured state-owned enterprises and reduced opportunities for the private sector to join the market • Sharing a background with China (Confucianism, socialism, and poorly functioning formal institutions) the practice of *quan he* in Vietnam (reciprocity in the cultivation of personal relationships) led to corruption, cronyism, favouritism and nepotism • These conditions have created a form of crony capitalism which encourages personal enrichment by party officials, their families, and friends	• With little evidence of immanent political or social change, the network-based economy in Vietnam may continue to exist in the medium term, to the detriment of both economic development and a more active civil society

REFERENCES

Almond, P., Edwards, T., Colling, T., Ferner, A., Gunnigle, P., Muller-Camen, M., et al. (2005). Unraveling home and host country effects: An investigation of the HR policies of an American multinational in four European countries. *Industrial Relations: A Journal of Economy and Society*, *44*(2), 276–306.

Aoki, M., Jackson, G., & Miyajima, H. (Eds.), (2007). *Corporate governance in Japan: In-stitutional change and organizational diversity*. Oxford: Oxford University Press.

Barro, R. J. (2012). Convergence and modernization revisited. National Bureau of Economic Research, Working Paper (No. w18295).

Bond, M. H., Leung, K., Au, A., Tong, K. K., De Carrasquel, S. R., Murakami, F., et al. (2004). Culture-level dimensions of social axioms and their correlates across 41 cultures. *Journal of Cross-Cultural Psychology*, *35*(5), 548–570.

Child, J. (2009). Context, comparison, and methodology in Chinese management research. *Management and Organization Review*, *5*(1), 57–73.

Gu, F., & Nolan, J. (2015). Performance appraisal in Western and local banks in China: The influence of firm ownership on the perceived importance of guanxi. *International Journal of Human Resource Management*, 1–21. http://dx.doi.org/10.1080/09585192.2015.1089063.

Guthrie, D. (1998). The declining significance of guanxi in China's economic transition. *China Quarterly*, *154*, 254–282.

Guthrie, D. (2012). *China and globalization: The social, economic and political transformation of Chinese society*. New York, London: Routledge.

Hamilton, G. G. (Ed.), (1996). *Asian business networks*. Berlin, New York: Walter de Gruyter.

Hamilton, G. G. (2006). *Commerce and capitalism in Chinese societies*. New York: Routledge.

Hamilton, G. G., & Shin, S. I. (2015). Demand-responsive industrialization in East Asia a new critique of political economy. *European Journal of Social Theory*, http://dx.doi.org/10.1177/1368431014568425.

Hofstede, G. (2001). *Culture's consequences: Comparing values, behaviors, institutions and organizations across nations*. London: Sage.

House, R. J., Hanges, P. J., Javidan, M., Dorfman, P. W., & Gupta, V. (Eds.), (2004). *Culture, leadership, and organizations: The GLOBE study of 62 societies*. London: Sage.

McSweeney, B. (2002). Hofstede's model of national cultural differences and their consequences: A triumph of faith-a failure of analysis. *Human Relations*, *55*(1), 89–118.

Nolan, J. (2011). Good guanxi and bad guanxi: Western bankers and the role of network practices in institutional change in China. *International Journal of Human Resource Management*, *22*(16), 3357–3372.

North, D. C. (1990). *Institutions, institutional change and economic performance*. Cambridge: Cambridge University Press.

Redding, G. (2005). The thick description and comparison of societal systems of capitalism. *Journal of International Business Studies*, *36*(2), 123–155.

Redding, G., & Witt, M. A. (2015). Advancing indigenous management theory: Executive rationale as an institutional logic. *Management and Organization Review*, *11*(02), 179–203.

Rowley, C. (1998). *HRM in the Asia Pacific region: Convergence questioned*. London: Frank Cass.

Rowley, C. & Abdul-Rahman, S. (Eds.), (2008). *The changing face of management in South-East Asia*. London: Routledge.

Rowley, C., & Benson, J. (2004). *The management of HR in the Asia Pacific region: Convergence reconsidered*. London: Frank Cass.

Rowley, C. & Warner, M. (Eds.), (2011). *Whither South East Asian management? First decade of the new millennium*. London: Routledge.

Sachs, J. D. (2006). *The end of poverty: Economic possibilities for our time*. New York: Penguin.

Walter, A., & Zhang, X. (2012). *East Asian capitalism: Diversity, continuity, and change*. Oxford: Oxford University Press.

Warner, M. (2014). *Understanding Chinese management: Past, present and future*. London, New York: Routledge.

Witt, M. A., & Redding, G. (2013). Asian business systems: Institutional comparison, clusters and implications for varieties of capitalism and business systems theory. *Socio-Economic Review, 11*(2), 265–300.

INDEX

Note: Page numbers followed by *f* indicate figures and *t* indicate tables.